I found the book to be engaging and compelling. It is obvious that Colly is writing from a deep relationship with Jim, both personally and professionally.

He is accurate with his portrayal Jim and Florida College and how Jim's family background and historical events blended to put him into the "right place at the right time" for FC and for his personal life, especially meeting Georgia Deane.

Jim loved his heavenly Father, his wife and family and just about all people with which he came into contact.

Jim thought of himself as a preacher first.

When he went into Clare Bridge he made it a point to preach each Sunday. Colly addressed Jim's comments about the "instrumental music element" there. One time when Connie and I came to be with him on a Sunday afternoon, he was waiting dressed in his suit with his bible in his hand. He was ready to go preach at Antioch (I think his most beloved work). I told him that Phil Roberts was preaching there now (it had been years since he preached there). Jim got upset and said that "no man should step into another man's pulpit like that!" Of course we redirected him, but his instinct was to preach.

Colly has captured Jim's persona perfectly.

I especially appreciate how he included the historical context of Jim's era and the impact of the Restoration Movement on his family and him.

Personally, I went to him many times with questions regarding "issues" and he would give me the historical context of the thinking on both sides and his opinion on the truth as taught by the word. Then, invariably, he would say "you need to contact (Melvin, Bob or some other knowledgeable bible person) and get their viewpoint.

— Mike Benson, Sr.

There are many books you read that have a slow start, but this one catches you right away. When I started reading, it immediately grabbed my attention. It was interesting, informative, humorous, and accurately described the life of James R. Cope and his love for the Lord. I couldn't put it down. He was an amazing servant and did much good in the kingdom that had lasting effects, even to this day. I know he made a lasting impression on me.

— Judy Bertram

Biographers are motivated by their desire to preserve a record of history, usually focused on a particular person. Sometimes, other goals emerge ... inspiration, information, context, and sometimes maybe curiosity. This biography, written by Dr. Colly Caldwell tells the story of James R. Cope, Sr, and the circumstances surrounding his life, including his influence on family, our Christian brotherhood, college students, and his community. Dr Caldwell is uniquely qualified to tell Cope's story. His 40-year association with Florida College overlapped most of Cope's presidency, and beyond. Cope served as president for 33 years, Caldwell served in the same office for 18 years. That's a half-century, and a major portion of the school's history. While their first relationship was that of teacher and student, they shared may years as co-administrators.

To understand Cope's role in recent history of education among Christians, one need to hear and share the background of his early life and exposure to many of the leading gospel preachers of the mid-20th century. Upon arriving in Tampa in 1948, as the new, young, president of the College, he began a life of being the influencer. Amid the challenges of running a college, funding a college, and maintaining a clearly defined view of Biblical principles, Cope became a leading voice of brotherhood education. Caldwell witnessed all this in person, in addition to interviewing dozens of people, family and associates, who also knew Cope's story. Given this record, readers will understand how Florida College became a steadfast bulwark of education for Christian families. Readers should find Caldwell's presentation of Cope's story encouraging, and rejoice in having this record.

— Olen Britnell

C. G. "Colly" Caldwell's work on James R. Cope provides a comprehensive retrospect of Cope's illustrious tenure as president of Florida College. A sweeping view of President Cope's family background and Tennessee roots, and consideration of the development of faith-based higher education, provide a sturdy foundation for a careful consideration of the opportunities and hazards that faced Cope as Florida College's long-serving president. This a fitting tribute by Colly Caldwell, who knows first-hand the work and service of the president's office.

— Brian Crispell

In Florida College's eightieth year of existence, Charles G. "Colly" Caldwell III has completed a biography of the college's second president, James R. Cope. In significant ways, his presidency determined the character, constitution and personality of Florida College. I was eight years old when brother Cope became president, and my father, Roland H. Lewis, was already on the faculty and administration. My parents became close friends to Jim and Georgia Deane through his thirty-three years of service.

In the book you will learn the background of his grandparents on both his father's and his mother's side, and that of his parents. You will find delightful stories of his childhood. You'll learn how he began preaching; how Georgia Deane accepted his marriage proposal only two weeks after they met; how and why Florida Christian College came to be; why FCC was changed to FC; and how, in the mid-1950s, the college's existence was severely threatened by a growing controversy over whether it could or should receive contributions from churches.

It's all here. The story of Florida College's existence and purpose—through the life of James R. Cope. Enjoy.

- Brent Lewis

Building on the Good: The Life and Times of James Rogers Cope, by C. G. "Colly" Caldwell, is both a biography and a tribute—the life story of a man who often encouraged others to "build on the good."

- Norene Thayer MacDonald

All who loved and admired James R. Cope will certainly treasure this new, definitive biography by Colly Caldwell. After extensive research on Brother Cope's family and work, along with multiple interviews over the years with him and his family, Colly has produced a comprehensive yet highly readable biography, a fitting tribute to the gospel preacher and educator whose influence will continue for generations to come.

The story begins several generations before James Rogers Cope was born. Cope's family roots include a rich heritage of family and faith, including a determination to teach and follow the patterns of Christianity revealed in the New Testament. Among Cope's forebears were influential restoration preachers and accomplished educators whose work impacted their times, the kind of work that Cope continued effectively in his own life.

This background, along with the story of Cope's early life and childhood in Tennessee, are presented in a narrative rich in anecdotes that make the story come to life and that offer the reader an intimate glimpse into James Cope as a person.

An important part of this study is what it contributes to the history of the institutional controversy among churches of Christ. Cope and others were committed to the biblical principle of congregational autonomy and stood firm in their opposition to churches establishing and supporting human institutions, including colleges.

Caldwell's work is an especially significant contribution to the story of Florida College, the school Cope served as its president for thirty-three years during a critical time in its history. James R. Cope's love and commitment to FC is a legacy that has impacted generations of young people for good—one that lives on into the present.

This book is a work that was decades in the making. Dr. Caldwell knew his subject in life. He sat at the feet of Brother Cope in his Bible classes at Florida College. He served under President Cope on the administrative team of the college for more than a decade. He looked to Jim Cope as his mentor, his brother in Christ, a fellow-worker in the Lord's work, and his friend. In many ways he followed in Cope's footsteps in his own work. Those experiences, combined with his rich knowledge of the history of the restoration movement, prepared Caldwell to be especially well-suited to write this book.

This book is, indeed, a labor of love. The story related herein carries forward the legacy of "building on the good."

— Dan Petty

In an era when college presidents often demolish Biblical foundations under cultural pressure and worldly pursuits, Caldwell's biography tells the life of a principled leader who built a college on God's design.

— John Weaver

Building on the Good

Building on the Good

The Life and Times of James Rogers Cope

by C. G. "Colly" Caldwell

FLORIDA
COLLEGE
PRESS

CONTENTS

Section 6: The School and the Church

Section 7: Building a Good Decade of Progress

Section 8: Building on the Good During Later Years of Presidency (1968-82)

Section 9: Good Days After Florida College (1982-99)

Appendices

At the end of each school year, the graduating seniors at Florida College are given the opportunity to present a Legacy Coin to the member of the faculty, staff, or administration who impacted their college career the most. This recent tradition is just one of the countless ways that bring to light how this little school on the banks of the Hillsborough River consistently "builds on the good."

Though the Coin Ceremony wasn't around when the author of this book was a student, I would hazard a guess to say that Dr. Caldwell would have given his Legacy Coin to Professor James Cope. As a third-year student, Caldwell sat at the feet of Cope as he taught upper-division Bible. But their relationship didn't end at graduation. The "legacy" of Cope's impact on Caldwell continued throughout their lives.

First and foremost, that's what this book is about. Caldwell has put together a thorough—yet thrilling—account of how Jim Cope related with the people around him. From his family and neighbors as a young boy to the countless Christians and college students he influenced up to his death, Cope knew that teaching and preaching were both about reaching others.

Much of this book also focuses on the fascinating history of Florida College. As a current professor there, I was intrigued to learn how some of the older traditions and practices of the school began; many of them were put in place by Cope himself. It renewed my passion for Our Dear FC as I read about all the sacrifices those early men and women had to make to ensure the school could "make the difference" it was designed to.

But even if you aren't necessarily interested in learning about the origins of Florida College, there is much in the following pages to keep your attention. Caldwell chronicles important controversial issues that impacted churches of Christ, Bible-based colleges, and the relationship between the two. We also get glimpses of the brethren who influenced Cope's journey in both preaching and the office of the president. I was surprised to see several familiar names listed in these chapters, including W. P. Hagewood, my wife's great-grandfather. More unexpected perhaps are the references to the ways Cope's life was involved in local, state, and even federal government. President Herbert Hoover, a distant cousin of my paternal grandfather, got multiple shout-outs.

The history book you are about to read shouldn't be prejudged to be a mundane series of dates nor is it too dense to understand. Caldwell writes in a way that is not only comprehensible but also compelling, humorous, even shocking at times. There are multiple laugh-out-loud moments throughout this biography, and even a few stories that made me audibly gasp.

Brother Cope was without a doubt an interesting and influential character. But what makes this telling of his story worth reading is that it is written by someone who really knew him. It's a book about a Florida College president written by a Florida College president. It's a book filled with anecdotes from the author's own recollections and adages and advice from the mouth of the subject himself. It's a book by someone who not only learned from Cope as a professor but loved him as a person.

And that's why I'm writing this foreword: Though I never knew Brother Cope, I know Brother Caldwell. I learned from him as a professor at Florida College and loved him as a person even before that. I have sat at his feet for over thirty years listening to anecdotes, adages, and advice from his own life. I don't just know him as President Emeritus Caldwell; I know him as "Coggy." Sure, I may be distantly related to other

PREFACE

One of James Rogers Cope's favorite concepts was "Building on the Good." He used that expression often in daily conversation. He included it in his sermon repertoire. He spoke of it especially in his addresses to the faculty, staff, and administration of Florida College. He instilled it within his children in the family. He taught it to students, whom he considered special charges to be mentored on behalf of their families as they entered into adulthood. He believed strongly that the college should maintain the policy of *en loco parentis*.

Because the "Building on the Good" philosophy was so apparent in his expressions about life, I have chosen it as the title of this volume. This is not the first time it has been used as a title to the life of James R. Cope. It was first used by me while serving as a section editor of a fiftieth anniversary book entitled "Making a Difference." That coffee-table book contains a history of the early years of Florida College. James R. Cope became its second president and continued in that position for thirty-three years. It was used also by Margie Garrett in the Florida College *FC Magazine* in an article honoring Cope when he died in 1999. It seems appropriate, therefore, to continue using a phrase that was so prevalent among Brother Cope's often-used expressions and to draw heavily in some sections of this volume on information in those two publications.

If we were to ask Jim Cope why he loved and used that phrase so often, he would have spoken first of our "building on the good" Word of God. Everything else in our lives should begin with a relationship with God and His Son Jesus Christ. Everything else in our lives should be examined in relation to the inspired Bible, particularly the New Testament revelation of Jesus and His divine will for mankind.

We will come back to that many times as we think about his life. For now, however, we believe he would think of "Building on the Good" next in terms of his family roots in the Upper Cumberland Valley of Middle Tennessee. That is where we begin.

Family was important to rural people in the American South. That was true of almost all those who lived in the Big Spring community of White County, up Highway 84 North from Sparta, leading toward Monterey, Tennessee. Sparta is about twenty-five miles south of Cookeville. It was the town most visited by the Cope family in Jim's youth.

The Cope family was not particularly prominent or even known by many folks beyond fifty miles from their homes. They did not have much money, but they were rich in values and character. They were simply well recognized by their neighbors and friends as being "good" country people who believed in God, the Bible, and the moral and spiritual teaching of Jesus Christ.

No doubt because family was so important to them, it is possible to trace Jim Cope's heritage through most of his great-great-grandparents.

APPRECIATION

I must express my gratitude to Adam Shanks who has tirelessly worked to produce this volume. It is impossible to know the hours he has labored to see to its design and availability to the readers.

Another special "thank you" is extended to Dr. Norene MacDonald Thayer, retired professor of English, who meticulously examined and corrected the text of this book. That is not intended to hold her accountable for misstatements and errors which are completely due to my mistakes. We are all indebted to Dr. Thayer for her contributions to this work.

Special appreciation is also due to Dr. Daniel Petty (retired Dean and professor of church history); to Dr. Brian Crispell (professor of history); to Dr. H. E. Payne, Jr., (Chancellor of Florida College); to Brent Lewis (former editor of Christianity Magazine); and to Judy Bertram (Assistant to the Florida College administration), who read the text; and to Olen Britnell (son-in-law of former board member S. O. Ward and presently a board member himself) who along with his wife, Jane Ward Britnell. offered insights and suggestions. Three members of the Cope family should be mentioned here: Michael Benson, Sr., (Connie's husband and Jim's son-in-law); Cathy Weaver, (Jim's daughter); and Dr. John B. Weaver (Jim's grandson and presently President of Florda College). We must not forget those who have now passed this life who are identified in the footnotes.

FAMILY TREE

James Rogers Cope [b. January 27, 1917; d. June 18, 1999]

Older Brother – Quill Evan Cope [b. March 28, 1912; d. September 24, 1968]

Younger Sister – Mary Hill (Cope) Luna [b. February 28, 1927; d. May 8, 2011]

PARENTS

Rogers Wallace Cope [b. November 17, 1882; d. October 19, 1945]

Dora Frances (Breeding) Cope [b. September 18, 1887; d. February 7, 1976]

GRANDPARENTS (paternal – Parents of Rogers Wallace Cope)

James Wallace Cope [b. October 18, 1856; d. June 13, 1889]

Ida (Rogers) Cope [b. 1857; d. November 25, 1882]

GRANDPARENTS (maternal – Parents of Dora Frances Breeding)

Evan Scott Breeding [b. June 20, 1848; d. August 13, 1929]

Fannie Jane (Weaver) Breeding [b. May 29, 1841; d. April 14, 1927]

GREAT-GRANDPARENTS (paternal – Parents of James Wallace Cope)

Wallace B. Cope [b. August 24, 1819; d. August 20, 1898]

Clarissa Jane (Sims) Cope [b. March 4, 1825; d. July 1, 1869]

GREAT-GRANDPARENTS (paternal – Parents of Ida Rogers)

George Washington Rogers

Amanda (Carnes) Rogers [b. June, 1831; d. April, 1858]

GREAT-GRANDPARENTS (maternal – Parents of Evan Scott Breeding)

Bryant Breeding [b. May 4, 1808; d. April 2, 1878]

Maria (Miller) Breeding [d. June 30, 1886]

GREAT-GRANDPARENTS (maternal – Parents of Fannie Jane Weaver)

Samuel David Peter Weaver [b. February 26, 1789; d. June 1, 1850]

Annie (Hickman) Weaver [b. February 9, 1794; d. July 23, 1884]

GREAT-GREAT-GRANDPARENTS (paternal - Parents of Wallace B. Cope

Andrew Cope [b. March 7, 1781; d. May 18, 1862]

Sarah (Wallace) Cope [d. April 14, 1822]

GREAT-GREAT-GRANDPARENTS (paternal – Parents of
  Clarissa Jane Sims)

Eli Sims

Rachel (Towsend) Sims

GREAT-GREAT-GRANDPARENTS (paternal – Parents of
  George Washington Rogers)

GREAT-GREAT-GRANDPARENTS (paternal – Parents of
  Amanda Carnes)

William Davis Carnes [b. October 23, 1805; d. November
  20, 1879]

Elizabeth (Billingsley) Carnes [d. 1859]

GREAT-GREAT-GRANDPARENTS (maternal – Parents of
  Bryant Breeding)

Father a Breeding

Mother a Tompson

GREAT-GREAT-GRANDPARENTS (maternal – Parents of
  Maria Miller)

Father a Miller

Mother a Brady

GREAT-GREAT-GRANDPARENTS (maternal – Parents of
Samuel David Peter Weaver)

John Weaver [b. March 31, 1762]

GREAT-GREAT-GRANDPARENTS (maternal – Parents of
Annie Hickman

Benjamin Hickman [b. September 13, 1762; d. May 5, 1838]

Judith Hickman [b. May 13, 1763; d. November 26, 1840]

Section 1

Building on a Good Heritage

Chapter One

Paternal Heritage: Carnes, Rogers, and Cope Families

James Rogers Cope's heritage on his father's side included three Tennessee families of special note: the Carnes, the Rogers, and the Copes. Each provided its own unique contributions to his personality and character. W. D. Carnes, James R. Cope's grandfather, was especially identified by him on the paternal side of his family because he served as a college president, a gospel preacher, a dedicated "Restoration" defender, and a role model in the development of Cope's occupational interests in educational administration.

The Carnes Family

In Scotland the name "Carnes" was "Cairns." Apparently most of the Carnes in America descended from two families of Cairns who immigrated to the colonies prior to the Revolutionary War. One family settled first in Boston. The other went from Scotland to Ireland and then immigrated to Baltimore. To the Baltimore Carnes, three brothers and a sister were born. Their immediate descendants spread geographically into the Carolinas and Georgia.

Alexander Carnes, Sr. One brother, Alexander, went from Baltimore to Virginia and served in the Continental Army during the Revolutionary War. Once, while he was home on furlough, a band of British soldiers raided his farm and tried to force his wife to reveal her husband's whereabouts. When she refused to tell them, they hanged her on a beam in the "loom room" where the servants were making cloth. Her life was saved by the servant women who quickly cut her down and revived her as the Tories left the farm. After the war, the Carnes' family moved to North Carolina, where Alexander bought land in both Rowan and Mecklenburg counties.[1]

Alexander Carnes, Jr. In 1804, Alexander Carnes, Jr. moved to the Lancaster district of South Carolina and married a cousin of John C. Calhoun named Mary Davis. Her family, like the Calhouns and Carnes, was radically committed to independence from the British crown. Mary Davis Carnes often told of a nervous neighbor who pled with Mary's mother to send to Charlotte, where her father, Mr. Davis, was serving with the Continental army, and call him home. The neighbor who sympathized with the Tory cause feared the consequences if the British found Davis in the immediate vicinity of his home. He wanted Mrs. Davis to urge her husband to sign an oath of allegiance to King George and argued that it was the only way she could save their land, their property, and their lives when Cornwallis' soldiers under Major Ferguson attacked the colonists at King's Mountain. Mrs. Davis promptly informed "the scoundrel" neighbor that she could not persuade her husband to desert the cause and that she would not if she could. A few days later, the Revolutionary

---

1   Joseph Malcolm Carnes, *Memoir of William D. Carnes, Combined with the Genealogy of the Carnes Family by William W. Carnes* (Beaumont, TX: G. L. Carnes, 1926), 1, 51-52.

soldiers were victorious at Kings' Mountain and the family courage was vindicated.

Four children were born to Alexander and Mary Davis Carnes: two daughters who died in infancy and two sons whom they named William Davis and Alexander Brown. All the children were christened by their parents into the orthodox Presbyterian faith, which they had learned from family immigrants who worshiped in churches established by John Knox and his disciples in their Scottish homeland.

Shortly after the birth of their second son in 1809, Alexander Carnes moved his family to the recently settled Warren County, Tennessee. He opened the first store in McMinnville and thus became the pioneer merchant in the new county seat. By investing his profits in town lots and surrounding farm acreage, he quickly built a reputation as an important area businessman.

Having established himself in Tennessee, Carnes returned to South Carolina to close out his business interests there. In payment for some old debts, he received a number of horses and mules which he drove to the coast country and sold to cotton and rice farmers. As he travelled home, Carnes was murdered in his Charleston hotel room by a thief who shot him in the head and fled with his money.

When his mercantile business and real estate in Tennessee was sold and all debts paid, the estate of Alexander Carnes, Jr., was valued at approximately forty-thousand dollars. It was divided into three portions. With her allotment, Mary Davis Carnes bought a farm and moved with her two small sons to Milton, a small community in Rutherford County about thirty miles west of McMinnville. The other two-thirds of the estate was entrusted to her brother in North Carolina, John

Davis, who promised to invest it for an inheritance for the two boys. When her younger son married, she sold her farm, divided the proceeds between the two boys, and spent the rest of her life in their homes. She died in Spencer, Tennessee, in 1851 in the home of her elder son, W. D. Carnes.[2]

William Davis Carnes. The tombstone that marks the grave of William Davis Carnes at Spencer, Tennessee, is engraved with the birthdate October 23, 1805.[3] He was four years old when the family moved to Tennessee.

From the beginning, Carnes was a bright child. Even his own mother could not say how he learned to read before he was old enough to go to school. From the beginning, he was ahead of his class although most students were older than he. The pursuit and later the dissemination of knowledge became a driving force in his life. As a child, he established a regular schedule of hours each day for study. He read all the books he could own or borrow.[4]

At age eighteen, a new and momentous influence came into the life of W. D. Carnes. Many Presbyterians in Middle Tennessee were becoming excited about a spiritual movement promoted by Barton Warren Stone of Cane Ridge, Kentucky. Stone was calling for members of all denominations to unite by forsaking their synods and man-made manuals of faith and returning to the simple New Testament patterns of first-century Christianity.[5] The Baptists were hearing a similar appeal

---

2   Carnes, *Memoir of William D. Carnes*, 1-3, 51-52.

3   Jim Cope and I visited the former site of Burritt College and the Spencer, Tennessee cemetery on July 15, 1984.

4   Carnes, *Memoir of William D. Carnes*, 3-6.

5   William Garrett West, *Barton Warren Stone: Early American Advocate of Christian Unity* (Nashville, TN: The Disciples of Christ Historical Society, 1954); John Rogers, ed, *The Biography of Elder Barton*

around Murfreesboro, the county seat of Rutherford County, from Alexander Campbell, a West Virginian who travelled extensively in Tennessee proclaiming that the church of Christ as revealed in the New Testament is non-denominational.[6] Many who had been reading Campbell's new periodical *The Christian Baptist*,[7] had become convinced that the church of the first century was something totally different in kind from the churches in which they were worshiping.

Many of those who accepted these non-denominational appeals also abandoned certain doctrines regarding the nature of man and redemption from sin associated with the writings of John Calvin, John Knox, and the Westminster Confession of Faith (1647). Those doctrines included total hereditary depravity, unconditional election, limited atonement, irresistible grace, and perseverance of saints, i.e., impossibility of apostasy. Additionally, many were discontinuing practices that they could not find authorized in the scriptures such as infant baptism, "modes" of baptism other than immersion, use of mechanical instruments of music in worship, non-weekly observance of the Lord's Supper, etc. Perhaps the most passionate demand of these disciples was the insistence upon worshiping in locally autonomous assemblies with no organizational ties to another church except as every

---

Warren Stone, Written by Himself: with Additions and Reflections (Cincinnati, OH: J. A. and U. P. James, 1847); *Barton Warren Stone, History of the Christian Church in the West* (Lexington, KY: College of the Bible, 1826-32, 1956).

6   Robert Richardson, *Memoirs of Alexander Campbell*, (Nashville, TN: Gospel Advocate Company, 1897, 1956); Earl Irvin West, *The Search for the Ancient Order: A History of the Restoration Movement 1849-1906*, (Nashville, TN: Gospel Advocate Company, 1964), vol. i. 36-52.

7   Alexander Campbell, ed., *The Christian Baptist* (Nashville, TN: Gospel Advocate Company, 1955). I-vii:1823-30.

congregation serves under Jesus Christ as Head of the universal body. These groups of Christians identified themselves simply as "Christians" or "disciples of Christ." The churches were identified as "churches of Christ" or "Christian churches." They no longer identified themselves individually or collectively as "Baptists," "Methodists," "Presbyterians," etc. They, therefore, left the mentality of denominational Christianity for a unified view of the one church of Christ. This, of course, required a changed concept of the church itself. It resulted in a view which was effected by careful study of the nature of the church in New Testament epistles and the "Acts of the Apostles."

Carnes listened carefully to an evangelist named Abner Hill and personally studied the New Testament.[8] Soon he determined he must be immersed for the remission of his sins. Within a year of his baptism, Carnes was publicly preaching. Several responded to his first sermon by asking to be baptized. He taught both his mother and his younger brother, who also accepted the appeal for a "restoration of the ancient order." This nineteen-year-old preacher became the talk of the community.[9]

These spiritual beginnings for Carnes took place in 1823 at Woodbury, Tennessee ,where Carnes had also accepted his first teaching position. The following year, Carnes joined his more experienced mentor, Abner Hill, and part-time evangelist Dr. William Jordan in travelling among the Sequatchie Valley and Lower Cumberland churches to preach the gospel.

---

8   Henry Leo Boles, "William Davis Carnes," in *Biographical Sketches of Gospel Preachers* (Nashville, TN: Gospel Advocate Company, 1932), 120-24.

9   Ivy Carnes, "Biographical Sketch of President W. D. Carnes," in James E. Scobey, ed., *Franklin College and Its Influences* (Nashville, TN: Gospel Advocate Company, 1954), IX, 203-13.

At the Smyrna church in Bledsoe County, William met the young woman whom he would take as his bride. She was Elizabeth Billingsley, the daughter Samuel Billingsley, an elder in the church. Her cousins John and Philip Mulkey were sons of her mother's brother and were already becoming quite well known as "restoration" preachers. They lived in the area surrounding what came to be Tompkinsville, Kentucky. At one of the services at the Smyrna church, Elizabeth confessed her faith in Christ and was baptized by Carnes.

Elizabeth was younger than William and was not yet ready for a serious romantic relationship. William left a few days after her baptism but something kept him from forgetting Elizabeth. The next year, he returned to preach in the Sequatchie Valley and while there courted and won the heart of Elizabeth Billingsley. They married June 1, 1825. Over the next ten years, five children were born into their family: three sons (Alexander Campbell, Alva, and Samuel Erasmus) and two daughters (Mary and Amanda).[10]

Over the years the Carnes' family acquired property. Their farms and mills prospered, but William was not satisfied with his work. As the children advanced through school and he helped them with their assignments, he decided he needed more education himself. With the help of a Professor James Garvin, who taught chemistry at East Tennessee University (now the University of Tennessee) in Knoxville, he studied several disciplines taught at college level. His studies did not include, however, Latin and Greek. He felt he should master those subjects in order to be truly educated.[11]

---

10   Carnes, *Memoir of William D. Carnes*, 8-12; William Walter Hill, "Grandfather Carnes" in "Chuicy's Family History," n.p. [cited 27 November, 2017]. Online: http://wwwchuicy.com.

11   Carnes, "Biographical Sketch of President W. D. Carnes," 206.

The urgency of Carnes' learning the classic languages was emphasized in his mind by his friendship with a highly educated agnostic lawyer named Whiteside, who questioned Carnes' intelligence for believing in Christianity. Carnes asked Whiteside if he had ever examined the evidence for Biblical faith. The lawyer confessed that he had not, to which Carnes replied, "Now as an intelligent man and a lawyer, what would you think of a juror who, when called into court, would declare himself ready to render a verdict without having heard the evidence?" Whiteside could not answer. He investigated and became a Christian.[12]

Although he had known what to say in that situation, Carnes knew that he did not have sufficient training to be equal to men like Whiteside in debating controversial religious issues. Therefore, when Campbell entered the preparatory department of the University and Mary and Amanda entered East Tennessee Female Institute, W. D. Carnes enrolled as a freshman at the University. In doing so, he left behind the opportunity to become wealthy.[13]

At the University, the younger students called Carnes "Old Pap." At the end of his first year, he had made such high grades in Latin and Greek that the university promoted him to the junior class, a move allowing him to complete his degree in three years. Upon receipt of the Bachelor's degree, he was appointed principal of the reparatory department, a secondary school attached to the university. Two years later, when he reached the masters' degree level, he accepted a professorship teaching English grammar and literature. "Old Pap," now thirty-seven years of age, became the academic hero of the campus. One young man conjectured to Professor

---

12   Boles, *Biographical Sketches*, 121.
13   Carnes, *Memoir of William D. Carnes*, 14-18.

Horace Maynard that Carnes would one day be president of the school. The professor replied, "He is too old."

While still a student in Knoxville, Carnes' religious fervor deepened. With two friends he began prayer meetings in the college chapel. In the beginning, a group of hooting, shouting, swearing students tried to disrupt their singing and prayers by playing fiddles and stomping their feet in a loud dance. The worshipers waited patiently until the opposition grew tired and left. The Christians then continued their services. Within a few meeting days, the demonstrations ceased and soon even their rebellious leader was converted. It was not long before the chapel hall was filled for regular prayer meetings and students were reaching out to the townspeople with the Gospel.[14]

Meanwhile, Elizabeth gave birth to two more sons in Knoxville: Joseph Malcolm and William Davis Carnes, Jr. A third daughter, Elizabeth Annette, was born in 1848 back at the family home in Sequatchee Valley after Carnes had left the university and was serving a brief term as principal of LaFayette Academy in Pikeville, Tennessee.[15]

Twenty miles to the north on the Cumberland plateau, two Christians, N. B. Huddleston and Isaac Newton Jones, were making plans to start a new college at Spencer, Tennessee. They approached Carnes offering him the presidency. The suggestion was especially attractive because they promised that he would be free to organize the college and develop whatever programs and curricula he judged expedient. He accepted, and "Burritt College" was born. The doors opened to students in January 1850. The new institution was named for Elihu Burritt, a self-educated blacksmith whose efforts at

---

14   Carnes, *Memoir of William D. Carnes*, 19-24.
15   Carnes, *Memoir of William D. Carnes*, 25-30.

writing were known throughout the region and "who intended that the youth of his community should get the benefits of education denied to him."[16]

For the next eight years, Carnes built Burritt College. The curriculum focused on the liberal arts and classics but included physical education courses for credit, a move disdained by many Southern educators. As best it is known, he also pioneered the coeducational boarding school concept, making Burritt the first college in the South to house boys and girls on the same campus. Not a few conservative parents radically objected. Only by building an annex to his own house to serve as the girls' dormitory and appointing his daughter Mary to be the live-in supervisor could he convince most that it was safe to send their daughters to Burritt. Although his ideas were innovative, the number of students was larger than facilities would accommodate that first year.

Carnes's solution to the need for housing and classrooms was to sell his farm at Pikeville to build three new buildings. In return, he was given additional ownership stock in the college property. In those days, administrators and faculty often bought stock or accepted part ownership in the buildings, land, and other capital holdings of the institution as part of their salaries. Together with shares Carnes had previously purchased, he now held controlling interest in the institution.[17]

---

16   Quotation inscribed on the state historical marker at the gate of Burritt College, Spencer, TN; Marion West, "Pioneer of the Cumberlands: A History of Burritt College, 1848-1938," unpublished manscript; E. G. Sewell, "Burritt College," *Gospel Advocate*, XLVII:21 (May 25, 1905), 329; M. Norvel Young, *A History of Colleges Established and Controlled by Members of the churches of Christ* (Kansas City, MO: Old Paths Book Club, 1949), 53.

17   Boles, *Biographical Sketches of Gospel Preachers*, 206.

Soon the student body tripled in size, and the future looked bright for the school. But trouble came to Burritt in 1857. Carnes had convinced the trustees to establish several controversial policies. One required that every student recite a Bible lesson each Sunday in the worship services. He believed that Bible study was necessary to a well-rounded practical education. Some objected to his attaching these school requirements to the church and its worship activity.

W. D. Carnes, President of Burritt College, 1850-58; James Rogers Cope's great-great-grandfather. Picture from www.therestorationmovement.com

Another policy imposed severe penalties on students who used alcoholic beverages. Several students were dismissed for drinking whiskey. Some of those suspended from school and sent home were from influential families who were known to manufacture liquor for considerable profit. Some of the fathers of these students defended their sons and branded Carnes a "fanatic" and a "tyrant." One such fellow was a local preacher. In spite of the opposition, Carnes was determined to keep the school clean from the influence of "white lightning." He went to Nashville and with the help of organized temperance organizations lobbied a bill through the Tennessee legislature prohibiting the sale of intoxicants within four miles of a chartered educational facility. In October, Carnes' home, including the girls' dormitory, burned down. No one was arrested but the community believed that the fire resulted from arson by opponents to Carnes' position on alcohol.[18]

While reeling from both personal losses and losses to the school, Carnes received an exciting letter from the trustees of East Tennessee University (now the University of Tennessee) offering him the presidency. Carnes accepted their invitation, sold his interest in Burritt College, and moved to Knoxville in September 1858. His tenure at the university, however, was short-lived and filled with misfortune. His son, William, contracted typhoid fever during the summer before the family left Spencer. The boy recovered, but a few months after President Carnes assumed office, Amanda fell ill and died. Still grieving for his daughter, "Old Pap" suffered another great trial. Doctors in Knoxville diagnosed Elizabeth, his wife, with incurable cancer. After her death, Carnes could never get his heart into running the university. The care of the younger

---

18   Carnes, *Memoir of William D. Carnes*, 31-33; Boles, *Biographical Sketches of Gospel Preachers*, 123.

children and other family matters had his attention. The less than two-year experience had been devastating.[19] Still, he is considered to have been the seventh president of the University of Tennessee.

Carnes next assignment grew out of a trip he had made in January 1859 to take care of some legislative business for the university. While in Nashville, he met with President Tolbert Fanning of Franklin College. Fanning was a strong restoration figure in Middle Tennessee. Fanning's school was a successful private junior college with ambitions of becoming a university. Fanning was looking for a new president so that he could resign and devote his time to preaching and editing a new periodical, the *Gospel Advocate*, which he had founded with the help of William Lipscomb in 1855. Fanning believed that Carnes was the ideal man for the presidency of the college because he already had educational background sufficient to lead it into the expansion programs he envisioned. Carnes was known to be a dedicated Christian committed to the same principles of restoration espoused by Fanning. After meeting others in Fanning's team and finding answers to some of his personal questions about the care of his children, Carnes decided to join their endeavor. He went back to Knoxville, resigned from the university, and spent the summer of 1860 travelling through West Tennessee and Mississippi, lecturing on education. He began selling stock in Franklin College and recruiting students.[20]

---

19   Charles E. Smith, "Pathfinder for Generations to Come," *The Tennessee Alumnus* (February, 1968), 5-7; Carnes, *Memoir of William D. Carnes*, 33-36.

20   James R. Wilburn, *The Hazard of the Die: Tolbert Fanning and the Restoration Movement* (Austin, TX: Sweet Publishing Company, 1969), 204-05.

Upon taking office, the new president introduced exciting new programs and built a new gymnasium. One year later, however, the Civil War ground the school to a halt. Like most others, Franklin College stood deserted during the next four years (1861-65).[21]

After the Civil War ended, efforts were made to revive the development of a university operated by Christians in Middle Tennessee. Franklin College reopened on October 2, 1865, but on October 28, a young boy accidentally set fire to the administration building while burning out soot from the chimney. The library, laboratories, and other facilities in that building were totally destroyed. Carnes's personal library valued at more than four-thousand dollars was also lost. There was no insurance. Insurance companies had not taken such risks during or immediately following the war. Neither could the impoverished Southerners support reconstruction of the college buildings because their own home repairs demanded whatever assets they could gather.[22]

Even so, many continued in their desire for the establishment of a university operated by Christians. Some suggested waiting until the national "Reconstruction" had been effectively begun. Others insisted upon going ahead by establishing a school at Manchester, Tennessee, in Coffee County, about halfway between Nashville and Chattanooga. Beginning in 1867, Carnes led Manchester College as its president. In its third year, a dam was built which turned the Duck River into a breeding ground for mosquitoes. Almost

---

21   William Davis Carnes, "Plans for Schools," *Gospel Advocate*, VI:11 (November, 1860), 331; Tolbert Fanning, "President Elder W. D. Carnes in the Field," *Gospel Advocate*, VII:10 (October, 1861), 14.

22   Tolbert Fanniing, "Franklin College," *Gospel Advocate*, VIII:1 (January, 1866), 14.

every home in Manchester was afflicted with malaria. Carnes himself suffered from the disease and had to leave or die.[23]

About the time Manchester College collapsed, the administration of Burritt College failed to maintain viability. Carnes' old friends called for him to return. Toward the end of this last term of five years beginning in 1874, the trustees with the president's approval hired Dr. T. W. Brents, a prominent preacher and former physician as a fund-raiser. Brents engineered a drive to sell stock in the college with a view toward providing new buildings and equipment.[24] He was so successful that soon a movement was underway to elect him president in place of Carnes, even though he had little background in the world of academia.[25] President Carnes was now past seventy years of age and was beginning to lose the effectiveness he once had. Under pressure he retired, and Brents took the reins of Burritt College. Brents offered Carnes a professorship, but Carnes chose instead to help a group attempting to start Waters and Walling College at McMinnville.[26]

Carnes' last work at McMinnville lasted only two months. The effort to build a college did not succeed. Carnes returned to Spencer because of illness. He developed an abscess in the liver and died on November 20, 1879. His body was buried beside his mother just down the hill from Burritt College at Spencer, Tennessee.[27]

---

23 Carnes, *Memoir of William D. Carnes*, 45-47.

24 J. A. Hill, "Burritt College," *Gospel Advocate*, XIX:38 (September 20, 1877), 580-81.

25 M. C. Kurfees, "The Life of Dr. T. W. Brents," *Gospel Advocate*, XLVII:36 (September 7, 1905), 564.

26 W. Y. Kuykendall, "Elder W. D. Carnes," *Gospel Advocate*, XXII:10 (March 4, 1880), 149.

27 Carnes, *Memoir of William D. Carnes*, 47-51; Smith, "Pathfinder

The Rogers Family

George Washington Rogers and **Amanda Carnes Rogers.** Amanda Carnes was the second of three daughters born to William Davis and Elizabeth Billingsley Carnes. Born in June 1831, Amanda died at the age of twenty-six in April 1858.

Amanda fell in love with George Washington Rogers, a merchant from Pikeville, Tennessee. They met while attending Burritt College and corresponded by mail after finishing their studies. In those letters, George several times asked Amanda to marry him. She did not respond. Finally, he wrote her a brief note in which he said, "I have expressed my affections to you and I am not going to bother you any more. I am on my way to Smithville to go into the mercantile business. Unless I hear from you, you will not be hearing from me any more." She responded, and one year from that day, they married.

Amanda Rogers was a strong-willed woman. Some thought she was a genius intellectually. Her parents considered her the most "devotedly religious" of all their children. Amanda's untimely death came soon after she had given birth to a daughter they named Ida. On her deathbed, Amanda asked her older sister, Mary Carnes Hill, to raise her daughter. Mary could not refuse. Two months later, Mary gave birth to a third child of her own, Ella. Several months after that, Mary learned that her mother, Mrs. W. D. (Elizabeth) Carnes, was diagnosed with cancer. Mary was now pregnant with her fourth child, Dora. In June, 1859 Mary took all the children to Knoxville to care for her dying mother.[28]

---

for Generations to Come," 7.

28   n.p. [cited 30 November, 2017]. Online: http://www.RoaneTNHistory.org.

After Amanda's death, her husband, George Washington Rogers, enlisted in the Second Tennessee Cavalry. He served in the Civil War and apparently died before 1863. There seems to be no family record of his burial place.[29]

Ida Rogers Cope. James Cope's grandmother, Ida Rogers Cope, was the orphaned daughter of George Washington and Amanda Carnes Rogers. Upon losing her parents early in life, she had been entrusted to the care of her aunt Mary Hill and her husband, a lawyer from Pikeville named William Jasper Hill. The Hills had five other children. They all lived with Ida's grandfather, W. D. Carnes, during the last part of the Civil War. Also in Carnes' home during that time was his daughter Annette.

During the winter of 1863, the family often suffered hardship because Carnes had not signed an oath vowing to refuse aid to Confederate soldiers. For six weeks the household existed on a diet of potatoes and water. Union soldiers had not found a patch of Irish potatoes which Carnes had covered with dead grass and weeds. Every night members of the family dug out enough potatoes for the next day with their bare hands and then restored the surrounding surface to what appeared to be undisturbed ground.[30]

For several years prior to her wedding, Ida Rogers was principal of the Female and Musical Departments of Sequatchie College in Bledsoe County, Tennessee. She taught piano and was a good artist in her own right.

Ida Rogers married James Wallace Cope, a young man who aspired to be a lawyer. She lived with her new husband

---

29   Interview with James Rogers Cope and Mary Hill (Cope) Luna, July 15, 1984.

30   Carnes, *Memoir of William D. Carnes*, 42.

little more than a year. She developed what they then called "childbed fever," probably resulting from blood poisoning and an infection in the uterus caused by the doctor's forceps used during childbirth. Two other women died of the same complication that year. She left her husband with a nine-day-old son, Rogers Wallace Cope.[31]

The Cope Family

Wallace B. Cope. James Cope's great-grandfather Cope was born on August 24, 1819, to Andrew and Sarah Wallace Cope. Wallace's mother died when he was three ,and his father remarried. Wallace was raised by his father and step-mother.[32]

During a fifty-two-year period of public service, Wallace B. Cope held several county government offices. He was a staunch Democrat and at one time served as Trustee of White County, Tennessee. Through all that half-century, he was also known as a prosperous farmer.

Wallace Cope was reared under the teaching and influence of Primitive Baptist parents who believed that the Holy Spirit would directly intervene into the lives of elect persons and miraculously save them. Wallace waited many years for the Lord to visit him in that way and let him know that he was among the chosen for salvation. Through all that time he remained very devout. His fourth wife was a member of the church of Christ. Through her influence, he listened to gospel preaching and read his Bible. After a difficult personal struggle, he obeyed the gospel. E. A. Elam baptized him. From the day

---

31 Interview with Mary Hill (Cope) Luna, July 15, 1984.

32 Andrew Cope was born March 7, 1781, and died May 18, 1862; Sarah Wallace Cope died April 14, 1822.

of his baptism until his death about a year later, he thanked God that he had been spared until he could learn the truth. His obituaries in the local newpapers indicate that he was among the most highly-respected citizens in the community. He apparently was known by all for his honesty. He had few enemies. He died August 20, 1898, at the age of seventy-nine from complications following surgery.[33]

James Wallace Cope. James Wallace Cope was the son of Wallace B. Cope and his first wife, Clarissa Jane. He had two brothers and two sisters, the only children of his father and all born to his own mother. He was graduated with honors from Burritt College and studied law with his brother-in-law, H. C. Snodgrass. He was admitted to the bar and became a prominent attorney in Cookeville, Tennessee. He also served as editor and publisher of the *Cookeville Chronicle* for one year (1878).

James Wallace Cope was born October 18, 1856. He married Ida Rogers in 1881.[34] He died of tuberculosis at the age of thirty-two on June 13, 1889.[35] He left behind his six-year-old orphaned son, **Rogers Wallace Cope**, who later became the father of **James Rogers Cope**.

---

33 "Wallace B. Cope," *Cookeville Press* (August 21, 1898); "Wallace B. Cope," *Sparta News* (August 22, 1898).

34 "Orange Blossoms," *Sparta News* (May 31, 1881).

35 "James W. Cope," *Sparta News* (June 13, 1889).

Chapter Two:

Maternal Heritage: Weaver and Breeding Families

James (Jim) Rogers Cope's heritage of special note on his mother's side included two other Tennessee families from White County: the Weavers and the Breedings. They depict the rural Southern family and provide a true insight into the social and cultural background that so deeply affected the character, attitudes, and values of Jim Cope. As we shall see, that is especially true of Scott and Fannie Jane Breeding, Jim's mother's parents.

The Weaver Family

John Weaver. Historians often identify the Battle of King's Mountain (October 7, 1780) as one of the major turning points in the War for American Independence. It stands with those at Lexington, Concord, Ticonderoga, Bunker Hill, Valley Forge, and Saratoga as decisive in the revolutionary effort. King's Mountain was a narrow ridge in South Carolina about six-hundred yards in length. It was positioned in a sixteen mile range of small mountains located about a mile-and-a-half south of the North Carolina state line just east of the Allegheny Mountains.

The hill was named for His Majesty King George by British Major Patrick Ferguson. Ferguson's army of 1125 men waited there for reinforcements several days before fighting broke out. Two nights before the battle, John Sevier and several other colonial officers gathered 910 riflemen in what is now Washington County, Tennessee. At dawn, they began a thirty-six hour ride on horseback across the Alleghenies, stopping briefly only once to rest and eat. Because of an all-night driving rain, they were forced to wrap their guns with blankets, sacks, and even the shirts from their backs to keep their powder dry for the ensuing battle.

Jim Cope's great-great-grandfather John Weaver was one of those 910 riflemen. They arrived about noon, were joined by a few soldiers from Virginia and North Carolina, and went immediately into battle. The Americans surrounded the mountain, with Sevier's men, including John Weaver, forming the right wing of the attack. The battle lasted only an hour. Two hundred twenty-four British soldiers were killed, including Ferguson. Another one hundred eighty were wounded, and more than seven hundred were taken prisoner. The horses, wagons, munitions, and supplies were confiscated. Only thirty Colonial soldiers were killed and about twice that many were wounded.[1]

After the war, John Weaver returned to Washington County, Tennessee (still North Carolina in 1783). He and his father, Samuel, bought farms near what is now Jonesboro, Tennessee, in 1784. He moved his family to White County, Tennessee (near Sparta) between 1796 and 1805. His body is buried in the Hickman family graveyard along the banks of Cherry Creek.[2]

---

1   "Descendants of John Weaver Hold Reunion," *Sparta News* (July 13, 1931).

2   Annie Breeding Bradley, *A History of the Breeding and Weaver*

Samuel David Peter Weaver and Annie Hickman Weaver. While yet a boy, Samuel (a name given to honor his grandfather) David Peter Weaver traveled with his family to their new home in White County, Tennessee. Upon reaching maturity, he married a South Carolina girl who was five years his junior. Their farm was on the mountain near a spring that flowed into Cherry Creek. Annie Hickman Weaver bore eleven children between 1823 and 1841. The youngest, Fannie Jane Weaver, was only nine years old when her father died at age fifty-one.

The Weavers were a hard-working and frugal family. Those traits passed to their children. Most of the Weavers were known as "savers" who hated to spend a dollar. They were farmers who cared little for the conveniences and luxuries of life so cherished by others. Samuel's family had no cooking stoves, kerosene lamps, or sewing machines while the children were growing up.[3]

Annie Weaver lived thirty-four years after her husband's death. Their eldest daughter, Mahulda, never married and stayed at home to care for her crippled mother. Annie had fallen, injuring her hip while pruning a grape vine in their yard. She never attended church worship services after that fall. Her Baptist ministers often came by to talk about religion and pray with her outside her home where she would be sitting. Mahulda put her mother in a homemade rocking chair and moved it first to one side and then to the other across the yard into the shade of a huge tree. Several of the other children lived nearby and helped with chores, especially the heavier work the two women could not do for themselves.

Families (Jackson, TN: Annie Breeding Bradley, 1948), 25-26.

3   Interview with Mary Hill (Cope) Luna, July 15, 1984.

Annie Weaver died at age ninety. As custom had it, some of the neighbor women came to bathe and prepare her body for burial. Black cloth was quickly made into a burial dress. The men put together a home-made wooden coffin and brought up a wagon to carry the body to the Hickman graveyard beside Cherry Creek. It was almost nightfall when they arrived at the cemetery. Her youngest daughter, Fannie Jane, wept as she made the beds the next morning, sorrowing that they had hardly been able to see their mother's face the last time because of the darkness. Often in those days, particularly in the summertime, when a large family was scattered, the body was buried and the funeral service was conducted later. Friends and family gathered in the white frame meeting house of the Board Valley Baptist Church several weeks after her death to hear her brother Jessie, a Presbyterian preacher, along with three Baptists, eulogize her and comfort the still grieving family.[4]

Fannie Jane Weaver Breeding. The youngest of the Weavers' seven boys and four girls was Fannie Jane. Her father's early death, coupled with the fact that the older children were establishing their own families, left the care of their mother to Mahulda and Fannie Jane. When the older brothers, Jeptha and William, enlisted in the Confederate army, the women farmed their land in Burgess Cove. Every morning they walked down from the mountain home place to the fields, and every evening they trudged back up to care for their mother. They planted corn and in the fall carried the produce of their harvest up the mountain in bushel baskets to store it out of sight of soldiers coming through Tennessee. When spring came, the "Yankees" discovered their crib and brought up five wagons to haul the corn away.

---

4   Bradley, *A History of the Breeding and Weaver Families*, 25-40.

After the war, Fannie Jane attended school for a short time at Cumberland Institute. While there, she met Evan Scott Breeding. She returned home, taught a subscription school, worked on the farm, and used her spare time spinning, weaving, and sewing for her own new home. Her wedding gift from her mother was a corn meal sack to be used for making a dress.[5]

The Breeding Family

Bryant and Maria Miller Breeding. Bryant Breeding's mother was a Tompson. Neither his mother's nor his father's given names were known to the Copes. Bryant was born May 4, 1808, and married Maria Miller about 1834. The family, which ultimately included eight children, moved to a farm near Cookeville, Tennessee, around 1850. Bryant Breeding was crippled before he was fifty and was considered too old to fight in the Civil War. He stayed home on the farm and supported his family during the War on four-hundred dollars cash which he had hidden securely by sawing out a piece at the end of a joist in their house.

Maria Miller Breeding was reared in the Hiawassee Valley region of East Tennessee. Her twin sister drowned in the Tennessee River. Maria often told with delight stories of the Indian tribes that lived in the mountains near her home. Her mother's maiden name was Brady and may have been part Indian herself. After the death of her husband, Maria continued to live at home with her two unmarried daughters, Minerva and Caroline.[6]

---

5   Interview with Mary Hill Luna, July 16, 1984.
6   Bradley, *A History of the Breeding and Weaver Families*, 21-24.

Evan Scott and Fannie Jane Weaver Breeding. Evan Scott Breeding was born June 20, 1848, at Livingston, Tennessee, in Overton County. He often told of a day in his childhood when his mother's old gander which carefully guarded its mate against the playful boys, grabbed his shirt-tail, and chased him out of the yard through the front gate. He was only two years old at the time.

Before he reached his teen years, the family moved to White County near Cookeville. His older brothers joined others and trained for the War. Scott sometimes went with them to the "muster," a term used to describe their military practice sessions. One day the boys were told by their father that they could go as soon as they finished tying up the flax out behind the house. Having worked as long as they could stand it, they set fire to the remaining flax and took off to "do their duty."[7]

When the Civil War ended, Scott had barely reached his seventeenth birthday. The hardships experienced during the four-year period of conflict made him realize the need for a good education in at least the fundamental skills required for "reading, writing, and 'rithmatic.'" The public schools left much to be desired in those days. They were not strong academically, and classes met only when the farmers could free their sons and daughters from working to support the families. The boy determined to work his way through a good school. He would need books, clothing, and a place to stay, but his father told him that if he could work it out financially, he would allow him to leave the farm. Scott went to his brother-in-law, Jim Eller, his oldest sister Jane's husband, and worked out an agreement to stay with them while going

---

7   Bradley, *A History of the Breeding and Weaver Families*, 24.

to Cumberland Institute during the winter. To pay for his room and board, he helped them "make their crop" the next summer.[8]

Cumberland Institute was a "subscription school" on Cherry Creek. It was operated at that time by Curtis McDowell. The teacher went through the countryside taking names and money from parents. He held classes only if enough students and dollars were raised to warrant his spending his time there.

Cumberland was recognized as the best school in that section of the state. A building was constructed for the school and some students lived in cabins on the property. McDowell was especially apt in teaching mathematics. He believed that a student who had no mathematical training had no practical education at all. Scott Breeding came to share that opinion and worked diligently with his own children to help them through difficult parts of their arithmetic homework lessons.

When he graduated from the institute, Scott took the teachers' examination and began school work in the Pistole community. A political disturbance arose soon after he arrived, and a rumor was started that his students were going to run him out of town. When he learned of the rumor, he took two old army pistols, hung them on the wall, and told the boys he would defend himself if he needed to do so. After their marriage, he trained his wife Fannie Jane to use the guns until she could put two bullets in the same hole. He also bored holes in the walls and doors so that she could shoot at anyone attempting to bother her without opening up the house for them to get in and harm her.

Evan Scott Breeding and Fannie Jane Weaver met at Cumberland Institute. He was twenty, red-headed, and

---

8   Bradley, *A History of the Breeding and Weaver Families*, 50.

about 5'10" in height. She was twenty-seven, black headed like all the Weavers, and six feet tall. They first lived on top of the mountain near her mother. In the early days of their marriage, they set a pattern for their family that was based on honesty, earnestness, hard work, and commitment to provide for themselves, their children, and neighbors they had the opportunity to help. That kind of integrity served them well.

After just two years of marriage, they decided to buy the Bohannon place. They lived there only a few months, however, before having to sell it because they could not make the payments. After that, they never again allowed themselves to be indebted to anyone. Their industry allowed them to secure a few acres several years later from Henry Taylor.[9] That property in the Big Spring area became the home place of Jim Cope during the years he was growing up!

Evan Scott Breeding and his wife obeyed the gospel in the fall of 1876. Fannie Jane had believed the Calvinistic teaching that the Holy Spirit works through direct, miraculous operation on the hearts of sinners. She had spent thirteen years at the mourner's bench trying to "pray through" to "get salvation." Her honesty forced her to the conclusion that she must be among the "non-elect." She had even allowed herself to be placed in a chair where candidates for conversion were wildly rocked and admonished by a woman to "Tell it Fanny, tell it Fanny." But she just could not "get it."

Almost frantic about their lost condition, Fannie and Scott heard of a gospel meeting at the Cherry Creek church of Christ. They determined to come down off Board Mountain at night to hear the preacher, a man named Reuben Cooper. His message was clear, and they wished it could be true that

---

9   Bradley, *A History of the Breeding and Weaver Families*, 14.

salvation was God's gift, given when one surrendered the human will and responded to the gospel invitation. Scott Breeding listened carefully each evening and wrote down every scripture Cooper cited. They then returned to the mountain to study by candlelight or kerosene lamp through the night. They learned the truth reading Bible references until daylight. Finally Scott said, "Fanny, this man is teaching what the Bible says." They were baptized by Cooper the next night.[10] From that time, they rarely missed a service of the local church of Christ and they exemplified the spirit of Christ to all in the community.[11]

After their conversion, the Breedings became intensely interested in the salvation of their friends and neighbors. They paid the subscription to *The Gospel Advocate* for many of them and ordered hundreds of religious tracts and booklets to hand out in the community. Sister Breeding became so convinced that *The Gospel Advocate* was teaching truth that she even took the patent medicines advertised in the paper in those days. She and her husband led many to Christ through the literature they purchased and gave to family, neighbors, and acquaintances.

The Breedings were deeply concerned about their children and committed to raising them to be good citizens and faithful Christians. They always tried to furnish appropriate motivational and inspirational examples for them to follow. In 1897, when Tennessee was celebrating its centennial year, they took the entire family to Nashville as an educational experience. Back home, Scott worked diligently in the community, encouraging the people to vote for good schools

---

10   Interview with James R. Cope, August 16, 1985

11   Mrs. A. F. Richards, "In Memory of Mrs. Fannie Weaver Breeding," *Gospel Advocate* (October 13, 1927).

and good roads so that the country children would have the same opportunities as those in town. He was a moving force in the election that provided taxation revenue for the establishment of White County High School.[12]

The Breedings read to their children and subscribed to several good journals, one of which was a children's paper. Many nights the father read by the light of the fire or a coal oil lamp while the children listened with rapt attention. They did not have radio or television distractions in those days. Scott often quoted the proverb, "Train up a child in the way he should go and when he is old he will not depart from it."[13]

Scott Breeding was a tender-hearted man. At times when reading a particularly touching story, tears ran down his cheeks. He religiously kept reading hours which meant that he was always well informed on current events and world affairs. He read mostly from the Bible, but he also read religious books, books on law, and, of course, the local newspaper. He bought the religious library of Ransom Geer, and, according to his daughter, read every book he bought. One by one, as he read them, he gave them away to gospel preachers. Among those books were Alexander Campbell's volumes entitled *Christian System, Christian Baptism, Living Oracle,* and the *Campbell-Owen Debate,* dealing with skepticism concerning God and the Bible. One of his favorite books was J. W. McGarvey's *New Commentary on Acts of Apostles.*

"Squire" Breeding (as he was called after increasing his land holdings to almost a thousand acres) was a truthful, sincere man of integrity, and he praised God for his prosperity. He never drank liquor, used tobacco, or spoke vulgar language.

---

12   Interview with James R. Cope, July 15, 1984.
13   Bradley, *A History of the Breeding and Weaver Families,* 49.

He was thankful and sometimes said that he knew of nothing he really wanted that he did not have. He did not hold grudges and always exhorted his neighbors and brethren in the church to look forward rather than backward. He was firm, but he controlled his temper. He was seen as a peacemaker although he said what he thought forthrightly. He tried to deal with issues kindly with strength.[14]

The Breedings upheld a truly high standard of morality in every way. The nearest town was Sparta and for the farmers, a trip to Sparta, took most of the day. The country storekeepers therefore offered items of trade (food, material for clothing, small hardware, etc.) that could serve as basic staples. The Breedings ran such a country store until their youngest daughter Dora married Rogers Cope. After several years in partnership, Rogers bought out Breeding's interest in the store.

Most of the trade was on credit. Breeding knew all of the families and trusted his neighbors. At the first of each year when transferring accounts to a new ledger book, he left some behind without forwarding them because he knew they could not be paid. Those would simply be forgotten by him. During long winter months when timber and mill workers could not work, he fed many hungry families, trusting them to come by and pay their bills in the spring. Many of those bills also never made their way into his ledger.

Scott Breeding was nonetheless quite a businessman. One summer he bought a large box of embroidered collars for ladies. They simply did not sell. One beautiful afternoon, Mrs. Martha Little, one of the best dressed ladies in the community, came in to the store. Breeding sized up the situation and offered to give her one of those collars if she would wear it to

---

14 Bradley, *A History of the Breeding and Weaver Families*, 56.

her Mt. Calvary Methodist Church meeting next Sunday. She did, and the next week he sold every collar in the store.

"Squire" Breeding was definitely a conservative in moral and spiritual matters. That was also his approach to politics. He served on the County Court for a time. He had strong convictions about almost everything, but he did not engage in bitter debates about politics. He sometimes said, "Sugar catches more flies than vinegar." That was his philosophy in any kind of dispute. He was firm, but he was kind. He once took his young son Wesley into Cookeville to view the public execution of the Brazzel brothers. Wesley sat on his father's shoulders about forty feet from the gallows and witnessed the confession of one, the obstinacy of the other, and the snap of the rope as each was hanged.[15]

The Breeding family were not only benevolent; they were also consistent in their religious faith and practice. Scott and Fannie Jane never missed a worship service. In fact, they gave a piece of their own property to the Big Spring church of Christ for the construction of a meeting house. They also deeded the ground immediately behind the new building to the community for a cemetery in which they and most of their friends were later buried.

Fannie Jane, like her husband, loved to help other people. She cared for the sick and sat with those who were dying. Her good deeds were often not known even by her own children until they later heard of them from the people who had received her kindness. Fannie Jane was a Weaver, however. Like the others in her family, she was thrifty and hated wastefulness.

---

15 Bradley, *A History of the Breeding and Weaver Families*, 52.

"Take care of the pennies, and the dollars will take care of themselves," was her philosophy. She cared little for luxuries. She took pride in her work and was seldom idle. She rarely was seen resting without some handwork on her lap. Most of her time was spent making clothing or cooking food for others she thought to be in need.[16]

In some things, Fannie could be a pessimist. She could see trouble before it came along. Two incidents are reported in a letter from Bill to Wesley after their mother's death. The first remembered the time when she had typhoid fever and thought she was dying. She had scalded a barrel several times to prepare it for kraut. She called Annie to her bedside and told her to scald it one more time before filling it with the kraut. "That should take care of them after my death," she said. The second incident occurred one summer when she planted peach seeds in a row and waited for them to come up. When they did, she took each sprout and planted it in a field with the remark: "Of course, I will never live to enjoy any of the fruit, but I rejoice in the idea that some or all of the children will." She lived for years and ate from those trees.[17]

One story of Sister Breeding's love for righteousness was related by J. T. Clark. After her death, the preacher told Jim Cope and his mother, "As I was leaving their home after one of my meetings at Big Spring, Sister Breeding called me out to herself, placed a heavy package in my hand, and said, 'Brother Clark, you know better than I where the gospel needs to be preached. I want you to pick out the place you think it ought to be done and take what is in this package for your support.' When I arrived home I took that package

---

16   Bradley, *A History of the Breeding and Weaver Families,* 53.
17   Letter from William Breeding to Wesley Breeding, February 28, 1937.

from my grip, untied it, and found wrapped in a paper bag ninety-nine silver half-dollars."[18]

A similar incident was learned from a letter sent to Jim Cope's mother by H. Leo Boles not long before Sister Breeding died. He said, "Tell Sister Breeding that the meeting I held resulted in several additions, and every time some person responded to the invitation I thought of her." Boles was under the same instructions as Brother Clark and had received similar compensation. The money came from selling chickens and eggs. She put it back for the gospel, and with it she bought religious literature or asked preachers to use it in spreading the gospel.[19]

Before she died, Fannie Jane Breeding told Jim Cope's mother that she had in the bank seven hundred dollars that she had deposited a little at a time. She wanted the family to see that it was spent helping someone through college so he could preach the gospel. Sister Breeding had been disappointed that none of her grandsons had decided to preach. She was, however, proud of a fine young man in the church named Will Floyd, whom she had taught in her Sunday Bible class. She suggested that he might make a good investment for the money because at her encouragement he was thinking about devoting his life to preaching. The summer after Will finished high school, H. Leo Boles held a gospel meeting at the Cherry Creek church. Boles had been reared nearby on the Calf Killer River and was at that time serving as president of David Lipscomb College. Will talked to Boles about wanting to preach, and Boles responded that Will needed a good college education before doing so. Boles told him to come to David Lipscomb and

---

18   Interview with James R. Cope, August 16, 1984.

19   Bradley, *A History of the Breeding and Weaver Families*, 74; confirmed by James R. Cope, August 16, 1984.

they would work out the money some way. When he went to school, the Breeding family loaned him Sister Breeding's money to help him finish. He attended classes at David Lipscomb two years and then moved to Gadsden, Alabama. He made a fine preacher and returned to the Calf Killer area for a meeting in which he baptized a large number of people. The winter came, and the family learned that Will's first child would be born soon. They wrote him a note at Christmas time expressing appreciation for his dedication and canceling the note on Sister Breeding's loan.[20]

Many years later in 1946, Will Floyd held a meeting at Livingston, Tennessee. His college roommate, Kurt Blankenship, had arranged for him to come preach in the services. Touched by Will's preaching, Sister Breeding's own second son, Bill, who had gotten caught up in business and fallen away from Christ, came forward and confessed sin, asking to be restored to the Lord to His church. Jim Cope said that Bill probably would never have even attended the meeting had it not been that Will Floyd was doing the preaching. Cope went on to say, "On that occasion Brother Floyd spoke at length of the influence of the Breeding family on his life. Surely the soul of Grandmother Breeding looked forth amidst the 'innumerable hosts of angels' and from the portals of the land of 'the spirits of just men made perfect' to sing the song of redemption and with the father of the prodigal son, shouted, 'for this my son was dead, and is alive again; he was lost, and is found!' Bill died a faithful Christian. His old mother had saved him through Will Floyd."[21]

Often the preachers holding late-summer daily gospel meetings at Big Spring stayed in the Breeding home. Sister

---

20 Interview with James R. Cope, August 16, 1984.

21 Interview with James R. Cope, August 16, 1984;

Breeding thought it her work in the meeting to be truly hospitable to the preacher and to all the visitors who came to worship. In the summer of 1892, W. H. Sutton came out from Sparta to conduct a two-week tent meeting. People came from all over the upper Cumberland area. The Breedings put up eleven beds in their home and all were used every night. They fed dozens of people with fresh vegetables, canned fruit and preserves from the cellar, lots of fried chicken, fresh biscuits, and hot cornbread.[22]

To Fannie Jane Breeding, the poor as well as those who came into temporary need were seen as prospects for a greater kind of service than benevolence. While she cared for their bodies, she talked to them about their souls and taught them the gospel of Christ. Sister Breeding did much to advance the cause of Christ in a very personal and quiet way. She spent great amounts of time weaving carpets with her own hands for the aisles and pulpit of the new church building. She said as she worked, "I was a 'Weaver' by name and by trade." She literally sheared the sheep, spun the raw wool into thread on the spinning wheel, and wove the yarn. She made it into clothing for her family and carpets for her own house, the houses of her children, and the house of the Lord. She did a majority of the janitorial work in the church meeting house as long as she was able. She almost always asked visitors in the services who lived outside the immediate community to go home with her family for Sunday dinner. Some Sundays there were two or three large families who accepted her invitation. She planted a garden each year and canned fruit from her peach trees, strawberry patch, raspberry bushes, and grapevines. She milked the cows and churned the butter. She fed the chickens and gathered the eggs. She drew water from

---

22   Bradley, *A History of the Breeding and Weaver Families*, 66.

the well and kept the house until the last week of her life of nearly eighty-six years.[23]

Fannie Jane Breeding was a determined kind of person. Her convictions on raising her children, serving her husband and family, obeying God, and setting a good moral example to all her neighbors were conservative and without compromise. And yet she was a sensitive person as you can readily imagine from reading her story. She said little when offended, sometimes carrying the hurt in her heart without letting it be known to others.[24]

Scott Breeding loved to tell Bible stories to his Sunday school class of boys and girls. All the classes assembled in little groups in the main room of the church building in those days. His class met on the west side about midway back. He loved the children and refused to give up his class until he became too old and infirmed to continue teaching. He often said, "The hope of our country lies in our children." He stood before the entire congregation each Sunday and asked to hear the memory verses of each person present. Almost everyone recited at least one Bible verse of Scripture and afterward he announced with pride the number of folks who had their memory work done. He often made comments afterward about the needs of the church and the activities of the brethren exhorting them to greater faithfulness or encouraging them to help one another when in sorrow, in need, or in wavering faith.

Fannie Jane also loved the children. By the time the Big Spring building was completed, she had reached her declining years. She prepared a special rocking chair and had it taken

---

23 Bradley, *A History of the Breeding and Weaver Families,* 18, 51-52.

24 Bradley, *A History of the Breeding and Weaver Families,* 58.

to the building. There in a front corner she worshipped and rocked babies for their mothers who were looking after older children. She wore a long black dress and a bonnet. She brought with her a basket containing the linen cloths for the Lord's table and the items used to symbolize the Lord's death. She made the bread and prepared the grape juice from her own vines. Unlike her husband, she was a singer. She loved the hymns and sang them enthusiastically from memory at home as well as in the worship of the church. She loved to gather the children together for singing on Sunday evenings.[25]

In this family, death took the wife first. After fifty-eight years of marriage, Fannie Jane suffered a fall and one week later on April 14, 1927, she died.[26] On the same day that she had fallen, her son Will's wife Ida had died. The trauma of losing both his wife and mother within a week was almost unbearable to Will.

Two years before his wife's death, Scott Breeding had fallen and suffered a broken hip. After she was gone, he lived alone until he suffered a stroke and became bedfast. Long ago his hair and long beard had turned snowy white from the red it had been. After he was paralyzed, Dora Frances and her family moved into the house to care for him. He died two years after his beloved wife, on August 14, 1929.[27] He was carried to his grave by his grandsons and buried alongside the body of his wife in the Big Spring cemetery in view of the home in which they had lived for more than fifty years.

The family showed the same care for one another in settling the Breedings' estate that the parents had always

---

25 Bradley, *A History of the Breeding and Weaver Families*, 66, 70.

26 "Mrs. Breeding Called," *Sparta News* (April 15, 1927).

27 "Death Calls Prominent and Aged Citizen," *Sparta News* (August 14, 1929).

shown for them. On a given day, the family all gathered at the home. They entered a room and selected from the things that they wished to keep in that room. They began with the eldest child and chronologically by age made their selections until all desired items of furniture, etc., were taken. Then they moved to the next room, and the second eldest child had first choice. There was not the first problem, and everyone was considerate of the wishes of the others. When the task was completed, all were allowed to make exchanges as they wished with one another. It was a loving family. Dora Francis and Rogers Cope with their family continued in the house for many years after their father's death.[28]

---

28   Interview with Mary Hill (Cope) Luna, July 16, 1984.

Chapter Three:

Parents: Rogers Wallace Cope and Dora Frances (Breeding) Cope

Rogers Wallace Cope.

Jim Cope's father, Rogers Wallace Cope, became an orphan at the age of six. A few days after his birth on November 17, Ida B. Rogers Cope became tragically feverish with a form of blood poisoning that apparently resulted from an infection in her uterus. The family came to believe that the condition was probably caused by contamination from the doctor's instruments used during childbirth. She died on November 26, 1882, when her son was only nine days old. She was twenty-four years old. James Wallace Cope, Rogers' father, was thirty-two when he contracted tuberculosis and died.

After his father's death, Rogers was taken to live at Pikeville, Tennessee. He was passed among relatives who cared for him on the Cope side of the family while discussing a permanent home for him. After a few months a bright light appeared in the darkness. Dora Hill Rhea had married five years earlier[1] but as yet had no children. She and her husband,

---

1   "Married," *Pikeville Advance*, January 30, 1884. The paper said,

Aquilla England Rhea, determined to take the child into their home and raise him as their own son. That decision came to be a wonderful blessing to all involved, particularly to Rogers.

Mary Madora ("Dora") Hill Rhea had grown up as the next to youngest child in her family. She was a first cousin to Rogers Cope's mother, Ida Rogers Cope (Jim's grandmother). Ida Rogers was two years old when her aunt Dora was born. Aunt Dora's mother, Mrs. William Jasper Hill (Mary Carnes), took Ida into her home when Ida's mother, Mrs. George Rogers (Amanda Carnes), Jim's great-grandmother, died. Dora and Ida had grown up together in the same household.

Aunt Dora's mother (Mary Hill) and Amanda Carnes Rogers were sisters, daughters of W. D. Carnes. Ida Rogers married James Wallace Cope, later Jim's grandfather. Aunt Dora, one of the natural children, said that if any favoritism was shown by her mother as they were growing up, it was toward Ida, the sister's child, because she was without her biological mother. The other children often got hand-me-downs while Ida got the new best. The girls actually grew up as sisters though they were first cousins. Ida Rogers married Jim Cope's grandfather, James Wallace Cope, but died when Jim's father was only a few days old.

Aunt Dora's mother, after being widowed, became a successful and much appreciated teacher at Lafayette Academy.[2] One of her brothers was an eye, ear, nose, and throat specialist at Harriman, Tennessee. He went to the

---

"A. E. Rhea, a worthy young man, unmarried, of Sparta, and Clerk and Master for White County, drove quietly into Pikeville last Saturday. He left Monday morning with a Hill which he proposed to convey across the mountains to Sparta, and seemed to be very happy as he went off singing his favorite music notes, 'Do-ra.'"

2   "Married," *Pikeville Advance*, January 30, 1884.

Christian Church because of his wife. Dora's older brother, Eddie, was a preacher and farmer near Pikeville, Tennessee. Still another brother, Lucius Davis Hill, was a lawyer elected to the Railroad and Public Utilities Commission of the State of Tennessee in a statewide election. Aunt Dora lived with the Copes from the time she was forty years old until her death at 92. She did much of the Bible teaching of the children while their mother was doing the work required of a housewife in caring for the family.

After twenty years of marriage, "Quill" Rhea, a city official in Sparta who served several terms as Mayor, succumbed to a severe kidney ailment known then as "Bright's disease" and now as "chronic nephritis." He died on January 10, 1904, leaving Aunt Dora a widow.[3] The question arose again, who would care for a family member left alone by death? Rogers and his young wife, also named Dora, stood up and took Aunt Dora into their household. She lived with them for the next forty-eight years. Someone has said that the family is "God's social security system." That proved to be true for Aunt Dora. She had raised a son who believed the family should care for children and senior relatives when they were alone in need.

"Aunt Dora" Rhea was the only mother Rogers Cope had ever known. In fact, she was the only meaningful "grandmother" Jim Cope had to spend time with him and influence his life. That explains my taking care to record this much detail concerning her background.

Jim's personal memory of his Grandmother Breeding was limited to one event in his childhood just a year or two before she died.[4] Jim had wandered into the dining room of the old

3   "Death of A. E. Rhea," *Sparta News*, January 11, 1904.
4   Much of the information upon which the reconstruction of

Breeding house. Grandmother Breeding was sitting by the fireplace. As he approached her, she pulled him up to her and gave him a big hug. She was in her eighties at the time, and Jim was eight or nine. That was awkward for Jim but later quite memorable because she was not the type to play with Jim when he was a little boy.

Having been orphaned, Rogers Cope appreciated many things in life that others took for granted. People loved him because of his optimistic approach to life and because of his love and appreciation for others around him. Before marrying, he did not have the kind of family relationships so common to Tennessee folk in his community, so he worked to keep his family stable and close in spirit to one another.

As a child, Rogers was all boy. Aunt Dora had to watch him constantly to see that he stayed out of mischief. Many times, she failed. Women wore black high-topped buttoned shoes in those days—at home as well as to church. They used a shoe hook to loop the tie on those shoes over the latches. Aunt Dora never knew where he got it, but one Sunday in church services, she looked up, and Rogers had one of those shoe hooks hanging on his eyelid. He was on the front row peering through it at the preacher. Jim got his mischief from his daddy.

Rogers was always into something as a young boy. One of the neighbors had a goose that disappeared.

James R. Cope's family background and his own early family history has been developed from stories he told to family and to me. Where Jim's memory can be tested, it has been found to be remarkably accurate. That is partially due to the fact that his family has delighted through the years in telling of what they considered to have been the "rich heritage" they shared.

The man said, "Rogers, have you seen my old goose."

"Yeah, I saw it."

"Where was it?"

"Aunt Dora got him, picked him clean, and we ate him."

"Oh, Rogers," the neighbor responded, "Aunt Dora would not do such a thing. What did she do with the feathers?"

Rogers instantly replied, "She fed them to the cow!"

Rogers was restless in church, and Aunt Dora always took something for him to eat. One Sunday she forgot to take his treat. An old African American friend lived at the bottom of the hill that led up to the church building at Sparta. They stopped and asked if she had anything Aunt Dora could take for Rogers to eat. She had made some thin cornmeal "hoecakes" that morning, so she wrapped one up for the boy to put in his pocket. Because of the delay, they arrived late after services had begun. Rogers broke away from Aunt Dora and ran toward the front of the auditorium. Rather than raise a commotion, she let him go. He went right to the "Amen" corner and perched on the front row. In a little bit, out came the hoecake from his pocket, and he ate it in front of everyone present.

From the beginning, Aunt Dora was interested in Rogers' education. She sent him first to the old Potter Bible School in Bowling Green, Kentucky, and then on to Burritt College. He came to be a careful, critical thinker and a well-read man. He loved to tell of a speech he made at Burritt College on the subject of Sam Davis's activities in Tennessee and Texas.

Rogers Cope was constantly active and always optimistic. He stood only five feet five and one-half inches tall, but his eyes flashed, and he never seemed old to his friends later in life. He spoke with a firm voice, yet he was loving and caring and sharing with all his friends and neighbors. He was never idle. He sometimes talked about how peculiar Bill Weaver was. Bill would get up at 4:00 in the morning, build a fire, and just sit there and look at it until about 7:30. Rogers could not imagine such a waste of time.

While a young man, Rogers went out to Dallas to work for a while, but he soon returned to White County. He married Dora Frances Breeding at the home of her parents on June 25, 1911. Elder J. D. Gunn performed the ceremony. Nine months and three days later, March 28, 1912, the first of their three children was born. He was named Quill Evan Cope in honor of Aunt Dora's deceased husband, Aquilla Rhea.

Rogers Cope operated a country store on Sparta's Rural Route #2 and made his living in the mercantile business. He became a traveling salesman, visiting the towns along the Tennessee River and selling his goods. He had one of the two cars in the county for a while. People went out to see the car when he drove by their farms, much as people in that part of the country stopped working to watch an airplane after World War I. When at home, he would meet people on the road walking to Sparta and give them a lift. He "carried" them to town in the morning and picked them up in the late afternoon for the ride back to their homes in the country. He loved people and used what he had to help them as he had the opportunity.

Once he gave a ride in the back seat of the car to a woman neighbor. The next day she called Jim's mother to tell her that she had seen a bed bug crawl off another man's shirt onto Rogers' collar. Sure enough, Dora Frances pulled back the covers of the bed and found bed bugs.

Jim sometimes rode with his father on rounds to the little country grocery stores of the Upper Cumberland Valley. In the car, they often sang hymns. One day when they finished singing "When the Roll is Called Up Yonder," Jim's dad thoughtfully asked, "Son, will you be there?" It was a perfect question for a young mischievous boy growing into manhood.

Rogers thought of himself as a local politician. He served on both the county school board and the White County Road Commission. He would often stay up at night with Frank Turner in order to figure out who could best talk to certain citizens to get their votes for the politicians he and "Uncle Frank" wanted in office. They knew everyone in the county. This activity laid the groundwork for Quill to run for White County Superintendent of Schools. They prepared so well that Quill was able to run unopposed. That was unheard of in White County politics.

His influence in the community was noted in an editorial in the *Sparta News* cut out of the paper by the family but without a date:

> The other evening a few citizens were talking about the opportunities and successes of young men when by chance Rogers Cope came along and speaking to the crowd as a whole passed on. One of those in the party remarked: 'There goes a young fellow, who without much backing or pull has succeeded much above the average man.' The editor of the *News* having known Rogers for some years was thinking about the remark and later asked him how he had gotten along so well. He replied: "I don't know that I have. I never had an easy job in my life, but have always tried to live on less than I made." This answer did not convey as much as the writer knows about Rogers. He was reared an orphan by his aunt, Mrs. Dora Rhea, who now

lives with him. He managed to get a fair education, is a good merchant, a progressive and successful farmer, and one of the directors of the Commerce Union Bank of Sparta and at present is chairman of the White County Highway Commission and can give a concrete statement of the workings of this commission to any one asking for this information. He also travels this upper country along the Cumberlands for Henry King and Company, the well-known wholesale grocers. Mr. Cope is plain of speech and you don't have to ask him the second time to know what he intends to say to you. However, he is considerate of the other fellow's feelings and opinions. But the point the News is making by this illustration is: What work and attention to business will accomplish rather than loafing and spending money foolishly, which sometimes belongs to the other fellow.

Squire Breeding had been a great believer in owning land. At one time he owned almost two-thousand acres. When he died, each of the children inherited a farm. He had already encouraged the young Copes to borrow money to increase their holdings. When the "Great Depression" hit in 1933, Rogers was financially backed against the wall. He had borrowed to buy over six hundred acres. He survived by increasing his traveling to sell grocery goods. During that time in order to keep the farms, he hired hands and paid each of them seventy-five cents per day. The going wage rate was fifty cents in those desperate times, but Rogers said that was not enough for those men to live and support their families.

Jim Cope's father could not lead the singing in worship. Mrs. Cope would pitch the songs for him when there was no other man present to lead the assembly. In good weather there would be about sixty to seventy-five in attendance at Big Spring services. Without visitors there were regularly forty-five to fifty-five at Sunday meetings while Jim was growing up.

Most of them were named Geer, Bradley, Breeding, or Cope. They met only on Sunday mornings except during gospel meetings, when they held services each evening for two weeks in October. On Sundays, the brethren met for both Bible classes and worship service. Five classes were taught, one in each corner of the auditorium and one in the middle up front.

Rogers Cope was a good Bible class teacher. He also maintained the treasury of contributions for the church. He made the fires during the winter and took care of upkeep on the building. Rogers spent most of every Sunday afternoon reading the Bible and the works of Josephus.

In 1939, Mr. Cope had to quit traveling because he was losing weight and did not feel well. Because his father had died of tuberculosis, he feared that he was also a victim of "consumption." The local doctor sent him to a clinic in Nashville. His primary concern at that time was hoarseness in his speech and irritation in his throat. The physicians at the clinic did not take a biopsy. Because of the family history, they too presumed that he had tuberculosis, even though his father had died when Rogers was six years old. The treatment and medicines they prescribed did little to make him feel better and did less to correct the problem.

In 1944, Jim heard of a more sophisticated clinic in Memphis and insisted that his father make an appointment. After staying a month and taking their treatments for tuberculosis, they took a biopsy. The diagnosis revealed a malignancy in his throat. Rogers had kept two stones surgically removed from his throat when he was a young man. They looked something like creek gravel. That condition may have been the forerunner of his cancer. For two years before his death, he was able to talk very little. When the cancer was diagnosed,

Rogers Cope was sixty-two years of age. He died the following year after having suffered for six years with the symptoms.

The Cope's only daughter, Mary Hill, was scheduled to return to Freed Hardeman College for her second year. Realizing that her father was going to die, she transferred to Tennessee Tech in Cookeville. On September 17, 1945, the morning before the school session began, Mary Hill prepared her clothing and took her baggage out to the back porch. A renter on the farm was coming to take her to Cookeville. Her father had not said a word to her about her plans and deliberately protected her from the full truth about his condition.

Jim was teaching at Freed-Hardeman College. Quill was still away in military service. Dad Cope came down the stairs and said, "Sweet, I'm going to have to ask you something. Your mother is going to need you this fall. You can go to school later. I'm a sick man, and I'm going to ask you to stay home with your mother." Mary Hill "never gave it another thought." She brought her bags back inside, unpacked her clothes, and stayed home. Her father suffered his first convulsion that night. Mary Hill was eighteen years old, ten years younger than Jim, and she "adored" her father.

Jim came home that weekend to start preaching in a gospel meeting in Sparta. It turned into a horrible experience. Knowing that he had to preach, the family tried to keep Jim from knowing just how critically ill his father had become. Some nights he had convulsions while Jim was preaching.

The next month was heart wrenching for the entire family. Jim had to return to Henderson. Quill was in New Jersey. Their father lived only one month longer and died on Friday, October 19, 1945, at the family home. Every night that last month, Jim's mother stayed up with him until midnight. Mary

Hill got up at midnight and sat with him until daylight. Mary Hill went every day to Sparta, a distance of ten miles, to get the day's supply of medicine. The doctor refused to give them but one day's supply of morphine for pain at any one time.

Three days before he died, Rogers asked for some boiled custard. Dora Frances was encouraged because he had not eaten in days. The doctor said, however, "Mrs. Cope, sometimes the candle burns brightest just before it goes out." Jim's father was rational until the last minutes before his death. Jim's mother sensed that the moment was near and sent Mary Hill out of the room before he died.

Andy T. Richie, Sr., preached Rogers Cope's funeral sermon. The largest crowd ever assembled in the Big Spring building attended his funeral. The old Big Spring church house was located just down the hill from the cemetery. Rogers Cope's body was buried on a beautiful October Sunday afternoon. He had never done anything "great" from an economic or political point of view, but from the perspective of family and neighbors, he was a God-given blessing to people as he helped them see the brighter aspects of life.[5]

Dora Frances Breeding Cope

After the death of Jim Cope's great-grandmother, Annie Weaver, at ninety years of age, her daughter Mahulda took care of the house for a while. Finally seeing that she could not continue, she sold the place and went to live with her sister, Fanny Jane Breeding. She was given her own bedroom, which she filled with furniture from the old homeplace. She was living there when Jim Cope's mother, Dora Frances Breeding,

---

5   "Rogers Cope," *Sparta Expositor*, October 22, 1945.

was born. As the child grew, Mahulda petted Dora Francis and treated her as if she were her own child. She worked at odd jobs or raised a pig each year to make extra money to buy something nice for Dora Francis. Any other child would have been terribly spoiled. She even asked if the child could share her room, and Mrs. Breeding agreed. Their special relationship continued until Mahulda died March 7, 1907.[6]

Born September 18, 1887, to Evan Scott Breeding and Fannie Jane Weaver Breeding, Dora Frances was the youngest child in the family. She was considered the "baby" or "younger sister" by the other children. When she was ten years old (1897), the entire family went to Nashville to celebrate the Tennessee Centennial. They caught the early train at Sparta, arriving in Nashville about 10:30 in the morning. They immediately went to Centennial Park and enjoyed the celebration over the next two days. It was one of those special educational experiences the Breedings were constantly providing for their children. Dora Frances attended Diderall Normal School, a private preparatory school operated by the Methodists. Her parents later sent her to Boscobal, a girls' finishing school.

Generally very thoughtful and conservative, Jim's future mother had her moments as a teenaged adolescent. On one occasion Dora Frances had a male friend coming from Livingston to visit her. They called him "Dr. Quall." It was early fall, and they had nothing "fitting" to feed him. Grandmother and grandfather were both living with them and getting older, so the work fell on the young ones in the house. There was also a couple who were farm workers living on their property named Lizy (pronounced with a long i) and Jim Randolph. Dora Frances had a pig her father had given

---

6   Bradley, *A History of the Breeding and Weaver Families*, 30.

her. Without telling her dad what she was doing, she and Jim Randolph went out after supper and killed the hog. The girl had not been involved in hog-killings before and was totally without experience in the procedures for preparing meat. She had heard them tell of boiling water to scald the hide, so she heated a teakettle full. Like the Methodists, she did not realize she had to "immerse" him. After the hog was properly dead, she poured the water on him and it loosened one little spot of hair. At that point, she knew she was into it. What should she do? It was getting dark and the parents had already gone to their room. She remembered a childhood poem: "Barber, barber, shave a pig. How many hairs to make a wig? Four and twenty, that's enough. Let the old barber dip his snuff." So she went in and got her daddy's straight razor and shaved that pig. It was a task that took all of the grizzly, rainy night to accomplish, and she caught a terrible cold. When her "doctor" boyfriend came to visit the next day, he found his young girlfriend a sick and disheveled "mess."

Dora Frances' father ran a store until after she married Rogers Cope. For several years her father and her husband shared a partnership in the business until Squire Breeding sold his interest to Rogers. Later, when good roads were built and automobiles became available to the people of the Upper Cumberland, the store was closed. Most heavy buying was done in town, and profits were slim out in the country stores. Rogers thought he could do better as a traveling salesman.

Dora Frances was a pessimist. That trait in her character made her seem older than she really was. Children thought of her as an old worrier. Her daughter, Mary Hill, said, "She crossed every bridge before she got to it. Some calamity was always getting ready to happen, and she had to get ready for it."[7]

Dora Frances and Rogers Cope were married on June 25, 1911. Together they became parents of three children: Quill Evan Cope, born March 28, 1912; James Rogers Cope, born January 27, 1917; and Mary Hill (Cope) Luna, born February 28, 1927.

Dora Frances always appeared much taller than her husband. She was 5'10" in height while he was only 5'5". Because of that disparity, she often did not walk with him in public. She was so sensitive to their height differences that when their pictures were taken together, she always chose to sit. He weighed about 135 pounds. She was larger boned and weighed something in the neighborhood of 150 pounds. His shoe size was the same as his daughter Mary Hill's. Dora Frances' nose was shaped like Jim's. She had a large mouth and soft pretty eyes.

Dora Frances never purchased ready made clothing in her life until she finally bought a winter coat shortly before she went to the nursing home. She was tall, and there were no shops offering clothing for tall women back then. She thought there was nothing appropriate for her on the racks. She was not a "dresser" or "fixy" in any way, and she was a modest Christian woman. She wanted to be neat, but she used no makeup. She always wore her hair in a bun, and she had little jewelry except her wedding ring. Rogers Cope had given his mother's wedding ring to Dora on the day of their marriage, and she wore it faithfully the rest of her life. Engraved inside were the Latin words "in hac fiducia mea" ("In this is my trust").

---

7   Interview with Mary Hill (Cope) Luna, July 16, 1984.

Dora Frances raised chickens. In 1927, she had on the farm five hen houses containing approximately two-thousand Rhode Island Reds and White Leghorns. Each year she sent the finest of them to the state fair in Nashville, and she often won prizes. She had one rooster worth twenty-five dollars. She shipped eggs all the way down the Tennessee River to Florence, Alabama. Poultry people often came out of Knoxville from the University of Tennessee to see her operation. Sometimes she would host a class of twenty-five to thirty students who had come to the farm. In appreciation, one professor designed a formal flower garden for her yard. Gardening was not work to Mrs. Cope. It was relaxation, she said.

When Jim was a little boy seven or eight years old, she made an incubator about the size of a large round dinner table. She used it to hatch the eggs during the cold winters. It took three weeks for them to hatch, after which they were taken out of the incubator and put into brooder boxes (again, about the size of the kitchen table). Too often the chicks would huddle and some would be smothered, particularly at night. So she sectioned off the brooder boxes with partitions. Each section held seven or eight chicks. She made Jim an apron and took him with her through the houses. She put the chicks in the apron to separate them into the different brooders. She took outing flannel and made strips to come down over the chicks to help keep them warm. One year many of her chicks died from a devastating disease that spread though that entire region of Tennessee. They buried hundreds of them in large feed sacks. Jim started a chicken cemetery. He got match boxes and buried many of them individually, preaching about the poor chickens and praying over them. Dora Frances sometimes said that Mary Hill was the "pullet who put her out of the business." It was shortly after Mary Hill was born that Dora Frances gave up the chicken business.

Like her mother, Dora Frances was deeply religious and concerned about her neighbors. She was baptized by T. B. Larimore. After her marriage, she prepared the bread for the observance of the Lord's supper by the church every week. She often killed four or five chickens on Sunday morning so that she could feed anyone who visited the church services. Like her predecessors, she always invited the preachers who came for gospel meetings to stay in their home. She kept close tabs on who was in need in their community. She made it a point to do something to provide for everyone who had less than she did. She would go to the "rag store" up on the hill to buy inexpensive clothing for them.

Jim Cope's mother loved hats with big brims. She would pay twice for a hat what she would pay for the material to make a dress. She never appeared at the church meeting house for worship without a covering on her head.

Dora Frances and Aunt Dora lived in the family house after Rogers died. Jim's mother had inherited the old home place from her parents along with considerable land. At one point she owned two-hundred-sixteen acres. Her father had bought the original farm and house from Henry Taylor, who kept a post office in the community then known as Taylors, Tennessee.

Jim's mother gained her strength as a strong, sturdy woman from farm work, cleaning out chicken houses, and helping her rural neighbors. She was also an independent, strong-willed person. But she was easy to care for in her old age. For a long time, she lived alone in the old house. She fixed her own supper and sometimes went to spend the night with a neighbor until she moved into a duplex with her sister, Mrs. Camp, in Sparta. Even then, she came home on weekends until finally she realized she must depend on others. The last five years of her life were spent with her daughter and son-in-law, Mary Hill and Roy Luna.[8] Dora Frances lived to be 88, dying in February, 1976. Jim Cope spoke lovingly of his mother before a large gathering during the funeral service at the Big Spring church building. Her body was buried beside her husband's.

---

8   Mary Hill Cope Luna was born February 28, 1927. She married Roy Madison Luna on April 23, 1948 at the Big Spring church building with James R. Cope officiating.

Section Two:

Building on Good Beginnings

Chapter Four:

A Back-Story: Tennessee 1917-32

The years of Jim Cope's upbringing were times of war in world politics and upheaval in American economics. Born in 1917, he left home for college in 1934 in the midst of the Great Depression.

Four days after the birth of the future president of Florida College, Germany notified the United States that unrestricted submarine warfare would be resumed in spite of an agreement the year before to protect passengers on merchant ships. That message ended American neutrality between the German and Allied military forces. President Woodrow Wilson had been elected but had not been inaugurated for a second term in the White House. Three more days into the life of Jim Cope, on February 3, 1917, a German submarine sank the *U.S.S. Housatonic*, and the United States severed diplomatic relations with Germany. By April 2, all-out war was inevitable. Wilson went before Congress to ask for a declaration of war, saying that "the world must be made safe for democracy." Four days later, on April 6, the President signed a bill approved by the legislature entering the United States into World War I. The Selective Service Act was adopted May 18, drafting young Americans into the military. Over the next year, almost five million Americans took part in the war effort, and more than a hundred thousand were slain in battle.

The United States, however, was not to be subjected to a long war effort. President Wilson proposed in January to negotiate peace on the basis of a Fourteen Point Plan. Later that year, the Germans were restrained at the Marne River and driven back to the Meuse. On November 11, 1918, the armistice agreement was signed in French Marshal Ferdinant Foch's railroad car in the Forest of Compiegne. Wilson went to Paris the following summer for a peace conference. Neither Germany nor its allies were represented. Wilson returned to America with the Treaty of Versailles, which included the controversial Covenant of the League of Nations, a proposal never ratified by the Congress of the United States.

The post-World-War-I years brought exciting changes to American society. Presidents Wilson, Harding, Coolidge, Hoover, and Roosevelt served the nation through that period. The "Teapot Dome Affair" marred the administration of Harding. Coolidge stabilized the government but refused to run for a second term. Hoover could not keep the nation from the "Great Depression." Jeannette Rankin, Republican of Montana, was elected in 1917 to become the first woman seated in the United States House of Representatives. The Eighteenth Amendment (1919) prohibiting the manufacture and/or sale of alcoholic beverages was ratified. The Nineteenth Amendment (1920) giving women the right to vote was approved by the states, and a unanimous decision written by Justice Oliver Wendell Holmes in the case of *Nixon v. Herndon* ruled that a Texas law forbidding African American people to vote violated the Fourteenth Amendment. In Tennessee, John T. Scopes was defended by Clarence Darrow and Dudley Field Malone in Dayton (1925) against charges of violating a state law that prohibited any teacher from teaching any theory that denied the Biblical account of creation. The chief voice of the prosecution, William Jennings Bryan, died just five days after winning the celebrated verdict. Dayton is approximately forty miles south-southeast of Sparta.

Airmail service was established between some major cities in 1918, and the first national radio transmission was begun when station KDKA in Pittsburgh broadcast the 1920 presidential election results. Jack Dempsey knocked out Jess Willard in the third round on the Fourth of July, 1919, to win the world heavyweight championship. He was defeated in 1926 at Philadelphia by Gene Tunney. Babe Ruth hit sixty home runs for the Yankees in 1927.

In 1922 Thomas Stearns Eliot published *The Wasteland*, DeWitt Wallace founded *The Readers' Digest*, Louis Armstrong joined King Oliver's jazz band in Chicago, and Herbert T. Kalmus developed "Technicolor." In 1924, George Gershwin performed his "Rhapsody in Blue" for the first time in New York City with Paul Whiteman's orchestra. Sinclair Lewis published *Arrowsmith* in 1925. Al Jolson appeared in "Jazz Singer," and Florenz Ziegfeld brought Jerome Kern's "Show Boat" with its show-stopping tunes, "Old Man River" and "Can't Help Lovin' that Man"to Broadway in 1927. The Ford Motor Company produced one million engines for Model A automobiles, and John D. Rockefeller, Jr., regained control of Standard Oil Company of Indiana in 1929. Charles Lindburgh had flown the Spirit of St. Louis across the Atlantic in 1927 and then became the object of national sympathy when his twenty-month-old son was kidnapped and murdered in 1932.

Wall Street suffered great disaster the week of October 24, 1929, and the nation went into its worst depression ever. Tennessee banks and agriculture surrounding the home area of

Jim Cope were hit hard as were those throughout the South, not only by the stock market crash but by a great drought in 1930.

Jim Cope's family experienced those hard times through his teen years. Its effects may be read into many of Cope's lifetime attitudes toward fiscal policy and personal relationships. For example, while president of the college, Jim constantly issued statements calling for faculty to turn off the lights when leaving a room.

There was, however, a popular new president of the United States. The nation's economic outlook appeared bleak for Tennessean farm people when Franklin Roosevelt entered the White House, but in his first one hundred days, he changed the direction of American life for years to come. His fireside chats with "my friends" were heard in Tennessee by farm people like the Copes, and their confidence was restored in the American dream. The majority considered themselves Democrats in those days, and Roosevelt won four consecutive presidential elections.

Chapter 5:

Building on a Good Upbringing

Infancy

During the first ten years of his life, Jim Cope was told that his birthdate was January 29, 1917. His family celebrated his birth on January 29 because his mother was convinced that she had delivered him on that day. In spite of that, a neighbor named Ann Cox, who lived with her husband in a log cabin on Grandfather Breeding's adjoining farm, argued with his mother that Jim's birthday was Saturday, January 27, and not Monday, January 29. Mrs. Cope remembered certainly that a huge snow had fallen on the ground the day Jim was born, and that snowfall happened on Monday. She asked Ann Cox why she was convinced and adamant that he was born on the twenty-seventh. Mrs. Cox said that on one of the logs in the old farm house they marked the days when their sows delivered piglets. The day Jim was born one of their old sows had a big litter, and they clearly had marked the twenty-seventh. Mrs. Cope was not going to change his birthdate because of a pig litter's arrival, and so she took Mrs. Cox's claim with a grain of salt.

The issue became serious, however, when W. C. Breeding's wife, who had been county registrar of vital statistics for the Eleventh Civil District of White County, turned over the county records to Mrs. Cope. Doctor Breeding was a country physician and Mrs. Cope's brother. His wife registered all births, deaths, and marriages in their part of the state. It was her job to send copies of all these records to the state department of health in Nashville. When Jim's uncle Breeding took a job with the health department in 1925, he moved his family to Nashville. Mrs. Breeding turned over the registrar's book and her position as registrar to Mrs. Cope. One day, two or three years later, Mrs. Cope was looking through the book. Curiosity got the best of her, and she looked up the record of Jim's birth. Dr. A. F. Richards, the Sparta doctor who delivered Jim, had reported that Mrs. Cope had delivered on January 27th. Jim's mother was shaken but convinced that a mistake was made. The whole family puzzled over how to settle the issue. In those days, the *Nashville Banner* ran a column called "The Query Box." Jim's elder brother, Quill, was a teenager by then and determined to find a solution. He wrote the Banner, told them about the snow, and asked the date of the last Saturday in January 1917. They published the answer, and the date was the twenty-seventh. That convinced his mother, and Jim became two days older than he had thought.

Jim Cope was born in a little frame house about half a mile down the road from the bigger white frame farmhouse that later became the Cope family "home place." The little house was the first property Jim's dad and mother bought. They purchased it and the surrounding farm from a man named Miller. It now sits along the south side of Highway 84 on a rural route outside Sparta, Tennessee, in the Big Spring area south of Cookeville.

Rogers Cope and Grandfather Breeding farmed and ran a country mercantile store together during Jim's early childhood. The boy was seven or eight years old when his dad started traveling to sell groceries and other goods. The mercantile store was located right across the road from the old home place on Grandfather Breeding's property.

The family were members of and worshiped devotedly with the Big Spring church of Christ. Jim remembers his grandfather making talks at the Big Spring church on Sundays when the preacher couldn't get there. Typically, in those days the preaching in numerous small rural churches in Middle Tennessee was done by itinerate preachers. Often they were teachers or students from David Lipscomb College. Sometimes these men would go to four different congregations each month. The congregations might have four men who regularly came on one of the four Sundays designated each month. A different preacher might come when a month contained five Sundays.

Brother Breeding "collected the verses." That was his phrase to explain how he went around the room calling upon old and young to quote some passage from the Bible memorized during the past week. In his talks he "comforted the sorrowing, rebuked the wayward and indifferent, and cheered the despondent." On one occasion when his grandfather was asking the children for their verses, Jim shouted, "Let every tub sit on its own bottom." On another Sunday, Jim astounded everyone by getting outside the Bible for another quotation: "Jump up, kitty cat, jump up higher. Jump up, kitty cat, Your tail's on fire!"

Jim was constantly disciplined by his mother and Aunt Dora in church until one Sunday when he was standing up on the pew looking back toward the audience. Mrs. George McLaughlin leaned over the seat, took him by the shoulders, shook him "until his teeth almost rattled," and said, "Jim Cope, sit down and behave yourself!" She proceeded to help him by physically turning him around and shoving him into a sitting position beside his mother. From that day forward, his demeanor in church was markedly quiet and reverent in appearance.

Picture of Quill and Jim

Jim's pre-school "busy-ness" was understood by all those who knew his personality. Aunt Dora took Jim to a big outdoor wedding in Aunt Mattie Pearl's yard. She dressed Jim in new clothes and told him to take care of himself so as not to get dirty. A rope was placed to guide the crowd and keep the aisles cleared. Jim, of course, disregarded the rope and found himself in the wrong place. Aunt Dora pleaded, "Jim, get back here behind this rope. Everybody will see you." Jim replied, "Well, that's what I'm here for all dressed up: to be seen!"

Elementary School Days

1st Grade (1922-23). Jim Cope began his formal education in the old one-room Big Spring school house, where children in eight grades were taught together. The little building sat alongside a creek that flowed out of a spring under the hill near where he had been born. Aunt Lulie Breeding was Jim's teacher from the beginning of first grade to midway through the third grade. It was aunt Lulie who taught Jim to read.

Aunt Lulie Breeding's husband was a physician. Wesley C. Breeding was born (February 1, 1870) and reared in Sparta. He practiced medicine in White County for thirty-three years. He moved to Nashville early in 1925 as Associate Commissioner of the Tennessee State Health Department. Dr. Breeding had been the first doctor in White County to own a microscope. He and two others led the fight to stamp out "childbed fever," which was found to be carried on the hands of attending physicians. During World War I, he produced written studies that showed that most men rejected as unfit for service suffered from malnutrition and hookworm.

Dr. Breeding married Lulie Johnson in 1899. They were parents of one son, Sam, and one daughter. Their daughter, Dorothy, married S. O. Ward, who served for many years

(1964-86) as chairman of the Florida College Board of Directors. Dr. Breeding had one brother (Dr. W. M. Breeding of Livingston, Tennessee) and three sisters (Jim's mother, Mrs. Harry Camp, and Mrs. George Bradley).

In Nashville, Dr. Breeding served for a brief time as an elder in the Central church of Christ, where C. E. W. Dorris regularly preached. His letter of resignation, dated July 27, 1932, indicates the conservative nature of his Biblical convictions in light of increasing movement in Central's eldership toward support of recreational and social activities:

> The events that have led up to my resignation are too well known to you for an elaborate repetition here. My opposition to the purchase of the Keim building for the purpose of establishing a so-called 'health club' under the auspices of the church, my opposition to the transfer of the church's equity in certain real estate without consideration, my opposition to the church entering into further speculative investments which would entail a further bonded indebtedness, and my opinion on other matters of more or less importance relative to the fiscal affairs of the church seems to have created in the mind of an active member of the congregation an opposition to my views which, as you know, has become so pronounced that I was placed in the unpleasant dilemma of accepting one of two courses; namely, that I should resign my eldership or continue to advocate the principles which I conscientiously believe to be right without a possibility of ultimate success. I have chosen to resign my eldership.

Aunt Lulie tried for years to help Jim speak better English. For example, when Jim was just a little tyke, he said something about "tators" to Aunt Lulie. She had replied, "It is not 'tators,' Jim—it is 'PO-ta-toes.'" A few days later, Aunt Lulie baked some sweet potatoes with the skins on them. Wanting one,

Jim tugged at her skirt and said he was hungry. She said, "Well, Jim, what do you want?" He hesitated and said, "Aunt Lulie, what was it you called your tators?"

Aunt Mary Bradley was an elderly woman who lived in a log cabin about thirty yards across the dirt road from the Copes' home. She was a fine woman but not a member of the church. Her house, however, was the only place Quill and Jim could go without asking permission. She loved the boys almost as her own, and the three of them could say anything to one another. Because he loved her so much, Jim told her, "When you die, I want your old walking stick and uncle Gussies' civil war knife and I want your glasses and false teeth." Jim got them all but the false teeth.

When Aunt Mary Bradley "got sick," Jim and Quill went over to her house. She was in the bed nearing death. Jim asked her if she could still kick. She said, "Yes, why?" Jim answered, "Well, Daddy said when an old mule got down to where he couldn't kick, he just knocked him in the head."

Jim was not inhibited, even with casual acquaintances. There was an old man in Sparta named McLoughlin. One day, Jim ran into this man on the street. He walked right up to him and said, "Mr. McLoughlin, I want some ice cream bad. Let's go into this drug store, and I'll set 'em up!" After they had eaten the ice cream, Jim said, "Mr. McLoughlin, now I've set 'em up, you'll have to pay for it." Jim didn't even know what it meant to "set 'em up," but Mr. McLoughlin thought he had been "set up."

Jim got some of his spirit and openness from his dad. Aunt Dora told of often visiting a certain family near home. Every time they would go, Rogers would ask for something to eat. On one occasion Aunt Dora told Rogers, "Today when we go, don't ask for something to eat. Be nice!" So they went and he didn't say anything. Instead, he walked the floors back and forth saying "pop, pop." They asked, "Dora, what is he wanting?" He was trying to be obedient, but they had to get him some popcorn. His personality was such that they all just laughed and let him have what he wanted.

Jim was not so subtle, however. During a gospel meeting, "Mama" told Jim and Quill to take only one piece of chicken so there would be enough for the preacher. After the prayer, Jim said right in front of their company, "Remember, Quill, what Mama told us—just one piece of chicken and that's it." His mother could have strangled him.

Brother J. T. Clark was well-known in that area. He held several meetings at Big Spring, including one when Jim was four or five years old. Brother Clark stayed with the Copes. So did others, especially family members who came on the weekends from all over the area to attend the meeting. They walked to service every evening, but toward the end of the week Aunt Dora was carrying (or dragging) Jim. After they returned home one night, Jim told Aunt Larue from Sparta that he sure would be glad when the meeting was over so everybody else could go home.

H. Leo Boles held the meeting in the summer of 1923, after Jim's first year in school. Before the meeting, Jim had picked up a habit of saying "doggone it" from his daddy. Aunt Dora and Jim's mother thought that expression was profane and convinced Jim's dad that he should not say it any more. They said it just was not right to say "doggone this" and "doggone that" all the time. Besides it was terrible that he had gotten Jim to saying it. They also convinced him that if he did not clear it up with Jim before the meeting. Jim would embarrass them all in front of brother Boles.

Jim's dad took him out for a walk, and after a while when they reached the barn said, "Son, we've got a problem. We are saying something we shouldn't say."

"What's that," Jim innocently inquired.

"We're saying, 'doggone it,' Jim, and it's all my fault. I started it without thinking. I shouldn't say it, and you shouldn't either. I'll make a deal with you. If you won't say it any more, I won't either."

Jim agreed but it continued to wear on his mind. One night at dinner as soon as the prayer was said, Jim looked up and said, "Brother Boles, Daddy and I have made an agreement."

"What's that, Jim," brother Boles asked?

"We agreed that we just won't say 'doggone it' any more."

The entire family was embarrassed but brother Boles laughed heartily. Many years later, at the orientation activities of David Lipscomb College, Jim was in the presence of other freshmen students and several preachers. Jim thought that brother Boles would not even remember him. The noted evangelist and president of the college came over to Jim and said, "Jim, are you still saying 'doggone it?'"

2ⁿᵈ Grade (1923-24). Mattie Pearl Gillen married Jim's first cousin Sam Breeding during Jim's early grade school days. They lived about two miles up the road from the church building. She liked to tell that one time grandfather Breeding gave Quill and Jim each a little pig. Quill said he was going to raise his pig, sell it, and put the money in the bank. Jim said, "Not me. I'm going to grow mine up and kill him and make sausage out of him."

In front of the family house in which Jim was born, the lawn was shaded out to the dirt road. The house sat on a slope with a rock wall holding up the dirt of the yard from the four-to-five foot bank that dropped down to the road. Jim often played on his tricycle, running it down the path from the porch to the steep steps at the front of the property. A piece of paper lying near the wall posed the challenge for Jim to see how fast he could pass over the paper with both wheels and turn before reaching the steps without turning the tricycle over and falling down the embankment. He came too close and tumbled over the edge into a concrete banister onto his head. Lucille screamed, "Jim's killed himself." His mother came running, grabbed him up, and rushed him to the doctor for stitches. He "bled like a stuck hog" and carried a scar through his lifetime from that day forward.

3rd Grade (1924-25). Jim was seven years old when he entered his third year of school. Quill had completed the eight grades taught at Big Spring and was ready for high school. The roads were bad in winter, and there were no school buses, so Aunt Dora decided to rent a little apartment in Sparta to make it possible for Quill to attend classes every day at the public school. She gladly helped Quill get his education by spending her only regular income, the rent payments on a store building her husband had left her. It was just enough to provide for his room and board. Aunt Lulie was Jim's teacher again during the first half of his third year of schooling, but when the Breedings moved to Nashville at the end of 1924, the children lost their teacher. The family was forced to send Jim into town also if he was to continue until the end of the year. His teacher there was Beulah Lee Kaiser.

Tom Cotton, a lifelong friend, had a sister named Dorothy who was the same age as Quill, five years older than

Jim, but he had a crush on her nonetheless. Jim thought she was beautiful and made her his secret sweetheart. One day at school, she hid from Jim behind the door because he had somehow embarrassed her. He found her and loudly declared, "I see you. You're the prettiest thing in the U.S.A."

Tom Cotton, lifelong friend, was asked, "What was the difference between Quill and Jim when they were growing up?" He said, "I'll just tell you what I thought about it. I always thought Quill was a little firmer headed than that boy sittin' over there." He went on to explain that Quill was more serious in those days and Jim was always into mischief. Quill "never got out of the way and never got a whippin' in school." Tom did not reveal how many "whippin's" Jim got.

During that time at Sparta Jim learned about tobacco. Jim looked up to a boy in the fourth grade who chewed Peach Tobacco, a brand popular in those days among the farmers. One day the older boy went to the store after school and bought a wedge to share with his friends. He gave Jim a big chew of the tobacco, and they walked around trying to look like men. Jim became so sick that he claimed it "broke him" of chewing tobacco forever.

4th Grade (1925-26). Jim went back to the country school for fourth grade. The Presbyterians had built a building in the France community that they could use for church meetings on Sunday and the community could use for school during the week. Margaret Little agreed to open a school there. In that school she taught all eight grades.

Jim had been reading well for two or three years because his parents and Aunt Dora insisted that everyone read from the Bible every day. Jim was not quite so quick with numbers. Miss Little taught him to multiply but he could never beat Reba Nell Angel, another of Jim's very pretty young sweethearts, to the board. Miss Little had the children race to the board when she posed a mathematics problem to see who could get the solution the fastest. Jim tried to beat Reba Nell but never could. In part, Jim had to accept that she was in the sixth grade, two grades ahead of him.

5th Grade (1926-27). Jim began the fifth grade when he was nine. School was started that fall out at Big Spring. It opened again under the tutelage of Frances Camp, Jim's first cousin. She agreed to teach grades five through eight. She was a large heavy lady who one day fell through the floor. Toward the front of the room, some old planks had gotten thin under the coal stove. One of the planks gave way, and Aunt Frances' leg went through up to her knee. Some of the older children pulled her out. Along with some other factors, that event kept Mrs. Camp from teaching more than a few weeks. The parents who were determined to keep their children in school were forced once again to go to classes in town. Aunt Dora again came to the rescue and rented a room from Mrs. Maxey, a seamstress who was a widow. Jim's teacher in town that year was Betty Lee.

After World War I, Jim's daddy had a chance to get some army surplus items to sell. Among them was a tent that the doughboys had used in France and a satchel containing an old gas mask. Jim played with the gas mask and used the satchel to carry books to school. The tent was large enough to sleep seven or eight of Jim's friends.

Jim also used the bag to carry home dead squirrels when he hunted in the woods. He killed his first squirrel on a land owned by Dot Breeding's father. He used the gun that later shot his brother Quill. Jim thought he had "shot a hole right through the heart of that squirrel." The animal dropped, and Jim just knew he was dead, but when he went to pick it up, it "nailed" him right through his finger.

Jim's mother had a group of Jim's fifth grade buddies (boys age eight through ten) out to the farm during the summer after school was out. The boys had a big time in the field with that tent. Jim supervised putting it up just as Tom Sawyer would have done. His mother gave them food, and they stayed out in the field three or four days, playing ball by day and camping out at night in the tent.

Mr. & Mrs. Cope went out to Monterey to visit the Sehorn family. Sam Sehorn had become a big teenage boy and had outgrown his forty-eight inch Shetland pony named "Maude." "Dad" paid $32.50 and bought that pony, along with its buggy, for Jim. The little mare was coal black with a star on her forehead.

In those days, the annual county fair provided some of the community's greatest excitement. There were two classes of ponies at the fair. One included ponies 48" to 56". There was a race for each class and then an open race for all ponies. Jim never could win the big race. Howard Grissom had a faster "horse," and Jim always came in second with Maude. One year Clotis Weaver brought his 56" pony and entered the race. Howard didn't race that year. In the big race, there were just two entries, Jim and Clotis. A huge crowd watched the race, primarily to see the little boy (Jim) on the little pony. Jim stood almost as tall as his little Shetland pony. As expected, the bigger pony ran off and left Jim early in the race. But when he got to the main swinging curve in the trace, the big horse turned off and headed for his feeding stall in the stables. Jim won the race before Clotis could get control of his horse. The crowd laughed and shouted as Jim brought his horse to the finish line.

Jim also had a little fox terrier puppy in those days. "Tony" had tan spots and loved to run and play with Maude. The house in which the Copes lived was about a half mile down the road from Grandfather Breeding's house and the store. Jim often rode down to the store on Maude with Tony running alongside barking. One day Jim let Maude have her rein racing down the hill toward the store. As she reached the bottom, just before starting up the rise to the store, Tony ran in front and Maude stumbled over him. Jim went over the saddle horn head-first onto the gravel road. The scrapes on his hands, knees, and face took weeks to heal. He later wondered how he reached maturity as prone to accidents as his youthful carelessness made him. Jim kept Maude four or five years after that.

6th Grade (1927-28). During this school year, Aunt Dora rented out the building in which her husband had operated a grocery store. After his death, she had managed a "racket" store in the building for a time before deciding to lease it to another merchant. The "racket" store was something like a "dime store," in which she sold inexpensive toys, what-nots, and other small items people bought for Christmas stockings, birthday favors, and other treats for special occasions. With the income she saved from the rent, Aunt Dora was finally able to put a down-payment on the house two doors down the street from the new church building in Sparta.

When Jim started the sixth grade, Aunt Dora moved into the house in Sparta. That year, the Sparta schools had different teachers in different grades and subjects for the first time. Jim studied English and reading under Willie Officer, the greatest grammar teacher he ever knew. He studied those subjects with her three years. She required students to stand up and read long passages in front of the class. Jim studied mathematics under Mrs. McCaskill and history under Will Story. The principal was Mal C. Wallace, and Jim was deathly afraid of him. Oliver Bradley (Jim's cousin) got a whipping every week from Wallace. Mr. Wallace spanked the children and everyone heard the pop of the paddle down the hall.

Chapter 6:

Building on Good Teen Experiences

Middle School

7th Grade (1928-29). The Cope family moved from the smaller house down the road to live with Granddad Breeding in the summer of 1928. The move was precipitated by Mr. Breeding's fall and subsequent crippling disability that resulted from a broken hip. Grandma Breeding's death the year before had been preceded by a similar fall from the steps of the porch of this old house.

The house had been constructed about 1894. Downstairs were the entrance hall, living room, front room parlor, dining room, and kitchen. All the bedrooms were upstairs. Jim's dad and mother slept in the back bedroom. Aunt Dora and Mary Hill used the center bedroom. Quill and Jim had the front bedroom. Aunt Dora, Grandmother Breeding, and Grandfather Breeding all died in the front room parlor downstairs. It had been turned into another bedroom when the older folks became unable to climb the stairs. There were large beautiful porches all around the house where evening hours after supper were passed until dark with elders watching the children play in the yard. While snapping beans, shucking and silking corn, or shelling peas, the adults discussed current news, the day's activities, or what was happening among the neighbors.

Jim's sister, Mary Hill, was ten years younger than he. Her birthday was February 28, 1927. One summer day when Mary Hill was just an infant playing in the yard, Jim was across the road at the store. He glanced at the house and saw Granddad in his wheelchair on the porch. Mr. Breeding had been a strong man, six feet tall, but, having broken his hip the year before, had become quite feeble. Since the house was encircled by wide porches, he could roll his wheelchair through the house and onto the porches to go almost anywhere he wished. He arose from his wheelchair and began to walk behind it as one would use a walker today. Seeing that his grandfather was losing his balance, Jim bolted across the road just in time to catch him as he fell from the porch. The boy was only eleven years old. Granddad no doubt would have been badly hurt. Grandfather Breeding died the next fall in August 1929.

On another day in that same season of year, Jim was specifically told to stay close and watch Mary Hill in the yard. His father came out onto the porch to check on the children and saw Jim across the road at the store "matching pennies" with another boy who lived over on the knob. Jim's dad sized up the situation and called Jim over under an old peach tree. He began explaining to Jim how he was failing a serious responsibility. All the time he was cutting a thin limb from the tree and making Jim watch as he trimmed off the leaves and knots with his pocket knife. When the talking was finished, Dad took hold of Jim and the two of them "danced all over the yard." Jim later said, "He wrapped that limb all around my legs."

Aunt Dora Rhea caught Jim in the store one day blowing up paper sacks to pop them. She explained that she had to pay for those sacks and told him not to do that anymore. In the midst of the rebuke, Jim asked, "Who does this store belong to anyway?" She replied, "To me and to your daddy, not to you!" Jim replied, "Well, give me dad's half of the sacks." Such comments definitely seemed impertinent to Aunt Dora, and surely they were even though Jim always had great respect for Aunt Dora. All his life when talking about his family, Jim was extremely sentimental, even tearfully so. He held all his seniors in the highest and deepest regard. Jim was just a mischievous lad in his growing up years, but he had to learn his lessons as he grew up.

Jim's real inner values were clearly established early in his concern about spiritual things. He had a sincere and tender conscience even about his own wrongs, including these childish words and actions that others criticized and he was punished for doing. At church worship services at Big Spring, Jim sat beside his granddad and found songs for him in the hymnal. The old cane bottom rocking chair in which brother Breeding sat for worship became a family heirloom. Jim pulled up a straight chair to sit by him, and they sang out of the same old songbook every Sunday. "Granddad was not much of a singer," Jim later said, "but he loved doing it."

Jim began to be concerned about his soul at an early age. He was baptized on September 30, 1928, when he was eleven years old. Horace Busby was preaching in a gospel meeting at the Sparta church. Jim was in town because he was again attending the Sparta city school that year. After the morning services on Sunday, Jim told Aunt Dora that he had decided to be baptized that evening. A little later, he went to play with the Walker boys over at Bronson Bend. Aunt Dora let him go but told him that he ought to be thinking about his sins. He did not get much pleasure out of playing that afternoon. Perhaps it was not so bad that he went to the Walkers' house. The boys talked about being baptized, and both Lloyd and William, who had already been thinking about obeying the gospel, decided to be baptized that night with Jim.

When the congregation stood to sing "Just As I Am," Jim stepped out into the aisle and made his way to the front to confess his faith in Christ. Lloyd and William followed him down the aisle. Joe L. Netherland, the local preacher, actually immersed them. Horace Busby had preached the sermon.

When he was baptized, Jim did not change his clothes in the church building. He ran down to Aunt Dora's house to do that. Unlike Big Spring, the Sparta building had a baptistery, a balcony, and a long tall steeple. It would seat about six hundred people. Not long after Jim's baptism, this old Sparta church building burned down. That weekend, Jim had stayed in town at Aunt Dora's place and seen the fire. He watched the volunteers fight it until it was extinguished. During the next few weeks, he went with other boys after school to the charred remains and used his hatchet to knock mortar off the bricks to save them for a new church building. After the fire, the Sparta church met in the courthouse until the reconstruction project was completed. The new building cost $50,000 in 1929.

8th Grade (1929-30). A field called "Gum Bench" ran along the ridge behind the Cope's farmhouse. The Copes grew corn up there. One blistery hot day, his dad sent Jim to Gum Bench to plow the corn with Old John, their mule. He was to use a "Geewhiz," a plow with feet that could be spread out. When Jim got hot while working, he resented having to work instead of being allowed to play ball with the other boys. He began to throw clods at Old John to make him run. The rows became crooked, and the job was not done well because he and Old John were "running down the rows," tearing up the tender plants. This was another of those well-remembered occasions when Jim's dad visited the corn patch and exercised parental discipline.

The summers were hot on the Cumberland plateau, but the winters were sometimes devastatingly cold. Everyone burned logs on open fires, and the children skated the pond when it was frozen. They got old chairs, put each other on them, and pushed them across the pond.

Jim always looked up to his brother Quill. Quill, born March 28, 1912, was five years older than Jim. Quill was a senior in high school the year Jim went through the eighth grade. Quill and Jim's cousin Dorothy Breeding, born May 10, 1906, who was eleven years older than Jim, had a profound influence on his life.

High School

Freshman Year - 9th Grade (1930-31). Jim never took a drink of whiskey in his life. Roy McDowell, a fellow freshman in Jim's high school class, drank on occasion. Jim went into a store one day to get some cheese and crackers, and Roy was there. His friend asked, "Do you want a drink of whiskey, Jim?" "I believe I do," Jim impulsively responded. Roy handed him the bottle and Jim turned it up and let it touch his tongue. But just as he did, he began to think about his mother and Aunt Dora. The bottle stopped, and for a long moment he paused. The tip of his tongue was as far as the whiskey got. He never took a swallow and never even came close to taking a drink again in his entire life.

Jim's sister, Mary Hill, was almost five years old by this time, and Jim was fourteen. She slept upstairs in the old house with Aunt Dora Rhea, whom she affectionately called "Aunt Dōtie." The roof was covered with galvanized tin, and the sound of the rain often lulled them to sleep at night. Outside the window loomed a large old spruce pine. The windows rattled, doing a little dance in their frames when the wind blew. In Tennessee, the thunder storms could be frightening to an imaginative young girl. To Mary Hill, the wind sounded like a coyote squalling. The discordant sounds of the rain on the roof and the rattling of the windows produced all kinds of images in her mind, from destruction of the house to madmen breaking and entering.

One night during an especially severe storm, Mary Hill awakened her aging aunt crying out, "Oh, Dōtie, Dōtie, something bad is wrong. We are going to be killed." Aunt Dora took her in her arms and softly spoke. "Don't worry, child. We have done all we can. We must leave the rest to the Lord." Mary Hill got quiet, but soon another great clap of thunder sent her running to her aunt. "Oh God," she cried, "just take care of us 'til daylight, and maybe by then we can take care of ourselves." Actually, Aunt Dōtie was a real source of spiritual help to all the children. She lived with the Copes until her death at age ninety-three. She was the only real grandmother Jim and Mary Hill ever knew. Remember, Jim often repeated that God's great "Social Security System" is families committed to taking in, caring for, and loving their own aged relatives. His family responsibly cared for its own, even taking them into their homes permanently.

Sophomore Year - 10ᵗʰ Grade (1931-32). In the spring of his sophomore year, Jim entered the inter-society debating tournament. He was now fifteen years old. His debate partner, Oliver Bradley, was a senior. The two young men were cousins: their mothers were sisters. Their team took the affirmative position on that year's national debate topic, "RESOLVED THAT THE UNITED STATES GOVERNMENT SHOULD ADOPT A SYSTEM OF UNEMPLOYMENT INSURANCE SIMILAR TO THAT OF GREAT BRITAIN." Jim and Oliver were members of The Star Society. Their counterpart was Girls for Progress (GFP). The male club rival was called The Forum. The girls' rival was identified as Euphemiums.

Quill had been a debater for Star, and Jim followed in his brother's footsteps. Bradley and Cope won the inter-society debate and went on to win the district final round. They were beaten in the finals of the state tournament at the University of Tennessee in Knoxville. Jim and his new partner lost the following year at their own school to classmates, but Jim won again during his senior year with Albert Breeding as partner. Mrs. Joe L. (Florence Nell) Netherland, the local preacher's wife who taught English and speech at the high school, drilled the boys and made them understand that certain words should be emphasized. That last year, the judges ruled against Jim and Albert in the finals of the Upper Cumberland district. A team from the Methodist operated Baxter Seminary run by Harry L. Upperman beat them.

Jim also tried out for the football team in his sophomore year even though it was obvious he was the smallest guy to walk onto the field. The first day of practice, while the offense was running some plays, a big teammate hit Jim, and he saw stars. He got up off his back and tried to catch his breath. That day, Jim found out that football was not for smaller boys. He was going to keep trying, however, until his dad found out he had tried out for the team. Quill had been a manager of the

Tennessee Tech Golden Eagles football team in Cookeville. Along the way, he had brought home an old pair of discarded football shoes. Jim's dad had seen those shoes on the back floor of the car and was watching to see who had put them there and why. When Jim went to sneak them out of the vehicle as he got out for school the next morning, his dad said, "Son, I believe I'd just leave those shoes in the car." After just one day on the football team, Jim went back to his debating.

Wanting to be a part of every activity with his classmates, Jim also went out for basketball, but he was put into a game on only two occasions. At the first of the season, Jim weighed ninety-eight pounds. He was the shortest "man" on the team at five feet seven inches. As a real "man" later, Jim stood five feet ten inches. He practiced hard, however, and the coach started him in a game against Allgood High School. Back then, they tossed the ball up at midcourt after every basket. Thirty points was a high scoring game. On the very first play, the tip went to Jim. He bounced the ball three times and shot a goal. Three times in succession he scored the basket. The coach took him out and never put him back in the game. Why? The coach explained, "You can score, but while you are making fifty points, the other fellow is making a hundred because you can't guard him." Jim soon saw that basketball was also not his game.

Junior Year - 11th Grade (1932-33). During his junior and senior years in high school, Jim served as Master of Ceremonies at the county fair. He called the pony rides and saddle horse shows, as well as the steers, mules, and horse competitions. He was known for the way he used the expressions, "Turn 'em on, boys," and, "Get 'em rackin'" in the gaited horse events. The citizens of White County raised a big tent on the high school grounds where the fair was held, and Jim announced the prizes in each category when the shows were over.

County fairs in Tennessee were the forerunners of the Tennessee Walking Horse shows that culminated each year in a championship event at Shelbyville, Tennessee. N. B. Hardeman, later a mentor of Jim and then president at Freed-Hardeman College, became a big walking-horse enthusiast with several prize-winning stallions and his solid-white mare, "Maid of Cotton," who won the National Junior Championship as a three-year-old at Shelbyville in 1947.[1]

During his high school years, Jim's dad often took his son to the courthouse, where he joined lawyer friends in talking about county politics. Mr. Cope even took Jim to the county caucuses where powerful political people in Tennessee gathered. The lawyers wanted Jim to finish his education, go to law school, and come back to Sparta to make a run for the legislature. They even said that they would back him in a race for the state senate when the time was right. They held out an even greater carrot to Jim, leading him to believe that he could then become a member of the United States House of Representatives and maybe even one of two United States Senators from Tennessee. Jim went to college planning to force them to back up their words. Later, when he returned to town after deciding to preach the gospel, Razzie Brady intercepted Jim on the street to tell him that some of the old fellows were disappointed that he would not be going to law school to be their congressman. He said, "They tell me you turned out to be a preacher. How come you changed your

1   James Marvin Powell and Mary Nelle Hardeman Powers, *N. B. H.: A Biography of Nicholas Brodie Hardeman* (Nashville, TN: The Gospel Advocate Company, 1964), 312.

mind?" Jim replied, "Yeah, I decided I'd rather go to heaven than to go to Congress."

Senior Year - 12th Grade (1933-34). Jim's political career began and ended with his election as president of his senior class in the fall of 1933. Only one boy in the White County High School class was younger than Jim, but Jim had the respect of his fellow students. He was only sixteen when elected president and seventeen when he graduated in the spring of 1934.

His biggest responsibility as president was sponsoring the senior Halloween party. He stuffed clothes with hay to create make-believe people. He fixed up old crinkling tin for the students to walk on. They stabbed the hay people with knives and splattered them with pokeberry juice to give the appearance of magenta-colored blood. Everyone attended, including the teachers.

Quill returned to Sparta to teach economics in the high school in 1933, Jim's last year. Jim did not take classes with his brother, but a pretty little senior girl in Jim's class named Mary Kate Smith did. Quill and Mary Kate did not date until she finished her degree at Peabody College for Teachers in Nashville and he was White County superintendent of schools. They later married and lived together happily until his death. While Quill did not study law, he nevertheless was drawn into the political arena by way of major appointments. After Quill earned his doctorate, Governor Frank Clemens called on him to be the Tennessee Commissioner of Education in his cabinet. Long-time Nashville preacher and personal acquaintance of Clemens, Robert Jackson, once asked the governor why he picked Quill Cope to be commissioner. He responded, "The first thing that attracted me to Quill Cope was his name."

After graduation, Jim took a job at Goff Funeral Home in Sparta. He earned a dollar a day. Jim's job was to keep the doors open during the daytime. In his second summer there, after a year at David Lipscomb College, Jim was paid ten dollars per week. These were depression days. Jobs were not easy to find, and everyone who could find work did whatever it took to support himself. Even the young people worked to help support their families. When he was not in town at the funeral home, Jim was milking cows, feeding animals, or plowing on the farm. They worked or starved in those days. Jim often came home from town after dark and went to the barn to milk and feed. He worked until noon on Saturdays before being free to walk four miles to play baseball with the other boys. He received no allowance. His allowance was playing ball Saturday afternoon.

These years on the farm and in a small Tennessee town had much to do with shaping Jim Cope's character. It also had a profound influence on the lives of his children. His daughter, Cathy, summed it up in a note to this author in which she said, "I loved my Daddy and grew to appreciate his country roots, especially when we were all together at the Tennessee family reunions, where we developed our knowledge of his people and conversed with aunts and uncles and played with cousins. I am grateful most of my own children got a taste of that heritage, not the least of which is the spiritual heritage that permeated my consciousness, especially in now my own twilight years. Daddy could truly relate to and converse at a grass root level with every type of person and was able to 'get inside their shoes.'"[2]

---

2   Cathy Cope Weaver, email dated September 13, 2024.

Section Three:

Building on Good College Experiences

Chapter 7:

Lipscomb Years (1934-43)

Origination of David Lipscomb College

The Nashville Bible School was opened October 5, 1891, by James A Harding and David Lipscomb in a large brick residence on Hermitage Avenue in Nashville, Tennessee.[1]

The original faculty consisted of Lipscomb, Harding, and Lipscomb's older brother, William.[2] Nine young men enrolled the first day. Each of them wanted to preach the gospel. A total of thirty-two students registered for this first session over the next few days. Two were female. Early in the year, Lipscomb had issued a call in the *Gospel Advocate* to those who might be interested in studying there. In September, he had written, "The school is not especially for preachers but to teach the Bible and all the branches that will be useful and helpful to the student."[3]

In its third year of operation, David Lipscomb, W. H. Dodd, and J. R. Ward bought a residence on two and one-

---

1   James A. Harding, "Nashville Bible School," *Gospel Advocate,* XXXIII:42 (October 21, 1891), 661.

2   Robert E. Hooper, *Crying in the Wilderness: A Biography of David Lipscomb* (Nashville, TN: David Lipscomb College, 1979), 273-75.

3   David Lipscomb, "The Bible School," *Gospel Advocate,* XXXIII:36 (September 9, 1891), 576.

fourth acres of land. It became the first property owned by the school. The deed declared that the Bible "shall be taught as a regular daily study to all who shall attend said school." It also required that the self-perpetuating board of directors be composed of members of churches of Christ.[4] A three-story extension was soon added to the main house. It contained a kitchen, dining room, chapel hall, classrooms, and bedrooms for boys. A separate two-story building was constructed to be a girls' dormitory and home for the Hardings.[5] To help pay their $5 per month tuition and $2.25 per week board fees, W. H. Dodd hired some of the boys to work in his newly established suspender factory in another small frame building. Dodd later merged the suspender factory with Robert Wickliffe Comer's Washington Manufacturing Company, a highly successful clothing industry in Nashville, until the rise of K-Mart and Walmart.[6]

Some of the faculty serving the growing school before 1900 included J. W. Grant (who replaced William Lipscomb), J. N. Armstrong[7] (who taught Greek), S. P. Pittman (spelling, English, and communication), W. A. Bryan (foreign languages), Leon Harding (Harding's son, music), O. W. Gardner (mathematics), and E. E. Sewell (English). Some students who later became well-known among brethren

---

4   Earl Irvin West, *The Life and Times of David Lipscomb* (Henderson, TN: Religious Book Service, 1954), 199-215.

5   Lloyd Cline Sears, *The Eyes of Jehovah: The Life and Faith of James Alexander Harding* (Nashville, TN: Gospel Advocate Company, 1970), 138-63.

6   M. Norvel Young, *A History of Colleges Established and Controlled by Members of the Churches of Christ* (Kansas Citiy, MO: The Old Paths Book Club, 1949), 85.

7   Lloyd Cline Sears, *The Biography of John Nelson Armstrong: For Freedom* (Austin, TX: Sweet Publishing Company, 1969), 27-41.

included R. H. Boll, E. G. Sewell, R. C. Bell, and C. E. W. Dorris.

During what proved to be the final two years of Harding's administration, the school was severely depressed financially. Harding took no salary at all, and teachers made possible the school's continuance by voluntary wage sacrifices. In those days, the board of directors served primarily as advisors and custodians of the property. The school operated with the faculty making almost all decisions. Harding's ability as an administrator came under such question that against his wishes it was decided by the board to incorporate the institution. It seemed necessary for the continuance of the school that it be placed on stronger financial footing and its financing brought into line with accepted best practices and business methods. A charter was drawn and issued on February 2, 1901, naming David Lipscomb, W. H. Dodd, J. R. Ward, C. A. Moore, J. C. McQuiddy, and W. R. Chambers as incorporators.[8]

Harding resigned as the school's superintendent that spring saying that the school was full and that he had never wanted to build a larger school than the Nashville Bible School had become already. He announced that he would move to Bowling Green, Kentucky, to establish a similar school made possible by the generosity of Clinton C. Potter and his wife, Mary, in memory of their son, Eldon. Harding's influence led almost one-half of the Nashville Bible School's student body to follow him although he made it plain that he would not seek to induce any student to leave Nashville. The only faculty member he took with him was J. N. Armstrong, his son-in-law. Potter Bible College continued until 1912, when Harding retired. Just prior to the outbreak of World War I in 1914,

---

8   Ibid., 87-88.

the Potters petitioned to operate Potter Orphan Home (later Potter Children's Home) on what had been college property in Bowling Green.

Harding's replacement in Nashville (1901) was William Anderson of Maury County, Tennessee. Lipscomb, acting for the board, hired him. Harding wrote in his new paper, *The Way*, that "brother Anderson is a very superior man. He is a teacher of much experience and skill. He is a preacher of splendid ability. May the school under his leadership continue to grow and prosper."

Through the recruiting efforts of J. S. Ward, the school opened that fall with only six fewer students than the previous year. Under the leadership of Anderson, the school did in fact prosper. In 1902, Dr. Ward wrote in the *Gospel Advocate* that all rooms for women were filled and total enrollment stood at 118 students.

Lipscomb preferred small schools, but he came to believe that Nashville was the logical place for a more permanent, comprehensive, expanded college. In November 1902, he wrote in the *Gospel Advocate* that he was donating the major portion of his beautiful seventy-three acre farm to the school. The property was located four miles south of Nashville's public square on Granny White Pike. A neighbor to the north, Oscar F. Noel, Sr., thought so much of Lipscomb that he joined three acres of his property to the sixty-two acres given by Lipscomb. The editor of the *Advocate* appealed for help in raising the funds for the construction of two buildings on the campus.[9]

Progress moved slowly, however. When the fall session

---

9   David Lipscomb, "The Needs of the Bible School," *Gospel Advocate*, XLVI, No. 1 (January 1904), 9.

began, the boys moved into a three-story dormitory later named Lindsay Hall for Texas donor Edwin L. Lindsay. The building did not yet have windows and doors. Sheets and quilts covered the windows and door frames. The boys climbed from floor to floor by way of ladders. The administration and classroom building (Harding Hall) was likewise unfinished. Most students endured the inconveniences in their living arrangements until the dormitory was completed. In fact, their awkward quarters seemed to bond students with one another and with the faculty who endured it together with them.

Daily recitations and examinations were required in all classes. Daily Bible classes and chapel assembly attendance were also compulsory. While the administration and faculty were all personally gentle characters, there was no lack of discipline. Improper language, use of tobacco, disorderly rooms, and willful disobedience were expressly forbidden. In 1903, the school's catalog stated, "Lax discipline and thorough scholarship are incompatible."

About a month into the summer vacation of 1905, William Anderson suddenly died of a heart attack. Dr. J. S. Ward was asked to administer the school until a new superintendent could be chosen and elected by the board. At the end-of-the-year commencement exercises, it was announced that E. A. Elam had been chosen to lead the school going forward. Elam was the newest member of the Board. He was also one of the editors of the *Gospel Advocate* and was a recognized and respected gospel preacher. Among the graduates at that ceremony was Henry Leo Boles.[10]

The Elam administration continued seven years (1906-

---

10   H. Leo Boles, *History of David Lipscomb College*, Unpublished manuscript cited in Young, 89.

1913). Brother Elam was a large man with amazing blue eyes and a gentle spirit. He often brought peace to churches that called for his advice in settling disputes. He was known to be one of the finest pulpiteers among churches of Christ. He travelled extensively in gospel meetings, enthusiastically inspiring brethren to greater faith. He came to be well known for his quarterly Sunday school literature aptly called *Elam's Notes* and used in many churches of Christ in adult classes.

Elam's connection with the *Gospel Advocate* gave the school unrivaled media exposure. The 1907 issues of the paper carried a front page appeal for support of the school in almost every issue. Even so, little financial support was forthcoming from individuals or churches.

During the 1912-13 school year, Elam decided that he could not continue his editorial duties and preaching opportunities while at the same time doing justice to the needs of the school. He retained his position on the board but resigned as president. He urged the board to select H. Leo Boles to lead the school.

Boles's father was a rural preacher. His great-grandfather was Raccoon John Smith, a pioneer preacher who was a well-known contemporary of Alexander Campbell and Barton Warren Stone. Boles was a graduate of Burritt College (1900) who taught school in Tennessee and Texas before enrolling as a student in the Nashville Bible School in 1903. After his second college graduation in 1906, Boles had been hired to teach mathematics and philosophy by Elam.

Under Boles, the college continued to grow. In Boles' second year, enrollment passed 200 students. Under Boles, new programs were established, and neighboring universities began to accept Lipscomb's academic credits. Boles encouraged teachers to increase their credentials by attending George Peabody College and Vanderbilt University. Boles, himself, completed a master's degree while serving as president. In addition, he managed the business affairs of the college, recruited prospective students, raised money, ran the school's farm, served as dean and registrar, taught classes every school day, and preached on Sundays.

When Boles took over the presidency, his mentor, David Lipscomb, was failing physically. After twenty-two years teaching Bible, the grand old man of Nashville Bible School was forced to give up his classes at the age of 82. On November 11, 1917, just ten months after Jim Cope's birth, David Lipscomb died at the age of 86.[11] Almost immediately efforts were initiated to change the name of the school, a move Lipscomb had resisted while alive. Even though almost all appreciated Lipscomb's dedication and recognized the appropriateness of naming the school for him, there were different opinions about the change. Removing "Nashville" from the name was not an issue because the school was reaching toward national recognition, and many of its students were now from other parts of the country. The real difficulty arose over dropping the word Bible from the title. Some thought it would weaken the spiritual emphasis and commitment of the school. However, others strongly felt that brethren should recognize that the school was not just for preachers and that the curriculum supported a full college general education in addition to Bible instruction. The change from "School" to "College" was not a source of controversy. After long debate, the board made its decision, and on March 4, 1918, the "Nashville Bible School" became "David Lipscomb College."

---

11   *Gospel Advocate,* "Special Issue," IX, No. 7 (December 6, 1917).

Shortly after World War I ended in 1918, David Lipscomb College went through a series of administration changes. Boles resigned after seven years in the spring of 1920. A. B. Lipscomb was chosen to succeed Boles. He appointed his brother, Horace S. Lipscomb to be the first dean of the college. Horace Lipscomb held a master of science degree from Vanderbilt and had done graduate work at both Harvard and Cornell. For eighteen years he had taught in Nashville's public school system. A. B. Lipscomb resigned before the end of his first year and H. S. Lipscomb was appointed both dean and president. He took the college into the Southern Association of Colleges and Schools and enlarged academic offerings.

H. S. Lipscomb could not, however, keep enrollment from declining. In 1923, he resigned, and Boles was brought back as president. With renewed vigor, he called upon A. G. Freed, former president of Freed Hardeman College, to move to Nashville and become vice president of the college and principal of the high school. Boles's second term as president continued until 1932, when he resigned from the burdens of administration to teach Bible and serve on the board of directors. In addition, he wanted to devote more time to preaching and writing.[12]

Boles' tenure had been stressful at a time when economic depression nationwide was threatening the survival of almost every college as well as every business venture in the nation. The college had recently suffered several disasters. On Christmas Eve 1929, Lindsay Hall was destroyed by fire. The building, valued at an estimated $75,000 at the time, was covered by only $8,000 insurance. Only three months later, Avalon

---

12   Leo Lipscomb Boles and J. E. Choate, *I'll Stand on the Rock: A Biography of H. Leo Boles* (Nashville, TN: Gospel Advocate Company, 1965), 142-56.

Home, the girl's dormitory burned. The college held insurance policies worth $12,000 on this $65,000 building. It was only due to Boles' determination, the board's commitment, and the faculty's dedication that the college was able to continue to operate.

Replacing, enhancing, and equipping these dormitories put David Lipscomb College in debt to the tune of a quarter million dollars. Interest alone on the brand new Sewell Hall for women and Elam Hall for men, after half the debt was paid through donations, was accruing at a rate of approximately $9,000 per year in the school's most desperate financial times. Boles also lost his trusted vice president, chief fund-raiser, and friend, A. G. Freed, in November 1931. The deaths of Mrs. Lipscomb, E. A. Elam, and Freed moved the school into a new era, and Boles decided to turn over the administration to younger men. In addition, Boles was holding meetings, working on the *Gospel Advocate*, and writing *Elam's Notes* quarterly from his home on Granny White Pike across the street from campus.

Upon Boles's retirement, the board asked Batsell Baxter, president of Abilene Christian College, to use his administrative experience to bring David Lipscomb College through these desperate financial times. Baxter had graduated from Nashville Bible School twenty years earlier and had strong emotional ties to the school. He accepted the invitation of the board. When he arrived and school began, he faced a 7% decrease in enrollment and a current operating debt of $11,000. Baxter turned the enrollment problem around, and in his second year the total enrollment in both high school and college reached 400. By cutting salaries in half and retrenching with program cuts, Baxter was able to bring the college balance back into balance.[13]

Baxter brought E. H. Ijams from Los Angeles to be dean. Ijams was preaching in California, but he had taught at David Lipscomb in the 1920s. Baxter and Ijams worked together well in bringing David Lipscomb out of its difficulties. In 1934, Baxter resigned to return to Abilene as the head of the Bible Department there, and Ijams was elected president at Lipscomb. Ijams first year as president was Jim Cope's first year as a student at David Lipscomb College.

Cope at David Lipscomb[14]

Every young person who leaves a loving home is faced with conflicting emotions. Jim Cope had always been a forward looking, optimistic personality who was filled with hope and anticipation. On the other hand, he was a faithful son who ached at the thought of being absent from the family table and the comforting presence of his father and mother. Just seventeen years old, the young man travelled the sixty miles to Nashville in September 1934 to begin his pursuit of independent manhood.

H. Leo Boles was the leading influence in Cope's choice of David Lipscomb College. At the time Cope graduated from high school, he wanted to study law at Vanderbilt and prepare to go to Congress. However, Boles' suggestion that

---

13   Young, 89-95.

14   The following section is copied with permission, but edited with additional material, from a chapter written by this author and published in Margie H. Garrett, ed., *Making a Difference Florida College: The First Fifty Years* (Temple Terrace, FL: Florida College Press, 1996), 41-43.

he spend two years of general education classes, including Bible, within the environment provided by Lipscomb was especially attractive to the Cope family. Boles told Jim that he could have both Lipscomb and Vanderbilt, the best of both opportunities. That was powerfully convincing.

Upon arrival at Lipscomb, Jim went to see Dean Arnold of the Vanderbilt law school. He asked the dean what courses he should take at Lipscomb to prepare to come to Vanderbilt, and Dean Arnold outlined a course of study for him. Jim stayed with a pre-law curriculum during his first two years of college. Even so, by the end of his first year, Jim was seriously finding that he really wanted to spend his adult life preaching. The thing turning him in that direction was exposure to godly men, women, and fellow students every day in a spiritual environment.

Although the Cope family had known Boles for years and he had been instrumental in bringing Cope to Nashville, the young man was never fortunate enough to study under Boles except in church services during gospel meetings. The year before Cope went to David Lipscomb, Boles left the faculty to devote full time to writing *Elam's Notes*, church Bible class literature for adults, and to editing the *Gospel Advocate*. E. H. Ijams was the new Lipscomb president when Cope arrived there in the fall of 1934.

Jim Cope attended David Lipscomb College from September 1934 to June 1936. His 422 classmates that first fall included twenty-five high-school valedictorians. He went on to live in Elam Hall for a total of nine years until 1943. Six of those years he lived in the same room. President Ijams took a special interest in young Cope and became "a great inspiration in [his] life." Ijams was a great listener. He would be quietly receptive and then move on decisions, often behind the scenes. Jim sometimes reflected on what brother Ijams taught him about administration: 1) before making a decision, get all the facts; 2) discuss options; 3) always choose what you know to be right with the Lord; and 4) don't be overly dogmatic (*arrogant*) but be firm. Ijams was always kind and approachable. He was a true gentleman, always smiling and reflecting kindness in his eyes.

Ijams was the first person at Lipscomb with whom Cope discussed his decision to put aside law and study the Bible. That was in September 1935. In October, Ijams arranged for Cope's first regular preaching appointment (first Sunday each month) at the Reed Avenue church. That began the first Sunday in November 1935, during Jim's second year in college. I. C. Finley and John Dillingham were elders at Reed Avenue at the time. H. Leo Boles was a member at Reed Avenue but was almost never there when Jim was there. He was always away preaching in gospel meetings or filling other pulpits when the preacher was away. Aunt Dora happened to be visiting Catherine and Rebecca Hill in Franklin when Jim began at Reed Avenue. They drove up to hear Jim's first sermon there.

One of Cope's freshman Bible teachers at David Lipscomb was Hall L. Calhoun. Calhoun had taught in the Bible departments of Bethany College and Kentucky University (then a private school operated by Christians) before coming to Lipscomb. Calhoun preached at the Central church in Nashville and spoke on radio every day. He died of a sudden heart attack early in September 1935, just prior to the beginning of Cope's sophomore year of college.

Cope's other freshman Bible teacher was R. C. Bell. P had previously taught at Potter Bible School. Jim commented many times that, in his view "If brother Bell ever had an evil thought, it would have busted his head wide open." It was Bell who brought Jim to see and appreciate the grandeur, glory, and goodness of God. In later years, Jim said that he could "still hear brother Bell spin the adjectives to explain the glory of God." As a freshman, Cope studied the books of Matthew and Acts under Bell, who was the first to challenge Cope to believe in the providence of God. One day while studying the Sermon on the Mount (Matthew 5-7), Jim asked, "Brother Bell, do you mean to tell us that if a man broke in to your house, you would not do anything to defend your home and family." Bell responded, "Brother James, I don't even lock my door. God will take care of us."

Bell's classes met in a large classroom that could seat seventy-five students in the basement of Elam Hall. Upstairs the rooms served as a dormitory for students. Jim began the year sitting on the back row, taking a course in the book of Matthew. One day after taking roll, Bell said, "James, I would like to see you after class. Could you come back at 3:00 this afternoon?" When Jim arrived, Brother Bell began, "I want to talk to you about your background and heritage. I have difficulty with you sitting on the back seat. That is not characteristic of your upbringing." After that kindly dressing down, Jim was always on the front row in class.

Jim also had classes with S. B. Pittman. From him, Jim learned more fully the need for Christians to have a strong disposition to help people. Pittman would be on his way to school when someone in need would stop him, asking for a handout. Pittman would give them everything he had on him. He was charitable but could be high strung and sharp tongued. He had gone to school with "Uncle Dave" Lipscomb and was still teaching when Jim left.

These teachers had more influence than they realized. By the end of the first year of college study, Cope was questioning his ambitions to practice law and go to Congress.

As he was working in town that summer, Jim attended the Sparta congregation on Wednesday evenings. Early in June 1935, A. R. Hill, the preacher at Sparta, asked him to speak on Wednesday night along with George Toms (Jim's roommate at David Lipscomb) and Terry Meeks (another young member who had gone to school at Louisiana State University to study pre-medicine that year). The boys would have about ten minutes each. Jim later joked that this would be the first and last time he preached for only ten minutes. Jim's title was "What Think Ye of Christ." He worked on it constantly all week and delivered it just as planned.

Jim's mother and dad were not there. Aunt Dora was present and heard his talk. After the lesson, Mrs. Fannie Richards, wife of A. Frank Richards, the doctor who had brought Jim into the world and an elder in the church, waited in the vestibule until everyone else was gone to talk to Jim. She put her arm around him and said, "Jim Cope, do you want to preach the gospel?" Jim responded with, "Yes, ma'am, I do more than anything else in my life." She gave him a big hug and replied, "If you want to preach the gospel, you can preach the gospel. Miss Fannie doesn't have long to live. My days are numbered, but I want you to know this. Wherever you go and whatever you are involved in, just know that Miss Fannie will be praying for you every day." Jim later said, "With that kind of a sendoff, it just makes you want to eat tigers!"[15]

---

15   James R. Cope interview with Colly Caldwell, February 12, 1987.

A few weeks after that, Cope was asked to preach for Hill on Sunday morning. Bob Gillam, a long time elder, said to Jim, "Next Sunday is my time to preach while brother Hill is away. How about you preaching for me?" His second presentation was on the theme "Buy the Truth and Sell It Not" from Proverbs 23:23. That summer was when his lawyer friends asked him what changed his mind about becoming a lawyer and he told them, "I decided I had rather go to heaven than to Congress." He was eighteen years old.

As earlier stated, brother Ijams got Jim a monthly appointment at Reed Avenue in the fall of 1935. He continued meeting that assignment until the fall of 1938, when he went to Donelson to preach full-time. During that time, S P. Pittman encouraged the brethren at Leipers' Fork in Williamson County (a group which later was instrumental in starting the Hillsborough church of Christ) to have Cope preach for them one Sunday a month. In addition, he often preached at Arkland (near Columbia in Maury County, about forty miles south of Lipscomb College). In 1936, he also added a regular appointment at Kingston Springs.

Jim Cope's influence as a preacher grew rapidly. In July 1938, when he was twenty-one years of age, he returned to Big Spring for a gospel meeting. He had preached in a similar meeting at Cherry Creek the week before. The world was on the verge of World War II, and the religious climate was intensified across the country. The meeting at Big Spring began on Wednesday night and continued for twelve nights. Crowds flocked to the building, and to accommodate them, the brethren accepted fans and borrowed chairs from Thurmond's Funeral Home, where Cope had worked in the summer after his senior year in high school. Cope's sermons were on fundamental principles of salvation. Fifty-five were baptized, and twelve were restored to faithfulness. On Saturday night before the meeting closed on Sunday, eighteen responded to the invitation. Boys and girls who had been Cope's classmates in school were baptized, among others.

Cope has often told of a talk his father had with him before he left home after the meeting. Rogers Cope said:

> Jim, I don't think this would happen to you. I don't want to think it, but I'm your father, and I think I need to talk to you a little bit. You have had an unusual gospel meeting. The people came from everywhere, and some couldn't even get in; they had to stand outside. You baptized people whose knees you sat on when you were a child. For a lot of people, this would turn their heads, but I want to remind you of something. Before either of us were ever born, the cause of Christ was established in this community, and this congregation has been here forty years. The thing I want you to remember is something Jesus said a long time ago, "other men labored and ye are entered into their labors" (referring to John 4:38). You have reaped where they sowed.

Jim's dad went on to remind him that many faithful Christians were now gone and some still there had been there 35 or 40 years (the Breedings, the Gilliams, the Geers, and the Weavers). Some of the finest preachers who ever lived had preached right there where Jim had preached that week (W. H. Sutton [father of Mrs. C. G. McGee], H. Leo Boles, Andy T. Richey, and J. T. Clark).

The next year Jim was invited to preach in a meeting at the Sparta church, where J. Ed Nowlin was the local preacher. Cope preached three times on Sunday and twice every other day, October 1-15, 1939. Thirty-eight were baptized and four were restored. Jim's sister Mary Hill, who was now eleven, was one of those baptized in that meeting. He returned to Sparta every other fall after that for the next ten years.

It was Ijams who got Jim started teaching school. In those days, the Cope family was struggling to keep him in school. Aunt Dora helped with the little money she had saved. Rogers Cope's business was diminishing as he became more and more ill. Remember, too, the country was still suffering a "Great Depression." Franklin D. Roosevelt was bringing economic ideas forward but he had only been president since January 1933.

In the summer of 1936, after Cope graduated from David Lipscomb College, President Ijams gave him a job looking after boarding academy students who lived in Elam Hall. Jim became big brother to these elementary school boys whose parents brought them to school for the week. They stayed in the dormitory Monday night through Thursday night before going home on the weekends. Cope was given his room and board for caring for the boys. During that time, from the fall of 1936 through the spring of 1938, Cope worked on his bachelor's degree in history at Peabody College, preached at Donelson, and lived in Elam Hall.

Over the next two years, Cope went on to earn his master's degree at Peabody and teach Bible and Tennessee history in the Lipscomb junior high school. In the fall of 1938, Ijams also asked him to serve as principal of grades one through six. He did that for two years and then spent the following three years from 1940 to 1943 on the Bible faculty of the college.[16]

---

16   Curry, Melvin D., editor. *Reemphasizing Bible Basics in Current Controversies* (Temple Terrace, FL: Florida College Bookstore, 1990), xvi-xvii.

In January 1941, Cope left Donelson to work with the Belmont church in Nashville. Jim had preached at Donelson for two years. M. M. Young (Matt), father of M. Norvel Young, was one of the elders. Norvel Young was preaching for the College church on the campus. Willard Collins was preaching at Old Hickory. J. P. Sanders was at Hillsboro Pike, and Clay Pullius was at Charlotte Avenue in Nashville.[17]

Early in 1943, Jim held a protracted series of nightly tent meetings on the corner of Demonbreun and 16th streets in the middle of Nashville's entertainment district (Music Row). J. B. Cox led the singing, and Jim preached to between 200 and 400 people at each service. After that meeting, Jim suggested that the elders at Belmont buy a tent and Jim would preach in meetings around Nashville in areas where either churches could be started or churches could be helped to grow. After moving to Tampa, Jim was forever wanting to help bring about the start of new congregations. For whatever reasons, the Belmont elders did not take to Jim's plan, however, and it was a significant discouragement to him.

Cope had continued to work at David Lipscomb until Ijams resigned the presidency in May 1943. He also resigned from David Lipscomb and Belmont that spring. As a much sought after young preacher, he decided to spend the summer holding meetings all over Tennessee and Kentucky. He was still an eligible bachelor, but he had little time for dating with a view toward settling down.

In the spring of 1943, Jim held a gospel meeting for the West End church in Nashville. The meeting was a great success. That led to his being asked to move to work with the

---

17   H. Leo Boles, *Gospel Advocate*, Aug. 13, 1942, 776.

West End church on a regular basis. He decided to take the opportunity at the end of the summer. He would go on to preach at West End until January 1945.

Chapter 8:

Freed-Hardeman (1943-44)

Origin of Freed-Hardeman College

The Freed Hardeman College family (now "Freed-Hardeman University") likes to count its history from schools operated in Henderson, Tennessee, almost continuously from the mid-1860s.[1] Henderson is located approximately 135 miles west of Nashville and 90 miles east of Memphis, 17 miles southeast of Jackson via Highway 45.

Shortly after the Civil War, A. S. Sayle operated a private school on land where Old Main Administration Building and Hall-Roland Hall now serve Freed-Hardeman. Late in that decade, on November 30, 1869, the Tennessee State Legislature officially chartered a school under the name "Henderson Male and Female Institute." In 1877, the name was changed to Henderson Masonic Male and Female Institute. That school opened in 1870 and was operated for fifteen years by faculty members. Leaders at various intervals were George M. Savage, John Bunyan Inman, and H. G. Savage.

In 1885, the school ceased operation. Primarily because of the persuasiveness of Inman, however, the school came under the influence of members of churches of Christ who

---

1   Freed-Hardeman University website, fhu.edu

were interested in its survival.[2] A Christian named I. J Galbraith found it expedient to more formally organize the administration of the college. The name was changed to West Tennessee Christian College. The charter included a board of directors and a president. John Bunyan Inman was chosen to be the first president evidencing an essential link to the former institute. After his death in 1889, Inman was followed by G. A. Lewellen (1889-93) and C. H. Duncan (1893-1895).

The school first experienced the influence of Arvy Glenn Freed in 1895. Freed came to the presidency of West Tennessee Christian College when he consolidated it with Southern Tennessee Normal College at Essary Springs, Tennessee. A 21-year-old student at West Tennessee Christian College by the name of Nicholas Brodie Hardeman took a horse-driven wagon the forty miles to Essary Springs to bring desks and other school equipment to Henderson.[3] Freed had established the school at Essary Springs primarily to train educators and had served as many as 450 per term.[4] Freed was given a ten-year lease to operate the newly combined effort.[5]

Just a year into Freed's presidency, the college received what was then a very significant donation of $5,000 from the family of J. F. Robertson of Crockett Mills, Tennessee. It was given in memory of the Robertson's daughter, Georgie, who

---

2   Earl Irvin West, *The Search for the Ancient Order: A History of the Restoration Movement 1849-1906, Vol. 2* (Indianapolis, IN: Religious Book Service, 1950), 361-62.

3   James Marvin Powell and Mary Nelle Hardeman Powers, *N.B.H. A Biography of Nicholas Brodie Hardeman* (Nashville, TN: Gospel Advocate Company, 1964), 100.

4   A. G. Freed, "Southern Tennessee Normal College," *Firm Foundation*, July 12, 1892. Cited in Young, *A History of Colleges Established and Operated by Members of the Churches of Christ*, 97-109.

5   Young, 101.

died at age 21. The donors designated the gift to build a new building on the campus in her honor to serve the growing student body. As a result, in 1897 school officials changed the name of the school to Georgie Robertson Christian College. N. B. Hardeman's first year to teach at Georgie Robertson was 1897.

Freed served as sole president from 1895 until 1902, when Ernest C. McDougal was hired to join with him as co-president. That arrangement continued until A. G. Freed resigned in 1905. N. B. Hardeman also resigned. He taught in the public schools and served twelve years as Chester County Superintendent of Education, a position he held even after returning to college life.[6] McDougal continued until early in 1907, when Georgie Robertson Christian College cancelled classes for the following year. Tennessee Governor James B. Frazier delivered its commencement address in June 1907. Powell and Powers report that speech as proving to be the school's funeral oration. A school by that name never again opened.[7]

According to Charles P. Roland, the closure was "for lack of funds because of a division in the supporting church."[8] Without funding from one side of the division among brethren in the churches, the college could not financially continue. M. Norvel Young explained that Freed and McDougal took opposing positions on what was coming to be a distinct and enduring division between "churches of Christ" and "Disciples of Christ" (or the "Christian Church"). Specifically, McDougal favored the use of instrumental music in worship and missionary societies supported by church treasuries. When

6   Powell and Powers, 101.
7   Ibid.
8   Charles P. Roland, tennesseeencyclopedia.net.

the school property was deeded to the Christian Missionary Society of Tennessee, Freed left and became president of Southwestern Christian College at Denton Texas. Georgie Robertson could not sustain itself, however, and the society sold the property to the city of Henderson.[9]

Later that summer, a group of businessmen in Henderson proposed to Freed that he keep the original educational mission alive. He corresponded with Hardeman, and they agreed. Accordingly, the National Teachers' Normal and Business College was incorporated. Over the next school year the college did not serve students but prepared for the following year by building the administration building. In the fall of 1908, A. G. Freed returned as president. N. B. Hardeman was named vice-president.[10] In assuming their duties with the school, the two men accepted a mortgage on the property and thereby essentially came to own the institution personally. In addition, together they assumed the costs of new buildings and other expenses over the next ten years. Their success was a significant accomplishment given the intervention of World War I (July 28, 1914 to November 11, 1918), which impacted both student enrollment and finances toward the end of that time. Both Freed and Hardeman preached in the Henderson church of Christ that opposed instrumental music in worship and missionary societies.

In 1919, Freed and Hardeman turned the property over to a college board of directors committed to its future well-being. In turn the board named the school Freed-Hardeman College for these two administrators who continued to lead the school until 1923, when both went on to do other work.

---

9   Young, 102-03.

10   Powell and Powers, 101-03.

Freed went to David Lipscomb College, and Hardeman preached in gospel meetings.

From 1923 to 1925, W. Claude Hall served as president. In 1925, Hall accepted the presidency of Western Oklahoma Christian College at Cordell, Oklahoma, and the directors of Freed-Hardeman recalled Hardeman. The school opened under the associate presidency of N. B. Hardeman and Hall C. Calhoun. At the end of one year, Calhoun resigned and Hardeman became the sole president in 1926. With the help of some major donors, he took the school through the "Great Depression," continuing in that role for the next twenty-four years until 1950.[11]

Cope to Freed-Hardeman College[12]

Jim Cope told that his "personal knowledge" of N. B. Hardeman began in 1923 or 1924, when he went to hear Hardeman speak in a school auditorium in Cookeville, Tennessee. Hardeman spoke about his trip to the Bible lands. Jim was six or seven years old at that time. Later, Jim heard him preach in a gospel meeting near home.

In October 1938, Hardeman preached the fourth of five series of sermons identified as "Tabernacle Sermons" in the Ryman Auditorium in Nashville.[13] Jim was twenty-one years old and teaching at David Lipscomb at that time. He attended

---

11   Ibid.

12   Parts of the following are copied with permission, but edited with additional material, from a chapter written by this author and published in Margie H. Garrett, ed., *Making a Difference Florida College: The First Fifty Years* (Temple Terrace, FL: Florida College Press, 1996), 41-43.

13   Hardeman did the preaching in five of these meetings over a span of twenty years.

almost every session.

The full transcribed text of each sermon appeared the following day in the local Nashville newspapers, the *Tennessean* (morning) and *Nashville Banner* (evening). The first four series of meetings were conducted in the Ryman Auditorium in Nashville, Tennessee. The first contained twenty-two sermons delivered March 28 to April 16, 1922. The second was twenty-three sermons delivered April 1 to April 22, 1923. The third was twenty-one sermons delivered March 18 to April 1, 1928. The fourth was eighteen sermons delivered October 16 to 31, 1938. The fifth was sixteen sermons delivered in the Nashville War Memorial Building and the Central church building November 1-8, 1942. The sermons in each of the five series of meetings were later published in book form

The meetings were striking in many ways. Efforts had been made to contact in some way every household in Nashville, inviting people to come. The Ryman Auditorium could seat between six and eight thousand people at that time, and it was packed for every service to the point of turning away hundreds. Hardeman was at his prime as a preacher, being careful to support every point with Scripture. The acapella singing was a lesson in itself to those from denominations who relied upon mechanical instruments to support their worship. It was estimated that there were over 150 baptisms[14] at the auditorium and in local church houses of worship as a result of the first series of meetings alone in 1922.[15]

It should be noted that as the institutional controversy

---

14 Earle Irven West, *The Search for the Ancient Order, Volume 4* (Germantown, TN: Religious Book Service, 1987), 159.

15 N. B. Hardeman, *Hardeman's Tabernacle Sermons, Volume 1* (Nashville: Gospel Advocate Company, 1953 printing), 9-14.

developed, Jim came to question the organization of the Tabernacle Meetings. Obvious efforts were made to maintain the local autonomy and independence of each congregation, but the fact was the meetings were a collective effort of about forty different congregations.[16] Such was also the case in regard to meetings in Houston, where similar efforts were made featuring Foy E. Wallace, Jr., preaching in what came to be called the "Music Hall" meetings. Wallace' sermons focused upon religious errors of "Premillenialism" (January 21-28, 1945) and Catholicism and Denominationalism/ Baptist Doctrines (January 1946). More than twenty Texas churches "cooperated" in those efforts that were organized by the Norhill church in Houston.[17]

Jim Cope had not been preaching at the West End church in Nashville long when he received a letter from N. B. Hardeman asking him to speak on the Freed-Hardeman College lectures on the theme "Dangers Confronting the Church." Jim worked hard on that lecture and put himself into it. The "dangers" he noted were issues to which he had given much previous thought. On January 28, 1982 (thirty-eight years later), he spoke on the last night of the Florida College lectures on the subject, "Heritage, Horizons, and Destiny." He told the audience that he had pulled out his old outline from the January 12, 1944, speech at Freed-Hardeman. He said, "I am intrigued by the identical or similar major dangers I listed regarding the future of 38 years ago and the future I see in the winter of 1982." Here are the 1944 "dangers":

> A tendency toward an inherited religion versus a divinely taught

---

16   Ibid.

17   Foy E. Wallace, Jr., *God's Prophetic Word* (Oklahoma City, OK: Foy E. Wallace, Jr., 1946); Foy E. Wallace, Jr., *Bulwarks of the Faith* (Oklahoma City, OK: Foy E. Wallace, Jr. 1951).

religion;

A tendency to lose sight of our plea of "speaking where the scriptures speak and remaining silent where the scriptures are silent";

A tendency to discount the Lordship of Christ in favor of human wisdom;

A tendency toward sectarianizing the body of Christ into group loyalties, such as papers, schools and power cliques which might stand between Christ and His church;

A tendency to institutionalize individual and congregational duties by shifting them to preachers or to human institutions;

Friendship with the world versus friendship with God;

A tendency to compromise the truth by not preaching all of it and applying it to existing moral and doctrinal issues;

A lack of personal consecration to the person of Christ, to the people of Christ, and to the word of Christ; and

Indifference toward the work of Christ versus a dedicated zeal in response to His commands.[18]

Alex Harlan, one of Hardeman's fellow horsemen, had encouraged Hardeman to watch Cope even before that lecture. Harlan owned the coal black Tennessee walking horse champion "Midnight Sun." Hardeman owned a solid white mare named "Maid of Cotton." Hardeman's horse

18 James R. Cope, "Heritage, Horizons, and Destiny," in *Their Works Do Follow Them* (ed. Melvin D. Curry; Temple Terrace, FL: Florida College Bookstore, 1982), 253.

won the National Junior Championship as a three-year-old at Shelbyville in 1947.[19] In 1944, Wirt and Alex Harlan of Franklin, Tennessee, bought the stallion they renamed "Midnight Sun." Midnight Sun was the first winner of the World Grand Championship at the 1945 Celebration. He repeated in 1946. According to the Walking Horse Club of Kentucky, "From then until his death from colic in 1965, Midnight Sun bred up to 100 mares per year, spreading his influence all over the Walking Horse breed. The majority of Celebration champions have Midnight Sun somewhere in their pedigrees, often multiple times."[20] The Harlans were well known throughout Tennessee and Kentucky as breeders. Harlan was a faithful member of the church and good friend of Hardeman. He had transferred his church membership following Cope from Belmont to West End.

While Cope was in Henderson for the lectures, he stayed with Hardeman, who encouraged him to come to Freed-Hardeman to teach. Cope told him that he could not leave his preaching. As reported by Cope in a lecture in 1981, Hardeman said,

> I can understand that sentiment, Jim. If I thought your influence as a preacher of the gospel would be lessened in the slightest, I could not in good conscience ask you to join our ranks. If you were to take a poll of those who know my life's work best, some would tell you that my greatest influence for good has been in the delivery of my Tabernacle Sermons and the books resulting therefrom. Others would say it has been through my debates. But none other knows as I know that my greatest and most

---

19   James Marvin Powell and Mary Nelle Hardeman Powers, *N. B. H.: A Biography of Nicholas Brodie Hardeman* (Nashville, TN: The Gospel Advocate Company, 1964), 312.

20   Walkinghorseclubky.com

far-reaching good for the cause of Christ has been in the daily classroom contact I have had for 40 years with the young men and women, particularly the young men, who have sat at my feet as I sought to impart to them an appreciation of the word of God and help them understand some things which will enrich their lives and make them effective as proclaimers of that word. Every day I am preaching throughout the world through my boys. My years are relatively few and we must have younger men to help those who come this way when those who have worked here have laid by our armor. I want you to think about that.

Cope did think about that. He was promised he could teach Bible every day, and the elders at West End encouraged him in deciding to go. He moved to Freed-Hardeman that fall (1944) and went back and forth to Nashville (West End) on weekends until January 1945. Following that (January 1945 to January 1947), he preached at Huntingdon and took other appointments. His last two and one-half years in Tennessee (1947-49), Jim preached in the Henderson church on campus.

Section Four:

Building on Good New Relationships

Chapter 9:

Georgia Deane (1944)

Jim and Georgia Deane Combs Cope

Jim "cut quite a figure," as they say in Tennessee, all through high school. He was good looking, smart, and very personable. Everyone liked him, and he had lots of girlfriends. Even after going away to college, he would bring home a picture of his latest heartthrob, but before he left to go back to school, the girls' pictures would be in his mother's trunk. She had eight or ten of them when Jim met Georgia Deane Combs, but it had been quite a while since she had put the latest out of sight.

Jim Cope's mate for life actually came into his world the summer of 1936, before he moved to Freed-Hardeman, although neither of them was aware of even the potential for a future relationship. Her name was Georgia Deane Combs. Her grandfather, James M. McFarland, was an elder in the church at Donelson, Tennessee, east of Nashville, where Jim had earlier preached. Cope had graduated from Lipscomb in June of 1936 after two years there. He was now attending Peabody during the week, working on a bachelor's degree. For three months in the summer of 1936, Jim had traveled each

Sunday to Gadsden, Alabama. Beginning January 1, 1937, Jim accepted the invitation of the Donelson elders to preach there two Sundays each month. In the summer of 1937, he held gospel meetings and continued preaching twice each month at Donelson. In January 1938, Donelson asked him to come every Sunday and on Wednesday evenings.

McFarland first married a widow who had three daughters. One of the girls later married Dr. J. S. Ward. After his wife died, McFarland seriously took on the task of raising her daughters. Soon he married again, a woman named Georgia Ellen. Their marriage produced two additional children, one of whom was Georgia Deane's mother, Naomi. Though Cope had seen pictures of the McFarland children and grandchildren, he had never met Naomi McFarland or her husband, Charles E. Combs. Jim did, however, get to know the McFarlands well. During his time at Donelson, both James and Georgia Ellen were ill and much of the time unable to come to worship services. Jim would go out to visit with them on Sunday afternoons. He would allow the elder brother McFarland to tell of other days, including some about his family. But the pictures didn't really mean a lot to Jim, and at that time there was no reason to have special interest in their granddaughter, Georgia Deane, who lived in Galveston, Texas. They came back every summer to visit the McFarlands, but Jim was always away in meetings and never met Georgia Deane or her parents.

Georgia Deane's other grandparents, the Combs, were influential members of the Una church, on Murfreesboro Road in East Nashville. Her father, Charles G. Combs, was the eldest of four sons (Charles, Elmour, Harry, and Wilbur). He also had a half-sister. He and Naomi married in 1915 during early phases of World War I. The Combs lived in Galveston, Texas, where Charles worked as a cashier and express agent for Wells Fargo. In the summer of 1941, the Combs family moved to Dallas. There Charles became general chairman of the Brotherhood of Railway Clerks for the region that included Texas and Louisiana.

The Combs had two daughters. The eldest, Murrel, was born on April 25, 1916, a year and a day before Georgia Deane was born in Galveston (April 26, 1917). Georgia Deane always called Murrel "Sissy." Murrel was already married to Charles Freeman when Jim and Georgia Deane met and married.

On June 4, 1944, two days before the "official birth date" of Florida Christian College, Jim Cope went to the Preston Road church in Dallas to hold a meeting. He stayed with the Robert Bell family. Bell was from Murfreesboro, Tennessee, and served as one of the elders at Preston Road. He was married to the former Katherine Tubbs, who was from Sparta and knew the Cope family well. The Bells' wedding was the first in the reconstructed Sparta church building after the big fire that destroyed it earlier. In fact, their wedding was held in the building before there was even a church service there. Jim remembered attending that wedding as a boy. He had been in the sixth grade at the time. Jim had also preached the funeral services for both of Katherine's parents. Brother Tubbs had been an elder at Sparta for forty years. He was the wealthy owner of the Sparta Spoke Factory that manufactured spokes for wagon wheels and later for early automobile wheels.

According to Jim, Roy Cogdill had recommended him to Bell and the other elders for the Preston Road gospel meeting. The very Saturday night he arrived, Katherine Bell began telling Jim about this intelligent, very beautiful, exceptionally faithful Christian girl, Georgia Deane Combs. She was not married, about Jim's age, and had a great job with a Dallas oil man. Though her family worshiped at the Sears and Summit church (later Skillman Avenue), Katherine had invited Georgia Deane to come to the opening day of the meeting. Later in the evening after Katherine had described this wonderful girl, Jim told this writer that he said to himself, "Maybe this is what I came to Texas for, in addition to the gospel meeting. I had told them jokingly at West End before going to Dallas that there were three things I want to accomplish on this trip: I want to hold this meeting, I want to find the girl that I want to make my wife, and I want to see Bonnie Parker's grave." (Bonnie Parker and Clyde Barrow were notorious thieves killed in a romanticized shootout in Louisiana in 1934 and buried in Dallas). The next morning, Katherine identified the certain place where the young lady would be sitting and instructed Jim to look for her.

Jim Cope saw Georgia Deane Combs for the first time from the pulpit. The building was a converted residence. There were classrooms on the first floor and the auditorium upstairs. Jim had been sitting on the front seat of the auditorium through the adult Bible class and early part of the service. He had not seen Georgia Deane come in during a short break before worship began. When he went to the pulpit, he looked out at the audience. Georgia Deane was sitting in the exact spot Katherine Bell said she would be. With her were her sister Murrel, whose husband was away, and a long-time girl friend named Walker from their time at Abilene Christian College. Both Sissy and Georgia Deane had spent two years at ACC.

That afternoon they met and talked at a potluck luncheon in the park. The next night, Jim asked Georgia Deane to go out with him after the service. That was their first date. They subsequently dated every night except one over the next three weeks (June 6th through 29th). The meeting at Preston Road continued through June 16. Jim was to start a meeting at

Ferris, Texas, the next Sunday, June 18. He stayed on with the Bells, and he and Georgia Deane drove the twenty-five miles down to Ferris every night in either her car or with the Dorans. Basil Doran, a prominent song-leader who often led singing in meetings with Foy E. Wallace, Jr., and others, was leading the singing for both of Jim's meetings.

Georgia Deane Combs was working at the time for Wesley W. West. He lived in Houston but had an office in Dallas. He supplied Georgia Deane a car, and she looked after his business in Dallas. In addition to his financial interests in the oil industry, West had owned a newspaper in Dallas. She helped him wrap things up when he sold it. Georgia Deane's job was important, and she had to work in the daytime while Jim preached during morning services. Most afternoons, Jim came by the office. The two of them talked before going to evening services and again out together afterward.

On Sunday night, June 20, Jim and Georgia Deane talked of marriage. That night she accepted his proposal and promised to marry Jim. They had met for the first time exactly two weeks earlier. Both were twenty-seven years old. She was less than three months younger than he.

Right away Georgia Deane decided she should go to Tennessee to meet Jim's family. She came to Tennessee the week of July 16. She stayed a week in the Cope family home and visited West End with her fiancé on July 23 before flying back to Texas. Jim began a meeting at Big Spring on July 24.[1] After that visit, the family loved Georgia Deane, and she loved them. They at once believed that she would be perfect for Jim. As a result, the two of them decided to go ahead with the

---

1   Jim Cope telling of his wedding at a luncheon in Sparta, Tennessee, on July 18, 1984.

wedding. Georgia Deane set the date.

Cope was scheduled to begin teaching Bible, history, and political science at Freed-Hardeman on September 18. The Sunday edition of the *Nashville Tennessean/Banner* announced that the wedding date would be September 1, 1944. Jim and Georgia Deane married in the back-yard garden of her parents' home in Dallas on a Friday. Melvin J. Wise performed the ceremony; Archie Waldron, W. R. Elder, Bob Bell, and H. Clyde Hale stood up with Jim. Mary Hill Cope, Murrel Freeman (Georgia Deane's sister "Sissy"), and Katherine Bell were maids of honor.

The newly united Mr. and Mrs. Cope spent the first part of their honeymoon on her boss's ranch near Johnson City, Texas, not far from where Lyndon Baines and Lady Bird Johnson would use their ranch for a presidential retreat. The foreman took the young couple out one night in a jeep with a big light on it and they saw jack rabbits that were sometimes hunted on the ranch.

One day Jim mentioned that his friend Claud Terry, who lived in Henderson, Tennessee, was able to purchase Cadillacs during the war when they came available. The foreman passed that information along to Mr. West, who called back saying if Jim could get Terry to get him a new Cadillac, he would give Jim his old one. Several months later, West came to Jackson to drive his new Cadillac home to Houston. Jim got his old one.

After a few days honeymooning on the ranch, Jim and Georgia Deane came back to Tennessee. They traveled to Chattanooga and up onto Lookout Mountain to see "Seven States" from a single site before going to Sparta. After a few days at home, they headed to Henderson taking Mary Hill with them for her freshman year in college.

Chapter 10:

N. B. Hardeman (1944-49): Early Debates and Controversy

The Copes' Freed-Hardeman Experience (1944-49)

Upon arriving in Henderson, the Copes lived in an upstairs apartment of a home owned by Crystal McKinney. She was a wonderful lady but not a Christian. They lived there until they bought their first house in 1948.

During the Copes' first year at Freed-Hardeman, Jim lost his father's presence in his life. Rogers Cope died of throat cancer on October 19, 1945, at the family home.[1]

The Copes were living in Henderson when their first daughter, Connie, was born. She arrived at 4 o'clock in the morning of April 23, 1947, one month premature. On Friday night the 18th, Jim delivered the baccalaureate address to the graduating class of Scott's Hill High School. It was the first of three such speeches that weekend. On Sunday, he preached three times. Georgia Deane's contractions began during the evening service. On Monday, before driving to the hospital in Jackson, Georgia Deane made what had become her much

---

1   That significant event in Jim's life has been described in chapter three.

cherished meringue cookies. Connie was not born until Wednesday after three days of labor. Jim and Georgia Deane would go on to have two other children. Their daughter Cathy was born two years later in July 1949 in Dallas where Georgia Deane's parents lived. The family was in the process of moving to Temple Terrace. James R. Cope, Jr., (Butch) was born four years later on July 10, 1953, in Tampa.

The five years the Copes lived in Henderson and were associated with Freed-Hardeman College were formative for Jim in many ways. Both his involvement in college work and his close association with leaders of brotherhood thought were especially significant. Additionally, at Freed-Hardeman, the impact of Jim Cope's personality caught everyone's attention. He was gracious, charming, and personally interested in everyone. In those days, he was slender and well-dressed, with glasses accentuating his vivid blue eyes.

From the beginning, Jim taught Bible classes in the Old Testament, the Gospels, Acts, and some of Paul's epistles. He sat in the one "Special Bible" class taught by Hardeman, and he taught it when Hardeman was out of town. Georgia Deane sat in on all of Jim's Bible classes at the college. Jim also taught American history and sociology. Students who planned to preach admired him so much that they imitated him in the pulpit.

Jim was in close and constant contact with N. B. Hardeman through that time. They spoke daily on campus and sometimes at the Hardemans' house and horse barn. Hardeman would reminisce or expound upon some Scripture, and Jim would soak it in.

Through the year 1948, Hardeman was a tremendous help in Jim's paration for debate. Early that year, Jim agreed to debate a Missionary Baptist preacher named L. H. Brown at Huntingdon, Tennessee. The discussion was later scheduled to be held September 6-11, Monday through Saturday, just prior to the start of the fall 1948 term at Freed-Hardeman.[2]

Ten years earlier, in April 1938, Hardeman had debated Ben M. Bogard in Little Rock, Arkansas, on some of the same topics. Bogard was then dean of the Missionary Baptist Institute in Little Rock and pastor of the Antioch Missionary Baptist Church in that city.[3] In 1924 Bogard and Doss Nathan Jackson became the principal founders of the American Baptist Association, later commonly called the Missionary Baptist denomination. Bogard was one of the best-known Baptist preachers and was their most prolific debater of that era. His debate with Hardeman was published, is read today, and stands as a classic in its genre.

Ben Bogard also debated Joe S. Warlick, W. Curtis Porter, and other able members of churches of Christ. Bogard's last debate (number 237 by his count with close to two-hundred of them defending Baptist doctrine against preachers from churches of Christ) was with Porter and was held at Damascus, Arkansas, in March 1948. Unfortunately for Cope, the publication was delayed until 1951, long after Cope's meeting with Brown and after Bogard's death in May, 1951.[4]

Jim not only discussed Biblical arguments with Hardeman; he also learned valuable lessons concerning how to present the truth in countering error. For example, in his debate with

---

2   James R. Cope, *Debate Notes on Missionary Baptist Doctrine, Second Edition* (Temple Terrace, FL: James R. Cope, 1954), p. i.

3   N. B. Hardeman and Ben M. Bogard, *Hardeman-Bogard Debate* (Nashville, TN: Gospel Advocate Company, 1938), p. 3.

4   W. Curtis Porter and Ben M. Bogard, *Porter-Bogard Debate* (Lufkin, TX: The Roy E. Cogdill Publishing Company, 1951), i-iv.

Bogard, Hardeman made one passage of Scripture the central, memorable theme of each thirty-minute speech. He presented a telling passage in its context, carefully applied it to the proposition at hand, and then challenged Bogard to dispute what it said. His method made his argument irresistible to many in the audience. Jim learned from his strategy.

Cope not only learned from Hardeman and from reading debates; he studied the writings of Foy E. Wallace (<u>God's Prophetic Word</u>, <u>The Certified Gospel</u>, and articles in the *Bible Banner*); A. G. Freed (<u>Sermons</u>, and <u>Chapel Talks</u>); Ashley S. Johnson (<u>The Great Controversy</u>); G. C. Brewer (<u>Forty Years on the Firing Line</u>); J. W. McGarvey (<u>Commentary on Acts</u>); Alexander Campbell (<u>Christian Baptism</u> and <u>The Christian Baptist</u>), and many other restoration writers. It was a training ground time in his life, and he always appreciated Hardeman's having tutored him.

The topics for the Cope-Brown debate were carefully crafted, but the issues were basic and clearly understood by the audiences. Each proposition was affirmed and denied the same evening in thirty minute speeches.

> Proposition I – (affirmed by Brown): "The Scriptures teach that the church of the New Testament, known as the Missionary Baptist Church, was established during the personal ministry of Christ."

> Proposition II – (affirmed by Cope): "The Scriptures teach that the church of Christ was established on the first Pentecost following the resurrection of Christ."

> Proposition III – (affirmed by Brown): "The Scriptures teach that the alien sinner is saved at faith before and without water baptism."

Proposition IV – (affirmed by Cope): "The Scriptures teach that water baptism is essential to the salvation of the alien sinner."

Proposition V – (affirmed by Brown): "The Scriptures teach that a child of God cannot so act as finally to be lost in hell."

Proposition VI – (affirmed by Cope): "The Scriptures teach that a child of God may so sin as to be lost in hell."[5]

Cope, of course, responded to the first proposition by pointing out among other things, that "There can be no New Testament without the testator's death, for declares Paul, 'Where a testament is there is of necessity also the death of the testator; for a testament is of force after men are dead: otherwise it is of no strength at all while the testator lives' (Heb. 9:16-17). Therefore, he said, "There could be no N.T. church till after Jesus died."[6] Tuesday, Jim took his time carefully pointing to the establishment of the church on the day of Pentecost by showing its fulfillment of God's prophecies on that day. There is no mention of a Baptist church.[7]

On Wednesday and Thursday evenings, the debate turned to the subject of the role and necessity of baptism in one's salvation.[8] Then on Friday and Saturday nights, the subject dealt with the Impossibility of apostasy or what Brown chose to call (like Calvin) the "Perseverance of the Saints."[9]

Jim Cope was a master in the classroom. The year following the debate (1948-49 school year), Jim had all of the preacher students in his classes. He taught his course material, but he

---

5   James R. Cope, *Debate Notes on Missionary Baptist Doctrine, Second Edition* (Temple Terrace, FL: James R. Cope, 1954), p. i-vii.

6   Ibid. p. 1.

7   Ibid. p. 29-40.

8   Ibid. pp. 41-78.

9   Ibid. pp. 80-106.

also spent time discussing the debate. He shared his arguments and debate notes with them, and they insisted he put them in permanent form. Five years later, after moving to Florida, Jim edited and printed a second edition to be shared with students at Florida Christian College and others who could use it in refuting Baptist doctrine.

While still at Freed-Hardeman College, Cope also carefully studied at length questions concerning the nature of the church and its relationship to human institutions (such as colleges, orphanages, etc.). Issues concerning that topic were being debated in the journals by Hardeman and the influential preacher, Foy E. Wallace, Jr. Cope was, of course, working in a college operated by brethren, and he knew he had to make up his mind for himself whether colleges could scripturally accept contributions from churches. It would be the first of several critical times in Jim's life when he was required to make conscientious decisions and stand firm with regard to church support of human institutions, specifically colleges in which he worked. It is to his credit that his decision was not the same as the conclusion of the president he reported to at that time.

Hardeman was seventy-three that year (born May 18, 1874). Cope was thirty. Hardeman's age, reputation, experience, position over him in the college, and their personal relationship caused Jim to want to show great respect while remaining true to his conscience. When he received a letter from Jack Meyer warning him not to get so close to brother Hardeman personally that it would influence his thinking on whether churches may support human institutions, he showed the letter to Hardeman. To Hardeman's credit, he replied, "Jack's right, Jim. You need to be careful that you do your own thinking."

Cope described the genesis of his own convictions on the subject while at Freed-Hardeman in a lecture he presented at Florida College on January 29, 1981.[10] The lecture was focused on the influence of N. B. Hardeman among Christians in his day. Cope was almost daily interacting with Hardeman in 1947. So his personal story is intermingled with first-hand reporting of Hardeman's reasoning and his own responses to it.

By way of background, as early as 1931 at the Abilene Christian College lectureship, G. C. Brewer advocated congregations supporting the colleges among brethren from their treasuries. He repeated that in 1933. At the request of Foy E. Wallace, Jr., who was editing the *Gospel Advocate* at that time, Brewer wrote a series of articles over the next several months explaining his position. Some opposed Brewer, and both sides of the controversy were given ink to espouse their positions. Those who disagreed with Brewer in those early days included John T. Hinds and F. B. Srygley. They wrote for the *Gospel Advocate*. W. W. Otey and C. R. Nichol led the opposition to Brewer and company in the *Firm Foundation.*[11]

Brewer thought that Foy Wallace was in agreement with his position early on, but Wallace denied it later, saying that he had only approved the airing of Brewer's position for discussion purposes among the brethren.[12] In 1936 and 1938 on the Abilene Christian College lectureship, Brewer repeated his appeal for churches to support colleges operated

---

10   James R. Cope, "N. B. Hardeman: Orator, Evangelist, Educator, and Debater," in *They Being Dead Yet Speak* (ed. Melvin D. Curry; Temple Terrace, FL: Florida College Bookstore, 1981), 133-55.

11   Cecil Willis, *W. W. Otey: Contender for the Faith,* (Akron, OH: Cecil Willis, 1964), 312-28.

12   David Edwin Harrell, Jr., *The Churches of Christ in the Twentieth Century: Homer Hailey's Personal Journey of Faith* (Tuscaloosa, AL: University of Alabama Press, 2000), 81.

by brethren and teaching the Bible. During this time, Wallace clearly opposed church contributions in an article published in the *Firm Foundation*. He said, "For many years the majority of our strongest preachers in these parts have opposed affiliating the church with the school and putting the college in 'the budget' of the church."[13]

Generally, individual Christians had supported colleges financially, but not churches. F. B. Srygley and Daniel Sommer met in Nashville in 1933 to discuss the issues involved. They came away agreeing that such colleges had a right to exist and teach the Bible, but congregational treasuries should not support them. Over the next few years the Great Depression (1929-33) was still influencing lives, and World War II (1939-45) had caused the issues among brethren to focus on the "war question" and premillennialism. The college question was discussed among preachers to some degree, but it was not the major concern.

By 1946, however, attention had slowly returned to the colleges and questions regarding "institutionalism." The controversy quickly heated up when G. C. Brewer debated Carl Ketcherside four nights (December 16-19) in St. Louis. Ketcherside was convinced that colleges did not have a scriptural right to exist and teach the Bible. He affirmed that teaching the Bible was the prerogative of the church collectively. Of course, family and Christians should do so individually. Brewer strongly defended the colleges and their right to church financial support.

Almost immediately, Brewer called N. B. Hardeman and informed him that a challenge to discuss these issues on Freed-

---

13   Foy E. Wallace, Jr., "Concerning Christian Colleges," *Firm Foundation*," January 19, 1937, 1, 3.

Hardeman's "Special Courses" in January had been issued to Brewer by Ketcherside. He had agreed subject to Hardeman's approval. Hardeman told Cope that he had said to Brewer, "Come on." The discussion would involve two, two-hour debate sessions on January 7, 1947. Brewer was already scheduled to speak that evening on the "College Question." The debate was much more impactful than a single speech would have been in spite of the fact that it was not reported in the *Gospel Advocate*.

Jim Cope felt that Brewer did not adequately deal with the question of church support in the Freed-Hardeman debate with Ketcherside. Hardeman seemed to agree. He apparently felt the need to write his own views and publish them in the *Gospel Advocate*. Before sending his article, he showed it to Jim and asked what he thought. At that time Jim saw that there were two issues involved. One related to the college's right to exist and teach the Bible, and the other to the college's right to be financially supported by the church(es). On the latter topic, Hardeman believed that churches should not put colleges "in their budgets" because that would bind them to the college. If, however, they made a single contribution for some purpose, that would not bind them to the college and would be an acceptable choice considered expedient on their part. Thus, Hardeman had included a statement that caught Jim's attention. Hardeman said, "If, however, a church believes any school is teaching the truth and is thus furnishing an avenue through which parents may train their children, and such a church desires to help the school to exist, it has the right to do so."[14] Jim suggested that Hardeman remove

---

14   N. B. Hardeman, "Position of Freed-Hardeman College Regarding 'Bible Schools,'" *Gospel Advocate* LXXXIX, 7 (February 13, 1947); 132, 144.

that statement. It was unnecessary because it did not help his argument for the right of the college to exist and because it would unsettle those who disagreed. Hardeman thought that Jim was "unduly concerned about its effect." Hardeman let his statement stand.

Jim later acknowledged that at the time in January he agreed with Hardeman's basic position. Over the next few months, however, while agreeing on the college's right to teach the Bible, he came to strongly disagree on the issue of church support. He said, "[A]t that time I was of the conviction that a church did not do wrong when it contributed to the school, but, growing out of the discussions over this issue, I became convinced that I was in error in my thinking and, before I had any plans of leaving Freed-Hardeman College, had urged brother Hardeman to adopt and publish a policy of refusing church gifts to the school." Hardeman would not do that. He replied, "That's what I believe and I am not about to change it."

On the day that Jim received the March 1947 issue of the *Bible Banner*, he made a visit to Hardeman's farm and found him in his horse barn. Jim sat down on a nail keg and told his mentor that "the *Bible Banner* had 'lowered the boom' on him because of the statement he had not deleted from his February 13, 1947, article." Cled E. Wallace, in an article entitled "Putting Schools Where They Belong,"[15] had agreed with Hardeman that the schools had a right to exist but had strongly disagreed that a church had the right to donate funding to a school if it chose. Hardeman responded to Jim, "I think I can take care of that in another brief statement."

---

15   Cled E. Wallace, "Putting Schools Where They Belong," *Bible Banner* Vol. 8, No. 3 (March 1947); 2-3.

Jim was much more concerned than Hardeman. He replied,

> Brother Hardeman, you are considerably more than twice my age and had been preaching almost 20 years when I was born. You have forgotten more than I have learned and I stand in awe of your knowledge and wisdom. Even so, I think I know that the Wallace boys are just like bulldogs—they never quit! If you feel that you may have made a judgmental mistake in approving church support of schools in your *Advocate* article, why not just say so in the *Advocate*? If not, it appears to me that the better course is to let the matter drop regardless of what is said in the papers. If you reply, you will be writing this time next year.

Hardeman did not drop it, and the battle raged throughout the year 1947 between him and the editors and associate editors of the *Bible Banner*. The controversy grew particularly hot and personal between Hardeman and Foy E. Wallace, Jr.

Jim and Hardeman discussed the increasing bitterness between Hardeman and Foy Wallace throughout that year. They discussed the distress this battle was causing in the brotherhood. Jim also talked several times with L. L. Brigance, a respected and older fellow teacher at Freed-Hardeman, about his concern for the brethren. He was aware that G. C. Brewer and Ira Douthitt both made visits to Henderson to discuss the problems with Hardeman. Brewer encouraged Hardeman in the dispute but Douthitt "was the most upset I had ever seen him," Jim said.

From February to November, Hardeman wrote six articles published in the *Gospel Advocate* dealing with the "*Bible Banner* Boys" and their position on church support of colleges. He implied that at least some of what schools and orphanages did was also the work of the church. It was in the article in the

October 23 issue that he wrote his now famous (infamous to many) comparison between churches supporting colleges and churches supporting orphanages. He wrote:

> I have always believed that a church has the right to contribute to a school or an orphanage if it so desired. In all that I have written there is no conflict on this matter. The right to contribute to one is the right to contribute to the other. Note the parallel: (1) The school is a human institution; it has a board of directors· it teaches secular branches in connection with the Bible. (2) An orphan home is a human institution; it has a board of directors: it teaches secular branches in connection with the Bible. The same principle that permits one must also permit the other. They must stand or fall together. Assuming that the school does the work of the church (which is subject to discussion), then may I ask: If the church can do part of its work-caring for orphans - through a human institution, why can it not do another part of its work -teaching the Bible - through a human institution?[16]

That article became a rallying statement for both positions held by "institutional" and "non-institutional" brethren. Freed-Hardeman College had truly become a catalyst for division across the brotherhood. In 1981, Jim Cope said that he had come to believe that "there has never been penned a clearer and more concise statement of the issue over which brethren have been divided in doctrine and practice" than the one in 1947 from Hardeman's pen: "They must stand or fall together." Cope continued, "Its acceptance opened the floodgate for a practice that split brethren and churches into opposing camps regarding their spending of the 'Lord's

---

16   N. B. Hardeman, "The Banner Boys Become Enraged," *Gospel Advocate*, LXXXIX, 43 (October 23, 1947); 844.

money.'"[17] Cope himself came to question if the church could support a school why could congregations not support any kind of organization with any kind of benevolent work including hospitals, homes for the aged, etc. Where would be the stopping place?

Two weeks later (November 6), Hardeman published an article entitled "Then and Now" in the *Gospel Advocate*, which he concluded by saying that he anticipated nothing new on the subject of churches supporting schools. Thus, "This article closes my part of the discussion."[18] Before saying that, however, Hardeman lashed out again at Wallace in a most personal way and responded to the charges and name-calling Wallace had uttered against him. Both men had crossed the line by placing such personal matters publicly before the brotherhood. Wallace was not through. When he saw what Hardeman had written, he delayed his November issue of the *Bible Banner* to respond. He denied much of what Hardeman had said publicly about helping Wallace out of financial difficulties in earlier days. He also denied that their personal issues resulted from Hardeman refusing to change his position on the "war question." He closed by saying, "Nothing in N. B. Hardeman's closing eruption of his pent-up animosity is true."[19]

Word of Wallace's response reached B. C. Goodpasture, editor of the *Gospel Advocate*. It apparently came from

---

17   James R. Cope, "N. B. Hardeman: Orator, Evangelist, Educator, and Debater," in *They Being Dead Yet Speak* (ed. Melvin D. Curry; Temple Terrace, FL: Florida College Bookstore, 1981), 146.

18   N. B. Hardeman, "Then and Now," *Gospel Advocate*, LXXXIX, 45 (November 6, 1947); 893.

19   Foy E. Wallace, Jr., "Stand By For the Facts," *Bible Banner*, Vol. 9, No. 9 (November, 1947) 16.

Lubbock, Texas, where the *Banner* was published. Jim Cope was in Hardeman's office talking to him when a call came urging Hardeman to apologize in the *Gospel Advocate* before the December issue of the *Bible Banner* was published. Cope understood that it was Goodpasture on the other end of the line. To his credit, following the call, Hardeman issued the following "Apology" copied here in full:

> "Some months ago I wrote an article on the position of Freed-Hardeman College. A number of articles have followed, both in favor of and in opposition to the position stated. Possibly some good has resulted from the arguments thus presented. It is regrettable that personalities have been injected. Truth and not victory should be the object of all controversy, and any effort to lessen the force of an opponent's argument by wit, caviling, ridicule, or reflection upon his character should be strictly avoided. This rule has been accepted to govern in all honorable debates. I have yielded to the temptation to violate this principle, and I offer to the brotherhood a genuine apology. Never again do I expect to descend to such low levels."[20]

Wallace and others did not accept Hardeman's apology. Wallace wrote, "No apology was made for what was said; he only apologized 'to the brotherhood' for saying it."[21]

While still in Henderson, Jim Cope was troubled by the personal attacks made during the controversy. In addition, he

---

20   N. B. Hardeman, "An Apology," *Gospel Advocate,* LXXXIX, 47 (November 20, 1947), 940.

21   Robert E. Hooper, *A Distinct People: A History of the Churches of Christ in the Twentieth Century* (West Monroe, LA: Howard Publishing Company, 1993), 208. See also Foy E. Wallace, Jr., "The Plain Facts vs. The N. B. Hardeman Falsehoods," *Bible Banner* X, 9 (December 1947), 9.

was conscientiously moved to go back and study the entire issue by a statement from James P. Miller. When things really became hot and feelings became raw, it appeared that there might be a division across the brotherhood over personal loyalties. Jim was in a meeting, October 10-17, 1948, with Miller and the local congregation in Evansville, Indiana, when Miller said, "You would not want to make a statement that you would admit was a matter of opinion that was divisive to the brethren." Jim told this writer that was the thing that motivated him to reconsider the right of a church to support a school.

Cope's Role at Freed Hardeman

It was widely speculated in the last two years of his time at Freed-Hardeman that Jim was being groomed by brother Hardeman to be the next president. That may have been true. Jim learned at some point that Hardeman had spoken to J. W. Akin about it, and Akin was favorable. According to Jim, brother Hardeman talked freely about retiring and leaving his position to someone else. He did not say to whom. In a discussion with this writer on February 18, 1988, however, he was asked if he ever thought that by coming to Florida Christian College he was giving up the chance to do something more influential at Freed-Hardeman. He replied that he never thought of that. He went on to say that his becoming president of Freed-Hardeman "was never really discussed between brother Hardeman and me all the time I was there." It may have been that brother Hardeman knew that the decision would probably not be entirely his to make. He may have been too smart to put that directly into the head of a young man. He may have been waiting to see how Jim would come out on critical issues among the brethren. The truth is, however, that Hardeman was not pleased when Jim decided to move on from Freed-Hardeman College, and their relationship changed after Jim announced he was leaving. Jim returned only one time to preach on the college lecture program.

Section Five:

Building a Fledgling College on Good Principles

Chapter 11:

Origins of Florida Christian College (1946)

Origination of Florida Christian College: "Laying the Foundation"[1]

A building is only as strong and secure as its foundation. The founders of Florida Christian College laid a strong and secure foundation that has been preserved.

Even before 1900, members of churches of Christ in Florida were expressing interest in building a school operated by Christians. Their interest was shared by T. B. Larimore, who, from 1871 through 1887, served as president of Mars Hill College in Florence, Alabama. Larimore's eldest son, Granville, practiced law in Tampa. Upon resigning his position at Mars Hill, Larimore conceived of a Bible college to be located either in Gainesville or Tampa.

In 1919, a number of interested Christians proposed an orphan home and school in the flat wooded area west of Avon Park. About that time a rumor spread that A. G. Freed

---

1   The following chapter is copied with permission, but edited with additional material, from a chapter written by this author and published in Margie H. Garrett, ed., *Making a Difference Florida College: The First Fifty Years* (Temple Terrace, FL: Florida College Press, 1996), 3-13.

was planning to start a college in Florida, but apparently Freed simply had advised with those who were interested in the project. Freed's name later ecame associated with Freed-Hardeman College in Henderson, Tennessee.

In the summer of 1942, G. A. Waters asked W. O. Norton, who was serving as president of Dasher Bible School in Valdosta, Georgia, to bring his family to his home in Oklawaha, Florida, for a brief vacation. Waters talked with Norton at length about establishing a school in Florida and took him to several possible sites. They discussed an elementary and secondary school like Dasher because both thought that much more support would be required to build a college.

In December of that year, Norton's interest was again piqued when P. L. Hunton told him that while preaching in a gospel meeting at Deland, he had learned of the potential sale of the Pineland College property. At Dasher's annual lecture program in March 1943, Norton called a meeting of Florida preachers whom he urged to get busy establishing a school. Among the fourteen preachers present were Thomas G. Butler, Walter N. Henderson, Glenn R. Shewmaker, L. J. Stanley, and J. Roy Vaughn. Stanley and Vaughn would later serve on the Florida Christian College Board of Directors.

In April 1943, Norton went to Deland, Florida, for another meeting. Some followed Norton's plan to establish an orphanage and school that the children of Christians could also attend. Their efforts resulted in the founding of Mt. Dora Christian Home and Bible School. Others wanted a college, and some of them became founders of Florida Christian College.

Because property near Deland was being considered, another meeting of those interested in starting a college was called there in May. Preachers and church members from all over the state attended. At that meeting, the Pineland College property was rejected as inadequate and too small. Garvin Toms and Leroy Miller told the assembly about a piece of property for sale in Temple Terrace. This property had been the site of the Florida Bible Institute, which Billy Graham had attended some four or five years earlier.

In October 1943, two meetings were conducted in Tampa. The first was disappointing with only J. Roy Vaughn, Leroy Miller, William Floyd, and Garvin Toms attending, but Toms and Miller were determined to take their cause to the brethren throughout the state and survey the level of support. They were encouraged by the results and by better attendance at a meeting on October 31. Calling the meeting to order, Toms informed those present that the property in Temple Terrace consisted of five buildings on approximately 150 acres of land that could be purchased for $100,000. Three thousand dollars was pledged toward the property and $1500 toward the support of the school in its first year. Roy Thurmon was selected as secretary to record minutes of this and future meetings. A committee of five (made up of Jesse Clark, J. S. Sweet, Lloyd Copeland, C. Ed Owings, and Roy Thurmon) was appointed to investigate procedures and problems associated with acquiring the Temple Terrace property and establishing a school.

The committee, of which C. Ed Owings was elected chairman, met several times over the next few weeks. Lloyd Copeland asked that the secretary contact several other schools operated by brethren and request copies of their charters, by-laws, and documents explaining the histories of their establishment. Jesse Clark moved that they notify property owners of their intention to negotiate for the purchase of the property. The committee determined to invite E. H. Ijams, president of David Lipscomb College, to come to Tampa to advise with them on how to avoid problems in founding a school. They decided if Ijams could not come, they would ask N. B. Hardeman for assistance. Ijams agreed to come on November 28 for a few days of discussion, and a general meeting of interested brethren was set for November 30. Ijams urged those present to go ahead with the project, saying that there would be no better time in the next fifteen years to establish a school in Florida. He advised them to begin with grades seven through junior college.

By January 24, 1944, the committee had received enough encouragement and financial pledges to take several significant steps forward. According to Lee Warren Boswell, they had $378 with which to begin a college. H. N. Donoho had given the very first money toward establishing the school. According to S. O. Ward, Donoho wrote a check for $1000 and told the other men to get a plan together.[2] He and his wife later left the school a forty acre orange grove that was operated for about five years at a profit of approximately $100,000 and was later sold for another $200,000. Mr. and Mrs. Boswell later gave millions of dollars at critical times in the college's history.

In the January 24 meeting, C. Ed Owings moved that the school be named Florida Christian College. He further moved that J. H. Clark be named treasurer to receive and deposit funds on behalf of the new college. The committee discussed men who should be considered for the presidency of this new school and also named several influential individuals who should be invited to join a statewide committee to promote the school. This list included H. N. Donoho, S. O. Ward, Lee

2   Meeting with S. O. Ward and James R. Cope, February 28, 1988.

W. Boswell, and C. G. McGehee.

On March 30, the new statewide committee met in Jacksonville with C. Ed Owings serving as chairman. Twenty-six men agreed that the new school would include a senior high school and a junior college. They unanimously approved a motion that money not be raised by soliciting the treasuries of congregations. This group voted to name the school "Florida College." Committees were appointed to investigate standards for accreditation, suitable sites, and proposed administrators for the school.

June 6, 1944, has been identified as the official birthdate of the college. Many of the men on the statewide committee that had met in Jacksonville went to Lakeland to join with others from all over the state for the purpose of establishing a school. There were twenty-seven to thirty men who attended that meeting.[3] The primary order of business was the selection of a board of directors. Before their selection, an objection was raised to a proposal passed in an earlier meeting to exclude men from board membership whose full time work was preaching. That proposal was unanimously annulled.

Ten men were selected to the board of directors: Lee Anderson of St. Petersburg, Lee Warren Boswell of Lakeland, Lloyd Copeland of Tampa, H. N. Donoho of Lakeland, T. H. Holsberry of Plant City, C. G. McGehee of Jacksonville, C. Ed Owings of Tampa, W. R. Starling of Miami, I. O. Taylor of Orlando, and J. Roy Vaughan of Miami. A motion made by W. N. Henderson, seconded by J. H. Harwell, and unanimously approved gave these ten men final authority and power over anything pertinent to the school. The torch was passed and the Florida Christian College Board of Directors

---

3   Lee Warren Boswell interview, February 29, 1988.

was established.

The first action of the board was to select its officers. C. Ed Owings was elected chairman. He was an elder in the Howard Avenue church in Tampa and a good man. I. O. Taylor was chosen to be secretary. A charter and by-laws committee and a finance committee were appointed. These committees included members who were not on the college board but who had been active in promoting the idea of a school in Florida. Garvin Toms served as chairman of the charter and by-laws committee, and S. O. Ward was made chairman of the finance committee even though he was not a board member at the time.

The Temple Terrace Campus

The first meeting of the board of directors was called for July 11, 1944, in Miami. At that meeting the official college motto, "A Friend to Youth," was approved unanimously. Total cash on hand available to the board was $1569.60. S. O. Ward presented reports from both the finance committee and the site committee. No action was taken on the site. Interested parties from throughout the state were encouraged to submit propositions on where the school should be located before the next meeting. In the meantime, some members of the board explored the possibility of negotiating the price for the property in Temple Terrace.

At the next meeting of the board in Orlando, September 6, several sites were considered: Temple Terrace, Lakeland, St. Petersburg, Miami, Palmetto, and Bradenton. At the insistence of J. Roy Vaughan, H. N. Donoho moved and the board voted unanimously to change the name of the college to "Florida Christian College" as originally proposed by some of those who first talked about establishing it.

The board again assembled in Tampa on October 26. Acting on a suggestion by Lloyd Copeland, the board added to its membership J. Lee Elder, an air-conditioning engineer from Jacksonville. The agenda focused on the property in Temple Terrace, and the board proceeded to negotiate the best price possible for this property. The choice of sites had been made.

On December 16, 1944, the board signed the original charter of the college. It was submitted to Hillsborough County Circuit Judge Harry N. Sandler in Tampa, and his signature officially recognized its approval by the State of Florida on December 21. The charter limited the number of directors to fifteen and set the second Thursday of April as the date for the annual meetings of the board. A committee was appointed to draw up a set of by-laws.

In Orlando on December 17, the board approved placing a $15,000 down payment with Sherman K. Smith on the property in Temple Terrace if negotiations for price and clear title could be worked out.

On February 9, 1945, the purchase of the Temple Terrace property from Sherman K. Smith was officially authorized. The total price for 18 acres on the west side of the river with 5 buildings and for 179 acres east of the river was $66,500.

Before the 1945 annual meeting, April 12, the board closed on the property in Temple Terrace and recorded the deed. A set of by-laws was discussed, revised, and approved. In these, the officers of the board were further defined. An election provided for the full complement of officers: C. Ed Owings, chairman; C. G. McGee, vice-chairman; Lloyd

Copeland, secretary; Lee Warren Boswell, treasurer; and J. Roy Vaughan, assistant secretary-treasurer. All board members were assigned to three-year rotating terms.

Selecting the First President

The next order of business was to select a president and open the school. Although some wished for a fall opening, others felt that the board would not have enough funding by September and the new administration would not be able to secure faculty and students by then. The board settled on first securing a president and allowing him to advise the board on a time to open. The list of names that was suggested for consideration indicates that those establishing the school were determined to bring the most qualified man available. The list included N. B. Hardeman, Homer Hailey, B. G. Hope, Norvel Young, H. A. Dixon, E. H. Ijams, Batsell Baxter, E. W. McMillan, Walter Adams, G. C. Brewer, and others.

Over the next few months, several were interviewed. Boswell and Vaughan visited Abilene Christian College in order to interview three men on the faculty and administration there. All encouraged the effort to establish the school, but none was prepared to move to Tampa at that time and take up the work.

As fall approached, one man became the prime candidate, and he was asked to meet with the board. He accepted and came to Tampa for a visit. On November 6, 1945, L. R. Wilson met with the board in Tampa. That afternoon, after discussing both doctrinal positions and administrative philosophy, he was chosen to become the first president of Florida Christian College.

In the December 1945 issue of a paper called *Florida Christian Advocate,* an article about a "mass meeting" of some 700 F.C.C. supporters held on December 7, 1945, reported that everyone assembled outside the building to witness the burning of the mortgage (the original $66,500)—conducted by—C. G. McGee, vice chairman of the Florida Christian College Board of Directors."

Opening Florida Christian College

Wilson immediately went to work to open the school in September 1946. One of his first appointments was Leonard Lewis to serve as academic dean. Lewis had earned a Ph.D. degree and for nine years had worked as superintendent of schools in the Del Rio, Texas, city school system. Wilson was primarily known as a preacher. Because of his experience in professional education, Lewis gave balance to the administration.

Both Wilson and Lewis understood the need to have a strong academic program accredited by regional and state bodies that would recognize the credit for transfer. Lewis was commissioned to write other schools and state agencies to determine requirements for meeting the highest possible academic standards.

Wilson and Lewis were authorized to negotiate for faculty with an $1800 to $2700 salary base per year. They needed approximately ten teachers to provide the proposed programs. By April 1946 they had hired Garvin Toms to teach Bible, Elvin R. Higgins to teach mathematics and natural sciences, Mrs. Elvin Higgins to teach English and speech, L. Griffin

Copeland to teach English and modern languages, Mildred Tinius to teach home economics, and Jean McCann to teach English in the high school. They still needed teachers in business and social science, a librarian, and a principal for the high school. The expected budget for salaries of all administrators and faculty totaled $44,540.

Almost immediately after his own appointment, Wilson had hired Roland Lewis of San Antonio, Texas, as business manager. Lewis was given charge of all office records. He was also authorized to receive, deposit, disburse, and account for all funds received by the college. Wilson reaffirmed that the college would not solicit congregations for contributions from their treasuries. He said, "The college is not an auxiliary of the church and is not founded for the purpose of controlling the church."

Several important changes had to be made in the physical facilities. The campus was overgrown and the buildings in disrepair. There were also some tenants living in the apartment building who would have to vacate before the start of school. Wilson determined that the old hotel (soon to be named Sutton Hall) should be used as a women's residence hall. The apartment building would house married faculty and male students. The smaller buildings would be used as classrooms and a bookstore.

Finances were obviously the biggest hurdle for the fledgling school at this point. Wilson estimated that a minimum of $200,000 would be needed in the first year to renovate or construct necessary facilities, secure library holdings, and pay teachers. An additional $100,000 would be required in endowment to satisfy educational accrediting associations. Thirty percent (sixty thousand of the $200,000 required to open the school) would be borrowed. Almost $33,000 had been raised by the time of the annual meeting in April. That included a $20,000 contribution from board member C. G. McGehee.

Almost everything in the way of physical equipment was needed: file cabinets, desks and chairs, classroom furniture, adding machines, etc. Roland Lewis made a number of trips to army bases and air fields in the hope of securing equipment no longer in use. The task seemed endless.

Student revenue from tuition charges and room/board fees would supply only a part of the college's expenses. Knowing that care would have to be taken in setting student costs, the administration asked Roland Lewis to consult the catalogs of other colleges operated by brethren with a view to keeping student fees in line with median acceptable costs elsewhere.

Wilson also secured a number of important gifts-in-kind for the college. Several benefactors in the Tampa area gave books to the new library. One Jewish philanthropist named Steinberg purchased the library of a retired Presbyterian minister and donated it to the college. It contained a number of reference works important to advanced Bible study and research. B. C. Goodpasture promised to contribute a collection of rare volumes on the Restoration Movement to be used as reference works by faculty and students. Goodpasture also introduced Wilson to several wealthy Christians in Nashville for the purpose of soliciting contributions. These included R. W. Comer, W. E. Stephens, Truman Ward, and A. M. Burton.

The founders of Florida Christian College were dedicated to a set of central beliefs that guided their actions. Foremost was a basic conviction that the school should be kept organically independent of churches. Since the school was not designed to do the work of churches, they insisted that care be taken to avoid official connection between the two. Neither should the school seek to influence the actions of churches. Decisions were made early restricting the school from accepting contributions from churches.

It was important to the founders that all members of the governing board of directors, all administrators, and all faculty members be faithful members of local churches of Christ. The college was established with a determined emphasis upon an environment consistent with faith in Christ. Daily academic Bible classes and daily attendance at devotional activities in chapel were required from the beginning. The founders believed that moral and spiritual training go hand in hand with academic learning and physical growth to complete the preparation of young people for life. That was the philosophy of the men and women who brought Florida Christian College into existence. Those guiding principles have been carefully guarded by subsequent boards and administrations.

Chapter 12:

Cope Selected to be President of FCC (1949)

Wilson's Departure from FCC

L. R. Wilson served as President only three years (1946-49). He said that he wanted to go back into full-time preaching. He told Griff Copeland that he wanted to do a little fishing.[1] When Wilson resigned, Dean Leonard Lewis also resigned. In fact, only two men who held some administrative responsibilities stayed to serve in the new administration. Roland Lewis continued as registrar and Griffin Copeland as chief librarian. There was no change at that time in board membership resulting from Wilson's departure.

The new president said that he would have kept all faculty members, but some made the choice to go elsewhere. Harold Fletcher (music teacher), Connard Hayes (Bible and business), James Jordan, Joy Lancer, and Billy Hood all left. Jean McCann and Leonard Tyler remained.[2]

---

1   Interview, Griffin Copeland, February 25, 1988.
2   Interview, James R. Cope, February 23, 1988.

Search for a Second President

On December 7, 1948, James R. Cope visited with S. O. Ward at Ward's sister's home in Nashville. Ward showed Jim some pictures of Hiroshima that had been taken the day after the atomic bomb had been dropped on that city on August 6, 1945. He also told Jim that it appeared L. R. Wilson was moving toward resigning the presidency of Florida Christian College. Ward was not yet a member of the board but later became a long-term chairman. His service on the board began in 1951, two years after Jim was made president. He was elected to the board to fill H. N. Donoho's seat. Donoho resigned from the board in 1950.

When Ward returned to his home in Lakeland, Florida, he told Lee Warren Boswell about a discussion he had with Gordon H. Turner. Turner had a state government job and preached at Lawrence Avenue in Nashville. Turner had heard that Wilson might be leaving, and Turner was interested in the job. The word was out. Roy Vaughn had spoken with E. H. Ijams. Ijams was at Dasher Bible School at that time in Valdosta, Georgia. Ijams came to Ward's radio station in Lakeland and talked with C. Ed Owings, Lee Warren Boswell, Lloyd Copeland, and Ward. These men inquired of Ijams how he would plan to take care of financing the operation of the school. According to Ward, he said, "Oh, you don't need to worry about that. It will take care of itself." They, of course, knew it would not take care of itself. Perhaps, they thought, after it was up and going, but they were starting from scratch. It seemed a strange statement coming from one who had taken over David Lipscomb College when it was down. In the end both he and they decided for Ijams not to come.[3]

---

3   Meeting with S. O. Ward and James R. Cope, February 28, 1988.

Another person of interest was George W. DeHoff of Murfreesboro, Tennessee. DeHoff apparently desired the position and came to interview the same weekend that Jim Cope came. DeHoff had some business experience operating a bookstore and was a noted preacher in Middle Tennessee. The board had DeHoff come to Tampa and Cope to Lakeland for worship services that Sunday.

In late December, 1948, Jim received a brief letter from S. O. Ward. Ward informed Jim that L. R. Wilson had formally resigned the presidency of Florida Christian College, effective July 1, 1949. Ward said, "I am in position to know that if you would be interested at all, some would like for you to at least come down and take a look at the possibility of becoming the next president." Jim had the impression that Ward had talked to some unnamed board members, including Lee Warren Boswell, who could set up a meeting consisting of Jim and the entire board. After talking with Georgia Deane, Jim agreed to travel to Tampa for the meeting.

A major factor in Jim Cope's interest in coming to Florida was what he saw as an answer to his conscience. Before marrying, he had wrestled within his own soul about doing foreign evangelistic work. In those days, Jim surveyed the state and looked on Florida as a mission field. There were not nearly as many churches of Christ in Florida as in other southern states, particularly Tennessee. He felt that if he came to Florida, it would give him that opportunity to take the gospel where it was needed. Not only was he qualified educationally to be president, but he had shown that he was qualified to preach the gospel. Both would satisfy his urge to do something that would benefit the kingdom of Christ in Florida. He could help weak churches and establish new ones where they were needed. Perhaps he could do more for the kingdom than if he went to Ireland, the South Pacific, or other places he had imagined needing the gospel.[4]

As already noted, there was considerable speculation that N. B. Hardeman was grooming Jim for the presidency of Freed-Hardeman College. Jim later thought that the Florida Christian College board no doubt reasoned that if that were true, and if he was good enough for Freed-Hardeman, he would be a good choice for them if they could get him to come. That would be a long-shot for them but worth the effort.

A Problem in Louisville

Before Cope's two visits to Florida Christian College to discuss the presidency, Jim got involved in a church controversy in Kentucky. James Arthur Warren of Paducah, Kentucky, was preaching for the old Taylor Boulevard church in Louisville. Warren had been taking classes at the Southern Baptist Theological Seminary. He had soaked in some of their modernistic teaching and was preaching it at Taylor Boulevard.

Early in January 1949, two of the Taylor Boulevard elders, L. L. Dukes and Paul Woodward, made a trip to Nashville to talk to some preachers who had held meetings at Taylor Boulevard while Warren was there. They apparently wanted to see if those preachers had sensed his defections. They also wanted some of them to come to Louisville and preach the truth on the issues involved. After seeing some brethren in Nashville, Dukes and Woodward came on down to Henderson. They talked to Jim and some others before going back to see James P. Miller in Paducah. At their invitation,

---

4   Meeting with James R. Cope, February 18, 1988.

Jim decided to go to Louisville along with Rufus Clifford and Eugene Clevenger.

On Sunday, Jim preached and a number of people in the audience resented his lesson. After the service, some of them began to chant, "Throw them out. Throw them out." Rufus Clifford spoke to Jim and said, "Let's get out of here, Cope." The two were walking down the aisle on the way out of the building when a woman hit Jim across the back with her umbrella. The incident did help, however, as Warren appeared to see some of his error.[5]

On the way home, Cope, Clifford, and Clevenger agreed to meet back at the David Lipscomb lectureship. Clifford was preaching full-time. Clevenger was teaching at Lipscomb. Jim was teaching at Freed-Hardeman. When they arrived in Nashville for the lectures, President Clay Pullius would not allow them to meet on the David Lipscomb campus. In fact, he called his professor, Clevenger, into his office and severely scolded him for being involved. The three preachers decided to meet at the home of W. H. Elder instead. In the meantime, someone had talked to Pat Hardeman. Cope assumed it was Clevenger who talked to Hardeman, but he did not know that. At the University of Illinois, Hardeman had studied some of the ideas Warren had been espousing in Louisville and was up on the arguments. In any case, Hardeman was present at the lectureship.

One day that week, Lee Warren Boswell was walking down the hall with W. H. Elder when he heard someone shout, "Hey Jim." Boswell's ears perked up and he asked loudly in his own way, "Jim who?" Somebody responded, "Jim Cope."

---

5   Meeting with S. O. Ward and James R. Cope, February 28, 1988.

Boswell replied, "He's the man I came to see." Jim later said that Boswell and Elder "cornered me and wanted to talk to me. That was when they made the arrangement for me to come meet the board at Florida Christian College." Jim went on to report that he told them he would write or call to confirm the meeting. He came for the first meeting upon that invitation.[6]

First Board Meeting with Cope

Jim went to Tampa that first time and met with the board in the basement of Sutton Hall on Sunday afternoon (February 13, 1949). He preached to the Lake Wire congregation in Lakeland that day and stayed two nights in the home of S. O. and Dot Ward. Dot was Jim's first cousin and Odell was sensitive to that fact. He had told the board about Jim, but he didn't want to push too hard for his selection. Jim was related to him, and Odell was afraid if he pushed too hard he might push the wrong way. Another factor in the mix was the position of W. R. Elder. Jim and Georgia Deane had stayed with Elder and his wife every Saturday night while Jim was preaching at West End in Nashville in 1944. But Elder also thought a lot of George DeHoff and was supporting him to be the next president.[7]

In an interview on February 18, 1988, Jim Cope explained that his thinking on church support of colleges was still in an "evolutionary process" when he arrived at Florida College. He had at first been somewhat sympathetic to Hardeman's views although he had been concerned. As he studied the issues for

---

6   Ibid.

7   Meeting with S. O. Ward and James R. Cope, February 28, 1988.

himself, however, he began to see the far-reaching implications of churches supporting humanly created institutions and could not find it to be scriptural. Because he had always been concerned and troubled about it, he decided that he would lay before the board of directors in their first meeting together a safe position that might be controversial but reassuring to his conscience.

When the board met in February 1949 to consider his hiring, Jim said to them, "Gentlemen, irrespective of what the school may have done or what you may think, if I accept the presidency, it will have to be that we will take no money from churches for the college itself." With that Jim Cope put himself on the line for the first time with the Florida Christian College Board of Directors.

Hardly had the words gotten out of his mouth when someone in the room spoke up and said, "We already have a policy not to accept money from churches." Jim became aware later that some board members had given money individually and made their checks to a church earmarking it to go to the college. Within a few months of his arriving in Florida, either the fall of 1949 or spring of 1950, the college received a check from a church in Cortez, Florida. Jim immediately sent it back.

He came without a commitment and left without making one. He was not ready for that, and they did not offer him the job in that first meeting. Both Jim and the board were much interested, but the Board wanted to talk it over, and he wanted to discuss pros and cons with Georgia Deanne. He would have other people to consider, especially his wife and young daughter. To be certain, he wanted it known there was not anything happening between himself and brother Hardeman that he knew about that would prompt him to want to leave Freed-Hardeman.

Not long after returning to Henderson, Jim received a communication asking him to come back for another meeting if he was interested in the presidency. He had discussed the proposition with Georgia Deanne and talked with brother Hardeman about the potential of an offer from Florida Christian College. He felt free to pursue the opportunity and communicated his interest to the board. A month later he returned to Tampa. It was generally accepted when he came for the second interview that he would be offered the position. That Sunday he preached to the Nebraska Avenue church and met with the board in the afternoon. He was offered the presidency, and he accepted.

Almost immediately, Cope sent a letter for publication in the *Gospel Guardian* to editor Yater Tant outlining the stance of the college under his presidency. Here is the letter:

Dear Brother Tant:

As you know I am to assume my responsibilities in connection with Florida Christian College, Tampa, Florida, July 1. I am sure that my brethren are looking our way with mingled feelings—some with confidence, some with misgivings, and some just wondering. Occasionally you will be asked your opinion concerning the school; hence, this letter for your own information and brethren who may be asking.

(1) Contributions from churches. Florida Christian college will not solicit contributions from churches nor will it accept them.

(2) Faculty. Every member of the teaching staff will be sound in faith and in good standing with his home congregation.

(3) Attitude toward other schools. It is our hope to be cordial toward other schools operated by Christians, but completely separate from them organically. We do not aim to be dictatorial toward any other organization nor do we propose to be dictated to nor play politics with any individual or group.

(4) Criticism. We purpose to profit by the constructive criticism of loyal brethren without counting them our enemies when they disagree with us in matters of judgment. We deserve their rebukes should we err in matters of faith.

(5) Point of emphasis. Florida Christian College proposes to not only declare emphasis on the Bible but it intends to make that declaration true. Either the Bible penetrates every fiber of school life or it merely takes its place as just another study in our curriculum. God being our helper, we do not intend the latter to happen now or later. Every student must receive at least one lesson in God's word every regular school day. Not only so, but we aim to make the Bible the chief consideration in every activity. If we fail in this, we shall fail in the purpose for which the school was founded.

(6) Preacher training. While we expect to have academic work accepted as readily by other educational institutions, we make no apology to anybody for placing emphasis on the teaching of young men desiring to preach the gospel and others desirous of doing religious work. We believe that the safety, security, and soundness of the church depend upon the kind and amount of teaching and preaching done. Those who take the lead in this matter are elders and preachers, and unless they are thoroughly grounded in the faith, innovations, error and inertia will abound; hence, we expect to have a Bible Department second to none. Our students

will be taught the issues and how to meet them. It is inevitable that some hobbyists will come our way and in such event we hope to sober them; however, we sincerely desire and expect that none shall become a radical or hobbyist because he has attended Florida Christian College.

(7) Academic ambitions. We have no objections to any institution's desire to improve its educational standing by seeking entrance into any recognized accrediting organization or agency. In fact, in the future we would like to be so honored, but let the following be once for all known and understood: if Florida Christian College must surrender any principle prompting its founding and existence in order to obtain entrance into any secular or educational accrediting organization, those organization can go their way and we shall go our own. We do not propose to sell principle for popularity even if it means the closing of our doors never to open again.

The foregoing is a statement of my personal attitude and that of the Board of Directors concerning some matters on which I believe brethren should be informed. We stand in constant need of financial support, personal good will, and the prayers of God's people. The road ahead is a rugged one, our problems are many, and our responsibility staggering, yet with the support of faithful brethren: and the help of God we must not, we shall not—we cannot fail!"

Cordially and faithfully,
James R. Cope, President-Elect[8]

Tant replied:

---

8   Fanning Yater Tant and James R. Cope, "Jim Cope and Florida Christian College," *Gospel Guardian*, Vol. 1, No 5 (April 2, 1949), p. 2.

Jim Cope And Florida Christian College

As our readers are well aware, the *Bible Banner* and the *Gospel Guardian* have consistently fought the idea of putting the colleges into the church budgets. We have sought to make it clear all along that we are not opposed to "Christian education" (We do not feel it right to restrict that term to the work done by the schools), and that we recognize the right of individual Christians to operate, promote, and contribute to schools of this sort. As we said in the original statement, "We are not 'anti' anything except anti-wrong.'"

It gives us a great deal of pleasure, therefore, to publish the following letter from Brother James R. Cope, newly elected president of Florida Christian College. The letter speaks for itself. It certainly sets forth the position which we believe to be scriptural. If all the "schools among us" had long since been as forthright and candid in their statement of, and adherence to, such a policy, we believe considerable misgivings could have been spared the brotherhood, and that much greater confidence could now be felt in their intentions.

With Florida Christian College adhering to the positions outlined in Brother Cope's letter, we feel she will deserve, and will receive, the wholehearted support of a grateful brotherhood. Christian parents can send their children to such a school with confidence and assurance.

Chapter 13:

Building a Good Administrative Team (1949-52)

Cope's Early Team at Florida College

The task of putting together a solid team of administrators and faculty is one of the most important jobs for a president anytime, much more at the beginning of his administration. Cope, of course, had knowledge of good educators and educational best practices growing out of his position at Freed-Hardeman. He also made a trip that spring to hold a gospel meeting with the College church in Abilene, Texas. That meeting brought him into contact with other academicians. The gospel meeting itself was successful as well. Glen Wallace was the local preacher. Seventeen were baptized during the week-long effort from April 3-10, 1949.

Clinton David Hamilton

The only administrator Cope brought with him to Florida Christian College from Freed-Hardeman College was Clinton David Hamilton. Cope was insistent that he did not recruit Hamilton, as that would have been disloyal to brother Hardeman. Nevertheless, the two men talked freely

HOMER HAILEY
A.B., M.A.
Vice President of the College

A. W. DICUS
B.S., A.B., M.A., Ph.D.
Dean of the College

CLINTON D. HAMILTON
A.B., M.A.
Dean of Students

ROYCE D. BROUGH
B.S., M.S., C.P.A.
Business Manager

ROLAND H. LEWIS
B.S., M.A.E.
Registrar

about the opportunities at a fledgling school in an expanding part of the United States. Hamilton decided to leave Freed-Hardeman and join Jim Cope in coming to Florida Christian College. Cope and Hamilton made a good team. However, Cope was wise enough to know that he needed an older, more experienced dean of the College. Jim was thirty-two years of age (born January 27, 1917). Clinton Hamilton was twenty-five (born March 13, 1924).

As a matter of fact, almost all of Cope's initial administrative team and Bible faculty were very young. Royce Brough had gone to Freed-Hardeman after earning a master's degree in business. When he indicated a desire to move, Jim asked him to serve as business manager at FCC and teach accounting and business courses. Griffin Copeland had been a student of Jim's at David Lipscomb. He was already developing the college library and teaching Spanish. Pat Hardeman's father was a half-brother to N. B. Hardeman (the same father but not the same mother). Pat had just finished his degree and was assigned social sciences and Bible courses. Like Pat Hardeman, Bill Humble had been Cope's student at Freed-Hardeman. Cope once said that Humble "knew as much in his political science class as I did." The two of them (Hardeman and Humble), along with Cope and Hamilton taught Bible courses in the 1949-50 school year. Eugene Clevenger was added to the Bible faculty the following year (1950-51). Harry Pickup, Sr., had been hired by Wilson to teach Bible and raise funds for the college in January 1949. Increasing student enrollment was seen by Cope as essential, however, and he assigned the task of student recruitment to Pickup soon after becoming president.

Richard Rivers had a master's degree from the Julliard School of Music and the Performing Arts in the Lincoln Center in New York. He was an excellent singer from Nashville. He came to lead the music program following Leonard Tyler's decision to leave the college and preach full-time at the North Street church in Tampa. Burthell Pauley came to teach education courses, and, of course, Cope brought Hamilton as dean of students. There were 149 students that year (1949-50) in the college and 27 in high school. There had been 98 total students in the 1948-49 school year.

Along with Clevenger, Cope added several other new faculty and staff in the fall of 1950: William D. Burgess taught biology and physical education; Rachel Kopel taught chemistry and mathematics. Magdalene Downey taught home economics. Jack Frost directed the chorus. Mrs. Frost was the school nurse. Mary Elizabeth Galloway was a librarian, working under Griff Copeland. That year Louis and Margie Garrett came to the college. He taught English, government, and psychology. She taught piano and high school mathematics in those early years. Paul Hutcheson came the following year (1951-52) to teach mathematics and chemistry.[1]

A. W. Dicus

At Freed-Hardeman the faculty, for the most part, was much more experienced and well-known in the brotherhood (President N. B. Hardeman, Vice-President C. P. Roland, L. L. Brigance, W. Claude Hall, etc.). In any case, Cope also named Hamilton "acting" dean until he could find the person he thought had the experience, age, and generally acknowledged maturity to lead the faculty and help the college in securing accreditation. Hamilton understood the advisability of Cope's philosophy and accepted his role.

In the fall of 1949, Jim was scheduled to preach in a gospel meeting in Cookeville, Tennessee (October 2-12).[2] Cookeville is the home of Tennessee Technological University. Jim found out that A. W. Dicus, a dedicated Christian, was planning to retire from his faculty position at the university. He

---

1   The "Royal Palm," Florida Christian College Yearbooks, 1950-52.

2   James R. Cope's hand-written chronological record of sermons preached over the years.

remembered that Dicus had been one of the three Tennessee Tech judges of Jim's high school debate team when they had gone to the state finals. Dicus had a doctorate, was experienced, and was a highly respected member of the faculty. Under his direction the school established its Curriculum Review and Academic Standards Committees. Dicus could bring many "best practices" to Cope's fledgling college. Dicus was also said to have invented the turn signal for motor vehicles. His patent ran out before it became standard equipment on all new automobiles.[3]

One night when Dicus came to the meeting, Cope confronted him after service on the steps out in front of the church building. He presented Dicus with the proposition of coming to Florida Christian College as academic dean of the college.

Dicus later said, "I don't think I slept a wink that night. The fact is, I had made a commitment to the Lord when I was relatively just a young man that if he would enable me to go on to school and get my doctor's degree (PhD) that I would go wherever He called me and my first consideration would be His kingdom. I just reflected on that and literally sweat all that night. I talked to my wife at daylight, the next morning and we decided to go."[4]

Dicus began working at Florida Christian College on January 1, 1950. He had retired from Tennessee Tech at age 60.

---

3   Margie H. Garrett, ed., *Making a Difference Florida College: The First Fifty Years.* Clinton E. Hamilton, ed., "New Directions: Controversy and Decision" (Temple Terrace, FL: Florida College Press, 1996), 52.

4   As told by Jim Cope, interview on February 18, 1988 with this author.

Homer Hailey

The other move Cope made to provide maturity and respectability to his team was bringing Homer Hailey to serve as vice-president of the college and head of the Bible department. That did not happen until the fall of 1951, however.

According to Melvin Curry, who succeeded Hailey as chair of the Bible department in 1973, "Homer Hailey brought to Florida Christian College a lifetime of rich and varied experiences. He had preached extensively in both local and meeting work, had taught at Abilene for eleven years, had earned a master's degree at Southern Methodist University, and had done two years of evangelistic work in Hawaii. In addition, he had published two books, which were well received by the brethren: *Attitudes and Consequences of the Restoration Movement* and *Let's Go Fishing for Men.*[5]

Jim's initial link to Homer Hailey was through Georgia Deane. She and her sister (Sissy) were in some of Hailey's classes at Abilene Christian College and were inspired by his teaching. Jim remembered meeting him and being impressed with him during the 1947-48 school year when Hailey came to Freed-Hardeman to make a presentation on the annual lecture program there. As already mentioned, in the spring of 1949 after deciding to move to Florida College, Jim preached in a series of very successful meetings at the college church. Seventeen were baptized during the meeting. In addition, Cope was able to get to know Hailey better during the week on a personal basis. A student, Bob Owen, had talked to

---

5   Margie H. Garrett, ed., *Making a Difference Florida College: The First Fifty Years*. Melvin Curry, , "Homer Hailey: A Teacher Who Walked Humbly with God" (Temple Terrace, FL: Florida College Press, 1996), 60.

Hailey about Florida College before Jim arrived in Abilene, so Hailey had some more recent knowledge of the young college and its new president, Jim Cope. Owen had gone to Abilene Christian after studying at Freed-Hardeman for one year. He would leave there and go to Florida Christian for his third year (1949-50). Eventually, Bob Owen, of course, followed Cope as President of Florida College (1982-91).

Cope also met with some of the students. Several later came to FCC to serve on his faculty. Cope later said that he knew then he should try to get Hailey to come to Florida College. He later said, "One of the best moves I ever made was bringing Hailey. It gave people confidence in our Bible department."[6]

Hailey had become concerned about what he saw as a trend toward liberalism at Abilene Christian College. He was increasingly finding himself uncomfortable with the positions of those around him in the christian education department. He was teaching principles in the New Testament that contradicted the sponsoring church arrangements and young preachers were increasingly accepting of the ideas he taught in his classes.[7] It would seem that he saw the writing on the wall.

Actually, this was not the first time Hailey had been invited to teach at Florida Christian College. In 1948, when the Hailey family returned from Hawaii where he had been preaching, he was given the opportunity to teach Bible at both Abilene Christian College and Florida Christian College. According to Ed Harrell, L. R. Wilson "flew to San Antonio, where Hailey was in a meeting, and urged him to move to Florida. Wilson told Hailey that he planned to leave the

---

6   Interview with James R. Cope, February 25, 1988.
7   Interview with James R. Cope, February 25, 1988.

presidency after another year to return to full-time preaching and that he wanted Hailey to succeed him as president." Hailey told Wilson that he was a preacher and teacher; thus he was not interested in Wilson's suggestion that he succeed him as president. Instead, he went to Abilene at that time.[8] Three years later, Cope flew to Abilene, met the Haileys in their home, and after three hours of discussions, Hailey agreed to accept Jim's offer.

The administration therefore consisted of:

James R. Cope, President

Homer Hailey, Vice President; Head of Bible Department

A.W. Dicus: Academic Dean

Clinton D. Hamilton: Dean of Students

Royce D. Brough: Business Manager

As it turned out, after Cope and Hamilton left Freed-Hardeman, a strong resistance, which Hardeman's daughter, Mary Nelle Powers called a "conspiracy," arose against Hardeman's administration on campus. Actually, there were some rumblings of discontent before Cope left, but the issues were not considered to be compelling by the board. During the following spring semester, however, many students joined a number of discontented faculty members in demanding that Hardeman, now 75, retire from the presidency. In March of 1950, the agitation reached a peak. According to the authors of *N. B. H.: A Biography of Nicholas Brodie Hardeman*, "Anonymous letters were distributed, mass

---

8   David Edwin Harrell, Jr., *The Churches of Christ in the 20th Century: Homer Hailey's Personal Journey of Faith* (Tuscaloosa and London: University of Alabama Press, 2000), 266.

meetings were called, students were urged to leave school...."
The board "yielded," and Hardeman "resigned."[9] Jim Cope
and Clinton Hamilton, of course, had nothing to do with
Freed-Hardeman's issues, but they were careful observers.[10]

In the first three years of Cope's administration at Florida
Christian College, the school was faced with challenges to
its stability. Nonetheless, Cope enthusiastically "desired to
develop Florida Christian College so as to attain accreditation
and to inform students fully as to what was expected of
them academically and socially in their particular school
environment," according to Hamilton. The challenges included
"raising necessary funds, becoming accredited, composing
a catalog of courses and academic rules, and meeting an
arduous time table for accomplishing these objectives."[11] Jim
was only thirty-two. He was the youngest college president in
the United States at the time.

One major challenge faced the college as the 1949 fall
semester began. Clinton Hamilton reports that he was notified
by the Veterans' Affairs Office of the Florida Department of
Education that it was withdrawing authorization for support
to veterans at Florida Christian College. Cope sent Hamilton
to Tallahassee to argue the case and had him write a full report
regarding how the college met all requirements for approval.
The state reversed its decision for the first two years of college

---

9   James Marvin Powell and Mary Nelle Hardeman Powers, *N. B. H.: A Biography of Nicholas Brodie Hardeman* (Nashville: The Gospel Advocate Company, 1964), 126-27.

10   Margie H. Garrett, ed., *Making a Difference Florida College: The First Fifty Years.* Clinton E. Hamilton, ed., "New Directions: Controversy and Decision" (Temple Terrace, FL: Florida College Press, 1996), 46.

11   Ibid.

work, and many veterans were able to continue their studies.[12]

It became apparent early that the college could not maintain a solid position regarding accreditation and grow in needed areas as a senior college. In the December 29, 1949 meeting of the board of directors, President Cope "recommended to the board that the senior college be dropped with the exception of Bible and religious education courses." Without having attained accreditation and with the challenges associated with its youth, Cope felt it could not gain accredited status as a senior college at that time. The board agreed, and the college took on junior-college status and was soon granted accreditation at that level. The college continued as a junior college for 45 years until 1994, when senior college status was granted by the Southern Association of Colleges and Schools during President Caldwell's administration.

Through all of this, Cope pursued ten goals and objectives for the development of the college that were set down shortly after he accepted the presidency. One can see his strong emphasis on academic credibility. Dicus and Hamilton were charged with bringing these objectives to fruition. They enthusiastically accepted the challenge:

- Achieve accreditation by the Southern Association of Colleges and Schools;

- Develop a comprehensive catalog that would be easy to understand by both students and the officials of other colleges;

- Secure adequate funding to assure the viability and vitality of the college;

---

12   Margie H. Garrett, ed., *Making a Difference Florida College: The First Fifty Years.* Clinton E. Hamilton, ed., "New Directions: Controversy and Decision" (Temple Terrace, FL: Florida College Press, 1996), 52.

- Expand the faculty by employing well-qualified teachers who could provide instruction that was standard among accredited institutions of higher learning;

- Develop a curriculum that was in concord with accredited colleges;

- Develop and publish a student handbook;

- Develop clear-cut academic rules and procedures so that the faculty could deal with exceptions and keep students well-informed of the standards they must meet in the college work;

- Bring the library into compliance with the accreditation standards;

- Plan for improving the current physical plant and for developing new ones;

- Maintain the atmosphere conducive to student development and academic quality.[13]

One of the major goals of Cope, Dicus, and Hamilton was always regional accreditation. The Southern Association of Colleges and Schools accredited Florida Christian College's junior college coursework on December 2, 1954, a remarkable achievement in light of the challenges it had faced in its early years.

---

13   Op. cit, 46.

Section Six:

The School and the Church

Chapter 14:

Preceptor (1951-55)

The *Preceptor* (November 1951 - April 55)

Constantly on the mind of any college or university president is the necessity of sound financial standing and underpinning of his non-profit institution. In the case of private colleges that are not funded by state or federal subsidies, substantial private contributions are necessary. The board had committed early not to accept government funding. They had also established policy refusing to solicit or receive church contributions. Jim Cope had insisted upon that policy when accepting the presidency. Not everyone on the board of directors, however, believed it to be unscriptural for a church to donate or for the college to receive church contributions if the brethren in those churches chose to send in support of the college's spiritual mission. N. B. Hardeman had received contributions on that basis without reservation at Freed-Hardeman College. Various responses to the issues involved developed in the minds of the leadership at Florida Christian College in the early 1950s. It is fair to say that President Cope was already committed when he arrived in Temple Terrace. His conscience would not allow him to accept any donation from a church treasury. Even so, the application of Biblical principles to the more extensive question of institutionalism took Cope, and also Hailey, some time to develop.

In the fall of 1951, Cope announced that he and several others on the Bible faculty would be publishing a new monthly religious periodical. In the initial editorial, he said, "Every generation must be taught anew the eternal principles of divine revelation; hence, each generation must rethink these principles and either accept or reject them. To studying, thinking, and accepting we are wholly committed."[1]

Originally, the editors had planned to call the paper "Reason and Revelation" after the title of a book published by restoration scholar Robert Milligan. Cope explained that "human reason apart from divine revelation is useless" but that "faithful soldiers have shown that reason has its proper place beside and in connection with divine revelation." After floating that name out among friends, however, the decision was made to use the more concise name *The Preceptor* for the journal. According to the editor, the term "preceptor" simply refers to "a teacher." He quoted Isaiah saying, "The word of the Lord was unto them precept upon precept, line upon line" (28:13) and the Psalmist, "Through thy precepts I get understanding: therefore I hate every false way" (119:104). He added, "It shall be one of the primary designs of this paper to strengthen the faith and brighten the hope of those whose trust is placed in God."[2]

In that first editorial, Cope acknowledged that the paper was born out of a sense of concern and urgency. He wrote,

---

1   James R. Cope, "The Preceptor," *The Preceptor* (November, 1951), 2.

2   Ibid.

The fight before us is no sham affair. We are not playing marbles. The time has come when infidelity's children are rapidly multiplying within the nominal membership of the church fathered and fostered by men posing as gospel preachers and friends of the word of God. The faith of innocent and unsuspecting disciples is in jeopardy. The futile fate of thousands may be forever determined if those who are robbing the gospel of its power, the church of its glory, and the Bible of its beauty are not revealed in their true colors that lovers of truth may take warning while time and opportunity afford. It is already too late to save some. Tomorrow may be too late to save many. May God give us all wisdom to observe truth, detect error, discern the adversary, and save our souls.[3]

Becoming even more specific, Cope went on to write,

But this is not all. These are times that try men's faith in another sense. The simplicity of the gospel order is so evident that "he who willeth to do his will shall know of the teaching," yet there are evidences within and among churches which make us fear for the future of Zion. Pride and a general spirit of worldliness give rise to "big time" movements and high pressure promotional campaigns, the fruit of which turns out to be a sale of the independence and autonomy of the local churches into super-organizations for doing the work God's plan places upon the local churches themselves. The same spirit prompted the formation of the human missionary society to displace the local churches almost a century ago and paved the way for mechanical instrumental music to enter and corrupt the worship and divide churches shortly thereafter. The present generation is not immune to the same attitude toward the ancient order of things. So long as this state of mind prevails just that long will continue a need

---

3   Op cit, 3.

for calling attention to the 'old paths' and exhorting brethren to walk therein."[4]

These are fighting words, of course. Yet Jim Cope and the other editors were determined not to allow their Bible discussions to devolve into personal conflicts like those that had appeared in the *Bible Banner*, *Gospel Advocate*, and other periodicals. Jim wrote,

> It is not our purpose that *THE PRECEPTOR* to be used as a medium for saints or sinners to settle their personal feuds and fight their personal battles. Too long there has been "stepping on toes" where there should have been "stepping on hearts." We hope to make *THE PRECEPTOR* of such character that it may be profitably read by brethren and passed on to unbelievers without apologies for personal bickerings and wranglings between or among those who ought to be discussing issues in the light of divine truth instead of killing off one another.[5]

As an indicator of the "tenor of writings" in the new paper, Cope wrote,

> We hope to present a balanced diet of positive and negative writings to our readers. As long as men hunger and thirst for righteousness there shall be need for wholesome and instructive food for thought. As long as there is error there shall be equal need for refuting it. We do not like to deal in personalities and we trust that such will not be necessary except as men are so identified with error that to deal with the error it becomes necessary to deal with the man espousing it. For such a procedure there is both divine precept and example.[6]

---

4   Ibid.
5   Ibid.
6   Ibid.

In that first issue, major articles appear from each of the other Bible faculty members who served as a kind of editorial board for the paper: Eugene Clevenger, Homer Hailey, Clinton Hamilton, Pat Hardeman, Bill Humble, and James R. Cope. Other well-known preachers and teachers were copied on transcribed presentations or articles lifted from other publications, expressing their views on questions arising out of the "institutional" issues confronting brethren. These included such names as Harris Dark,[7] Earle West,[8] G. K. Wallace,[9] Bryan Vinson,[10] Jack Meyer,[11] Jack Hardcastle,[12] Vaughn Shofner,[13] Bill Fling,[14] Wesley Jones,[15] and others.

---

7   Harris Dark, "Congregational Independence," *The Preceptor* (December 1951 and January 1952), 22-23, 16-17. This was a transcribed sermon presented to the Chapel Avenue church of Christ in Nashville, Tennessee in the spring of 1950.

8   Earle West, "New Testament Examples," *The Preceptor* (July 1952), 15-16; and a three part series originally published by the *Gospel Advocate* and reprinted in the *Preceptor* by Bill Humble entitled "Congregational Cooperation," (June, July, and August 1953), 17, 10-11, 6-7.

9   G. K. Wallace, the transcript of a ""lecture delivered in the University Place Christian Church, Oklahoma City, Oklahoma and stenographically reported" entitled "The Difference Between The Christian Church and the Church of Christ," (October, November, January 1952-53), 14-17, 8-9, 14-16.

10   Bryan Vinson, "The Mission of the Church," *The Preceptor* (February 1953), 2-3.

11   Jack Meyer, "What Is the Difference Between the Christian Church and the Church of Christ," (November 1953), 16-17.

12   Jack Hardcastle, "Some Thoughts on the Care of Orphans," *The Preceptor*, (April 1954), 14-15.

13   Vaughan Shofner, "Church Kitchens," *The Preceptor* (October 1954), 9.

14   Bill Fling, "Caring for Orphans," *The Preceptor* (November 1954), 20-21.

15   Wesley Jones, "Church Autonomy," (January 1955), 6-7.

From the opening prospectus, it was apparent that Cope was the principal mind behind the effort. He insisted, however, that they were a "team" and each would share the burden of the "technical work."[16] Although not exclusively, each wrote from a different topical perspective or theme. Eugene Clevenger emphasized attitudes among brethren. Pat Hardeman discussed theological issues. Bill Humble wrote articles based on Restoration History. Clinton Hamilton dealt primarily with Catholicism. Homer Hailey explained texts from Scripture. Even so, all appear to have been sympathetic with the non-institutional mindset and with the purposes of the journal. All wrote with principles of Biblical interpretation and divine authority at the center of their thought processes.

Jim Cope wrote in each issue of *The Preceptor* from November 1951 to May 1955 when the paper was transferred to Luther Roberts and Dean Bullock in Denton, Texas.[17] Roberts published the paper for one year. In 1956, Stanley Lovett took over the editor's position and published the paper for many years.

Cope's first effort in the new paper to deal with the current situation in churches was a study of John 17:20-21. He pointed out that for brethren to be united, they must come together on the Word delivered by the apostles from Christ. He concluded that "persons who have never done what the apostles' 'word' teaches them to do to be 'one in us,' are outside 'us'—the Father and the Son, God and Christ—and therefore cannot possibly be united on the basis of 'their word.'"[18]

---

16   James R. Cope, "Who Is the Editor?", *The Preceptor* (January 1952), 5.

17   Luther Roberts in a news release, *Gospel Guardian*, (May 19, 1955; Vol. 7, No. 3) 13.

18   James R. Cope, "That They All May Be One," *The Preceptor*

The following month under the title "Consistency and Character," Cope wrote:

"One of the fundamental reasons the Restoration Movement commended itself to the sober thinkers of the time and progressed as it did was the position of its leaders to surrender former views in the light of new found truths. Once they were convinced of error, they gladly gave it up and espoused the truth learned."[19]

In the early part of 1952, Cope concentrated his writing in *The Preceptor* on the organization and leadership of churches of Christ as they are presented in the New Testament. He wrote concerning the differences between "pastors" and "preachers," outlining the purposes of each, and concluding, "Elders need to meet their responsibilities and preachers need to 'preach the word.'"[20] In two other articles he wrote that churches should not seek to displace the duly qualified elders with an opposing view of a majority of members. Such disposes of God's authorized leadership in a local church.[21] Preachers also need to be careful to abide in the doctrine of Christ and not use degrees and titles attained in human institutions and programs of study to enhance their image religiously in the church.[22] As

---

(November 1951, Vol. 1, No. 1), 18.

19 James R. Cope, "Consistency and Character," *The Preceptor* (December 1951, Vol. 1, No. 2), 4.

20 James R. Cope, "Pastors and Preachers," *The Preceptor* (January 1952, Vol. 1, No. 3), 4-5.

21 James R. Cope, "Majorities and Manners," *The Preceptor* (February, 1952, Vol. 1, No. 4), 4-5; "Majority versus Elder Rule," *The Preceptor* (March 1952, Vol. 1, No. 5), 4-5.

22 James R. Cope, "Abiding in the Doctrine," *The Preceptor* (April 1952, Vol. 1, No. 6), 4-5; "Preachers and Degrees," *The Preceptor* (May 1952, Vol. 1, No. 7), 2; "Attitudes," *The Preceptor* (June 1952, Vol. 1, No. 8), 10-11.

the year progressed, he gave attention to a number of gospel subjects that he would refer to as first principles: baptism, the Lord's supper, the kingdom of Christ, and salvation by grace.[23]

When the editors moved into the second volume of the paper, Jim once again took up the controversial issues being discussed among brethren. Laying groundwork for addressing how brethren had lost sight of the nature of the church as revealed in the New Testament, Cope published a three-part series that he entitled "The Espoused Bride." In it, he methodically outlined from a positive, scriptural point of view the proper designations of elders and preachers, conditions of membership, and the spiritual nature, work, worship, and organization of the church as seen in the first century.[24]

Then beginning in April 1953, Cope presented an eight-part series entitled "The Problem of Institutionalism." These were significant enough that outlining them here seems necessary to understand Jim Cope's thinking.

(No. 1). **"We Are Debtors"** (to God and to those gone before us); **"An Introspection"** (seeking to establish one's position in light of ancient landmarks while freeing oneself from personal considerations of family, trusted friends, and brethren); **"Possible Attitudes"** (1. "The task is impossible," "There is little, if anything, I can do; consequently, I shall do nothing; " 2. "Things are going pretty well as they are; though

---

23   James R. Cope, "Baptism, a Confession," *The Preceptor* (July 1952, Vol. 1, No. 9), 10; "The Lord's Supper, a Confession," *The Preceptor* (August 1952, Vol. 1, No. 10), 16-17; "The Church is the Kingdom," *The Preceptor* (September 1952, Vol. 1, No. 11), 16-17; "Salvation by Grace," *The Preceptor* (October 1952, Vol. 1, No. 12), 10-11.

24   James R. Cope, "The Espoused Bride—The Church," *The Preceptor* (December, 1952, Vol. II, No. 2, 10-11; January, 1953, II, 3, pp. 17-18; February, 1953, II, pp. 4, 18).

I may have some personal misgivings, I shall refrain from drawing fire to myself...remain quiet and be content to drift with the tide"; 3. "God is my judge. It is my responsibility to please Him in all things"); **"Human Limitations and Divine Authority"**; and **"The Fruits of Disregard"** ("wounded hearts, weakened faith, and divided churches").[25]

(No. 2). **"Changes are Evident"** (in customs and conditions, but not principles and commands from God); **"Indifference and Interest"**; **"The End of Wisdom"**; **"The Proper Attitude in Study"**; **"Pertinent Issues"**; and **"Questions"** (having to do with current concerns among brethren regarding: I. Missionary Society; II. Publishing Society; III. Educational Institutions; IV. Benevolent Homes; V. Evangelism).[26]

(No. 3). **"A Problem That Must Be Faced"** (Institutionalism in the church); **"No Partisan Interest"**; **"Dependence and Progress"**; **"The Divine Test"**; **"The Modernist's Attitude"** ("attitude of all who are willing to set aside any precepts or principle of divine wisdom").[27]

(No. 4). **"Principles are not Proved by Uninspired Examples or Practices"** (Not by what we have always done in matters such as instrumental music, majority rule, deacon rule, athletic teams, Christmas trees and Easter egg hunts, and sectarians leading the church in prayer).[28]

---

25 James R. Cope, "The Problem of Institutionalism (No. 1)," *The Preceptor* (April, 1953), Vol. II, No. 6, pp. 4-5).

26 James R. Cope, "The Problem of Institutionalism (No. 2)," *The Preceptor* (May 1953), Vol. II, No. 7, pp. 12-13, 19).

27 James R. Cope, "The Problem of Institutionalism (No. 3)," *The Preceptor* (June 1953), Vol. II, No. 8, pp. 9, 23).

28 James R. Cope, "The Problem of Institutionalism (No. 4)," *The Preceptor* (July 1953), Vol. II, No. 9, pp. 6, 17).

(No. 5). **"Principles are not Proved by the Teachings of Uninspired Men."** After citing some statements from respected preachers of the past, Cope said, "If a proposition cannot be proved by the New Testament, it cannot be proved by an appeal to the sainted dead regardless of their greatness. If a proposition can be proved by the New Testament, an appeal to uninspired men is wholly unnecessary and uncalled for.[29]

(No. 6). **"Principles are not Proved by Sentiment."** Illustrations of men choosing religious positions based upon personal emotions and sentimental feelings were the following topics: premillennialism, instrumental music, methods of evangelization, schools in which the Bible is taught, benevolent homes such as orphanages and homes for the aged, and centralization into brotherhood wide campaigns and church-cooperation.[30]

In this same issue of the *Preceptor*, Cope led with an article entitled "Is the Missionary 'Method' Revealed?" In it he argued that the New Testament reveals a definite divine pattern for a church doing the evangelistic work God gave it to do. He shows at length how that pattern does not include one church becoming or using a sponsoring church to oversee the work.[31]

(No. 7). **"The Divine Standard," "Possible Misunderstandings," and "Some Clarifications."** In this article, Cope recognizes that "any person who discusses issues over which there are divergent views always runs the

---

29   James R. Cope, "The Problem of Institutionalism (No. 5)," *The Preceptor* (August 1953), Vol. II, No. 10, pp. 14-15).

30   James R. Cope, "The Problem of Institutionalism (No. 6)," *The Preceptor* (September 1953), Vol. II, No. 11, pp. 8-9).

31   James R. Cope, "Is the Missionary Method Revealed," *The Preceptor* (September 1953), Vol. II, No. 11, pp. 2-3, 9, 21, 23).

risk of being misunderstood, misquoted, or even maligned." Therefore, he reaffirms that he is not opposing the preaching of the gospel, "visiting the fatherless and widows," or teaching young people in schools, as some were apparently charging. "Even though that person may not agree with our views of **how** such works should be done, we nevertheless affirm **they should be done**," he said.[32]

(No. 8). In this last article in the series, Cope returns to the fundamental **"Nature of the Church."** He again stresses **"Local Churches Established," "Local Churches Equipped," "Independence and Autonomy," "Autonomy Disregarded and Independence Destroyed," "A Gradual Development,"** and **"History's Warning."** He concluded by saying,

> If one church may speak for or act in lieu of another church in any or all matters, it may also speak for or act in lieu of all other churches in any matter or in all matters. If there is a scriptural principle that will prevent one it will also prevent all other infringements upon the autonomy and independence of any and every local church on earth, either in part or in whole. If not, why not? It has happened before. It can happen again.[33]

Jim Cope addressed other subjects over the course of *The Preceptor's* publication, but his principal concern was how certain attitudes and practices were affecting the churches. "The Issues," as they came to be called, challenged two primary and essential concepts: the very heart and soul of New Testament authority and New Testament teaching concerning the nature

---

32   James R. Cope, "The Problem of Institutionalism (No. 7)," *The Preceptor* (October 1953), Vol. II, No. 12, pp. 4).

33   James R. Cope, "The Problem of Institutionalism (No. 8)," *The Preceptor* (June, 1953), Vol. III, No. 1, pp. 4, 19).

of the church. Practically, the overriding abuses were being observed in two clear principle violations of essentials to local church autonomy as Jim Cope saw it. First, does the New Testament authorize churches to contribute from their congregational offerings to humanly formed and governed organizations (such as missionary societies, schools, homes for the aged, orphanages, hospitals, etc.). Second, does the New Testament authorize a church to receive contributions from other churches to support a cause under the oversight of the elders of the receiving church and claiming to do the work of all supporting churches (certain other missionary societies, orphanages, etc.). Such is being designated "the sponsoring church arrangement." In response to the first, separate human organizations other than the local church are doing the churches' work for and doing it instead of the church. God did not authorize the building and maintaining of separate organizations to do the church's work. That does not comply with the all sufficiency of the church to do what God has commissioned it to do. In response to the second, elders are not authorized to oversee the work, or any part of the work, of any congregation(s) other than the one "over which they had been made bishops" (Acts 20:28) and which is "among you" (1 Peter 5:1-4).[34]

In *The Preceptor*, each of the editors eventually had something to say about these "issues." It was Jim Cope,

---

34   James R. Cope, "Societies, Schools, Papers, and 'The Editor'" *The Preceptor* (November, 1953); "The All-Sufficiency of the Church" (December, 1953; January and February, 1954); "The Missionary Method Again" (January, 1954); "When Does Cooperation Become Centralization?" (March, 1954); "Independence and Episcopacy" (April, 1954); "The UCMS and the Sponsoring Church" (January, 1955); "County, State, Regional, National, Rome" (March, 1955); "Is There a Parallel?" (April, 1955).

however, who carried the ball and provided the detailed articles on these matters throughout the four-year history of the paper's being published by the men on the Bible faculty of Florida Christian College.

As time passed, Clevenger, Hardeman, and Humble drifted away from the non-institutional fellowship and positions they had taken in *The Preceptor*. Eugene Clevenger, who was a roommate of this writer's father at Freed-Hardeman College in 1939-40, went on to teach at Abilene Christian College. Bill Humble left the college to preach in Kansas City, followed that by preaching for a church in Louisville, completed his doctorate at the University of Iowa, and became a professor and administrator at Abilene Christian. Pat Hardeman went to the University of Illinois to get his doctorate[35] and came back, having redirected his thinking on numerous theological, doctrinal, and practical issues of concern to brethren. "After repeated clashes with the college administration over such issues as social drinking, mixed gender swimming and dancing, and other issues, Hardeman left Florida Christian to teach at Tampa University."[36]

Early in 1955, Jim attended the annual lecture series on the campus of Freed-Hardeman College (January 10-14). While openly acknowledging that he differed with some on the faculty with whom he had worked closely in his five years teaching there, he applauded President H. A. Dixon for his "practice of affording opportunity for divergent views to be fully expressed and honorably examined both at their lectures and in their classes." He also expressed appreciation for the manner in which Guy N. Woods conducted the "Round

---

35   James R. Cope, "Florida Christian College Begins Seventh Year," *The Preceptor* (November 1952), II, 1, 15.

36   Harrell, 305; Cope Interview

Table" open-forum sessions each day. Jim even encouraged his readers to join the "Friends of FHC" giving program in support of the college. He concluded, "I am glad I went to Henderson. I love my brethren more, and my hopes are brighter that in the future God's people may live and work in peace. May we all learn to do justly, love mercy, and walk humbly with our God."[37]

Even so, there were some "unpleasantries during the last day of the Freed-Hardeman Lectures involving Leroy Garrett."[38] The first involved the Open Forum. An open letter signed by twenty-six brethren (including James R. Cope, E. R. Harper, James D. Willeford, Basil Overton, etc.) explained what happened:

> About noon of January 14, Brother Leroy Garrett of Dallas, Texas, came to the campus of Freed-Hardeman College, and at 3:00 o'clock in the afternoon presented a question to the Open Forum, which was being conducted during the lectureship. The question was, "Is Freed-Hardeman College doing a work of the church?" Brother Guy N. Woods, the chairman of the Open Forum, stated the question and gave Brother Garrett at least one-third of the hour to discuss his view in answer to this question. Others, of course responded and Brother Garrett seemed to feel that because some replied to him, that he was being persecuted. It is our conviction that Brother Garrett was treated with eminent fairness by Brother Dixon, Brother Woods, and everyone connected with the lectureship. We believe that this statement should be made in view of

---

37   James R. Cope, "My Visit to Freed—Hardeman, Some Reflections," *The Preceptor* (February 1955), IV, 4, 18.

38   James R. Cope, "The Garrett Incident at Henderson," *The Preceptor* (February 1955), IV, 4, 18-19.

developments that took place immediately following the Open Forum.[39]

Shortly after arriving on campus, Brother Garrett had also become involved in discussions about his views with students and visitors on Freed-Hardeman's right to exist. President Dixon was notified and calling brother Garrett aside, told him that he was welcome to raise the issue in the Open Forum, but he would have to ask him to avoid "agitating students concerning his views." He invited Brother Garrett to his office to discuss the matter with C. P. Roland, R. L. Witt, and himself. That meeting lasted an hour, and, according to Dixon, Garrett "refused to comply with any of our requests in regard to conduct on our campus," insisting that "he had been invited to our campus and that he was going to our young men's dormitory to talk over these things with students there." Dixon informed him "that such a visit to the dormitory would be out of order and that it could not be permitted. When he refused to agree to abide by the president's requests, Dixon "informed him that his course of actions would compel us to appeal to civil authorities." The meeting concluded on that note, and they went to the Open Forum. Following the session described above, Garrett persisted in further discussions with students and visitors until Dixon was able to get him to return to the office. Witt and Dixon tried to get him to agree not to visit the dormitories. When all failed, Dixon called the mayor of Henderson for assistance. The mayor sent a police officer with a warrant for Garrett's arrest. Dixon agreed to his release if he would agree to cease "further disturbance on our campus." He would not and spent the night in jail. In the morning, Dixon contacted the mayor and personally paid all

---

39   E. R. Harper and 25 others, "Open Letter," *The Preceptor* (February 1955), IV, 4, 20.

costs, withdrawing any charges against Garrett.[40]

Jim Cope was present when these events took place at Freed Hardeman and published these notices about what happened in *The Preceptor*. It is significant here because a somewhat similar event took place in 1972 in Temple Terrace during the annual lecture program at Florida College. W. Carl Ketcherside attended the lectures and entered the men's dormitory where Bible majors lived and talked to the students about his doctrinal views without asking for or receiving permission.

Cope did not have Ketcherside arrested. He had witnessed H. A. Dixon's actions seventeen years earlier and, although having defended Dixon, was surely glad it did not come to that pass at Florida Christian College. In any case Carl Ketcherside, although aggressive, was not of the same disposition as Leroy Garrett. Perhaps also both Cope and Ketcherside were anticipating a meeting arranged by brethren in the University church that night following the lecture program. Robert Turner had been asked by Harry Pickup, Jr., and the brethren at University to engage Ketcherside in a one-night discussion of his views.

Ketcherside had by this time totally done a hundred-eighty degree about-face in his convictions regarding whom we may fellowship as faithful Christians. He had formerly been aligned with the views of Daniel Sommer and Leroy Garrett. It was an astounding change from extremely conservative to radically liberal positions. Among other things, Ketcherside was now advocating acceptance of mechanical instruments of music in

---

40   H. A. Dixon, "Leroy Garrett's Visit to Freed-Hardeman," *The Preceptor* (February 1955), IV, 4, 20.

worship and receiving into fellowship pious persons who had not been scripturally baptized. He called them "brethren in prospect."

As reported by Ray Ferris, "On January 25, 1972, at 10:00 p.m. an overflow crowd gathered at the meetinghouse of the University church in Tampa, Florida. For approximately three hours, or until one o'clock in the morning, a lively exchange took place. For thirty minutes Carl Ketcherside set forth his views on the question of fellowship, and immediately following, Robert Turner spoke for thirty minutes on the same subject. Then for about two hours the audience participated in a question and answer session with the two speakers, plus Harry Pickup, Jr., and Ferrell Jenkins, who spoke and joined the panel."[41] Pickup was regularly preaching at the University church in those days and apparently was instrumental in arranging for the meeting. Jenkins had spoken with Pickup about having known Ketcherside in St. Louis and was asked to actively participate.[42]

Although they had not espoused his views, Ketcherside mentioned in his opening speech that Pat Hardeman, Bill Humble, and G. K. Wallace had changed their positions on significant issues, having been members of Florida Christian College's faculty.[43]

In anticipation of this lecture series, Harry Pickup, Jr., had prepared three studies entitled "The Fellowship of Jesus" to be presented each morning, Tuesday through Thursday, at 10:50 in the college auditorium. After introducing the subject and

---

41 Ray Ferris, "The Ketcherside Discussion in Tampa: Was It Wise," *Truth Magazine* (April 6, 1972), XVI: 22, 6-7.

42 Conversation with Ferrell Jenkins; December 21, 2020

43 Ray Ferris, "Carl Ketcherside's Strange Views on Fellowship," *Truth Magazine* (April 13, 1972), XVI: 23, 10-12.

the circumstances calling for it to be studied, Pickup's outlines printed for the lessons included both his understanding of "Concepts of Fellowship," and "False Concepts of Fellowship." He then analyzed Ketcherside's views in a speech he entitled "Context of Fellowship" in which he pinpointed the questions at issue and provided his understanding of the Biblical teaching on each point.[44]

During Pickup's Thursday presentation, this writer sat with Jim Cope. Both of us listened carefully to Pickup. Toward the end of his speech, Jim passed me a handwritten note that I still have in my possession. It says,

> I have never seen any practical application of Carl's "song and dance" except as it provides a stage for himself to perform upon. If everything he says be true it doesn't change one iota of the things that divide us, per se. He admits he hasn't changed one basic concept over these things yet I've not heard of his teaching anybody about what he believes on any of these divisive matters. He creates another sect, heads it himself without its having local structure except as he does here, and encourages the sentiment expressed by Melanie's stepfather at University Tuesday night.

The feeling expressed was frustration that there is no real objective basis for fellowship if Ketcherside's views are followed to their logical conclusions.

---

44   Harry Pickup, Jr., "The Fellowship of Jesus," *Florida College Lecture Series 1972* (Temple Terrace, FL: Florida College, 1972) 13-23.

Chapter 15:

Defining Moments (1954-56)

James R. Cope and the Florida Christian College Board

Jim Cope's articles in *The Preceptor* were not in line with the thinking of the chairman and some members of the Florida Christian College Board of Directors. The Board during the 1940s and mid-1950s consisted of the following:

Lee Anderson (St. Petersburg, FL)	1944-54
Lee Warren Boswell (Lakeland, FL)	1944-91
Ralph S. Church (Winston Salem, NC)	1955-59
Lloyd Copeland (Tampa, FL)	1944-91
H. N. Donoho (Highland City, FL)	1944-50
Jesse L. Elder (Jacksonville, FL)	1944-61
Robert Y. Griffin (Florence, AL)	1954-64
David E. Harrell, Sr. (Jacksonville, FL)	1953-64
Sam C.. Hastings (Pensacola, FL)	1949-91
Charles M. Hendrix (Orlando, FL)	1951-53
John R. Hoile (Columbia, SC)	1954-59
T. H. Holsberry, Sr. (Plant City, FL)	1944-62
O. C. Horne (Lubbock, TX)	1954-57

E. A. Howard (Orlando, FL)	1953-55
Wilbur C. King (Wauchula, FL)	1955-64 (chair 1962-64)
Clifford G. McGehee (Jacksonville, FL)	1944-56 (chair 1952-56)
E. J. Moore (Pensacola, FL)	1950-60
C. Ed Owings (Tampa, FL)	1944-62 (chair 1944-52; 1956-62)
L. J. Stanley (Miami, FL)	1949-69
W. R. Starling (Miami, FL)	1944-59
I. O. Taylor (Apopka, FL)	1944-53
J. Roy Vaughn (Miami, FL)	1944-49
S. Odell Ward (Lakeland, FL)	1950-88 (chair 1964-86)
R. H. Whitehead (Gainesville, FL)	1949-66

C. Ed Owings was selected to be the original chairman of the board. He was one of the elders of the Howard Avenue church in Tampa. In 1952, Owings stepped down from the chairmanship but remained on the board. The vice-chairman, Clifford G. McGehee, was elected chairman. He lived in Jacksonville and was an elder in the Riverside church there. His views on church support of human institutions such as orphanages, the *Herald of Truth*, and colleges were in direct conflict with those Jim Cope had been offering for consideration in *The Preceptor*. McGehee was a friend of Foy Wallace and also of B. C. Goodpasture and Roy Vaughn, who were both associated with the *Gospel Advocate* in Nashville.

Interestingly, Vaughn was married to a sister of D. Ellis Walker. Walker was the local preacher at Riverside, where McGehee served as an elder.

According to Cope, late in 1955, C. G. McGehee invited Jim to come to Jacksonville and preach at Riverside on December 11 while Walker was scheduled to be away. Unbeknown to Cope, McGehee also invited C. Ed Owings and Lloyd Copeland from Tampa and W. R. Starling, an elder in the Central church in Miami, to come and have dinner at his home that day after the morning services.

Following their meal, McGehee asked Jim if he thought churches were going to divide over the support of colleges and orphanages. Jim replied, "Yes, I think they will." McGee then stated that he did not think the president of Florida Christian College had any business opposing churches supporting orphan homes, colleges, or the *Herald of Truth*. He then told Cope that "he would withdraw his money which secured the accreditation of the College if the young president did not cease his preaching and teaching against church support of human institutions and sponsoring church arrangements." McGehee went on to say that he could not support Jim's presidency at the school if Jim continued to write in opposition to churches doing so.

To that, Jim replied,

> The board employed me to operate the College, not to stultify my conscience. You wanted a man when you employed me who was also a gospel preacher, one true to God's book. I was a Christian and a preacher before I became involved in school work. I settled the matter as to who would control me in my preaching when as an 18-year old boy. I committed myself not to go beyond the things that are written. To date I have been true to that pledge. My soul is not for sale.[1]

Jim went on to say,

> All you have to do is call for the board to ask for my resignation, and if that is passed by the board, I will leave the next day. I am not going to play politics. I will serve as I was elected to serve

---

1   Quotation from a hand-written note by James R. Cope in possession of the author.

until the board tells me to leave. The board will have to make its decision, and I will have to make mine.[2]

Over the three months between that exchange in Jacksonville and the next board meeting, it appears that there were several "mini-meetings" of groups of board members. On the night before the board meeting, several board members met in Tampa to discuss what each was thinking. The next day, Chairman McGehee asked for the minutes of that meeting. He was told that there were no minutes; it was not an official board meeting. McGee was also reminded of his gathering in Jacksonville and that it was known there had been several similar meetings up and down the state in recent times. The chairman did not pursue his request, knowing that there had been other meetings and that he had personally been involved in some of them.[3]

The official board meeting was scheduled to begin at 10:00 the next morning. They would not leave until almost 11:00 that night. Before the meeting was called to order, Jim was asked to leave the room and the board went into executive session. The ultimate question was going to be whether or not a majority of the board would vote to retain Jim Cope and reaffirm certain guidelines for the college's policies regarding refusal to take contributions from churches. His critics on the board wanted an understanding with Jim about his writing and sermons. They would also have to have a definite commitment that he would not follow the line he had chosen to go or they would get a new man. Jim waited in his office with Clinton Hamilton, Franklin Puckett (a more recent Bible teacher), and Homer Hailey all day. If the board chose to let Jim go, the others would resign and leave as well.

2   Interview with James R. Cope, February 23, 1988.
3   Ibid.

Chairman McGehee had contacted a number of preachers over the country. When he came to the board meeting on March 6, 1956, he brought with him letters from at least twenty of them, all of whom became strong advocates of churches' supporting institutions. Much of the morning was consumed in reading those letters and discussing them. Some of the other members of the board had letters from other preachers who supported the administration. S. O Ward had received a letter earlier from Roy Vaughn expressing concern about the school. Vaughn asked Ward to talk to Jim and see if he could change Jim's mind. In Ward's view, Vaughn and B. C. Goodpasture were developing a growing attitude of distrust for Cope and Florida Christian College's board of directors.[4]

About 1:00, the board took a break. S. O. Ward left the room. A student came up to him on campus and asked, "Who is the president of the College?" Ward responded, "Why, Jim Cope is the president. Don't you go to school here?" The student replied , "Yes, but people are saying Cope won't be the president after this meeting." Ward said, "Is that right? What do you know about it?" He replied, "I just talked to my father in California. I could, if I wanted to, tell you who is going to be the next president." Ward responded, "That's interesting. Tell me about it." "Well," the boy said, "You don't seem to know anything to tell me, so I won't say anything to you." Before the boy walked off, he said, "You will find I'm right. We will have a new president tonight. Cope's gone." He did not say who the next president would be, and Ward could not be certain how news of the board meeting's agenda had gotten all the way across the country.[5]

---

4   Interview with S. Odell Ward and James R. Cope, February 28, 1988.

5   Ibid.

As the afternoon went on, the discussion became intense. Lee Warren Boswell, Lloyd Copeland, and Sam Hastings spoke up noticeably against the college soliciting church contributions. They were for retaining Cope in the presidency. C. G. McGehee, W. R. Starling, O. C. Horne, and E. J. Moore provided the opposition. When time came for a vote, twelve of the seventeen current members raised their hands in favor of retaining Jim Cope as president.[6] They also reaffirmed the unanimous decision of the founding Board on March 30, 1944, that "money not be raised by soliciting the treasuries of congregations."[7]

When he saw that the decision was going against his position, Chairman McGee rose and exited the room saying, "Gentlemen, I cannot go this route. My support ends. I will be at my hotel down-town until 8:00 a.m.. If you all decide different, contact me. If not I am through forever."[8] "Accordingly, on March 14, 1956, he sent the board a letter informing it that, effective on May 31, 1956, he would cease his $20,000 per annum gift."[9] That $20,000 was the basis on which accreditation was granted by the Southern Association of Colleges and Schools.

The chairman knew how important that gift was to Florida Christian College. Jim Cope reported that Benton Cordell Goodpasture, editor of the *Gospel Advocate,* said after that meeting that Florida Christian College would not be opening

---

6   Ibid. Also Cope's handwritten note in his preaching list of sermons.

7   Margie H. Garrett, ed., *Making a Difference Florida College: The First Fifty Years* Clinton E. Hamilton, ed., "New Directions: Controversy and Decision" (Temple Terrace, FL: Florida College Press, 1996), 74-75.

8   Interview with S. Odell Ward and James R. Cope, February 28, 1988.

9   Garrett, op. cit., p. 75-77.

that next fall. Goodpasture must have known that McGehee would not give the school any more money.[10]

Jim Cope also knew how important the annual McGehee contribution was to FCC. Within three weeks, Jim made a trip to Longview, Texas, to solicit help from J. W. and Nellie Akin. Later, Cope said that when he told them the story of the conflict and that McGehee had pulled out his contribution, brother Akin became visibly angry. Akin said, "Brother Cope, you just tell that fellow McGehee to take his money and leave with it. Nellie and I will stay with you. We'll take care of you as long as we live." Jim admitted that upon hearing that, he broke down weeping, to which Nellie said, "Brother Jimmy, dry your eyes. John and Nellie are going to stay with you." The Akins later pledged to give $20,000 per year as long as they lived. He was made an honorary board member in 1960 in appreciation of their gifts to the college, and a building was named in their honor.

Cope later said, "That's how close the school came to going down the drain." McGehee's contributions were not the sum of it. When word got out about the stand of the board and the reasons for it, the number of continuing financial supporters took a nosedive. Before that, the Living Links program had over 2,500 annual donors. Three years later, there were only 400 committed givers. Also student enrollment dropped immediately with many cancellations. Administrators, led by Harry Pickup, Sr., took to the telephones and recruited or saved enough to keep the school open. Brethren who disagreed with Cope and the board influenced the securing of both dollars and students. Within a reasonable time, those board members who had sided with the chairman or sympathized with his position

---

10   Interview with S. Odell Ward and James R. Cope, February 28, 1988.

either resigned or did not stand for reelection. McGehee did not return after that March meeting but apparently did not officially withdraw his membership on the Board until his term expired. C. Ed. Owings was again elected chairman and the board was united.[11]

Jim was painfully open with the Southern Association about both the loss of funding and the reasons for it. Dean Clinton Hamilton explained the situation to the accrediting agency, and its leaders came back with the decision "that the Association would work with the college because it was refreshing that there had been no compromise to keep financing."[12] At the next board meeting on April 12, 1956, several members stepped up and made pledges to continue programs the board had previously authorized. Contrary to Goodpasture's prediction, the college would continue to serve students.

---

11   Ibid.
12   Garrett, op. cit., p. 77.

Section Seven:

Building A Decade of Progress

Chapter 16:

Lean but Productive Years (1956-65)

The decade following the crisis in the board of Florida Christian College was truly a time of both turmoil and development in American life, as well as in Florida Christian College.

Dwight David Eisenhower (1952-60), John Fitzgerald Kennedy (1960-63), and Lyndon Baines Johnson (1963-68) were United States Presidents. The Korean War (1950-53) was ended, but in 1965 under President Johnson, thousands of American troops were sent to Vietnam, and the world recognized that it was in what has been called a "Cold War" between the United States and the Soviet Union. That lasted four decades (1947-89). Although not in open military warfare during the Kennedy administration, America held its breath at least once each year:

a) during an invasion of the Bay of Pigs by Cuban exiles (1961);

b) during the erection of the Berlin Wall (1961);

c) during the strategic Cuban Missile crisis (October, 1962); and, of course,

d) with the assassinations of President John Kennedy

(November 22, 1963), Civil Rights advocate Martin Luther King, Jr., (April 4, 1968), and Senator Robert Kennedy (June 5, 1968).

There was also the growing threat of China's rising to power and the menacing presence of Fidel Castro in Cuba just ninety miles from the southern borders of Florida.

Internal division was even more apparent in the daily lives of Americans. *Brown v. Board of Education of Topeka* (1954) had propelled a major change in the landscape of civil rights in communities over the nation. That decision was followed with a bus boycott in Montgomery, Alabama (1955), school integration in Little Rock, Arkansas (1957), a major civil rights march on Washington (1963), and the Civil Rights Acts (1964 and 1965).

Even so, advancements in science and technology worldwide were phenomenal. The early 1950s had brought the introduction of the Xerox machine (1950), the first business computer, Univac (1951), the first United States transcontinental television transmission (1951), the discovery of DNA double helix (1953), and the introduction of the polio vaccine (1954). Later 1950s and 1960s saw the introduction of even more amazing discoveries. Medical science saw the first successful human heart transplant (1967) and the introduction of Medicare benefits to aging Americans. Space exploration saw the launch of artificial satellites beyond earth's atmosphere with the Russian Sputnik (1957) and the American NASA project Mercury (1958). A man orbited the earth (1961) and a human being exited the capsule and actually walked in space (March 18, 1965) and on the moon (June 20, 1969). The times were both challenging and exciting.

Within the brotherhood, times were hard in the days following the showdown over church support of the college. The college had been deeply impacted by the challenges of brethren in the debate concerning church sponsorship of human institutions. Enrollment and contributions tanked, and the future looked glum. It appeared that the predictions of preachers and editors in Nashville and elsewhere that the college would fold might be on the horizon.

Other "faith-based" schools across the country faltered under the pressures placed upon them by the very young people they served. Short skirts, bawdy entertainment, mind-altering drugs and alcohol, and general disrespect for the law, the rules, and classroom decorum challenged the administrators and faculty on every hand in academia across the country. It was a time of protests. Many schools experienced demonstrations and rioting. It took wise, strong leadership to navigate the waters of unrest that made many spiritually minded parents unwilling to send their college-age students so far from home. At Florida Christian College most students were respectful and remained faithful Christians while away from home, however. The board, Cope, Hamilton, and the faculty did not capitulate to the general social environment. President Cope continued his leadership, looking for the good. He never considered giving up, leaving the presidency, closing the college, or failing to preach his convictions on congregational support of human institutions.

Instead, the administration doubled down. Student recruitment efforts were in full swing during that same period of time in order to bring projected student revenue to meet budget numbers in the following school year. Cope often said to those on his administrative team, "There is little we could not accomplish if we had sufficient students and dollars!" In those years Cope was serving as business manager as well as covering the many duties of the presidency.

When the student count reached a low mark, the president sent Harry Pickup, Sr., then Director of Public Relations and Student Recruitment, to New Jersey to find students from the cold Northeast who would like to study in warm Florida. It proved a good thing personally for a number of students who read the Bible for the first time, met husbands or wives who taught them the gospel, and got a good education away from unfavorable conditions in New England. But it was not so good for the environment of the campus when the number of non-Christians became such that their presence influenced the desired culture of the school. The student recruitment policy had to be modified.

With the support of James "Dudy" Walker, the president authorized a spring bus trip carrying the college chorus across the South. Its success in interesting students in attending the college was immediate. Alumni in each city hosted the students in their homes and provided a venue for the program. They were faithful to advertise widely. Large crowds attended. In the early years, the first half of the programs consisted of hymns known by the audience. The second half, still a capella, was composed of secular music, often from Broadway musicals. The trips lasted ten days. Cities included Atlanta, Nashville, Louisville, Athens, Birmingham, and others in areas where a larger contingent of supporters were eager to help.

At a meeting during the annual lectureship on January 25, 1965, Jim announced the creation of the Florida College National Council. Fifty men and women who were already dedicated supporters of the college were asked to make suggestions for enhancing the effectiveness of the college and serve as a sounding board cabinet for the president. Of course, they would be the first ones to which the president would go for financial help.[1]

An even more abiding solution to student recruitment adopted first by the Cope administration and expanded by presidents Owen and Caldwell proved to be the establishment of **summer camps.** In the beginning they brought high-school students to campus for a week at a time. It introduced them to one another, giving them a resemblance of campus life as it would be if they came to school at this college. Most were already Christians, and the association would continue and grow if they came to school. That association and the wholesome activities were good for the young people whether they enrolled or not. The camp activities included daily Bible classes and evening devotionals. The camps also gave opportunity for college personnel to encourage the students to choose Florida Christian College for their first experience with higher education.

The idea for the camps apparently grew out of an event conducted July 11-16, 1954, and directed by Bob and Janelle Owen, Paul and Doris Andrews, Frank and Corine Andrews, and Roy and Patricia Lanier. Observing the obvious success of that summer gathering of students, a full-fledged program was developed and expanded by Harry Pickup, Jr., during the Owen administration. Camps were started over the country and run by faithful alumni. When Caldwell left office, there were twenty-two camps scattered geographically over the contiguous United States all the way from the eastern seaboard states to California, Oregon, and Washington.

---

1   Jane Ward Britnell, "Rebuilding Years: 1961-1970," Margie H. Garrett, ed., *Making a Difference Florida College: The First Fifty Years* (Temple Terrace, FL: Florida College Press, 1996), 109.

Jim Cope was always ready to take advantage of new opportunities to further his projects. In May 1957, he discovered that WFLA Radio conducted ongoing Federal Communications Commission Public Service spot announcements. He applied to fill that time slot at 10:05 pm. For several weeks, he provided a "thought for reflection" at the end of each day, followed by patriotic music from the Florida Christian College chorus. It raised awareness of the college throughout the hearing audience just before the station signed off each evening.

In December, Jim announced that Channel 13, the newly formed WTVT television station in Tampa, had granted the college a permit to air an academic Bible quiz program called "College for the Asking" each week. The idea was for viewers to call in and try to "stump the panel with their Bible questions. The program featured a panel composed of Florida Christian College administrators and Bible faculty. Usually the panel consisted of Bible faculty chairman Homer Hailey alongside President Cope, Dean Clinton Hamilton, and Professor Franklin Puckett. Bob Owen was the moderator. The program was relatively popular in the Tampa area until much of the local programming was replaced by the station's national affiliation.

Chapter 17:

Contributing Partners (1956-64)

Florida College's fiscal year runs from June 1 to May 31. Each year annual fund-raising efforts were in full swing in the spring to meet budgeted requirements by May 31. For a small school like Florida Christian College, meeting the budget meant receiving hundreds of small donations and a few major gifts that were not designated for special capital expenditures or other special purposes. Often board members stepped up to supply the non-designated funding at the annual board meeting in May. In those years, Cope often appealed to board member Lee Warren Boswell of Lakeland to provide essential giving to balance the budget at the end of the year. Numerous times Boswell came to the rescue.

As already noted, fund-raising was a major challenge in those years. Jim's first major donation from Tennessee after the board decision to retain him as president came from Mrs. A. B. Barret, the widow of the founding president of Abilene Christian College. Cope had become acquainted with the Barrets while he was in Nashville and Henderson in the early 1940s. Barret had preached in Murfreesboro, Tennessee, after returning from Texas to his home state of Tennessee in 1920. When his wife, Exie, sent the contribution, Allan Booker Barret had been deceased since 1951. Mrs. Barret liked Jim and wanted to help the young, struggling school. Her gift was a milestone for Cope.[1]

In 1957, Paul Hutchinson of El Centro, California, donated $60,000 for the building of the A-frame auditorium that came to be the recognizable symbol of the Florida College's campus. Hutchinson's gift was a huge contribution in that day. It was followed by a decision of the board to sell one-third of some land then owned by the college in the Imperial Valley of California. The Hutchinson gift was given in memory of Mr. Hutchinson's late wife, Mary Lena, and was officially named for her and for her husband on March 5, 1961 when it opened for daily chapel exercises. The theater seating was given by board member, R. Lee Warren Boswell, and his wife, Margaret Eades Boswell.[2]

Later, in 1963, Cope announced that Hutchinson had signified his intention to leave his entire estate to the college.

> Hutchinson described "an investment in Florida College today as an investment in the America of tomorrow" and said the "greatest joy of my life has been to see the great pleasure and appreciation of these young people. I enjoy seeing the good that this money has done. People should not wait until they die to put their money to work for young people." Hutchinson prefaced his gift with the statement, "I have more confidence in the college today than when I made the original gift and am delighted to see that others have been inspired to help also."[3]

---

1   The reader may learn more about A. B. Barret from the Introduction of A.B. Barret's book, *The Shattered Chain*, Henderson, Tennessee, 1942-1943. (See under his name in *therestorationmovement. com*).

2   Making a Difference, p. 86.

3   James R. Cope, "Florida College" (*Truth Magazine*, April 1963), Vol. VII, No. 7, p. 5.

Another major gift came to the college following the tragic death of Wilbur C. King in an automobile accident in July, 1964. King was serving as chairman of the Florida College board of directors at the time. He had willed a portion of his estate including his Wauchula house, a cattle ranch, and an orange grove to the college. He had stipulated that the proceeds of the sale of these properties be designated for an endowed fund to provide loans to young men committed to serving the Lord in their lives and enrolling in Florida College.[4]

In 1965, Jim and Georgia Dean moved the family from the old Spanish house they had lived in for the past sixteen years to a newer home constructed on the large adjacent lot behind it immediately around the corner at 301 Greencastle Avenue. William C. Hammontree, a local member of the board and sometime business manager of the college, designed the house and was charged with overseeing the building of this stately residence with tall columns at its front entrance.

Cope secured major gifts toward the building of two other major buildings on campus in the years 1966-67. He had earlier befriended Fred K. Conn, a prosperous land owner and lumber mill operator from Mississippi. Conn had been chosen in 1927 by then Secretary of Commerce Herbert Hoover to supervise government aid for flood relief at Yazoo City, Mississippi. Working with the Red Cross, Conn was very successful. That experience apparently initially motivated his philanthropy and community service. In 1957, he received a letter from Jim Cope expressing appreciation for the service rendered by the Conn Memorial Foundation, established in 1954. Ground was broken on November 14, 1966, for the

4   Margie H. Garrett, ed., *Making a Difference Florida College: The First Fifty Years* (Temple Terrace, FL: Florida College Press, 1996), 110.

construction of Conn Gymnasium. It came as the result of a gift of $60,000 from the Fred K. Conn Foundation.[5]

In 1967, President Cope applied for and received a donation of $250,000 from William F. Chatlos to be applied to the construction of a new administration and library building. Chatlos was an architect from Connecticut, who earned his wealth constructing homes, apartments, and office buildings. Investing wisely, Chatlos established a philanthropic foundation in 1953 to provide funding to Bible colleges, religious and social causes, and medical concerns. He said, "You can't measure your worth by the values we place on our possessions. A calamity of only a few seconds can change all that. Real worth is determined by what you do with what you have ... be it large or small."

When President Cope announced the gift, he said, "Mr. Chatlos was intrigued by Florida College's emphasis on character building and by our free enterprise system."[6]

Cope announced two other bequests at the same time and declared that increased support by Tampa area businessmen is "an indication of local confidence in the college." He pointed to a gift of $10,000 for surfacing the parking lot near the auditorium and to a gift from John T. Lewis of a valuable set of periodicals to be housed in the college library. Lewis was a dedicated gospel preacher from Birmingham, Alabama.

Another significant gift was a $5,000 check secured by Jim and Lindy McDaniel from Phil K. Wrigley, owner of the Chicago Cubs major league baseball organization. Lindy McDaniel had attended Florida College and in 1964 was a

---

5   https://connfoundation.org/wp-content/uploads/2021/08/Mr.-Conn-Brochure-Scanned.pdf.

6   Ibid., 114.

relief pitcher with the Cubs. He had a twenty-one year career in the major leagues (1955-76), during which he pitched for five major league teams (St. Louis Cardinals, Chicago Cubs, San Francisco Giants, New York Yankees, and Kansas City Royals). He always had an agreement with management that he would be allowed to go to worship on Sundays before going to the ball park. Upon retirement from baseball, he regularly preached the gospel in his home state of Oklahoma and around the country. The gift was used to upgrade the intramural athletic facilities. The intercollegiate baseball field was later named for McDaniel.

Jim Cope was born during the presidency of Woodrow Wilson in the midst of World War I. His teen years were spent in rural Tennessee during Herbert Hoover's Great Depression, yet he only spoke fondly of his "growing up" years in middle Tennessee.

One of the donations most cherished by Jim could not be calculated in dollars. Shortly after the new auditorium was dedicated, Jim made one of his regular trips to Sparta, Tennessee, for the annual Cope family reunion. While there, he of course visited the family home in the Big Spring community and the church building where he and his family had regularly worshiped in his childhood days. The congregation had been established by Jim's grandparents. During the visit, he was shown the old church bell that had called the people together for worship every Sunday morning in early days. As a boy Jim had often rung that bell with his father looking on. He was so moved by seeing it sitting on the floor in disrepair, no longer used, that he asked if he could restore it and preserve it at the college. With their approval, he brought it to the College and mounted it on the rear peak of then new Hutchinson Auditorium. At first he had it rung at the beginning and close of each school year, during the opening day ceremonies and at graduation, beginning April 6, 1962. On each of those occasions, the bell tolled the number of years the school had been in existence. In 1981, Margie Garrett, then Director of Development, suggested that the bell should be rung more often. "Why not each day, calling the students to chapel as the bell had been rung to call people to worship." Of course, Jim loved the idea, and the daily practice was begun while the annual observances continued. The bell has pealed each school day since, calling the students to chapel. It is one of the great traditions of the school.

Jim Cope was sometimes criticized for his forthright appeals for money to keep the college in operation and out of debt. His success is securing major gifts came from a deep belief in his cause and his own personal charm. He often declared that he was not ashamed to ask for help because of the value of his cause and the blessed benefit to the donor.

Connie Adams, noted preacher and editor among churches of Christ, reflected on Cope's charisma in an article in *Truth Magazine*, September 18, 2012. The following excerpts provide an insight into Jim's personal character. They also provide insight into Cope's ability to raise the funds essential to the operation of Florida Christian College.

> Brother Cope had a very warm personal side. My own father who had very little formal education felt perfectly at ease with this man who could "walk with kings, nor ever lose the common touch." His east Tennessee rearing never left him. He was a delight to have as a guest in our home. He could kick off his shoes and unwind after a service. Someone said he was so relaxed he could "wear" a chair. He could go out in the yard and shoot baskets with the boys (I saw him do this when he was well past

50). He loved to hear and tell good jokes. He used to tell some to students in chapel before going back to classes. Once, when Weldon Warnock, my brother Wiley and I were doing a show one afternoon to raise money for tennis courts, we talked him into helping us with a stage joke. He was disguised until the very end when I asked for a hand for our assistant and the audience was greatly surprised to learn it was the school president.

He held a meeting in Akron, Ohio at Brown Street while we lived there *(August 1-6, 1965, cgc)*. One night I sat down beside him on the front row just before time to begin. He was looking over a brief outline for his sermon that night. It was written by hand on a jagged piece of a paper sack. I kidded him that it did look like the president of a college could have a more prestigious looking outline. He grinned and said, "Aw, it works fine this way."

Near the end of my sophomore year, he called me into his office one day to tell me he knew that Barbara Colley and I planned to marry that summer and that my folks were hard pressed to help me settle my school bill for that year. He said he knew a man who might be willing to help me on that but that he did not want to be identified. During the summer I was in a meeting in the panhandle of Florida when a letter came from brother Cope which said that this unnamed man had settled my account. To this day I do not know who the man was, but it was brother Cope who made this come together for me and I shall always be grateful."[7]

---

7   Connie W. Adams, Truth Magazine, September 18, 2012

Chapter 18:

The Academy (1958)

From its first classes beginning in 1946, Florida Christian College also conducted a high school. Luther Savage was the first principal. Julia Greenfield taught high-school English, Gladys Bonner taught mathematics, and Myrna Wallace taught history. There were six seniors, nine juniors, and ten sophomores in the 1946-47 class.[1] In addition to duties at the college, Roland Lewis, served as principal of the high school in its second year, 1947-48.[2] He continued in that role until it was decided to drop the high school program in the early nineteen-fifties and concentrate efforts on post-secondary programs.[3]

In the fall of 1958, the board of directors allowed Cope to add an elementary school program to the school's offerings. Officially at first it was named "Florida Christian Training School." Later it came to be known as the "Florida College administroatr

s." On campus it was called "The Little School."

---

1   *Royal Palm* 1947 (Florida Christian College Yearbook).

2   *Royal Palm* 1948.

3   Roland H. Lewis, "The High School of the Early Years," Margie H. Garrett, ed., *Making a Difference Florida College: The First Fifty Years* (Temple Terrace, FL: Florida College Press, 1996), 35.

That first year there were thirty-eight students in grades one through six. Roscoe Knight served as principal and taught grades five and six. His wife, Betty, taught grades one and two. Kay Payne (wife of college faculty member Harry Payne, Sr., and mother of future-president Buddy Payne) taught third and fourth grades and served as the librarian. Margie Garrett taught music. The second year the enrollment doubled and seventh grade was added.[4]

Knight served as principal from 1958 to 1963. Between 1963 and 1971, a series of four different teachers served as interim principals and reported to president Cope, having been assigned the administrative duties: Grady Palmer, Fred Moore, and Kay Payne. In 1971, Jim appointed Mari Smith to the principalship; she served until 1984.

Jim felt there was a special need and that such a school would be attended by faculty and staff children and students from the Temple Terrace community. The public elementary schools had become increasingly over-crowded, and classroom discipline was a serious problem. Jim noted that people in his acquaintance would support a school "having no double sessions, but having small classes and competent teachers." In addition, they would appreciate the fact that their children were being taught from the Bible by Christians and were being engaged in daily chapel exercises and other devotional events.

Another strong factor in Jim's decision was the fact that all of his own children were now of school age. Connie was eleven, Cathy would be nine, and James R. ("Butch") Cope, Jr., was five and ready for kindergarten when school started in

4   Nancy Hamilton Bourquardez, "Florida College Academy," Margie H. Garrett, ed., *Making a Difference Florida College: The First Fifty Years*. (Temple Terrace, FL: Florida College Press, 1996), 90.

September. He could hardly bear the thought of their being trained by non-believers in an environment without the kind of discipline and personal care he had experienced in those Tennessee schools at Sparta. He and Georgia Deane—Jim would say "especially Georgia Deane"—wanted their children to be taught conservative values, godly morals, and Biblical knowledge. That was an especially poignant motivation for Jim and Georgia Deane as parents to want the kind of environment and teaching the academy would provide. They had been surprisingly blessed on Sunday evening, January 14, 1958. Jim preached at Temple Terrace on the meaning of the resurrection. When the invitation was offered, Connie stepped up to the front of the audience and asked her dad to baptize her into Christ.

Chapter 19:

Preaching and Teaching

Immediately following the historic meeting in which his administration was reaffirmed by the board, Cope flew to Baytown, Texas, for a gospel meeting. He preached twice each day from Sunday through Sunday, March 11-18, 1956. A. Hugh Clark was the local preacher, and the two men spent the week together discussing the issues facing brethren across the country. Clark was already among the leading opponents of institutionalism in Texas.

After the Baytown meeting, Jim travelled to Longview, where he met with Mr. and Mrs. Akin. As already seen, this dedicated couple saved the day with their promise of future financial aid. Jim went home Monday encouraged but still not totally at ease regarding the future of the college. The following Saturday he was back on the road. On Sunday, he began a gospel meeting with the Fourth Street church in Cullman, Alabama. Sunday night's lesson was devoted to a discussion of James 1:27. He argued that the passage was speaking of individual responsibility and did not authorize congregations' building, maintaining, and supporting institutions or taking from the treasury to support non-Christians as proposed by institutional brethren. He observed that if it did authorize general benevolence from church treasuries, it would not authorize building and maintaining separate institutions (orphanages, homes for unwed mothers and the aged, etc.). He said that he would address that question more fully later in the week. On Thursday evening he preached on "The Organization and Operation of the Lord's Church." Robert Pressnell was preaching at Fourth Street at the time, and Roscoe Knight led the singing. Knight would go on to be a legend at Florida College in the classroom and on the intramural field.

In October 1956, Jim held a meeting with the Riverside Drive church in Nashville, Tennessee. Robert Jackson was the local preacher, and W. P. (William Preston) Hagewood was one of the elders. The building was packed each evening and Jim preached with fervor. Most of his lessons in gospel meetings were focused on how to be saved and how to live in Christ. Again, however, he used the Thursday night sermon to teach on current institutional issues. This time he focused on the difference between "Individual and Collective" action, explaining that Christians have personal responsibilities that congregations are not authorized to fund from their treasuries. His principal passage was 1 Timothy 5:3-16, which gives guidelines for the care of widows. He emphasized verse 16 and pointed out that families (individually) are to care for their own widows, and the church is not to be charged. Jackson, a former Methodist who had come out of denominationalism, saw Cope's position clearly. He, with Riverside's elders leading the way, became identified as non-institutional brethren in the midst of Nashville's center of opposition "to the Antis."

Soon, the Franklin Road church in Nashville also took a strong stand in this controversy, learning from the preaching of Harris Dark and others. In the fall of 1959 (Sunday through Sunday, October 11-18), Franklin Road conducted a series of meetings with different speakers pointing out the Biblical seriousness of the issues confronting brethren. Manuscripts of these twelve sermons were published by the church and distributed widely. They dealt with the following topics presented by the following speakers:

"Give Us a King" by Harris J. Dark

"Contending For the Faith" by Charles M. Campbell

"The Organization of the Church" by Charles M. Campbell

"Speaking as the Oracles of God" by Irven Lee

"The All Sufficiency of the Bible" by E. L. Flannery

"Divisions, Who Is Responsible" by James P. Miller

"According to the Pattern" by Stanley J. Lovett

"Church Cooperation" by Cecil B. Douthitt

"The Glorious Church and Its Purpose" by W. Curtis Porter

"The Care of the Needy" by Herschel Patton

"The Individual Christian's Responsibility" by Bennie Lee Fudge

"When Should One Change?" by James A. Allen[1]

Jim preached in thirteen gospel meetings in 1956, approximately one per month.[2] Each Sunday when home,

---

1   Copies of these manuscripts were published in eleven booklets (Campbell's lessons are published together in one) by Norris Publishing Company, Russellville, AL, 1960.

2   Cope's meetings in 1956: Asheville, NC (January 25-29); Disston Avenue in St. Petersburg, FL (February 19-March 4); Baytown, TX (March 11-18); Cullman, AL (March 25-April 1); Huntingdon, TN (April 22-29); East End in Detroit, MI (June 3-10); Eastside in Dayton, OH (Monday night, June 11); Taylor Boulevard in Louisville, KY (Wednesday night, June 13); Central in Johnson City, TN (June 17-24); Southside in Springfield, MO (July 23-29); Bear Wallow, KY (August 9-19); LaFayette, TN (August 20-24); Westside in Beaumont, TX (September 30-October 7); Riverside Drive in Nashville, TN (October

he preached twice at Disston Avenue. Most of the meetings began on Sunday and continued through the following Sunday. A meeting at Bear Wallow, Kentucky, continued eleven days. A meeting in Pinellas County/St. Petersburg was designed to help establish a congregation in the Cross Bayou area of the county. It continued over three Sundays, a full two-week period with preaching each evening for fifteen days. Jim dreamed of starting more congregations in the St. Petersburg area and in other locations in the Bay area. He was instrumental in the beginnings of the Drew Park congregation in Tampa, where Doug Burgess, Harry Payne, Sr., and others came to preach. In 1956, Jim also preached in some one-night services while traveling between meetings. In all his preaching, he was careful not to use the pulpit to promote the college. He clearly informed each congregation that Florida Christian College would not accept financial contributions from churches. On one occasion a check was sent from a church to the college. It was promptly returned with the explanation that on principle the college would not receive contributions from churches.

Jim Cope obviously considered his preaching and Bible teaching to be primary objectives in his life's work. He never ceased wanting to be in the pulpit or in the college classroom teaching Bible. He especially enjoyed teaching Bible to those young men who would go out and preach the gospel. For example, in the 1963 fall semester, he taught a course two days a week on the New Testament book of Hebrews. His class began early, before chapel on Tuesdays and Thursday mornings so as not to interfere with his administrative work or weekend meetings. His syllabus was entitled, "Hebrews:

21-28); and Brush Creek in Kansas City, MO (November 4-11).

The Epistle of Better Things." This author especially enjoyed that class. The times were rife with controversy, and brother Cope was in the middle of it. He would come to class and bounce arguments off the boys, and we would talk well past the bell. Some days he would tell us to memorize the current section in the three-page outline of Hebrews in the syllabus as our assignment for the day and then tell us about his study of the church and human institutions. Of course, next class we would have to make up time studying Hebrews. He was a master with that as well. In the spring, the text was Romans. Several were baptized at Disston Avenue during his time at home.

The controversy among brethren severely impacted his opportunities to preach away from Tampa. Only over the next decade, he only held on average approximately one-half the gospel meetings he had before. The meetings away were entirely with congregations opposing church support of human institutions. In 1957, for example, he preached in only five gospel meetings.[3] He had conducted thirteen the year before. Cope understood why. He felt that some elders did not wish to bring the controversy before their congregations. Apparently others in the regions of the country where Cope was well known did not ask him to come or cancelled earlier plans to have him because of his stand on the controversial subjects. Still others seemingly hesitated in order to not be labeled as agreeing with him by neighboring churches or by advocates of institutionalism in positions of influence (prominent preachers, elders, editors, schoolmen, etc.). It

---

3   Spring and Blaine in St. Louis, MO (May 13-19); Hayes Ave. in Detroit, MI (June 3-9); Westwood in McMinneville, TN (June 16-23); Hickory Heights in Lewisburg, TN (July 28-August 4); and Tarrant City northeast of Birmingham, AL (October 6-12).

would have been impossible—and Jim did not desire—to judge the motivation of individual cancellations, but some caused him pain.

Even so, the places Jim was invited to preach in that decade for the most part had dedicated preachers who opposed the institutions at issue. Many became friends of Cope and the college because of his stand. Cope had long extended days and nights with them, discussing "the issues," giving them an important insight into his reasons for the stand he took as president of Florida Christian College, and their sharing with Cope their reasons for agreeing with him.[4]

Jim Cope's passion for leading the lost to Christ motivated him to publish several eight-page color booklets that dealt with God's plan for salvation. He spent considerable time preparing a series dealing with questions people ask about baptism. "Let the Bible Speak Your Questions Answered," he wrote on the front of each booklet. His titles were "What is Baptism?" "Why Be Baptized?" and "Who Should Be Baptized?"

In January 1962, Cope published a forty-two page booklet that he entitled *Voices in the Wilderness*.[5] The voices were those of Thomas and Alexander Campbell and other pioneer preachers who proclaimed a slogan, "Where the Scriptures speak, we speak; and where the Scriptures are silent, we are silent." The

---

4   Over the decade of most intense opposition, these men included H. Elwood Phillips in Gainesville, FL; Bryan Vinson in Tulsa, OK; James P. Needham in Owensboro, KY; W. R. Jones in Baytown, TX; Roy E. Cogdill in Nacogdoches, TX; Bobby Thompson in Miami, FL; Jack Holt in Cullman, AL; A. C. Grider at Preston Road in Louisville, KY; Delton Porter at Locust Street in Mt. Pleasant, TN; Harris Dark at Perry Heights in Donelson, TN; Loren Raines at 40th and Emerson in Indianapolis, IN; Bill Fain at Southside in Seattle, WA; and a host of other notable men.

5   A reprinting of this booklet is included in the appendix of this book.

booklet was taken from sermons Cope had been preaching in gospel meetings. It traced the history of the division between the "Christian Church" (Disciples of Christ) and churches of Christ over missionary societies and instrumental music. Cope then asserted that the present-day development of benevolence societies, specifically orphanages and schools supported by churches, follows the same path while setting aside the requirements of New Testament authority. His point was to show churches of Christ that they were not listening to those who before had kept them from the errors of "Christian Church" institutionalism.[6]

In the "Afterword" to *Voices in the Wilderness* Cope responded to critics.

> I have sometimes been asked if I believe that an orphan "home" constituted as a human board to direct activities under it has a right to exist. Certainly I do! Frequently I have been reported as being 'anti-orphan home' and in many instances "anti-orphan".... I am not now nor have I ever knowingly spoken one word against the right of any individual or group establishing whatever arrangement of and by themselves might enable that person or group of persons to feed, clothe, shelter and nurse fatherless children for whom they are responsible.

He closed the booklet with these words:

> As enterprises independent of the church benevolence societies ('homes') have a right to exist. When these or similar enterprises begin looking to and calling upon churches of Christ for support and when churches respond, both 'homes' and churches have assumed a role for which there is no divine religious authority.[7]

---

6   James R. Cope, "Voices in the Wilderness," (Temple Terrace, FL: Published privately by James R. Cope, 1962), 1.

7   Ibid., 40-41.

Another booklet was written and published by Cope in June 1964. Several months earlier, in November and December of 1963, Batsell Barrett Baxter had presented a series of three sermons before the Hillsborough church in Nashville in which he defended the institutional position. Particularly of concern to Cope was Baxter's defense of churches contributing to colleges. Those sermons were published in a thirty-two page booklet entitled *Questions and Issues of the Day in the Light of the Scriptures*. In those years, Baxter was highly influential. He was chairman of the Bible Department of David Lipscomb College. He was a staff writer of the *Gospel Advocate*. He was featured speaker on the *Herald of Truth* television and radio program. He was regularly preaching for the large Hillsborough Road congregation in Nashville. His sermons/booklet dealt with his assertions concerning the hermeneutical issues, the application of specific passages of Scripture, the work of the church, and the expediency of supporting human institutions in doing the Lord's work.[8]

Baxter's analysis was fairly comprehensive. Cope saw a special opportunity to respond directly in writing and to present his views to a broad audience. Both men were "school men." Both were gospel preachers. Both were widely respected. Cope's booklet, *WHERE IS THE SCRIPTURE? A Request for Scriptural Authority in the Light of Questions and Issues of the Day Being a Review of Batsell Barrett Baxter's Tract*, was as lengthy as its title...eighty-four pages. It, too, was comprehensive in stating the opposition to churches supporting humanly organized and operated institutions. On the cover he identified the booklet as "an analysis of

---

8   Batsell Barrett Baxter, *Questions and Issues of the Day in the Light of the Scriptures* (Nashville, TN: privately published, 1963).

the position of those who advocate church contributions to schools and other human enterprises operated by Christians."[9]

Throughout the "tract," Cope continually called for Scripture while asserting that there was no authorization for churches to build or maintain institutions with the "Lord's money." This was not a matter of expediency. It was corrupting the very nature of the church as God designed it and revealed it in Scripture. Cope's introduction included these words: "I request nothing more than an unbiased consideration of my remarks. Good and honest hearts will weigh every criticism carefully and prayerfully." Such was his spirit throughout the division that occurred among churches of Christ.

Of course, Jim could not have handled the rigor of all this work and all these many challenges without the dedicated staff that helped to manage his office in those years. His aide ("assistant" or "secretary") for the decade of the sixties was Mrs. Elizabeth Woolf (1959-71). Jim depended on Elizabeth and saw her as his right hand "man." Preceding Mrs. Woolf were Evelyn Buchanan (1955-56), Bobbie Jean Henry Johnson (1956-57 and fall semester 1958), and Virginia Davis (1957-58 and spring semester 1959). In addition to all the tedious jobs at which Elizabeth was so capable, she greeted dozens of dignitaries, gospel preachers, alumni, and other guests before escorting them into Jim's office. She also shielded him from some who would just take his time.

Virginia Davis was also a good assistant for Jim. Her legacy, however, was not to be in the president's office but as the men's dorm mother on campus. As often as not, rather

---

9   James R. Cope, *WHERE IS THE SCRIPTURE? A Request for Scriptural Authority in the Light of Questions and Issues of the Day Being a Review of Batsell Barrett Baxter's Tract*, (Temple Terrace, FL: privately published, 1964).

than "spanking" the boys for their pranks, she laughed with them and even joined in. She wrote a book about her, and their, escapades in the residence halls entitled *Mama, Come Get Me*. In it she told of writing a letter to the President.

> My two dorms have had no hot water since the students arrived. In six days these 130 boys have become quite rancid.
>
> My two dorms have no telephones. In six days 260 parents trying to reach 130 sons have become quite irate.
>
> My two dorms have no drinking fountains.
>
> My two dorms do have two drink machines but neither works. (Add to this no campus student center or snack bar.)
>
> My two dorms have no janitors, brooms, mops or toilet paper.
>
> My two dorms have no garbage collection.
>
> For my two dorms I have no assistant or assistance. And there is no nightwatchman.

Mrs. Davis went on to suggest that Mr. Cope let the students know in chapel that he was aware of the their needs. Jim took her suggestion to heart and read her letter verbatim in chapel. It was humorous to everyone present the way he read it, but Jim saw to it that Virginia and the boys got everything she mentioned in her letter. It evidenced both his humor and his readiness to respond to the needs of students.[10]

"Mama" told that on another occasion, President Cope came over to the dorm to speak to her about a problem.

---

10   Virginia M. Davis, *Mama Come Get Me! An Anecdotal Portrait of Florida College* (Temple Terrace, FL: Florida College), 118-19.

Apparently, it had been reported that boys were leaving their undershorts in the shower room. His solution was to make a rule that the boys put their names inside their underwear so they could identify them with their owners. Of course, "Mama" wondered how she would ever enforce that "rule." She thought quickly and said, "Why don't I put a notice in the shower rooms to the effect that any articles of clothing left there will be discarded in the trash." "Well now," Jim responded, "that may be the solution to the whole thing right there. You do that and see how it works."[11] Another great decision made and acted upon!!!

---

11   Ibid., 86-87.

Chapter 20:

Florida Christian College to Florida College

After much discussion within the board, administration, faculty, alumni and friends, the Florida Christian College Board of Directors voted unanimously at its February 18, 1963, meeting to change the name of the college from Florida Christian College to Florida College. The long-awaited change was announced during the annual lecture week that followed the board meeting.

For several years informal discussions had questioned the use of the word *Christian* in the name of the College. Dropping the word *Christian* from the College's name might have caused concern among conservative thinking members of the churches had it not been pointed out by some prominent preachers, including Cope, that the word *Christian* is never used in the New Testament as an adjective. It is a noun and always refers to a believing person, not to a school, country, journal, or any humanly created and designed institution however committed it may be to following Christ and the New Testament. That being seen, constituents almost unanimously accepted the change with the caveat that the administration always remember to be faithful to the spiritual doctrines, convictions, and values of the Scriptures and its founders.

That a change was to be forthcoming had been considered by the board of directors and announced the year before at the February 1962 lectures. No formal decision on a new name was made at that time in order to give opportunity for feedback from the various college constituencies. To that end, President Cope sent out a "Request from Florida Christian College" for feedback including "comments, criticisms, and suggestions" from friends and supporters. It passed along three names presently being considered: Florida Suncoast College; Florida Coastal College; and Florida Westcoast College.[1]

To obtain as much feedback as possible, the President sent a copy to Cecil Willis, then editor of *Truth Magazine,* with the proposal that the "Request" be printed in that journal. Willis wrote back that he was glad to do so. He went on to say that he had harbored reservations about the use of the name *Christian* since his student days and suggested that simply the name "Florida College" might be considered.[2] Willis was not the only one offering that possibility. As it turned out, Florida College was approved by the board of directors as the school's name.

Under date of February 24, 1963, the Sunday *Tampa Tribune* carried the following story in which President Cope explained some aspects of the change:

Florida College is the new name of Florida Christian College, President James R. Cope announced during a progress report concluding the annual lecture series last week. "Cope said college officials intended to change the name of the junior college for

---

1   James R. Cope, "Request from Florida Christian College." Memo in Florida College library.

2   Cecil Willis, Letter to James R. Cope, February 1, 1963, Letter in Florida College library.

a number of years and that confirmation was received from Tallahassee recently.

Commenting on the name change, Cope said the 'Christian' in the name 'leave many people under the impression that the college is church supported and church controlled, whereas neither of these conclusions is accurate.'

Florida College was used frequently as the school's name during the formative years, he declared and letterheads originally carried that name before the school opened.

The junior college president said the primary reason for including 'Christian' in the school name probably had been to emphasize character training and 'a study of the Bible as a required part of the curriculum.'

I would like to make it clear that the dropping of the term 'Christian' from the name does not mean that we have in any sense altered our emphasis upon the Bible as the basis for character building.

"This institution is not a theological seminary but a standard junior college with the Bible offered as required study of those who attend."

On August 11, 1964, Jim was the guest speaker at the Civitan Club in downtown Tampa. At that time it was disputably the most influential gathering of the city's business leaders next to the Chamber of Commerce. He spoke eloquently of his view of the mission of Florida College:

We want a school where college students learn right and wrong while they learn about money and government, where manhood is identified because of its respect for womanhood, not for panty raids and telephone booth squeezes; where womanhood is identified with virtue and refinement, not by non-virgin clubs and back alley coarseness; where the sanctity of the home is upheld rather than scoffed at by infidel professors advocating free love; where Americanism is identified by respect for the Stars and Stripes rather than by compliments for the Hammer and Sickle; where the capitalistic system is presented with appreciation rather than apology, where prayer is an occasion of acknowledging God rather than its absence being an occasion of denying Him; and where the Bible, the Word of God, is believed rather than belittled. If such an institution is worth anything to this community and the world, we are glad that we have had a little part to building it. If it is not of value, we confess that we know of little in this world that has value.[3]

---

3   Jane Ward Britnell, "Rebuilding Years: 1961-1970," Margie H. Garrett, ed., *Making a Difference Florida College: The First Fifty Years* (Temple Terrace, FL: Florida College Press, 1996), 106.

Chapter 21:

Lectures and Notable Outside Speakers

The fifties and early sixties demonstrated Cope's willingness to face headon the issues and controversies of the day. That is illustrated in the fact that on the 1953 lecture program, John T. Lewis was given the topic, "The Christian's Relationship to Civil Government." Lewis held that while we must "meet our obligations to civil government," we are citizens of the heavenly kingdom of God." He took positions on both the "war question" and the "covering question" with which most brethren disagreed.[1] On that same program, G. K. Wallace was asked to address the subject, "Things That Divide Us," and James Walter Nichols spoke on the college lectureship defending the *Herald of Truth*. Both were advocates of church sponsored institutions.

L. R. Wilson had organized the first lectureship program, which was conducted in February 1947. James R. Cope later expanded the lectures from twelve to thirty-one speeches. That offered options in separate venues each hour during the day. Other colleges had used this same type of program to

---

1   Ottis L. Castleberry, *He Looked for a City: A Biography of John T. Lewis* (Fairmount, IN: Cogdill Foundation, 1980), 183.

offer special Bible studies to constituents, air brotherhood issues, and to publicize the college. That was particularly true at Freed-Hardeman, where Cope had taught. Notably also, Wilson's friend, B. C. Goodpasture, was a featured speaker on the first program. L. O. Sanderson, author of many hymns and at that time a leading voice in the church's music worship, led the singing. N. B. Hardeman spoke on the February 1949 lecture program, just prior to Cope's coming to Tampa, on the topic "The Church vs. Human Institutions." Annual lecture programs featured lively "open forums" through the 1950s and periodically thereafter. Current issues were vigorously discussed. Franklin T. Puckett moderated the discussions in those early days. Men holding opposing positions regarding the institutional questions and other issues were invited to speak on the lecture programs and were allowed to air their views.[2]

In 1951, James Cope used the lecture series to have an open discussion of the institutional issues. He chose Otis Gatewood to speak on behalf of the institutional position. He chose James W. Adams to speak in opposition to the sponsoring church and other church supported human institutions. James D. Bales was also given time to speak in favor of the institutions. Glowing reports of these sessions declared that both sides were heard graciously and without unbecoming speech.[3] In 1954, Cope and the Bible faculty focused the lectures on keeping the church undenominational. They further highlighted the ideal character of the church as seen in the New Testament

---

2   Ferrell Jenkins, "The Lectures," Margie H. Garrett, ed., *Making a Difference Florida College: The First Fifty Years* (Temple Terrace, FL: Florida College Press, 1996), 236-37.

3   Harrell, *The Churches of Christ in the Twentieth Century*, 285-86; Yater Tant, "Those Florida College Lectures," *Gospel Guardian*, March 15, 1951, p. 4.

while pointing out the trend away from non-denominational Christianity observed in institutionalism.

In 1953 and 1954, lecture outlines were made available to the audience. Speakers submitted their work ahead of time, and the college put them together using a mimeograph machine. In 1955, the speakers were encouraged to expand their outlines, and the enlarged copies were bound together off campus.

In 1974, brother Cope decided the lecture manuscripts should be permanently bound in hardback book form. They have been published by the college in that format since that time.

The hymn singings were important to the atmosphere of the lecture programs. Jack Frost, a fine song leader and the choral director at the college, led afternoon song services for several years. In the only times this biographer ever heard brother Cope lead singing, he directed the lecture crowds on the final nights in the first verse of *God Will Take Care of You* before the closing prayer. He often led it at the close of worship services in the local churches where he preached. At his funeral, it was the final song before his body was taken from the auditorium.

In March 1960, the annual lecture program was delayed three weeks while the college anticipated the completion of the new Hutchinson Auditorium. When that did not happen on time, plan B called for the day-time lecture venue to be moved to the outdoor amphitheater on the banks of the Hillsborough River. Twenty-four hours before several hundred people were expected to arrive on campus, a Florida storm came in. The winds blew, the rains poured, and the river flooded. The water rose to within four inches of the top of the railing at the riverside bank below the amphitheater. The administration was forced to move again. Activating plan C, day-time lectures that year were held at Sutton Hall in the main lobby, the dining hall, and the college library. Night lectures were moved up Busch Boulevard to Chamberlain High School as planned beforehand to accommodate the larger crowds.

The following year (1961), the lecture program was entitled "Ancient Faith and Modern Thought." It was designed to challenge atheism, intellectualism, communism, secularism, humanism, and materialism. Alongside Roy Cogdill, James Adams, Clinton Hamilton, Homer Hailey, and Ed Harrell, Jim Cope spoke on the virtues of supernaturalism as opposed to the many ways in which modernism chose a godless world for its belief system. Of course, modernism had invaded the protestant denominational world as well. The following year (1962), Cope spoke again, this time on the "Historical Development of Benevolence Societies." In 1965, he spoke on the "Moral Implications of America's Public Health Enemy #4" (#1 heart disease; #2 cancer; #3 venereal disease; #4 alcoholism).

In addition to lecture programs providing an opportunity for distant brethren to visit and get to know the college and particularly its Bible faculty, Jim Cope was dutifully aware that the college must maintain good relationships with the surrounding civic and social environment. That maintenance, of course, meant establishing connections within Temple Terrace's secular community. But it also meant acknowledgement of the value of the school in the larger city of Tampa, the state of Florida, and beyond.

On the front page of the January 25, 1965 issue of the Florida College student newspaper (*The Beak*) a list of Cope's involvement in community service over the past sixteen years included the following:

President of North Hillsborough Rotary Club.

Charter member of the Board of WEDU, Channel 3 television station.

Member of the Tampa chapter of the American Red Cross.

Member of the Tuberculosis (T.B.) Association.

Member of the Tampa Safety Council.

Member of Awake and Survive.

Member of Tampa Chamber of Commerce.

Member and Vice-President (later President, cc) of Temple Terrace Chamber of Commerce.

Member of the American Cancer Society

On September 15, 1955, President Cope introduced United States Senator George Smathers to the students, faculty, and guests from the city to speak in chapel. Senator Smathers was taken with the college and saw it as a fitting place for furthering his campaign effort. For the college, the occasion was the tenth opening ceremony of the school year.[4]

In January 1964, President Cope accepted a request from Tom Anderson to speak at Florida College. Anderson had heard of the college's conservative philosophy of education and patriotic views. Anderson was a social and economic conservative activist and popular speaker. He was also an "evangelical Christian" who unashamedly expressed his faith. He was chairman of the American party with political ambitions. He would later run for Vice-President of the United States in 1972, President in 1976, and Governor of

---

4   *Tampa Tribune* (September 11 and 16, 1955I).

Tennessee in 1978. His speeches were most notable for his catchy phrases and adamant opposition to communism. His newsletters were entitled *Straight Talk*. His book bore the name *Silence Is Not Golden. It Is Yellow.*

On March 10, 1966, Jim served as host to Paul Harvey on the Florida College campus. Harvey was the singularly most noted newscaster and commentator on national radio networks in his day. Millions stopped what they were doing at noon to listen to his broadcast. Harvey spoke in Hutchinson Auditorium to the student body in the afternoon and then in the evening to an open invitation audience at McKay Auditorium in downtown Tampa. The Florida College chorus opened the program that evening with patriotic songs prior to Harvey's speech. The evening was concluded after President Cope presented Harvey with an "In Freedom's Name Award."

In April 1966, Jim brought R.. J. Cordiner, retired president of both General Electric and Schick Corporation, to speak to the students. In chapel, Cordiner noted to students that most successful men in big industry came from small towns and small educational institutions rather than large Eastern cities and schools.

In 1971, Jim reached out to United States Senator Lawton Chiles. After learning about the school, Chiles chose to send his daughter Tandy to Florida College. The next April, Chiles spoke at the Spring Banquet. That same month, Cope awarded an honorary Doctor of Humane Letters degree to John C. Council, *Tampa Tribune* publisher and long-time Florida College supporter.

Building on the Good During Later Years of Presidency (1968-82)

Chapter 22

Jim's Brother, Quill

On January 20, 1981, Ronald Reagan took office in Washington, DC, as the fortieth President of the United States. He served eight years in that office until January 20, 1989. James R. Cope's college presidency had been continuing thirty-two of its thirty-three years when Reagan was inaugurated. The prior four terms of the United States Presidents were served by Richard Nixon (January 20, 1968-August 9, 1974), Gerald Ford (August 9, 1974-January 20, 1977), and Jimmy Carter (January 20, 1977-January 20, 1981). Each POTUS left office with baggage. Nixon resigned before completing his second term. Ford and Carter were thought to be good men but unsuccessful presidents. Cope's long tenure as president of Florida College would end successfully with his retirement at age sixty-five on June 30, 1982. It was not without challenges, but it was concluded with the admiration of almost everyone.

As seen earlier, Jim's brother, Quill Evan Cope, was about five years his senior. Jim almost revered his big brother and followed literally close behind him everywhere Quill went in their youth. Tom Cotton, a distant relative and close family friend spoke of Quill as the "serious boy." He read the Bible from cover to cover from youth and continued to do so with his wife and children. Jim, Tom said, was "mischievous," all the time doing something to get himself called down by his mother.[1] At one point in his early college career, Jim thought about quitting college. Upon hearing of it, Quill drove to Nashville to talk him out of it. Jim didn't quit.

Quill married his one and only love, Mary Kate Smith, on November 25, 1939, in White County, the Saturday following Thanksgiving. They went on to be parents of two sons, John Rogers Cope and James Carl Cope. At the time of Mary Kate's death on her 92nd birthday (August 15, 2012), she was grandmother to four boys and a girl and great-grandmother to two more boys. The Copes' loyalty to family was never questioned.

Well-known preacher Robert Jackson told Jim that he and then Tennessee governor Frank G. Clement (1953-59; 1963-67) once had a conversation about Quill. Clement told Jackson that the first thing that attracted him to Quill Cope was his name. Quill was the Tennessee State Commissioner of Education from 1952 to 1958, during most of Frank Clement's first set of two-year terms as governor. He also held that post for a time under Governor Buford Ellington. Before serving in Tennessee State government, Quill had been superintendent of schools in White County. Mary Kate was an elementary school teacher until she left the other children to raise her own. Even then, she supported Quill's position and was often seen in school classrooms and at official functions promoting educational projects she dearly loved. When Quill left the governor's cabinet, he became the fourth president of Middle Tennessee State University in Murfreesboro. He served the university continually for a decade from 1958 to 1968 leaving that office on September 1, 1968, just twenty-three days before his death on September 24, 1968.

---

1   Visit with Tom Cotton on July 16, 1984.

Quill and Mary Kate were both strong Christians from youth and deeply committed both to the Lord and to each other. While in Nashville, they were members of the Franklin Road church of Christ. It was said in those days that Franklin Road and Riverside Drive were the two among a hundred congregations identifying as churches of Christ in Davidson County that took an aggressive stand in opposition to institutionalism.

The first two or three Sundays after they moved from Nashville to Murfreesboro in 1958, Quill and Mary Kate attended worship across the street from the president's home where J. Leonard Jackson preached. In earlier days, Jackson had been sympathetic to conservative views and had even recommended to Dorris Rader that he attend Florida Christian College. But in 1958, Jackson had become a critic of the "antis." Jackson knew of Quill's conservatism, and Quill thought the sermons were personally directed at him. In any case, he was uncomfortable there and was in a quandary as to where they should regularly attend and place their membership.

At that time there seemed to be two immediately viable choices, but the preachers, Virgil Bradford and Richard Weaver, were locked in a "first-class fuss" in their bulletins. Quill was again uncomfortable because of his perception of the spirit and attitude the "fuss" portrayed. Quill and Mary Kate decided to attend worship at East Side with Bradford but to hold off placing membership. They were aware that a new conservative congregation in the University Heights area was being formed by some sound conservative brethren. As it turned out, both the president of the university and the brethren at University Heights desired to bring Harris Dark to Murfreesboro. He had been preaching at Franklin Road in

Nashville. Dark had a doctorate degree in mathematics. Quill offered him the chairmanship of the mathematics department. The brethren asked him to come preach for them. It was a perfect marriage. Quill helped the new congregation get established and taught a Sunday school class for them until his move to Knoxville.

Quill was a "visionary." MTSU grew tremendously during his tenure from a student body of 2000 to more than 6800. The campus underwent many changes. Among them was a new administrative building, which the State Board of Education named in his honor in 1965. He worked his vision that the university should have "a beautiful campus, an excellent instructional program, loyal alumni, and a friendly student body and faculty and be a people's college by meeting diverse area needs."[2]

When he announced that he was leaving MTSU, he revealed that he was taking a newly formed position at the University of Tennessee as head of the Department of Continuing and Higher Education." He said, "It has always been my intention to someday return to teaching." He was accepting "the UT post because of the challenges to improve public education in Tennessee through that position."[3]

According to Mary Hill Luna, Quill's sister, a year before leaving MTSU Quill said, "The laws are changing so much. If I can't live with my values and enforce them where I am supposed to be in charge, I'm just going to have to give it up." He told the family about a couple in the last quarter of

---

2   James C. Free, *"Sidelines Student Newspaper"* (September 28, 1968).

3   Keel Hunt, "Last Rites for Dr. Quill E. Cope, Former MTSU President, Held Today," *Daily News Journal,* (Murfreesboro, TN: September 28, 1968), 1-4.

their senior year found living together unwed on campus. The discipline committee of the university accepted what they were doing. Quill bemoaned, "I knew then I could not accept what was coming."

Quill announced his resignation from the presidency in June 1968. He would hold title to the office until September, when a new president took charge. He and Mary Kate planned, however, an extended vacation trip out west lasting the rest of the summer. Before leaving on their trip, they bought a house in Knoxville and moved their furniture and other belongings.

Upon settling into the house after the trip, Quill and Mary Kate decided to go out to the farm and get some flowers and bushes from the old home place to transplant around their new house in Knoxville. Tradition in the South still calls on folks when they move to take plants as remembrances of their family home and roots. Quill was just fifty-six, and he and Mary Kate planned to live in Knoxville for the next decade. The plants would be something to cherish from Quill's upbringing.

After supper on a Monday afternoon, Quill and Mary Kate had a pleasant evening together. They watched the Andy Griffith Show, laughed, and talked casually during the rest of the evening before turning in for the night. Quill's favorite name for Kate was Katie Mae. Mary Kate remembered his calling her Katie Mae that night while they were laughing at Andy, Opie, and Barney. She also said that while she was restless, she had noted how soundly he slept that night.

Tuesday morning, September 24, 1968, seemed to promise a normal day. Mary Kate was fixing breakfast when Quill came into the kitchen. He was up, showered, and fully dressed for work. He had already gone over his notes for his morning class at the University of Tennessee. He was well prepared. A newspaper was on his desk and he had written something on it to use in his lesson with his favorite ball-point pen.

As Mary Kate did not quite have his breakfast ready, Quill wandered back out of the kitchen and down the hall to the spare bedroom. The house was a three bedroom home, nice but modest for one accustomed to a university president's home. There were still boxes of packed up books in there and some other of Quill's things not yet permanently placed. The house had hardwood flooring. In that room on the floor near the closet was a four by six oval throw rug that was known to slide on the slick wood flooring.

Mary Kate was finishing breakfast when their son, James Carl, who was staying with them while going to school at the university, came into the kitchen and sat down at the table. Now that the food was ready, he began to eat. Mary Kate could not later remember if she had heard the shot or if she had set the skillet down at the exact time, but something caused her to say, "Jim, go see about your Daddy."

Of course, he went, and when Jim stepped into the bedroom, he found his father on the floor across the room. At first Jim thought his Dad had suffered a heart attack. Not taking time to move his Dad, Jim rushed to get a doctor who lived in the neighborhood. Still supposing it was a heart attack, the two of them rushed to Quill's aid. Their perception of what happened changed when they looked more closely at his now deceased body. The rug under him was moved over from its normal placement. Quill had been shot in the head.

The funeral director told the family that the bullet came from an upward trajectory and loosened his teeth. The coroner told James Carl that the bullet went in above his right eyebrow. The family assumed that Quill for some reason was going through his hunting and fishing equipment and the gun went off accidentally. Perhaps he slipped on that rug as he fell. The gun was thrown away from his body into the corner. Usually, one would expect the gun to be under the body or in the hand of the victim when purposely self-inflicted.[4]

The gun was a twenty-two caliber rifle his brother Jim had when they were boys at home. Quill had taken it while Jim was at Lipscomb and for some reason kept it. It was known to have a fast trigger. One time years ago, Jim was walking by the barn and tripped over some barbed wire fencing. The gun accidentally discharged. A friend in Murfreesboro later told Mary Hill and Mary Kate that he had borrowed that gun from Quill about six weeks earlier to shoot rabbits in his garden. He thought he had cleaned it out but he would always wonder if he had left a bullet in the chamber.

As they were packing to move, Quill and Mary Kate had talked about what to do with his three guns and live ammunition they had from earlier hunting trips. They certainly did not want anyone to get into them while they were away on the trip or absent from either house. They spoke of going out into the back yard and burying the bullets. Instead, they decided to wrap up the ammunition, put it in a box, heavily tape up the box, and put it in the garage under other packed belongings. They apparently left the guns in the house thinking they were not loaded. Days after Quill's death and funeral, Mary Kate found the box of ammo still sealed up in the garage.

When the coroner's report was issued, Quill's death was ruled a suicide. That was how his death was publicized in

---

4   Visit with Mary Hill Luna, July 15, 1984

the local news sources. The family was devastated. Some of them urged Mary Kate to challenge the coroner's report and seek the insurance money legally. She said that it was not worth it to have to endure all the effort, expense, publicity, and heartache. Nonetheless, knowing all the circumstances surrounding that time period in Quill's life and knowing Quill, they never believed that he willingly took his own life. His wife, sons, brother, and sister adamantly denied that he did that to himself or to them!

Chapter 23

Challenges at Florida College

For the most part, the administration of the college maintained stability through its first two decades (1949-68). With Cope at the helm, A. W. Dicus served as Dean from 1949 until the end of the 1955 school year, when he retired. It seemed the natural course of events to name Clinton David Hamilton dean of the college to succeed Dicus. Hamilton served in that role for thirteen years.

The challenge for the president came in the summer of 1968 with Hamilton's resignation. Cope and Hamilton had come to Florida Christian College together from Freed-Hardeman College in 1949. They had gone through the difficult times caused by the institutional controversy together, with Hamilton's being one of the president's closest advisors.

Hamilton had become quite well known around the state in educational circles. He had been the voice of the college to the Southern Association of Colleges and Universities in obtaining cherished regional accreditation, which Jim had promised when he first came to FCC. Hamilton had led the school academically and had succeeded in raising the credentials standing of the faculty significantly. In addition, he had been chosen to be the Executive Secretary of the

Florida Association of Colleges and Universities, a body where membership was composed of all college and university presidents, public and private, in the state.

Cope was not surprised when Hamilton was offered the Executive Vice-Presidency of Broward Community College in Fort Lauderdale, but in many ways he was disappointed when his friend accepted it. It was a new and prestigious challenge for Hamilton in those days. At that time in his life, Hamilton felt he needed that. Hamilton later said to this author that he believed at the time it would also provide him opportunities for a broader service in the kingdom of Christ. His colleague sincerely wished him well. Only God and Hamilton now know how he fully evaluated that decision at the end of his life.

President Cope met Dean Hamilton's departure with a major realignment of his administrative team. In 1968, he named Louis Garrett dean and dean of Students. He moved Bob F. Owen from the dean of students' position to become assistant to the president stationed in the business office. Roland Lewis was registrar, Harry Pickup, Jr., director of public relations, and Margie Garrett bursar. That arrangement continued until 1974 when Louis Garrett resigned. Roland Lewis became the dean of the faculty, C. G. "Colly" Caldwell was named dean of students, and H. E. "Buddy" Payne, Jr. became the registrar.

One of Jim's major concerns was maintaining Scriptural sound teaching by the Bible faculty. He felt the staff was in good hands while Homer Hailey was chairman, but Hailey returned to Arizona after the 1972 spring semester. From his new home in Tucson, he wrote his commentaries on Job,

Isaiah, Daniel, the Minor Prophets, the Gospel of John, and the book of Revelation.[1]

Melvin Curry had been hired in 1963 and became chair of the Bible department upon Hailey's departure. The president believed that it was best if new men be experienced preachers who knew firsthand how to deal with doctrinal challenges and local church issues. If the Bible staff was recognized among the brethren as faithful and experienced, it would bring confidence in the instruction the younger generation was receiving.

In 1969, Cope and Hailey brought Ferrell Jenkins and Roy Cogdill on board. At that time, brother Cogdill was preaching in the Par Avenue church in Orlando. He commuted two and three days per week over the two years he taught in the college. Jenkins had earned a Masters degree from Harding Graduate School in Memphis and had been preaching in Akron Ohio, and St. Louis Missouri. In 1971, they hired C. G. "Colly" Caldwell to teach Bible and religious history when Cogdill went back into other duties involving local preaching, meeting work, writing, and debating the issues identified with institutionalism. Jenkins was later named Chairman of the Bible department by President Caldwell when Melvin Curry left that position. Caldwell, who had been preaching for the Mooresville Pike church in Columbia, Tennessee, continued as a tenured Bible faculty member for forty-seven years (1971-2018). He would also serve as dean of the faculty (1981-1991) and president (1991-2009).

Jim was especially good at recruiting the right people for the right job. He was personally responsible for Hailey, Dicus,

---

1   David Edwin Harrell, *The Churches of Christ in the 20th Century: Homer Hailey's Personal Journey of Faith* (Tuscaloosa, AL: University of Alabama Press, 2000), 331-34.

and Hamilton coming in the early days of his administration. That talent was true not only for administrators. For example. Jim held a meeting at Huntington Beach, California, the second week of June, 1970. He stayed in the home of Don and Jean Canavello. That fall they moved to Temple Terrace and became the new dormitory supervisors in Wilson Hall.

Chapter 24:

Campus Growth

Jim Cope first learned of William F. Chatlos from Wilbur King, a member of the Florida College board of directors. King suggested that Cope reach out to Chatlos as a potential donor. Chatlos lived at Golden Beach, Florida, near Miami. He was a wealthy industrialist and philanthropist with a keen interest in education for future leadership. The president contacted Chatlos and was invited for a visit. Chatlos listened, asked questions, and the two immediately became friends. Although he would never set foot on the campus, Chatlos donated $250,000 toward the construction of the new Chatlos Administration and Library building. The building was dedicated on Sunday afternoon, March 31, 1968.

The ground floor library had been operating from the beginning of the spring semester, following a "Book Walk" in which students and faculty hand-carried boxes of books and other library materials in shelf-order from the old library to the new facility. They had come back two-days early from holiday visits home to do this task. They made 1735 trips moving more than 15,000 volumes.[1] The second-floor administrative offices, including Cope's, were not completed until the following year, 1969. Jim Cope

---

1   Garrett, 121, 144.

donated his personal library in 1992 to be housed in the Chatlos building.

Opening day of school 1971 brought the 25th anniversary of the College's operation. A celebration was certainly in order. President Cope invited every dignitary he knew of from the West Coast of Florida. Several came, along with many friends from among Christians in the area. Tampa mayor Dick Greco and Temple Terrace Mayor George Fee were among the guests. Both were seated with Mr. and Mrs. Lloyd Copeland. Copeland was a faithful Christian, a founder of the college, a member of the board of directors, and a member of the Tampa City Council. The special honoree was C. Ed Owings, first chairman of the board of directors and thought to be originator of the motto "Friend to Youth." At a special point in the program, Jim was to present a large red and white cake designed to recognize this special anniversary. He had asked Mr. Owings to receive the first piece on behalf of the board of directors. Jim cut a nice big slice, turned around quickly and landed the cake in Owings bare right hand which he had immediately put forth to avoid the cake's falling to the ground or flying onto the pants of his fine suit. Embarrassing for the president, but all had a good laugh.[2]

There were always the financial challenges that had faced the college from the beginning. "Our challenges could all be met if we had enough students and enough dollars," said President Cope. In large measure, no doubt, the stand of Jim Cope in opposition to institutionalism in the church and the college's open stand against immoral

---

2   Pictured in 1971 *Royal Palm*, p. 31.

trends in the nation's social fabric had forced the board of directors to take on indebtedness. The downturn in donors and students had to be reversed. That called for a successful campaign to retire the debt and secure the budget, which had reached above the three-quarter million dollars mark in 1972. Of course, Jim reached out to alumni, the school's National Council (a body of friends across the country), and the newly organized Century Club (all donors who would contribute $100 annually). He also went to the Tampa business community. Largely with the help of a number of sympathizers in the Tampa Bay area, the debt was retired within the following three years. The Tampa Merchant's Association also contributed scholarships to boost the recruitment of worthy students.[3]

For thirty years, the Temple Terrace municipal building housing city government offices had occupied a space right in the middle of the Florida College west campus. It was constructed in the classic Mediterranean style and was considered to be a historic building by community leaders. Along with Sutton Hall, it had originally been built for the Temple Terrace Golf and Country Club. After numerous attempts, on August 20, 1979, the College was finally able to purchase it for $145,000.

The building was originally constructed in 1925 for a night club and gambling casino, the very opposite kind of operation that would have been approved by the school. In the days prior to the Second World War, it was called El Morocco and faced the ninth hole of the golf course. President Cope was told that Babe Ruth tended bar there

---

3   Garrett, 136-37.

in the baseball off-season. After major renovations largely executed by alumni Andy and Lily DeKlerk, this structure became the student center and mail room.[4]

One of Jim's plans for the college involved a footbridge across the Hillsborough River to connect the main campus to athletic and intramural facilities on the east side of college property. Proposals were made and engineering drawings were completed when the decision was made by the United States Corps of Engineers to reject the college's request for permission to cross the river. The bridge was discussed by Cope's administration into the 1970s but was never built.

With the retirement of debt, Cope and the board began to make plans for further development of the college's academic offerings. The president sincerely desired to become a four-year college but inflation hit the nation's economy, enrollment did not increase as expected and the plans were stalled until 1991 when they were revived by the board and President Caldwell's administration.

---

4   Garrett, 169-172

Chapter 25:

The "Solving Family Problems" Meeting Series

In his gospel meetings, Jim generally preached sermons that would deliver the good news of salvation in Christ that led to baptism. He knew how to preach first principles and touch people's hearts so that they would come to Jesus. His efforts in that regard had motivated many to begin life in Christ from the time of his earliest gospel meetings. Even so, in every meeting he had given some time to discussions of current issues threatening the church. One of those threats to both the church itself and to individual Christians was problems in the family. He believed that at the core of family problems was a failure to develop proper attitudes toward Biblical authority and commitment to Christ.

Jim's series of lessons dealing with issues and problems in the family can be traced back to a message he delivered on Sunday morning, January 12, 1968. He was addressing the Brandon church, where he was regularly preaching when he was home. The lesson was entitled "Christ in Your Home and Mine." It precisely addressed the content and tone of his attitude toward what it means in general to live as a Christian in all relationships. Two months later on March 2, he presented that sermon again. He was preaching before

271

the Second and Walnut church in Paragould, Arkansas, in a gospel meeting. Back home, the next weekend (March 9), he preached at Brandon in the morning and that night delivered a lesson he entitled "The Christian and His Relationships." In his mind a plan was developing. Those two sermons became the foundational lessons in a meeting series of lessons he preached to congregations all over the country. He later called the series *Solving Family Problems*. He published his outlines in a forty-two page booklet.[1]

Having decided what he thought was really needed in lessons on the home, Cope prepared seven lessons:

Christ the Standard in all Relationships (or The Christian's Authority in all Relationships)

What is Happening to Our Families

Christ in the Home (or Christ in Your Home and Mine)

Parental Responsibilities

Discipline in the Family

How Shall a Christian Choose Recreation

Problems of Young Christians (or A Young Christian's Faith in a Faithless World)

The theme of each lesson was the involvement of Christ in all aspects of the home. Believe it or not, Jim delivered some or all of these lessons to 249 churches between January 1968 and November 1987. That included thirty-two times in 1971;

---

1   Cope, James R. *Solving Family Problems* (Temple Terrace, FL: privately published and copyrighted 1971, edited 1976). This booklet is reproduced in the appendix of this book.

fifty-one times in 1972; forty-five times in 1973; and twenty-five times in 1974.

Jim was fit to be tied when he missed an appointment to present his series in Flagstaff, Arizona, on July 13, 1970. It was the first time in thirty-five years that he had missed a commitment to preach. His plane had engine trouble in Phoenix. He opened 1975 with a hernia operation on January 2, but he was again on the road with the Timberland Drive church in Lufkin, Texas, preaching his family series January 12-15. The response to this series of lessons was overwhelming. It became the hallmark of his later years of preaching.[2] To attempt a recital of the experiences Jim had in all these congregations would require a volume larger than this.

Such a commitment of time, however, brought with it its own issues. Especially over the four year period from 1971-74, Jim was away from the college and his wife and son virtually every week or weekend. Butch was still at home. Jim had recently performed the marriage ceremonies of his two daughters in Hutchinson Auditorium on the campus of Florida College. Connie wed James Michael Benson on December 20, 1968, and Cathy married John E. Weaver on December 19, 1969. He married James R. Cope, Jr. to Jennie Lynn Barrow whose family lived in Temple Terrace, on June 24, 1976. Georgia Deane was a very special first lady and mother to their three children. She was totally committed to Jim's preaching. She saw herself as having an important role to play in his work, taking care of his home. Jim agonized over

---

2   A listing of the dates, locations, and local preachers where Cope presented the "Solving Family Problems" series is contained in an appendix to this biography. Interestingly, it provides identification of where many well-known local preachers were working when Cope visited.

being away from her and from their son Butch at that time in his son's growth to manhood.

Through the period of time around 1971-74, Jim was continuing to serve as the college president while having to delegate school business affairs, student and faculty issues, campus activities, and administrative oversight and coordination to other administrators. Had he not had a sympathetic board of directors and a team of fellow administrators including Homer Hailey, Bob Owen, Louis and Margie Garrett, Roland Lewis, and Harry Pickup, Jr., it would have been impossible. Some criticized him for being out of the office so much, but he responded that the opportunities were too important to turn away from them. He was doing the Lord's work. He argued also that he was taking advantage of the travel opportunities to recruit students and raise dollars for the college in every city to which he travelled. He was very careful, however, to avoid any direct mixing of his pulpit work and his school work.

In 1972, Jim joined Roy E. Cogdill and Cecil Willis on a tour to the Bible lands. He had always wanted to go. On October 8, Jim preached to the group on board a ship off the coast of Rhodes. His sermon was "God's Answer to Honest Doubt." The following Sunday, Cecil Willis preached, and Jim led the prayer beside the Sea of Galilee near Capernaum. Interestingly, the Cypriot cruise ship *Sounion* on which Jim had preached, sank March 4, 1973 in Beirut harbor, Lebanon just five months after his trip. An explosion in the engine room tore a hole in the ship shortly before it was to leave for Haifa, Israel, with 250 American passengers on board.[3]

---

3   New York Times, www.nytimes.com <1973/03/05 > archives.

Jim's one known venture into hymn writing developed from a poem he wrote sometime around 1970. On one of his trips to the West Coast to deliver the family series in 1972 (June 18-22), Cope stayed in the home of R. J. and Pauline Stevens at San Bernardino, California. Jim wanted R. J. to help him set his poem to music. He had deliberately held back trying to develop the music in anticipation of that meeting. Stevens was well-known for his interest in helping churches with their worship in songs and for dozens of hymns he had written. He was also called upon by Cope to direct the singing during the Florida College lectures for many years. Exposure in doing that led numerous churches to have R.J. direct singing during their gospel meetings and annual lecture programs. R.J.'s father, M. Roy Stevens, was a well-known preacher who had conducted training sessions in song leading in churches. R. J. had studied music at Abilene Christian College, the University of Houston, and Oklahoma A&M College (now Oklahoma State University). He went on to establish the R. J. Stevens Singing School, which continues to this writing under the leadership of his son, Tim, and his associates Dane Shepard and John Kilgore. R. J. also helped compile and edit *Hymns for Worship*, a widely used hymnal in churches of Christ. During that week, Jim and R. J. spent hours working on the project. When Jim left San Bernardino, he took with him the hymn "King Most High." It has become a regularly used spiritual song in many churches. Jim's words and R. J.'s music were copyrighted later in 1986:[4]

From the earth, from the sky, breaks forth the joyful cry, "Our
Lord is King most high!"

Crucified, He revived, that's why He's King most high.

---

4   Related to the author by Tim Stevens, June 18, 2024.

Humble birth, held no worth til angel voice sang forth, 'A King is born this day!

Then the earth was aware its hope had come to stay.

Words He gave me to say, by works He led the way--this Lord and King to be.

Then alone, blood atoned, His life He gave for me.

Darkest pow'r He overcame, life for me He regained; a Prophet ne'er to die;

Priest for e'er on His throne; Lord, God, my King most high.

Chorus: My Lord is great and good and He will hear my cry;

He'll ever live and ever reign, my Lord and King most high.

Chapter 26:

Secular Speeches

While Jim's public speaking was overwhelmingly Biblically based or scholastically focused on behalf of the college, the times in which he lived and the mission of the school brought him to speak often in secular situations. In many of those venues, he encouraged patriotism as citizens of America. One special occasion was the Civitan Convention in Nashville, TN, on May 25, 1973. His speech was entitled "Which Way America?" In these later years of his presidency, he began the practice of reciting the Pledge of Allegiance each day in chapel as a kind of dismissal ritual. That became a tradition in the culture of the institution. He despised the brazenness of those who justified burning our American flag and promoted principles of socialism and communism.

Jim saw the mission of Florida College to include providing an environment where students would be educated against communism, socialism, and hedonism. He was dedicated to the school's supporting the tenets of the founding fathers of America as well as those of the founders of Florida College. Further, he was truly concerned about the influences on young people in his times. He saw Florida College as a refuge to which parents of young Christians could send their children. In the seventies, when the so-called "love children" rallied for world peace while actively rebelling against authority, manners, and morals, Jim stood up against "free love," unwholesome rock music, immodest dress, and inappropriate behavior. In a speech to students and parents and friends of the College, he said:

> What does this tear-it-down crowd have to offer instead of the "Establishment?" Exactly nothing. They would have you believe that the 'Establishment' is blind—totally blind—to burning problems of civil rights and economic opportunities and to youth problems such as the draft and the Vietnam war. They would convince you that every problem has a simple solution and that solution is revolution through agitation, confusion, and violence. They would burn down the house to remove the cobwebs.[1]

Traditionally, the President spoke at the opening of each school year. He often used that platform to remind the students of their moral and civic responsibilities. Jim also promoted those values in a paper he occasionally sent to alumni and friends over the country. He called the paper "Shake Friend." In his speech at the opening of the 1975 school term and later copied in "Shake Friend," he said:

> I hope and pray that this year's student body may catch the spirit of 1776 by experiencing a new birth of appreciation for the America our founding fathers dreamed about. I also pray that at the same time you will drink deeply of the spirit of 1946 which marked the beginning of the first session and the first generation of Florida College. If the spirit of '76 and '46 can be rekindled and kept meaningful, our nation and this school will survive and become everything the founding fathers of both envisioned for their respective offspring. To this end we, to whom the torch has been passed, pledge "our lives, our fortunes, and our sacred honor."[2]

---

1   Garrett, 123-124
2   Garrett. 154.

Jim addressed the student body at the close of the 1967-68 year with a parable:

> In a strange town you inquire concerning a road which, you have been told, will take you to your destination. A would-be helper responds, "Take the second street to the left and the third to the right. Pass the school on the corner, take the second one-way going south to the fourth street where you will see a traffic light and just beyond this one turn left, and you are on the road you want." As you move ahead, hopeless confusion fills your mind. You are lost. How different had that person said, "Follow me. I will take you where you would go." Too many times a college environment that should lend personal confidence and stability to inquiring youth lends only guides who need guidance; questioning minds are fed a babel of doubt and disorder. How different at Florida College!"[3]

---

3   *Royal Palm* – 1968, p. 39

Chapter 27:

The College's Right to Exist and Teach the Bible

It seemed personally ironic and terribly frustrating to James R. Cope that after his long history of declaring the distinction between the school and the church and declining contributions from congregations, he should now have to defend the school from the charge of doing the work of the church. He said, "The contention that certain kinds of human institutions displace a local church is not new; but, so far as I know, since almost 20 years ago Florida College Inc., has not been a target until within the last few months."[1]

Cope was right. Some brethren had opposed colleges operated by Christians almost from the beginning of New Testament Christians in America. When the opposition claimed that such organizations were unscriptural, it was most often on grounds that the schools were usurping the mission of the church. The assertion was that by implementing organization other than the local church to teach the Bible, they act without authority and denigrate the church. The claim was

---

1   James R. Cope, "A Review of 'Bible Departments and Colleges,"Authored by Ralph Williams and published by Red Bluff church of Christ, Pasadena, Texas" (Marion, IN: *Truth Magazine*, September 16, 1971), XV, 44, p. 7.

that collectively teaching the Bible was solely the prerogative of the church and that creating any other organization to teach the Bible or prepare preachers is unscriptural.

Prior to the Civil War, several influencers in what has been called the Restoration Movement established colleges in which the Bible was taught as an essential element in the curriculum. Walter Scott served one year as president and professor in newly formed Bacon College at Georgetown, Kentucky, in 1836. Alexander Campbell founded Bethany (West Virginia) College in 1840. Tolbert Fanning established Franklin (Tennessee) College in 1844. In 1849, a group of twenty-seven "stock holders" organized Burritt College in Spencer, Tennessee. They chose twelve men to be trustees. In its second year of operation, they selected W. D. Carnes, destined to be James R. Cope's great-great-grandfather, to be its president. These schools all had either to close or suspend operation during the Civil War (1861-65). Most brethren welcomed them back when the conflict ended. In those days, they gave little consideration to their right to exist while receiving funding from both churches and private individuals.[2]

The introduction of controversy over the organization of the American Christian Missionary Society changed the landscape in the late 1840s. The attention of brethren was drawn to the question of congregational financial support of separate institutions claiming to do the work of the church. That included evangelistic, benevolent, and educational institutions. Alexander Campbell had been a leader in the Baptist "anti-mission" movement during the 1820s. He had argued that there is no authorization in the New Testament

---

2   M. Norvel Young, *A History of Colleges Established and Operated by Members of Churches of Christ* (Kansas City MO: The Old Paths Book Club, 1949), 11-81.

for churches to relegate their evangelism responsibilities to a separate institution. Now having made an aboutface, he was the first president of the American Christian Missionary Society, commonly called the ACMS.

In 1856, Benjamin Franklin (not the American patriot) established a monthly periodical which he entitled the *American Christian Review*.[3] Largely because of the developing controversy over the issionary Society, Franklin increased the frequency of publication in 1858, and the paper found its way into anxiously awaiting homes every week. At first Franklin had an open mind concerning the society, but by late 1866, he firmly opposed it. In the South, David Lipscomb and Tolbert Fanning revived the *Gospel Advocate* after the Civil War. Its editors and principal writers opposed the society. This set the stage for the publication of the *Christian Standard* in Cincinnati. Isaac Errett, its editor, vigorously defended the society.[4] The debate was on, and brethren everywhere made what constitutes Bible authority and church work/organization the hot topics of current Bible study.

During the next quarter century, the colleges continued to operate virtually unopposed. Bethany, Franklin, and Burritt were not particularly vulnerable. The periodicals, the *Millennial Harbinger, American Christian Review, Christian Standard,* and *Gospel Advocate* were almost universally unquestioned as to the colleges' right to exist. Representative

3   Joseph Franklin and J. A. Headington, *The Life and Times of Benjamin Franklin* (St. Louis, MO: John Burns Publisher, 1879), reproduced and distributed by Old Paths Book Club, 1956), 267ff.

4   Marshall E Patton, "Concerns About Non-Church Sponsored Separate Organizations (Schools and Papers)" in Melvin D. Curry, editor, *Their Works Do Follow Them* (Temple Terrace, FL: Florida College Bookstore, 1982), 76-77.

of the attitude of most brethren was Alexander Campbell's statement in an article entitled "The Bible Colleges," appearing in the *Millennial Harbinger*:

> Colleges are not instituted especially for the benefit of qualifying men for preaching the gospel. Sacred history and the Bible in colleges as a text book, with regular systematic lectures thereon, are just as necessary to properly educate school teachers, lawyers, doctors of medicine, farmers, merchants, mechanics, etc., as to educate preachers.... Colleges, as far as religion is concerned, must be a blight to any community, if irreligious, if conducted without religion and the Bible.[5]

When the Nashville Bible School opened in 1891, Isaac Errett effectively charged David Lipscomb with inconsistency. Errett claimed that the Missionary Society was no more unscriptural than the college. Of course, he was editing a periodical that was doing the same thing on paper, teaching the Bible, that the college was doing in the classroom. Lipscomb responded that the school was simply doing what every Christian should do in teaching the Bible and was not usurping any function of the church.[6] According to Lipscomb, it was not a theological seminary. It was simply meeting every Christian's responsibility to teach God's word at all times in any occupational pursuit. It was Christians operating a business rather than the church operating and/or financially supporting a mission society.

Coming into the twentieth century, the leading opponent of colleges operated by brethren was Daniel Sommer.[7] He

---

5   Alexander Campbell, "The Bible Colleges," Millennial Harbinger, Third Series, Vol. VII, No. 9 (September, 1850), 511.

6   David Lipscomb, "Missionary Societies," Gospel Advocate, Vol. XXXIII, No. 5, (Feb. 4, 1891) 70.

7   William E. Wallace, *Daniel Sommer 1850-1940, a Biography*

had long opposed missionary societies and instrumental music, and he argued that the colleges had no more Biblical authority than either of those. Sommer had purchased Ben Franklin's *American Christian Review* periodical and used it to write his views on a number of subjects. That paper morphed into Sommer's Octographic Review and later once again The *American Christian Review*.[8]

Some of Sommer's positions were considered by many brethren to be extreme and on some he even did an aboutface in later years.[9] He opposed Bible class literature, calling it "lesson leaves of human origin." He opposed "located" or "full-time" preachers. He called them "preacher pastors" and referred to their work as "evangelistic oversight." In the place of the "pastor system," Sommer advocated what was called "mutual edification" through Bible readings rather than sermons from "professional preachers." He discovered that this practice did not edify but provided the opportunity for less informed novice brethren to take advantage of the circumstances to ineffectively preach.[10] Because of these views, Sommer lost a measure of credibility, and the Christians and churches following his lead were identified as "Sommerites."

Sommer joined with conservative brethren who opposed colleges operated by the brethren receiving financial support

---

(privately published, 1969).

8   Matthew C. Morrison, *Like a Lion: Daniel Sommer's Seventy Years of Preaching* (Murfreesboro, TN: DeHoff Publications, 1975), 149-59.

9   Earl E. Robertson, "Daniel Sommer, Thunder on the Right," in Melvin Curry, Ed., *They Being Dead Yet Speak* (Temple Terrace, FL: Florida College Bookstore, 1981) 220-40.

10   Cecil Willis, "The Saga of Daniel Sommer, II", Marion, IN: *Truth Magazine*, (October 1, 1970, XIV; 46), 3-5).

from church treasuries. But he also opposed colleges' including the Bible in their curricula receiving individual contributions from Christians. He argued that sending funds to a "church school" was parallel to supporting a missionary society. To Sommer, such contributions were also a misappropriation of the Lord's money. If a Christian was giving according to his prosperity into the church's first-day-of-the-week collections, he would not have the means to give to a school. Such, of course, was another of Sommer's extreme inconsistences. Brethren, for the most part, were forced to recognize that Sommer willingly took contributions from individuals in support of his paper.

It would not be inappropriate to note that Jim Cope studied carefully Sommer's arguments on all these issues. Sommer's arguments did have an influence upon Jim's conclusion that colleges should not take contributions from church treasuries. Cope, however, disagreed with Sommer's view concerning non-church-supported colleges.

Over the next half-century, the issue of non-church-supported entities' (schools, papers, and other collective religiously motivated enterprises) teaching the Bible was sometimes discussed but infrequently debated. Sommer debated B. F. Rhodes and had a written discussion with J. N. Armstrong in 1907. Leroy Garrett and Carl Ketcherside also publicly opposed the colleges. Ketcherside debated G. K. Wallace in 1952, and Garrett debated Bill Humble in 1954. There were other opponents, but for the most part, they were a small minority.

On March 7, 1971, the bulletin of the Red Bluff church in Pasadena, Texas, carried a ten-page article written by the local preacher, Ralph Williams. It was entitled "Bible Departments and Colleges." In this article, Williams argued that the "N.T.

recognizes but ONE Divinely ordained arrangement for God's people 'collectively' to carry on Gospel edification work." He went on to say that "no question was being raised about the right of brethren to enter the field of higher education which is purely secular as a business enterprise. Certainly brethren have the freedom to join their talents, form corporations and engage in any kind of business pursuits that are legal and ethical." "The question rather," he continued, "is WHERE is the Scriptural right to collectively organize, pool talents and money, in order to teach the Word."[11]

Upon seeing the article, Cope decided to respond. He said, "I replied to the Red Bluff bulletin because I believed the time had come for me to defend the right of Florida College to exist as chartered."[12] Not knowing the extent of Red Bluff's large mailing list that included numerous preachers and brethren outside the Red Bluff church, Jim questioned how to distribute his response. He discussed his problem with Cecil Willis, and the editor agreed to publish it in *Truth Magazine*. It would, however, be lengthy and costly. As it turned out, the entire exchange (Williams' original article was included) required thirty-two pages of print. To avoid any collusion between the Red Bluff church and/or Florida College, Jim went to an unnamed donor who paid for the printing and mailing of Jim's part of the additional cost to *Truth Magazine*. The Red Bluff elders financed the reprint of William's article in the magazine.[13]

In his response, Jim Cope affirmed that Florida College

---

11   "A Review of 'Bible Departments and Colleges,' Published by Red Bluff Church of Christ, Pasadena, Texas." Copied in *Truth Magazine* (Marion, IN: September 16, 1971), XV, 44, 5-6.

12   Op cit., 33.

13   Ibid., 33.

is a human institution, a business enterprise offering a service to be purchased. He denied that it does any work peculiar to any local church. He said, "If Florida College displaced any local church, it would be wrong in whatever area it deprived a local church of its uniqueness in God's plan. Florida College, Inc., is not and cannot displace a local church of Christ for its conditions of membership and its purposes and actions differ from those of a local church!"[14]

Cope further affirmed that the right to teach the Bible and/or worship while engaged in business activity is inherently present in the conduct of Christians in any individual or collective occupational pursuit of life. He said,

> I want to know: how can a collectivity of Christians enter into any 'secular business enterprise' without being honor bound to purpose, work, and pray that the ultimate result of their combined business efforts may be the spread of the word of God? How can such a group of men demand honesty, purity of speech, sobriety, and chastity of its employees without teaching God's word to their employees? Are we now being told that we should demand these character qualities of employees without telling them that such character and conduct are demanded by God in His word? When a cooperative of Christians tells its employees or customers that they must not lie, steal, use profanity or get drunk on its premises, if this company is not teaching God's word, whose word is it teaching? Does it do wrong by telling them to do right?"[15]

Of course, Williams and Cope both dealt with many of the same arguments articulated in past decades.

In 1974, Cecil Willis signed a proposition affirming: "It

---

14   Ibid., 13.
15   Ibid., 12.

is scriptural for individual Christians to organize, operate, financially support by contributions, and to utilize liberal arts educational enterprises, in which the Bible is taught as a regular part of the curriculum (as is practiced by Florida College)." Jesse G. Jenkins, a highly respected Texas preacher, signed in opposition to the proposition. The debate on that topic took place in the Pasadena Texas High School auditorium September 23-24. On September 26-27, Jenkins affirmed, "It is unscriptural for brethren to form a collectivity that solicits contributions from individual Christians, and that employs and oversees men in the work of teaching the Bible (as is practiced by Florida College)." James W. Adams was Willis' moderator and Robert Craig assisted Jenkins.[16] Jim Cope attended two nights of this discussion.

Willis opened the discussion by asking a series of questions.

> Number one, Could one attend North Texas State University and take Bible classes which are offered there? Number Two, Is it wrong to study Bible taught by a Christian at Florida College but right to study the Bible taught by a denominationalist at North Texas State University? Number three, Could one study Bible History as a course in ancient history? Number four, What portions of the Bible can anyone teach without unintentionally or incidentally be training a preacher? Number five, Could one scripturally take the seventeen Bible courses offered at North Texas State University but then for it to be unscriptural to take the same courses at Florida College.[17]

Jenkins rejoined with five questions of his own.

> Number One: What would Florida College have to start doing

---

16   The Willis-Jenkins Debate (Marion, IN: Cogdill Foundation, 1976), 3-4.
17   Ibid., 31

through its Bible department that it is not already doing, to be doing a work of the church or to be a rival to the church?"

Number Two: What basic difference is there between teaching the Bible and preaching the gospel?

Number Three: What collectivity has God specified in and through which saints are to collectively support the teaching of the word?

Number Four: Is there not an inherent contradiction in the idea of secular support of Bible teachers.

Number Five: If it is right for the college to receive contributions from individual Christians to support and oversee men to teach the Bible, to train young men in Bible instruction to equip them to preach the gospel of Christ, to hold daily worship services and hold an annual gospel lectureship program, would it also be right for the college to have a Sunday assembly in which the Lord's Supper is served[18]

In a 1975 written debate in *Searching the Scriptures*, Marshall Patton affirmed and Darwin Chandler denied the right of Christians to "collectively teach God's word through service organizations such as Florida College."[19] Patton argued, as Cope had done, that the college is a business selling services. That fact distinguishes them from the Lord's church. "If the church," he said, "were to so function, it would be wrong!" He went on to affirm that the college is in a "different category" as an organization. It does not purport to do the work assigned to the church, supplant the church, or in any way reflect upon the all-sufficiency of the church.[20]

---

18   Ibid., 31.

19   Patton-Chandler Debate (*Searching the Scriptures*, August 1975, Vol. 16, Nos. 8-10).

20   Ibid., 345.

Chapter 28:

Local Church Work

When at home, Jim most always had a standing appointment to preach in one of the local congregations. He and a few others who had come to work at the college helped to establish the Temple Terrace congregation shortly after coming to Florida in 1949. In those days, he was also holding gospel meetings across the country almost every week. In January of 1957, Jim agreed to work with the Disston Avenue church in St. Petersburg on Sundays when he was home. That continued until the fall of 1966.

As already seen, Jim was always interested in establishing new congregations in areas where brethren were not meeting. At 8:45 on the morning of June 15, 1962, thirty-nine persons (about half adults) met in the Cross Bayou section of Pinellas County. Jim's sermon was titled "Why Are We Here?" It was apparent that they were there for the first service of a new congregation. Jim was back at Disston at 11:00 a.m. and 6:00 p.m. He preached a fourth time that day at Cross Bayou at 7:30 p.m. The heavy schedule of preaching four times on Sunday continued through April 1963 when Jim turned the Cross Bayou work over to others and continued preaching at Disston Avenue. During this time, Georgia Deane and the children worshipped with the Temple Terrace church.

In the fall of 1965, the brethren at Brandon asked Jim to come and preach for them. He was at Brandon from November 1965 to June 1974, at which time the church contracted with a full-time man and Jim left the work. He went to Antioch, where he preached from June 1974 to May 1982. Then he went to the Forest Hills church in Tampa and worked there until December 1987.

Jim never forgot the need for a congregation to serve retired Christians in the Sun Center area south of Brandon/ Riverview. He had considered it while observing those people living in the center having to drive to Brandon or Palmetto for services. So he talked to Earl Kimbrough, who was then preaching at Brandon. They offered worship and soon had a regular group meeting together. They identified it as the East Bay church of Christ. Cope and Kimbrough shared preaching duties until Jim's retirement from preaching. In the late 1990s a building was built on a lot facing U. S. Highway 301, and the congregation continued to flourish.[1]

---

1   A discussion with Richard Conger, longtime member at East Bay church, August 3, 2024.

Chapter 29:

Heart Surgery

In Jim's preaching records, he provided the sequence leading to his heart surgery. Early Friday morning, February 29, 1980, during a gospel meeting in Flagstaff, Arizona, Jim was awakened with severe heart pain. The condition continued until he decided to go to the emergency room at the nearest hospital. He was admitted for observation about 4:30 in the afternoon. He immediately called to cancel his part in the evening service. Later he telephoned brethren in Winslow, Arizona where he was to begin his series on the home on Sunday. After tests and some medication relieved the pain, he insisted on being discharged so that he could catch the 11 a.m. flight to Tampa on Saturday, March 1. He flew to Tampa, where a very worried Georgia Deane met him at the airport and took him home. She had already called their physician and fellow Christian, Dr. Leon Wayne Mitchell, who promised he would stand by if needed over the weekend. If no serious heart incident occured, Dr. Mitchell would meet with Jim at 11:30 a.m. on Monday morning, March 3. At that time Jim's pain had eased, and neither he nor Dr. Mitchell considered it to be immediately life threatening. Dr. Mitchell arranged for a heart scan and catheterization at Tampa General Hospital on Wednesday, March 5.

That morning (March 5), Jim dictated a letter to Colly Caldwell. He said,

I am just back from meetings in California and Arizona, ran into some chest complications during exceedingly cold weather and at high altitude (7800 feet in Flagstaff), and decided that I would seek medical advice. I had several checks and my angina is acting up a little bit. I am going in this afternoon at the suggestion of Dr. Mitchell for a heart scan. Nothing enormous, but he feels it is a precautionary measure which in the years I have had this ticker problem we have not done. I think he has thought about it a time or two before but thinks now I should do it. After all, I am ten or twelve years this side of my original angina introduction. I would just as soon you wouldn't tell anybody this at the present except Lynda. You know how easy it is for everybody to have you dead with a heart attack while you are still going.

The scan was taken, and the next afternoon (March 6) Jim was told it reflected the urgent need for open heart surgery. From his hospital bed he dictated to Mary Cannon, his office assistant, an addendum to his yet to be signed letter to Colly.

After my scan it wasn't long till I learned that my situation is much worse than I had thought though Dr. Mitchell I think felt it could be this way. By the time you have received this letter I will either be through the surgery for a bypass—at this point I don't know whether it is double or triple, probably the latter—or else will be on the verge of the operation. I have not yet talked with the surgeon, Dr. Pupello, who is said to be the best in the whole area and the one that the whole staff here and Dr. Mitchell recommends, but I am certain that he will get to it as soon as he can. I don't think it would be on Saturday or Sunday but could be early tomorrow. I will have Georgia Deane or Mary to call you as soon as they know what the situation is .... I believe that everything will work out for the best here, that I will have a successful operation and that I may be spared for many more years to do the work that I feel so direly needs to be done in my latter years.[1]

The surgery took place on Tuesday, March 11, beginning at 7:30 a.m. It required a triple bypass. Georgia Deane called the Caldwells in Nashville that evening with the news that the surgery had gone well and that Jim was alert and articulate in the intensive care heart unit of Tampa General Hospital. The following morning (March 12) Caldwell penned the following:

Dear Jim, We were all so glad to hear last night that you had come through the surgery successfully and that everything looked as good as could be expected at this stage. We have hardly thought of anything else since we heard about the whole problem. In his prayer Monday night at the table, Chuck added the phrase, "... and help brother Cope to be safe," so you can know we were all thinking about you and praying for you.

Colly closed his letter to Jim, "Keep everything together and don't sneeze."

Jim left the hospital ten days later. He went home on March 21. He received an unbelievable deluge of cards, letters, calls and various other communications from all over the country as word of his surgery spread. He did not preach for five Sundays, March 9 through April 6. He made up for it, however, by holding thirteen gospel meetings between May 26 and November 23.[2]

---

1   James R. Cope letter to C. G. "Colly" Caldwell, March 5-6, 1980.

2   The meetings were at Somerset KY (May 26-30); Woodbury

After the Caldwells returned from Nashville, early one morning on his regular walk before daylight, Jim passed the Caldwells' house on Mission Hills. Colly was again serving as dean of students, a position often tested by students in any of the institutions of higher learning. Late the night before a group of boys had left the dorm with rolls of toilet paper that they proceeded to spread over the Caldwell's lawn, bushes, and up into their trees. Jim was a mischievous boy himself in more youthful days and had done more than tee-peed a dean's yard. So after a good laugh, he proceeded to clean up the yard. No one in the house was aware of the mess or of Jim's cleaning it up until days later when Jim told Colly and Lynda they owed him one.

TN (June 1-6); Kingston OH (June 8-12); Benton IL (July 11-16); Celina TN (July 17-20); Jasper AL (August 3-7); Bradley AR (August 8-10); Skyview in Pinellas Park FL (September 14); Cullman AL (September 28-October 3); Dickson TN (October 20-24); Forest Hills in Tampa FL (November 9-14); Purcell OK (November 16-18); and Greenville TX (November 20-23).

Section Nine

Building on the Good After Florida College (1982-99)

Chapter 30:

Retirement

Jim retired exactly thirty three years to the day from taking on the presidency of the college. He was now sixty-five years of age. He was said to have been the youngest college president in the nation at age thirty-two, when he took office in 1949. To mark his service to the community and recognize his retirement, the Temple Terrace Chamber of Commerce honored him with a dinner on October 21, 1981. It was attended by almost every mayor, council member, and dignitary in the city over the past thirty years who were still alive. Jim had served as both president of the Chamber of Commerce and the Tampa North Rotary Club.[1]

The largest retirement events at the college took place during the annual lecture program in January 1982. Approximately fifteen hundred alumni and friends attended. Many gospel preachers and fellow Christians who had known Jim personally through the years were there. The board of directors sponsored a special evening of "Tribute to James R. Cope" immediately following the Tuesday night lecture and a reception Wednesday afternoon on his birthday. Jim gave the lectureship address on the last evening of the lectures. Caldwell introduced him and reminded the large audience of how Jim

---

1   Garrett, 172-73.

had defended his conscience before the board in 1955 and set the course of the school in refusing to accept funding from churches. Cope spoke that night about the church in the New Testament from a sound spiritual perspective. The title of his message was "Heritage, Horizons, and Destiny." Following his lecture, the college chorus presented a special tribute in song to Mr. and Mrs. Cope.

At the close of the semester as the final school year of his presidency concluded, the faculty and staff gathered in Sutton Hall's dining room for a retirement dinner honoring the Cope family. His children and grandchildren were present, along with the official college family including the board of directors. Everyone was deeply moved as they contemplated the end of an era.

Chapter 31:

After Florida College Activity

The last two decades of the twentieth century are often remembered as the "Yuppie days." The first of those decades is often identified as the "Reagan Years." In general, America was basking in prosperity. Young and middle-aged men gorged themselves with electronic consumer products in materialistic extravagancies to the point of obsession with the latest fads. Women openly demonstrated for equal wages in the workplace and for positions in jobs formerly held almost exclusively by men. It was a time marked by the development of cable television, the internet, and wireless telephones. Ronald Reagan was credited with the Soviet Union's collapsing under Nikita Khruschev and with the "Cold War's" abating significantly. Sandra Day O'Conner was selected to become the first woman to occupy a seat on the United States Supreme Court. Socially, Americans feared contracting AIDS which became for many a symbol of a decadent lifestyle. Racial unrest in the United States continued with rioting in major cities such as Los Angeles and Chicago. This was the socio/political environment in which the students who came to Florida College had grown up.

Bob F. Owen followed James R. Cope as president of Florida College in the eighties (1982 to 1991). C. G. "Colly"

Caldwell served in that role for almost two decades spanning the beginning of a new millennium (1991 to 2009). Jim Cope was named chancellor but was quietly disappointed that he was never given a seat on the board of directors following his retirement from the presidency.

When at home, Jim preached in the Antioch church beginning June 30, 1974. This small group of Christians worshiped in a building located at the intersection of Macintosh and Thonotosassa Roads in northeastern Hillsborough County. It served a rural constituency between Temple Terrace and Plant City as did a small group a few miles on east in the Cork community. The congregants at Antioch claimed that theirs was the longest serving group of faithful Christians in Hillsborough County. Jim's last worship service working with the brethren at Antioch was on Wednesday evening, April 28, 1982, the week he retired from the presidency at Florida College. He had served the Antioch Christians well for almost eight years.

Jim was not retiring from his preaching, however. He continued to hold gospel meetings across the country for several years. When at home, he shared preaching responsibilities with Dennis Reed at the Forest Hills church in Tampa west of the college. His regular work with Forest Hills began May 9, 1982 and continued through 1987.

Jim's good friend Earl Kimbrough preached in Brandon and became interested in establishing a congregation in the Sun City area south of Riverview. Sun City was basically a retirement community in which lived a good number of Christians who had difficulty traveling north to Riverview, Brandon, or Tampa or south to Palmetto or Bradenton. As always, Jim became excited at the prospect of a new congregation. Encouraged by Kimbrough, he determined to help start that group. That effort provided his last regular preaching opportunities.

As the decade of the 1980s came toward its end, Jim became aware that his memory of recent events was sometimes failing him. He could tell you of his days in Tennessee and the early days in Florida. He had trouble, however, with more recent times and with things people told him currently. He often called Georgia Deane to the phone when talking about things to remember and asked for them to be repeated to her so he would not overlook or fail to remember something important or something he should do. It was difficult to witness the progression of his loss through the next ten years. Jim had always had a tremendous memory and, before declining, was one of the quickest and sharpest minds this writer has ever known.

Late in 1989, Jim was asked to speak on the up-coming Florida College annual lectureship program. The topic assigned was "The End of the Journey." He was to speak the final night of the series to a full house in Conn Gymnasium (February 1, 1990). He spoke primarily about the "institutional" controversy and the direction in which many churches were going since the division. His manuscript addressed the dangers of compromising truth and how those promoting institutionalism would go further and further away from scriptural authority. He did, however, refer to his personal journey, a journey that, unknown to himself, would not end for another nine years. When one reads his manuscript, not leaving behind any personal enemies seems to have been his greatest private concern. He said,

As I approach the end of my personal journey on this earth, I make this appeal to every man, woman, and child who hears or reads these words: "If you have ought against me, or if I have sinned against you without proper apology and correction, as far as human ability permits, please, let us correct the wrongdoing while we live because the day of judgment before God will be too late!."[1]

---

1   James R. Cope, "The End of the Journey," in Melvin D. Curry, ed., *Reemphasizing Bible Basics in Current Controversies* (Temple Terrace, FL: Florida College Bookstore, 1990), 206-15

Chapter 32:

Georgia Deane

Like Jim, Georgia Deane was comfortable with everyone. All who knew her loved her. She truly "ministered" to her family's well-being, to the students and personnel of the college, and to the needs of her fellow Christians. She was perfect for Jim. He considered it providentially so!

She also came to be a favorite person in Temple Terrace. George Jenkins, founder and president of the Publix supermarket chain, called upon her several times to cut the ribbon opening a new store. Through it all to herself, however, she was just a woman standing beside her husband, looking for opportunities to serve him, her Lord, and her family. Shortly before her passing, Lynda Caldwell asked her advice on becoming the president's wife. Her answer was simply, "Be yourself."

Obviously, Jim's being away from home so much was difficult for his wife and family. It seemed she was always on the road to the Tampa airport. Often twice in a week she would make that trip across town. Her only consolation was a stop at her favorite Mexican drive-through on the way home from delivering Jim to airside to purchase a couple of their special tacos for lunch or dinner.

Superseded only by her commitment to meet her responsibilities to the Lord, it was her daily duties for family that defined her in the eyes of her friends. Her parents lived down the street with her widowed sister (Sissy), who was then their principle caregiver. Sissy did not drive, so for many years taking them to church, to doctor's appointments, or to wherever they needed to be fell upon Georgia Dean. Nannie Combs died in 1973. Granddaddy Combs passed away in 1986. She and Sissy saw to their every need. Sissy outlived Georgia Deane and passed in 1995.

Cathy Cope Weaver spoke of her "mother's dedication to her obligations and tasks at home."[1] That spoke volumes concerning Jim's wife and companion for life. Cathy noted that none of her mother's children could remember ever coming home when Georgia Deane was not there.

Georgia Deane was always careful to be modest in demeanor and appearance. She never wanted to violate her sense of decency or be seen in any sense to violate principles of her faith. She would die before offending Christians around her. She would work in the house or yard in jeans or modest pants, but she would never wear those to campus or church. Harry Pickup, Sr., was not so sure women should wear "breeches" at all, and heaven forbid Georgia Deane run afoul of sweet brother Pickup's sensitive conscience. She loved him and her husband too much to do anything that might reflect upon them. She did, however, wear trousers to church on a few occasions when the weather was terribly cold or rainy. She rolled up the legs so as not to show the pants and put over them a large-sized skirt or a lengthy trench coat to hide them.[2]

---

1   Cathy Cope Weaver, email message, September 13, 2024.

2   Michael Benson, Sr., interview, February 14, 2025.

The Copes had eight grandchildren. Mike and Connie had two girls and a boy in that order of birth (Michelle, Heather, and Michael, Jr.). Cathy and John also had a boy and two girls. The boy was born before the girls (John B., Amy, and Mary Beth). Butch and Jennie had a boy and a girl (Ryan and Jessica).

Cathy said,

> In the early years of our childhood, being 4 years apart, Butch and I were big buddies. Connie and I were 2 years apart and she was the mature reader in the family, curled up with a book, but we all got along together. However, Butch and I were literal playmates but often I was the "adult" leader when we played school, him being the student and me being his teacher. At the other end of the spectrum we played on pine needle-filled tree swings, played cowboys and Indians and Tarzan and Jane together outside (and dressed the part), and in the summertime in Dallas at my own grandparents' house we made mud pies and could almost cook them on the concrete driveway in the hot Texas sun. Most often we would then meet up with Daddy in Sparta for the Tennessee family reunion. As an aside, we were all very close to Aunt "Sissy," my mother's widowed sister who lived with and cared for their parents, who eventually all moved to Tampa.[3]

Following her mother's passing, Cathy wrote a beautiful personal poem about her mother in which she said,

> "No one will ever sing her praises,
> No one will ever praise the songs that are her,
> Save only those who do so in her epitaph.
> Even then, a dirge and chiseled lines
> Will be much less than what she is about.
> Not because the hymn is short

---

3   Cathy Cope Weaver, email message, February 14, 2025.

Nor because the headstone can contain no more;
Rather because no one really knows."

One night in July 1990, the Copes had dinner with us, Colly and Lynda, at the Caldwell's home on Mission Hills Drive. During the evening, Georgia Deane revealed that she had been diagnosed with terminal stomach cancer that had spread to her liver. It was a great shock to their good friends.

As per their custom, the Copes had gone to the Breeding family reunion in Tennessee. During the festivities, Georgia Deane had come down with severe stomach pains so bad that she could hardly walk. Jim always preached to the small congregation at Celina when there, so it was decided that they would put Georgia Deane on a plane out of Nashville to Tampa instead of her riding home in the car. Mike and Connie had not gone to the reunion that year. They met her at the Tampa airport and took her home. She was very sick. The next morning they took her to their doctor, Leon Wayne Mitchell, who ordered a complete battery of tests. When the results came in, Dr. Mitchell called Mike and Connie with the results and told them that he had arranged an appointment with an oncologist. It fell Mike's lot to call Jim who broke down and immediately started home. The prognosis was devastating—six months to live.[4]

As it happened, Georgia Deane lived six months with the disease just as the oncologists predicted. She passed peacefully on Monday, December 3, 1990, in the college-owned president's home with Jim and her daughter Connie at her bedside. Her life on earth had continued seventy-two

---

4   Michael Benson, Sr., interview, February 14, 2025.

years, seven months, and seven days. The family and friends' visitation took place in Puckett Auditorium on Wednesday, December 5. The funeral followed Thursday morning in Hutchinson Auditorium on the campus of Florida College. Bob Owen spoke of earlier days and Earl Kimbrough of more recent times. Colly Caldwell addressed the large audience with the following eulogy.

GEORGIA DEANE COPE

BIRTHDATE, April 27, 1917

PASSED AWAY, Monday, December 3, 1990

SERVICES, Thursday, December 6, 1990

Funeral Address by Colly Caldwell

There is a wonderful phrase in the apostle Peter's instructions to married Christians which speaks of their "being heirs together of the grace of life" (1 Peter 3:7). If she allows her beauty to center in the gentle and quiet spirit, the hidden person of the heart which trusts in God, as she maintains moral purity and follows the leadership of her husband in the home; and if he gives honor to her, understanding her needs, their prayers will not be hindered and they will be heirs together of the grace of life.

The ultimate "grace of life" inherited by the children of God is, of course, that undeserved eternal blessing of the life beyond. There is, however, in addition for those who love and pray and share and care as Jim and Georgia Deane Cope have these past forty-six years, a certain shared "grace of life" upon this earth. God caused Solomon to write, "He who finds a wife finds a good thing, and obtains favor from the Lord."

We share sadness today, but through our tears we smile and feel a profound sense of joy that Georgia Deane is part of our lives. We also cannot help but be happy as we look by faith at the wonderful experiences she has now entered. And we feel an excited sense of encouragement in the memory of all the wonderful experiences she brought into our lives by the grace of the good providence of God. In all of those ways, she would not like for this to be an unseemly sad time for us.

Every one of us will always remember Georgia Deane as among the most graceful and beautiful women we ever knew. The bright colors in her clothing, the radiant glow in her eyes, the captivating smile that brightened her entire face, and the charm of her expressions (both facial and verbal) were inescapable, they drew us to her like the brilliant light of the sun or the fragrant aroma of a rose in full bloom. Certainly they drew Jim to her.

But like the wife envisioned by Peter or the worthy woman described by Solomon, her real beauty was inner, not her outward appearance. As she added years, she added even more modesty, grace and charm. Age seemed only to enhance her beauty and the calm and quiet spirit that accepted change with dignity and poise. Such only added to our pictures of her beauty and made her appearance even more pleasant to all of us. Where her beauty was really found, however, and it was always so, was in her character, the kind of character that God has blessed by providing her with the "grace of life."

To me, and I think to most of you, the beauty in Georgia Deane's life centers in two great qualities. First, her understanding of who she is. Sister Cope committed her life to Christ, and first and foremost she wanted to be a faithful Christian. She saw herself simply as that, no more, no less, and in that fact she seemed always to be herself. She was equally at home with those of us who have little as with those who walk with kings, and she wanted us to be so, to be ourselves before God and men. She entertained very important people with grace and charm, but she loved to be with those very important people with whom she could share a taco and talk about family and church. I never knew her to seek any kind of recognition for herself. She simply served others, ALL others, often at great cost to her own personal needs, when it was easy and when it was not.

That brings us to say that her beauty is also found in our knowledge that the guiding principle in all the beliefs and values in this woman was one articulated by her Lord when he said the "greatest among you shall be your servant." Truly she was as giving a person as I have ever known. Even in dying she put others before herself. Perhaps especially in dying, she showed her love in how much she cared that her loved ones were all okay. I wish all of you could know as we know that to end the suffering of these last days was her wish for Jim, Connie, Sissy and other family much more than for herself.

And she was thankful, a gratitude that was articulated almost unbelievably to me when she said that God was blessing her by her illness in letting her experience the love her family and friends showered upon her in visits and cards and beautiful flowers and words. That was an experience she saw as a great gift given by the Lord.

One time a man asked Jesus, "Who is my neighbor?" I cannot imagine Georgia Deane asking that question. First of all, she considered everyone who contacted her to be important to her and a part of her life. She sewed up the students' ripped clothes, she made little marangue "Connie Kisses" by the thousands, she fed and cared for the brethren, because others were important. Beyond even that, I think Georgia Deane would never have ask that question because she thought more in terms of "family" than "neighbors." The church is her family. The people, all the people here at the college are her family. Her friends are "family" to her.

Of course, she has her own immediate family whom she literally served until the moment she left us and whom in many ways she will continue to serve through all she has already done. She came out of a wonderful Tennessee family of Christians. Her grandfather McFarland was an elder in the Donalson church near Nashville, and her grandmother was a fine Christian named Georgia Ellen. Her mother was named Naomi after that wonderful mother in the Bible, and her father, Charles Combs, was a dear man who walked along the streets of Temple Terrace greeting us in his own way. Georgia Deane and Sissy gave themselves to their father's care as long as he was with us. Her sister, Sissy, who is here today, was almost her twin, a year and day separated their birthdays, but there was not a year and a day separating their love and devotion to one another as the dearest and closest of sisters.

Isn't God's Providence wonderful? Let me tell you a story. When Georgia Deane's parents married, they went to Texas on their honeymoon and never returned to make their home in Tennessee. Brother Combs worked in Galveston for the old Wells Fargo company until 1941, when his job moved the family to Dallas. It was there in the summer of 1944 that Jim Cope came to the Preston Road church to preach in a gospel meeting. On the opening day, he met the young woman who would be his bride for life. He had preached for four years on a regular basis at Donaldson, where her grandfather McFarland then in his nineties, had served as an elder, but Jim had never seen Georgia Deane, except perhaps in a family picture or two, until now. During the next two weeks she heard him preach every evening, spent almost every moment during the daytime hours in his presence (at his insistence we might add) and before he returned to Tennessee, she had promised to become his wife.

Can anyone doubt her loyalty and dedication to Jim? "The heart of her husband safely trusts in her." She has been his love and she bore his children. She has been his friend and confidant, and she never violated his trust or broke his confidence. She has been his helper, intellectually and emotionally and he has always been proud to have her at his side. They read the Bible together, and they prayed together; we know they have shared, and we trust they will share the eternal "grace of life" together.

She has been his homemaker in the truest and fullest sense of all that that means. She has cared for so many in their home. She has literally fed thousands. She did it for Jim, and she gave all that from her love, and it was not easy to do. Ask my Lynda. A private, quiet life would have fit her personal desires much more.

Jim could well have written the words of that beautiful song we often hear on the radio: "It must have been cold there in my shadow; you always walked a step behind; I was the one with all the glory; while you were the one with all the strength; I never once heard you complain." And had he written these words, Jim would have gone on to say, "It might have appeared to go unnoticed, but I've got it all here in my heart; Did you ever know that you're my hero, and everything I'd like to be? I can fly higher than an eagle, cause you are the wind beneath my wings."

Her children call her blessed. She gave so much to them without regard for herself, beginning in the labor which brought them forth. When Jim had to be gone to find help for this school, to preach the gospel of Christ, or help others by defining a good home for other families, she took the support of his work and the family as her mission in life. She cared for Connie and

Cathy and "Butch" and nurtured them and loved them and their mates, Mike and John and Jenny, unselfishly. Her touch was gentle and comforting. Her voice was pleasing. Her nature was sympathetic. She was fulfilled as a wife and mother. She loved her grandchildren and her new great-granddaughter. She certainly wanted to share the "grace of life" with them.

I do not believe that love ceases when one moves to be with the Lord. Jesus spoke of the concern of one who had passed into the spirit realm for his five brothers on earth. Be that as it may, I know our love for Georgia Deane did not suddenly stop when she went away. She will always be there in Jim's heart and in the hearts of her family, in mine and Lynda's, and in all of yours. And she would want us to love one another as well so we can share the grace of life with her when we all get to heaven.

I want to close with some verses from God's word. The Bible passages I find myself wanting to read today are not the passages that speak of death and mourning. I think Georgia Deane might like for us to read one like this:

Be devoted to one another in brotherly love. Honor one another above yourselves. Never be lacking in zeal, but keep your spiritual fervor, serving the Lord. Be joyful in hope, patient in affliction, faithful in prayer. Share with God's people who are in need. Practice hospitality. Bless those who persecute you; bless and do not curse. Rejoice with those who rejoice; mourn with those who mourn. Live in harmony with one another. Do not be proud but associate with people of low position. Do not be conceited. Do not repay anyone evil for evil. Be careful to do right in the eyes of everyone" (Rom. 12:10-17).

As we pray for God to comfort Jim and this wonderful family, let's pray also for God to bless Georgia Deane's extended family, all of us, with the same spirit she had so that we might practice the words we have read in our lives as she did so that we all may share the "grace of life" with Georgia Deane with God up there and we with God down here.

Chapter 33:

Jim's Final Chapter

After Georgia Deane's passing, Jim's life was understandably changed. He lived alone in the college-owned president's home before moving to a smaller house nearby. He took his noon meals most days in the college cafeteria and Connie saw to his other daily meals and household needs. He terribly missed the love of his life. I have sat next to him in chapel as tears rolled down his cheeks. In our home we have heard him ponder what Georgia Deane was doing in her new home.

During that time he strengthened some of his most cherished local friendships. He especially enjoyed being with Dominic Accetura and James Needham. Dominic was an Italian immigrant who had moved to Florida from Gary, Indiana, upon retirement to volunteer lawn services on the college campus. Those services included keeping up the President's lawn. Needham was a longtime preaching acquaintance working at that time with the Ninth Avenue church in St. Petersburg. Jim loved to fish, and Needham proved to be the perfect fishing buddy. Needham told of Jim's appearing at his front door one evening with his pajamas in a paper sack, saying, "I came to spend the night and go fishing."[1]

---

1   James P. Needham, "James Rogers Cope, A Man for All Seasons,

The last almost three years of Jim's life were spent at Clare Bridge, an assisted-living facility on Fletcher Avenue in Tampa. The move there had been precipitated by a heart attack while he was living alone in the house on Mission Hills Drive, where he had lived for several years since the fall of 1991. With Connie's devoted care just a few blocks away, it had been a good living situation for him. But during those years, Jim's health declined.

Late one night he called his son-in-law Mike Benson, telling him he was having severe chest pains. Mike, in turn, immediately called for an ambulance and hurried the four blocks over to Jim's house. The EMTs arrived almost simultaneously and rushed Jim to the University Hospital emergency room. Doctors did not subject him to surgery, but his general condition was not the same after this experience. All agreed he should no longer live alone. Clare Bridge could provide more fully for his current needs.

The family was pleased with Clare Bridge. Not only did it see to Jim's prescriptions and medical needs, but there was also provided much appreciated socialization to this entertaining people person. In addition, they had a worship service in which Jim was allowed to preach. Each Sunday he dressed in his suit and tie and delivered one of his meeting sermons. He seemed excited that he could properly influence the situation. Most of the attendees were denominational in their former practices and accustomed to singing spiritual songs with instrumental music. Both the Bensons and the Caldwells remembered his somewhat proudly saying, "If I weren't there, there is an element that would have played that piano over there in the service."

Has Crossed Over," *Truth Magazine*, Volume 43, 1999.

Jim passed peacefully Friday night, June 18, 1999, at Clare Bridge. Memorial services were conducted the following Tuesday morning in Hutchinson Auditorium on the campus of his beloved Florida College. A large crowd of family and friends were present.

James Rogers Cope: Funeral (6/22/99)

Born: January 27, 1917

Dies: June 18, 1999

Memorial: Florida College Campus; Hutchinson Auditorium

Tuesday, June 22, 1999, 10:00 a.m.

Funeral Address by Colly Caldwell

There was a preacher, many years ago, who came to be a very wise and world-renowned man. He came from good parentage. He held high position among his people. He experienced life to its fullest enjoying many wonderful successes and relationships but overcoming also many personal heartaches and professional crises, criticisms, and disappointments. Men came from afar to hear him speak and glean words of wisdom from his sayings. With God's help, he wrote his prayers, his songs, his messages to the people, and his proverbs in books that we still read among the inspired writings that we call Scripture. In one of his books, he wrote: "To everything there is a season, a time for every purpose under heaven. A time to be born, and a time to die.... He has made everything beautiful in its time" (Ecclesiastes 3:1,11).

When we come to that time when a man of distinction dies, our minds race through memories so multiplied that we cannot catalog them, and our hearts almost burst from the myriad of emotions that pour over our spirits. In these last few days, I have thought first and most intensely about the inner person I believe that I knew (and to whom I related in so many ways): the intensity of his feelings, his nature, his reactions, his dreams. Bob is going to talk about some of brother Cope's heroic deeds and about his first love, preaching the gospel. I would like to talk with you just a few moments about Jim as just a human being, for that is how I will most remember him.

FIRST, I WILL ALWAYS REMEMBER HIM AS A SENTIMENTAL, EMOTIONAL MAN WITH A SOFTER SIDE.

I was privileged to know Jim as a man who loved intensely his family and friends, the church, his school, and most of all, the Lord. Solomon said: "Two are better than one, because they have a good reward for their labor. For if they fall, one will lift up his companion. But woe to him who is alone when he falls, for he has no one to help him up" (Eccl. 4:9-10). Jim stood by his friends. He prided himself on his ability to sense the character of other people, and, as a result, he inspired loyalty in others. His students of fifty years ago at Freed Hardeman still love him and call him their favorite teacher of all time. His fellow administrators would go to the mat with him and for him in an instant.

His sentimental side showed itself in many ways, but perhaps most when he thought of his beloved Georgia Deane and his children, Connie, Cathy, and Butch.

We all remember that series Jim did on the family and how much it helped so many across the country at a very critical time for families. The inspiration and intense feeling he had for that situation came from his love for his own family. In spite of all the traveling Jim did on behalf of the school and in the many gospel meetings he held across the country, Jim loved to be with his family and with his beloved soul-mate, Georgia Deane. I know there were times when it seemed his work had taken him away from them, but it was only out of a sense of duty and need, a greater obligation to God, that he boarded those planes and left the children and their mother. I know the feeling of the knot in the pit of a preacher's stomach when he goes off to where he has never been and leaves behind his loved ones.

The sense of family in brother Cope came from his roots in the rural White County of Tennessee in the Big Spring community outside of Sparta. Jim's character was formulated there in the culture he experienced in a white frame farmhouse on a dirt road and in a little church house where his Grandfather Breeding required every member to memorize a verse every week and grandmother wove the carpets for the building by hand. That heritage never left his soul.

Jim's dad and mother did not have much of this world's goods, but their home was filled with love. They knew how God values family, and they held sacred His will. Jim's father, Rogers Cope, was orphaned at age six and taken in by Uncle Quill and Aunt Dora Rhea. When Aunt Dora was widowed at age 40, she came to live in Rogers' home until her death at age 92. Jim talked often to me about the family. Rogers Cope died painfully, not long after Jim's sister, Mary Hill, followed Jim to Freed-Hardeman. Jim's mother lived to be 89, and Jim's eyes always watered when he spoke of her to me. Jim's sister, Mary Hill, is with us today. His brother Quill died tragically after retiring from the presidency of Middle Tennessee State University in 1969.

Solomon said, "Again, if two lie down together, they will keep warm; but how can one be warm alone?" (Eccle. 4:11). Jim's great love was Georgia Deane. They met in the Preston Road church building in Dallas and were engaged two weeks later. He always spoke of her with pride and affection. He thought she was not only beautiful but brilliant and good and everything he could ever want in a companion. Eight and one half years ago (Dec. 1990), we gathered with Jim and their children in this building to bid her goodbye. I often sat beside him in chapel, and for many months I watched him weep quietly during the singing of certain songs that reminded him of her.

Their children (and his grandchildren) were his pride. Like most of us fathers, he may not have said it often enough, but he loved you, Butch, and respected your character; he adored you, Cathy, and would do anything for you; and, Connie, he knew even through his dementia how wonderfully you cared for him, and his every word to me always articulated trust and appreciation and love toward you and Mike.

SECOND, I WILL ALSO REMEMBER HIM AS A MAN OF INTENSE COMMITMENT.

Solomon said, "When you make a vow to God, do not delay to pay it, for He has no pleasure in fools. Pay what you have vowed. It is better not to vow than to vow and not pay (Eccle. 5:4-5).

That showed itself in his preaching in ways Bob will talk about. It also showed itself when he talked about Florida College. It is amazing that at such a young age (32) he cast his lot here when he could have been so much more secure in a well-established college where his reputation was already stellar. For the next 33 years he served as president, often when the going was extremely tough. In that work, too, he was often controversial. He had moments with the board on the one hand and with the faculty and staff on the other. His decisions were sometimes disputed, often misinterpreted, and misunderstood by those who did not see his goals and vision. I hope everyone here today recognizes that Jim knew full well that he could be wrong in his head but right in his heart. He realized that in his job there would be major decisions affecting everybody that simply could not please everyone. He would make the call and then look for the good in every person and ask for support.

He talked to me often of his respect for those who I thought had tested him so hard in meetings that he could not possibly like them. Actually, some of those meetings hurt him deeply. But he loved us all and wanted to do the best for us he could.

Jim's personality was something like that of a dedicated, determined salesman—I suppose I use that figure because he always had a financial investment going—but he brought that personality type into his work for the college. He believed in what he was doing, and his persuasive manner, coupled with that look in those dark blue eyes, made you feel strongly about it, too. He could be tenacious. He could make you almost ashamed not to do what he wanted you to do because of the intensity he felt about it. He made me, and many others, come to Florida College when we had no way to know how we would feed our families on the pay. He also got me into administration, and I am still trying to figure out whether I should thank him or not. He caused others to give, whether they had money or not, to help young people get wisdom along with an education.

THIRD, I WILL ALWAYS REMEMBER HIM FOR HIS SPIRITUAL HUMILITY:

I think there were some who saw him fight for truth who would not believe what I am about to say to you. I never saw in Jim the least hint of Pharisaic pride often exhibited in those who are blessed with special opportunities among God's people.

Solomon said, in the book of Ecclesiastes from which we have been reading, God "shall judge the righteous and the wicked" (3:17).

The apostle Paul said, "All have sinned and come short of the glory of God." Jim realized at an early age that he needed the salvation that is offered in Christ. He never thought of himself as a great man. He just thought he was doing his job.

I remember well coming out of a service one night when I was about thirty years old. I had just heard Jim preach what I thought was as great a sermon as I had ever heard. I overstated my praise and turned it to reflect my estimate of his spiritual condition. Jim smiled and put his other hand on mine. He said, "You really don't know me as well as you think." That was his way of saying that he knew his weaknesses and sins. He knew that before God, he was like us all, a sinner, a man tempted and tried, fallible and mortal.

Solomon said, "I know that whatever God does, it shall be forever. Nothing can be added to it, and nothing taken from it. God does it, that men should fear before him" (Eccle. 3:14). Jim would want us to admonish you to be faithful to God, to "fear God and keep his commandments, for this is the whole of man."

Jim had a favorite poem by Rudyard Kipling that speaks to his spirit and to the direction of his life. Its title is simply "IF." He often quoted from it when he was speaking at memorials such as this. I will close with part of it at Connie and Cathy's request:

If you can keep your head when all about you
  Are losing theirs and blaming it on you,
If you can trust yourself when all men doubt you,
  But make allowance for their doubting too;
If you can wait and not be tired by waiting,
  Or being lied about, don't deal in lies,
Or being hated, don't give way to hating,
  And yet don't look too good, nor talk too wise:

If you can dream—and not make dreams your master;
  If you can think—and not make thoughts your aim;
If you can meet with Triumph and Disaster
  And treat those two impostors just the same;
If you can bear to hear the truth you've spoken
  Twisted by knaves to make a trap for fools,
Or watch the things you gave your life to, broken,
  And stoop and build 'em up with worn-out tools:

If you can make one heap of all your winnings
  And risk it on one turn of pitch-and-toss,
And lose, and start again at your beginnings
  And never breathe a word about your loss;
If you can force your heart and nerve and sinew
  To serve your turn long after they are gone,
And so hold on when there is nothing in you
  Except the Will which says to them: 'Hold on!'

If you can talk with crowds and keep your virtue,
  Or walk with Kings—nor lose the common touch,
If neither foes nor loving friends can hurt you,
  If all men count with you, but none too much;
If you can fill the unforgiving minute
  With sixty seconds' worth of distance run,
Yours is the Earth and everything that's in it,
  And—which is more—you'll be a Man, my son!

As most of you know, many years ago now, when the old church building was replaced at Big Spring, Jim secured the bell that had called the rural people of that community to services on Sunday mornings. He brought that bell to Florida College and placed it on this building to call students to chapel each morning. That is one of the grand traditions of this school, and its sound can be heard not only over the campus but from several blocks away throughout the community. As we leave with Jim's earthly body this morning, the bell will toll, once each year for the thirty-three years of his presidency.

Appendices

Voices in the Wilderness
(Institutionalism)

Solving Family Problems

Churches where "Family" Series was
Presented

VOICES
IN THE
WILDERNESS

A STUDY IN THE DEVELOPMENT OF BENEVOLENCE
SOCIETIES AND THEIR SUPPORT

By James R. Cope

HAVE CHURCHES OF CHRIST "ALWAYS" SUPPORTED ORPHAN HOMES?

WHEN DID THE OPPOSITION BEGIN?

IS IT REALLY TRUE THAT PERSONS NOW LIVING REMEMBER THE ORIGIN OF THE FIRST ORPHAN HOME SUPPORTED BY CHURCHES OF CHRIST?

DEDICATION

TO MOTHER
" ... and a sword shall pierce through thine own soul ... "

TABLE OF CONTENTS

1. Two distinct ·peoples -"Churches of Christ" and "Disciples of Christ"

2. Churches of Christ:

a. "Distinct and separate in name, work, and rule of faith"

b. "Purely congregational and. independent in policy and work," having "no general meetings or organizations of any kind"

3. Eight hundred Tennessee churches "generally oppose all innovations upon the primitive order"

4. Observations on Lipscomb's statement

B. W. T. Boaz "Quarterly Report" on Tennessee Orphan Home Supporters: 1911

C. G. C. Brewer articles on "The Budget System": 1935

1. Series on "Organizations": 1933

2. Practice of churches at Memphis, Tennessee, and Cleburne and Sherman, Texas, in supporting schools and orphan homes

3. Appeal for churches to "pay David Lipscomb College out out debt, to equip and endow it"

4. Declares churches still "have to be convinced ... that it is right for churches as such to contribute to" schools and orphan homes

5. Observations

V. THE OPPOSITION SPEAKS: 1897 -1951

A. "Behold, how great a matter a little fire kindleth!"

    B. Opposition is in proportion to intensity of innovation's force

    C. Isolated cases establish neither general practice nor scriptural authority

       1. True of sprinkling and pouring

       2. True of instrumental music

       3. True of missionary societies

       4. True of opposition to church support of schools and orphan homes

    D. Scriptural practices need no reenforcement from history

    E. Voices in the Wilderness

       1. 1897-S. L. Barker

       2. 1897-J. J. Limerick

       3. 1916-C. E. Wooldridge

       4. 1919-C. M. Pullias

       5. 1930-A. B. Barrett

       6. 1931-Foy E. Wallace, Jr.

       7. 1931-F. B. Srygley

       8. 1934-F. B. Srygley

       9. 1946-Guy N. Woods

       10.1951-G. K. Wallace

VI. THE REALITY OF DIVISION: 1962

    A. Restating the Issue

    B. Who Must Bear the Blame?

THANKS

A host of brethren who have heard me present much of the material in this booklet have insisted that I put it in print. Their expressions of confidence that it will do good is my only· excuse for presenting it in this form. For their encouragement and for the grace of our Father which has made it possible I am grateful.

In this work I have repeatedly indicated that there may be information which I have not seen nor heard. If I am mistaken in evidence presented or in conclusions drawn from it, he will be my friend who points up my error.

James R. Cope

Temple Terrace, Florida

January 23, 1962

CHAPTER I

A Slogan Based on Scriptures

"Where the Scriptures speak, we speak; and where the Scriptures are silent, we are silent." So spoke Thomas Campbell near the beginning of the Nineteenth Century while still a Presbyterian. These words, however, were not only to lead Mr. Campbell out of and away from Presbyterianism but were to become a slogan which would shake the religious world to its foundation. In fact, they were so revolutionary that hardly had they fallen from Campbell's lips until a dear friend and fellow-Presbyterian said, "Mr. Campbell, if we adopt **that** as a basis, then there is an end of infant baptism." Not perceiving the full implications of this announcement at the moment, Mr. Campbell, nevertheless, recognized its soundness and straightway replied, "Of course, if infant baptism be not found in Scripture, we can have nothing to do with it." (Richardson's **Memoirs of Alexander Campbell**, Vol. I, pp. 237, 238.) True to the principle proclaimed, Thomas Campbell analyzed his own "sprinkling in infancy" and later, as a believer in Christ, was baptized for remission of sins. He would not allow the tradition of his fathers to keep him from obeying God.

The Slogan's Scriptural Basis

Almost eighteen centuries earlier, the Holy Spirit had announced the same principle which Thomas Campbell announced to a small group of Presbyterians. The Spirit had said, "Whosoever goeth onward and abideth not in the teaching of Christ, hath not God: he that abideth in the teaching, the same hath both the Father and the Son." (2 John

9.) He had also said that "if any man speaketh" he should speak ... as it were oracles of God" (1 Pet. 4:11), and that men should "learn not to go beyond the things which are written." (1 Cor. 4:6.) Like Jesus who, speaking as "one having authority and not as the scribes," confounded the Jewish teachers and awakened the multitudes because of His appeal to the word of God, so Campbell and other pioneer preachers called the deceived and confused people away from the creed-bound preachers of their day to the simple but living word of the living God. They urged their hearers to forsake traditions of men for the truth of God. "To the law and to the testimony!" they cried. "Nothing else will do," they declared. And they were eminently correct for Jesus had said, "He that rejecteth me, and receiveth not my sayings, hath one that judgeth him: the word that I spake, the same shall judge him in the last day." (John 12:48.)

Truth Opposes Tradition

Tradition had said, "Let us sprinkle or pour water upon men and call it 'baptism'," but truth had said, "We are buried with him in baptism." (Rom. 6:4; Col. 2:12.) Those who loved truth more than tradition forsook tradition for truth. Tradition had said, "Let us baptize babies," but truth had said, "He that believeth and is baptized shall be saved." (Mk. 16:16.) Babies could not be baptized at Christ's command because they could not believe. Tradition had said, "We may have our church associations, our intercongregational arrangements, even our presiding elders, archbishops and popes," but truth had revealed nothing larger than a local congregation of saints with its bishops and deacons (Phil. 1:1), none of which exercised themselves to control anything other than the work and souls committed to their charge by the Holy Spirit. (Acts

20:28; 1 Pet. 5:2-5.) These are but a few of the traditions surrendered in the light of truth newly learned.

Truth Conquers Tradition

The success with which these preachers pushed their anti-tradition plea while they urged their pro-Scripture appeal is evidenced by the tremendous impact they made upon the religious society of that distant day. By the hundreds and by the thousands the multitudes became excited as they became enlightened by the simplicity of the appeal to return to the ancient order of things religious. They laid aside their human creeds, their denominational names, their human organizations, their man-devised governments, and obeyed the gospel of Christ. Onward they marched as a mighty phalanx. Forward they moved as a mighty army. Methodists said, "We must forget Wesley and return to the apostles." Presbyterians said, "We must forsake John Calvin and return to the New Testament."Baptists said, "Let us cast aside our manuals and go back to the Word of God." Catholics 'Said, "Let us forsake Rome for Jerusalem." It was not. easy for many of them, but it was safe for all of them. Truth was prevailing over tradition for the first time in centuries!

The spirit characterizing these truth-seekers was one of freshness. They weighed everything in the light of the New Testament. If they could not find where any practice had been commanded by Christ through His apostles they rejected it. With them it was a direct statement or command; an approved apostolic example or a necessary inference for whatever they taught and practiced. If the apostles taught it they practiced it; if not, they repudiated it. Regardless of what they had once felt, thought, or said they now surrendered minds, sentiments and wills to the decrees of the sacred Scriptures. Fleshly ties and blood relations felt the impact. They knew that the peace made possible by the Prince of Peace came only after the sword of the Spirit had cut through the walls of sin which separated men from God, for Jesus had said, "Think not that I came to send peace on the earth: I came not to send peace, but a sword ... and a man's foes shall be they of his own household." (Matt. 10:34, 36.) Nevertheless they knew that the very kingdom for whose borders they were battling was a kingdom of "joy and peace," and that they had been promised "the peace of God which passeth understanding" as a result of their relationship with Christ the King. (Rom. 14:17; 'Phil. 4:7.)

CHAPTER II

Development of Division: 1849 - 1919

But, alas, the movement fell upon stormy seas as winds of division and strife rolled down from the domain of the ruler of the darkness of this world. Brother began to oppose brother. Again, man's foes were they of his own house. Even among some who had shouted the loudest to flee fast and far from Rome came also the suggestions and urgency of forming organizations and introducing innovations upon the ancient order which neither they nor their followers could find commanded by the Christ which they professed to serve. Alexander Campbell, great and good man that he was, led hundreds away from the fundamental principles to which he had formerly directed them. Perhaps more than any other person in Restoration History, Campbell stirred the fires and fanned the flames which eventually brought divisions among the people who were once united upon the simple plea: "We speak where the Scriptures speak; and we are silent where the Scriptures are silent."

A. Campbell's Changed Views: 1823 vs. 1842

In the first issue of **The Christian Baptist**, August 3, 1823, Alexander Campbell expressed his opposition to all organizations of a "religious nature" outside the Lord's "societies called churches" as follows:

> "The societies called churches, constituted and set in order by those ministers of the New Testament, were of such as received and acknowledged JESUS as Lord Messiah, the Saviour of the World, and had put themselves under His guidance. The ONLY BOND OF UNION among them was faith in Him and submission to His will ... Their churches were not fractured into missionary societies, Bible societies, education societies; nor did they dream of organizing such in the world. The head of a believing household was not in those days a president or manager of a board of foreign missions; his wife, the president of some female education society; his eldest son, the recording secretary of some domestic Bible society; his eldest daughter, the corresponding secretary of a mite society; his servant maid, the vice-president of a rag society; and his little daughter, a tutoress of a Sunday school. They knew nothing of the hobbies of modern times. In their church capacity alone they moved. They neither transformed themselves into any other kind of association, nor did they fracture and sever themselves into divers societies. They viewed the church of Jesus Christ as the scheme of Heaven to ameliorate the world; as members of it, they considered themselves bound to do all they could for the glory of God and the good of men. They dare not transfer to a missionary society, or Bible society, or education society, a cent

or a prayer, lest in so doing they should rob the church of its glory, and exalt the inventions of men above the wisdom of God. In their church capacity alone they moved. The church they considered 'the pillar and ground of the truth'; they viewed it as the temple of the Holy Spirit; as the house of the living God. They considered if any other obJect of a religious nature. In this capacity, wide as its sphere extended, they exhibited the truth in word and deed. Their good works, which accompanied salvation, were the labors of love, m mm1stermg to the necessities of saints to the poor of the brotherhood. They did good to all men but especially to the household of faith. They practiced that pure and undefiled religion, which, in overt acts, consists in 'taking care of orphans and widows in their affliction, and in keeping one's self unspotted by (the vices of) the world'."

Nineteen years later Campbell reflected an entirely different attitude. He wrote in the **Millennial Harbinger** of 1842, p. 522, as follows:

" ... We cannot concentrate the action of the tens of thousands of Israel in any great Christian effort, but by co-operation ... We can have no thorough co-operation without a more ampie, extensive and thorough church organization."

American Christian Missionary Society Founded: 1849

The evolution of Campbell's thinking was gradual but it was complete. The eventual result was the founding of the American Christian Missionary Society in Cincinnati, Ohio, in October,, 1849, with Mr. Campbell himself elected president of the organization whose constitution set forth its purpose as follows:

"The object of this society shall be to promote the preaching of the gospel in destitute places of this and other lands."

The same constitution established an "Executive Board'", and, in addition to possessing the usual powers of such an organization, this Board was to act as follows:

> "They shall establish such agencies as the interests of the society may require, appoint agents and missionaries, fix their compensation, direct and instruct them concerning their particular fields and labors, make all appropriations to be paid out of the treasury, and present to the society at each annual meeting a full report of their proceedings during the past year."

It is interesting to observe that Dr. L. L. Pinkerton who formally opened the Kentucky Female Orphan School at Midway, Kentucky, the first week in October, 1849, served as Chairman of the Convention which established the American Christian Missionary Society the third week in October, 1849. From the beginning both of these institutions drew contributions from churches. Pinkerton, was also redited with introducing the melodian into the Midway Church just ten years later (1859) and then denied verbal inspiration of the Bible within another ten years (1869).

Society Opposition Gradual but Intense

From the beginning of the American Christian Missionary Society there was serious discussion, though perhaps not at first wide-spread, regarding its scriptural right to exist. As time passed, the opposition increased. The opponents of the Society stepped up their opposition in direct proportion to the intensity with which the proponents of the society pressed its claims upon local churches. The Society's friends branded its opponents as "radicals," "hobby-riders," "trouble-makers," and "church-splitters." They spoke of such opponents as being "anti-cooperation" and "anti-missionary." Popularly they came to be identified by the society supporters as "antis." "Progressives" and "digressives" were used by the "antis" to describe the "liberals." A few years after the Society controversy began, instrumental music was introduced into the worship of a few churches. This innovation came in 1859 at Midway, Kentucky.

Reflective of the attitude expressed above is the following excerpt from an article, "Love the Brethren," by W. E. Daugherty in the **Christian Standard** (considered by the "antis" as a "digressive" paper) of August 29, 1896, p. 1114:

> "I was once what some of your scribes call 'anti.' In those days I could hardly report a meeting, or write a line for any of our papers without 'spatting' at some of the 'Digressive' wanderers, as we 'Antis' called you then and as you are still called."

"Official" Division: 1906

In time, churches favoring missionary societies and instrumental music came to be distinguished from others by the names of "Christian Churches" and "Disciples of Christ." Between these latter groups there now exists practically no fellowship. For government purposes the 1906 Federal Census set forth "Churches of Christ" and "Disciples of Christ" "officially." The "Disciples" group is now much too liberal for the "Christian Church" since it has gone even to "open membership" in many places and has greatly enlarged the Missionary Society to include widow and orphan benevolences, colleges and universities, and other cooperative activities. The "Disciples" are identified with a much more liberal attitude toward the inspiration of the Scriptures than the "Christian Church" and are identified with the "Federal Council of Churches of Christ." As early as 1907 the

Christian Standard, a mouthpiece for persons identified with the more conservative element (Christian Church) opposed vigorously the Federal Council. In fact, there is now such a cleavage between the two groups that in 1956 A. T. DeGroot, identified with the "Disciples,", wrote a book, **Church of Christ Number Two**, wherein he speaks of these conservatives in the same general class with "Churches of Christ (anti-organ and anti-missionary society)."

"Progressive" Organizations Multiply and Merge

The United Christian Missionary Society was the inevitable development of churches sending funds to numerous self-governing institutions. The churches rapidly became little more than pegs upon which these human institutions were hung. With the development of extra church organizations and with these various institutions begging hundreds of churches for places on the "church calendar" and money from the church treasury, the same reasoning that gave rise to one society governmentally independent of but supported by churches ("It is merely an expedient method for a church to do its work," its supporters said) logically demanded a unifying of the multiplicity of extra organizations into one giant body; hence the **United** Society in 1919. Some of these other smaller societies in addition to the American Christian Missionary Society were the Christian Woman's Board of Missions, the Foreign Christian Missionary Society and various educational, benevolence, health, recreational and cultural organizations.

The United Christian I\lissionary Society: 1919

The Constitution of the U.C.M.S. sets forth the aims and objects of the Society as follows:

" ... to preach the gospel at home and abroad; to maintain missionaries, preachers, and teachers in America and other lands; to promote religious education in the churches; to establish and conduct schools, orphanages, hospitals, and homes; to pension and support disabled ministers and missionaries and their dependent families; to assist in the erection of churches and other buildings for religious purposes; to disseminate religious information and encourage a missionary and benevolent spirit in the churches; to solicit, receive, hold in trust, and administer funds for these objects; and to engage in any other form of Christian service that will help to bring in the kingdom of God, in which His will shall be done, as in heaven, so on earth."

Warnings to "Antis" by "Antis" Watching Floodtide

In the **Gospel Advocate** of October 20, 1932, H. Leo Boles wrote on "The 'United Christian Missionary Society'" in which he pointed out the tendency toward consolidation of various organizations in the United Society. After quoting the foregoing objectives of the society, he said:

"It is strange that' religious people would organize institutions and form the by-laws of those institutions with the wisdom of men and set aside the New Testament church and still claim to do the will of God on earth as it is done in heaven! St. Louis Missouri, was selected as the headquarters of this new society.

"These boards still conduct their own educational and financial campaigns; hence there is still some competition and overlapping of efforts. Many strong men among them opposed the uniting of all their organizations into one big organization; quite a few of them are still opposed to the 'United Christian Missionary Society.'

"There is no end to organization when once a departure is made from the New Testament pattern. It will be well to note the steps that were taken which resulted in this tremendous organization now known as the 'United Christian Missionary Society.' The steps are as follows: (1) 'Cooperative meetings'; (2) 'Organized cooperation'; (3) 'Bible Society'; (4) 'The American Christian Missionary Society'; (5) many organizations too numerous to list; (6) finally, the 'United Christian Missionary Society.' The steps were taken gradually and carried them over the same road that resulted in the organization of the Roman Catholic Church and all other gigantic denominational organizations. Those who have studied these things and have observed the dangers in them are grieved at the least departure from the New Testament pattern. Occasionally brethren who claim to follow the New Testament and who claim to be loyal to the congregation in its autonomy call for 'preachers' meetings,' 'elders' meetings,' 'cooperative meetings,' 'tabernacle meetings,' 'union meetings of all the churches,' and 'get-together meetings of the leaders' of the churches in a certain city or vicinity. These are steps along the road and are impregnated with great danger."

The very year (1919) that the United Christian Missionary Society was established C. M. Pullias wrote a front page editorial in the July issue of **Tidings of Joy** and among other things said:

"The main principle violated by the missionary society is combining of all the congregations to do what God has assigned to one. There is no work that cannot be done by the power of God ... that which the church has not the power to do, then should not be considered. Besides this, we might say this way of a few getting together and saddling on the church of Christ orphan homes and schools or anything else is a very serious thing, and will in the course of time prove to be a curse to the church ... All such combines are wrong and in them the man of sin is working, just as in Paul's day, and in the course of time he will be revealed to the sorrow of the church. (2 Thess. 2:3-10.)"

We mention the writings of H. Leo Boles and C. M. Pullias in this connection to reflect their thinking at the time church centralization of funds and the resulting loss of church oversight of church resources were reaching floodtide among Disciples of Christ. Liberal thinkers formally opened the gate in 1849 when they established the American Christian Missionary Society. They and their spiritual descendants had kept the current running swiftly through all succeeding years. Brethren Pullias, Boles and many others had, seen something in the experiences of Disciples' Churches which caused them to sound the warning notes among those who had not gone with the missionary society movement. They knew that the seventy years between 1849 and 1919 composed a period of dissention, strife, division, and heartache produced by the "man of sin." These seven decades revealed his usurping presence first in the field of evangelism and later combined evangelism with benevolence and secular education. They knew that what happened before could happen again, and they did not hesitate to lay the blame for the discord at the feet of those who had promoted the innovations and combines.

CHAPTER III

Benevolence Societies — A Backward Look: 1884 — 1962.

Just how far back have churches identified with the "Restoration Movement" made contributions to societies dealing in the care of needy persons, particularly widows and orphans? This question should not be difficult to answer; yet we are wholly dependent upon secular history for that answer, since the New Testament is completely silent concerning these institutions. The apostolic Word mentions none of them and is silent regarding church support of them in exactly the same way it is silent regarding sprinkling, infant baptism, instrumental music in worship. and missionary societies in evangelism.

"Gospel Defender" Editor Speaks

Apparently some people, even those in responsible places, think churches of Christ have always supported these institutions. Here, for example, is part of an editorial appearing in the **Gospel Defender**, August, 1960, p. 2:

> "Orphan homes have been an established and accepted means of practicing pure religion for many years before the Missionary Society was organized. The brethren who stood so firmly against the Missionary Society digression accepted without hestitation the scriptural principles of establishing such homes. They saw no parallel, dragon of terror, that the modern advocates of Anti-ism shout so loudly about. Were these great men so stupid that they could not see what the modern advocates of Anti-ism of the last ten years say is so plain? Or is it possible that these modern advocates have departed from an establishing and accepted principle?"

Then follows four quotations from the **Gospel Advocate**. The first two written in 1912, another in 1913, and the last in 1928. Three of these quotations had to do with Tennessee Orphan Home and the other with Belle Haven Orphans' Home, Luling, Texas. Three of the statements reflect congregational donations to these two orphanages. Then the **Defender** editor concludes:

> "It is evident from the foregoing that the **Gospel Advocate** and its writers stand today and the same ground and for the same spiritual principles as they did years ago when they so courageously fought against the departures from the truth by those who espoused the Missionary Society digression. Indeed, who has departed?"

Obviously, there are certain points made by this brother, which he expects his readers to accept without question. What are some of these? Notice, please, the following: We are expected to believe (1): that orphan homes were established and an accepted means of practicing pure religion many years before the missionary society was organized in 1849; (2) that brethren who rejected the missionary, society accepted orphan homes "many years" before the missionary society was established; (3) that older brethren saw no parallel between orphan homes and missionary societies; (4) that "Anti-ism" was born within the last ten years; (5) that opponents of church donations to orphan homes have departed from the faith. We shall have occasion to consider these points shortly.

"'Always' — All My Life Churches Have Done It!"

Brethren frequently accept a practice because others before them have engaged in the practice and, without measuring the practice by the Scriptures, they measure it by what they have seen others do. Recently a brother said to me, "Churches have 'always' supported orphan homes. All my life the church where I grew up has donated to one. I can't remember when that congregation wasn't sending money to it!" I did not doubt that this man had stated the facts regarding the practice of the church where he "grew up." I did not question his word when he said that church had thus acted "all my life." The man was not sixty years old, yet he assumed that what he had always seen, churches of the Lord have always done! In this conclusion he was mistaken. Churches have not "always" supported these institutions. Both inspired and uninspired church history deny that this conclusion is warranted. To many it is surprising to learn how short-lived is both the benevolence societies among us and the time churches have supported them.

The Record Speaks

What, then, are the facts regarding the benevolence institutions and their support by churches?

At the risk of being tedious I present here a number of quotations which speak for themselves. I trust that the reader will read each of these statements keeping his mind upon two particular points - (1) the peculiar type of institution being discussed and (2) the date identified with its beginning. The first general division of quotations and observations cover the institutions established and supported by Disciples of Christ after the establishment of the American Christian Missionary Society in 1849 and before the separate listings of "Disciples of Christ" and "Churches of Christ" in the U.S. Census of 1906.

Benevolence Societies Among "The Disciples"

In his **The Disciples in Kentucky**, pp. 303-307, A. W. Fortune declares:

> One of the finest institutions supported by the Christian churches of Kentucky is the Christian Church Widows' and Orphans' Home. This home is in Louisville, and was established

bythe Christian churches of that city ... This Louisville home for the widows and orphans was the first to be planned by the Disciples and the first to be put in operation. The first home in Louisville was put in operation six years before the home in St. L:ouis was opened, which was the first of those maintained by the National Benevolent Association ....

"On March 28, 1872, a charter was obtained from the legislature of Kentucky for the establishment of the Christian Church Widows' and Orphans' Home in Louisville .... The business depression of 1873 and the years following greatly delayed the enterprise .... A constitution was adopted January 14, 1879 .... By-laws were adopted at a meeting, January 27, 1879, and plans were formulated to raise the necessary funds to put the home in operation. For some reason the plan failed and the project was dormant again for about four years ... At a meeting, January 2, 1883, a board of control was organized by the members of the church (Floyd and Chestnut Street Christian Church) to establish a widows' and orphans' home in Louisville, which should be under the auspices of the Christian Brotherhood of Kentucky .... The first children to be received into the home were Myrtle and Alice Montgomery of Shakertown. The application for these children was approved May 21, 1884."

In Garrison's Religion Follows the Frontier, p. 254, . we read as follows:

"With the organization of the Board of Ministerial Relief and the National Benevolent Association, in the 'nineties,' the Disciples registered their discovery of certain social responsibilities, for superannuated ministers and for the orphans, the aged and the sick, which had hitherto escaped their attention."

Errett Gates, author of **The Story of the Churches -The Disciples of Christ**, p. 274, declares:

The National Benevolent Association was organized in 1886, and did work principally in St. Louis, Missouri; it did not become national in its activities until about 1901 when it appointed a general secretary to urge its cause on behalf of the orphaned young and the aged upon the entire. denomination. Since then it has rapidly consolidated the local state benevolent enterprises of the Disciples under its auspices, and has increased its income ....

In **The Story of a Century**, published in 1909, pp. 166, 167, J. H. Garrison, long-time editor of **The Christian-Evangelist** which came to be the mouthpiece of the "liberal wing " of the Disciples, ties together in one package schools, missionary societies, and benevolence societies related to churches, and says:

"These organizations have come into existence one by one as the need for them has been felt, and they have grown and prospered just to the extent that they have ministered to the welfare of the cause .... It scarcely needs to be said that none of these organizations possesses, or claims, any authority over the churches. On the contrary they are the instruments of the churches for carrying out their desires and purposes in respect to education, missionary work, and benevolence. They are voluntary co-operations seeking to express that unity of faith and purpose which we have, and to more effectively accomplish, by united effort, our common ends and aims."

Throughout the period that the Disciples of Christ were getting their various social welfare institutions under way churches were dividing over missionary societies and instrumental music. We have been unable to find any indication that the anti-missionary society churches ever donated funds to any of the benevolences established and promoted by those who favored the former innovation. It would seem that if there was a clear line of distinction between the benevolence.

and missionary societies that somewhere there would be an indication of rather widespread church support of the existing benevolence institutions or an effort made to start some by the antimissionary society brethren back in the 1880's or early 1890's when so many churches were dividing over the preaching societies.

Benevolence Societies Among Churches of Christ

In 1909 the oldest benevolence society (orphan home) now supported by churches opposing missionary societies was established. This was the Tennessee Orphan Home, headquartered at first in Columbia and later moved to Spring Hill.

The following information was given by J. C.' McQuiddy in the **Gospel Advocate**, Sept. 15, 1910, pp. 1036, 1037, under the title, "Tennessee Orphan Home":

"This home, located at Columbia, Tenn., was formally opened on Monday, Sept.· 5, 1910 ....

"This beautiful four-story brick building did not have an existence even in thought eighteen months ago. The idea of such an institution had not entered into the heart of man until very recently ....

There were two addresses made, one by Dr. Dinwiddle, preacher for the Methodist Church in Columbia, and the other by R. H. Boll, our associate and front page editor ....

"While members of the church of Christ conceived and originated the plans of the home and have given more largely to its support than any other people, still other religious bodies of the county and the county itself have taken a deep interest in the work. It is a poor religion that cannot unite with any one in feeding and clothing the poor .... Doing the will of the Lord is neither commending nor condemning the errors of others. May God help us all to rise superior to religious prejudice and bigotry and not to know anything ... save Jesus Christ, and him crucified!'

"The Home is to be controlled by directors who are loyal and true to the Word of God. Only men who have proved their love for the truth will be selected to the sacred trust of looking after the interests of the institution."

In the **Christiari Chronicle**, December 2, 1960, p. 13, we read:

"The Tennessee Orphan Home was established in 1909 with three Scotten children, who were left homeless by the death of their father. Their father was a member of West Seventh Street Church of Christ, Columbia, Tennessee."

On page one the same publication says:

"Other of our older homes are Tipton in Tipton, Okla., founded in 1922; Potter Orphan Home in Bowling Green, Ky., 1915; Boles Home at Quinlan, Tex., 1926; Sunny Glenn Home at San Benito, Tex., 1936; and Southern Christian Home at Morrilton, Ark., 1926."

The same article declares:

"Fifteen hundred children are being cared for through the facilities of Children's Homes in the United States operated by members of the churches of Christ ...."

"These 1500 children are housed in 27 locations throughout 12 states—mostly in the South and Southwest. Total property owned by these homes nears the $10 million mark."

The article continues with information about the number of homes in these twelve states. Texas leads with eight; then comes Oklahoma and Tennessee with three each; then California, New Mexico, Arkansas, and Kentucky have two each; and one each is found in Florida, Alabama, Indiana, Kansas, Colorado, and Arizona.

In the thirty-year period following 1909 when Tennessee Orphan Home was founded five other benevolence societies identified by the **Christian Chronicle** as "homes" came into being. (We are under the impression that Ontario Children's Home, Ontario, Californiai should be added to this list since it was chartered in 1929.)

In the twenty-year period following 1939 twenty-one other benevolence societies were established. (**The Potter' Messenger**, Nov. 1961, says that there are now twenty-eight orphan homes.) So far as we have been able to ascertain only one of these, Christian Home at Lawrenceburg, Tennessee, which was completely endowed by its founder, draws no support from churches. Reflective of the "home fever" spread we find only one other home yet in operation which was founded within the decade following the first one, five in the second decade from 1909, and all the rest in the last thirty years, most of which have been started since the end of World War II. The fire was slow to start. It is now a conflagration.

Conclusions from the Record

In view of the foregoing statistics it would appear that any effort to argue church support of orphan homes on the basis of churches having supported them "always" or even since before the missionary society was founded is completely without factual evidence. We are face to face with the **fact** that churches rejecting missionary societies did **not** build and maintain orphan homes or other benevolence societies separate and apart from themselves prior to the founding of the missionary society in 1849. Furthermore, **those churches which supported missionary societies and used instruinerital music were of that school of thought which produced and promoted the first benevolence societies into· the treasuries of these churches!** Again, for twenty-five years following the opening of the first orphan home by anybody connected with the Restoration Movement (1884-1909) and thirty-seven years from its chartering (1872-1909) there were hundreds of churches which **never** subscribed to missionary societies; yet to date (so far as we have seen) no one has presented any evidence that **any one** of these churches donated its funds to such institutions, much less that such was a **general practice** among the churches. In addition, it should be remembered that the oldest home now supported by churches rejecting missionary societies is barely fifty years old!' I do not claim that my research in the area of church support of benevolence institutions is exhaustive. Nevertheless, I am persuaded that it is thorough enough to draw some conclusions of a general nature — conclusions based on fact, not on tradition, as follows:

(1) Churches of Christ have not "always" supported benevolence societies—"homes" for the fatherless and widows—apart from the churches themselves.

(2) These societies were not established, much less looked upon and supported as "benevolence homes," "many years prior to" the establishment of the American Christian. Missionary Society in 1849. Even among Disciples of Christ the first began operation in 1884;

(3) The foregoing being true, those who represent the record otherwise misrepresent the facts. They mislead people when they suggest that pioneers who rejected missionary societies encouraged **churches** to contribute to orphan

"homes."

"Latter Day" Claims

We are now ready to consider another matter which is frequently produced in an effort to convince people that churches were building and maintaining benevolence homes in the early days of the "Restoration Movement." This, if established, would prove nothing regarding the scriptural authority for the practice. At best it would show that **some** brethren and churches engaged in it, not that it was a universal or even a general practice. At the same time, even from the evidence presented to "make out the case," it is seen that the use of the term "home" to describe the institution in question was accommodative, not official, But now to the case in point -the Kentucky Female Orphan School, officially opened on October 3, 1849.

Kentucky. Female Orphan School: 1849

The current editor of the **Gospel Advocate** apparently feels that he has an unusually strong case in the Kentucky Female Orphan School's being called "that home of female orphans" by Alexander Campbell in 1856, since twice within recent years he has called attention to this statement by Campbell in his paper. In the October 13, 1960, issue of the **Advocate** he writes of "Alexander Campbell and the Kentucky Female Orphan School," mentions that John. T. Johnson, a pioneer preacher, called upon churches in the heart of Kentucky to support it and then gives a quotation from, Campbell in the **Millennial Harbinger** of 1856 after he had visited the School at Midway. The Advocate editor says:

"It is worthy of note that Campbell spoke of the Orphan School as 'that home of female orphans .' It was intended that the school, or home, should exist for the purpose of 'clothing, feeding, and educating orphan girls.' (**History of Kentucky Female Orphan Home** [sic], page 29.)"

Observations

The. following points are also "worthy of note" in connection with Kentucky Female Orphan School and Alexander Campbell:

(1) Without exception, so far as I am able to ascertain, the Kentucky Female Orphan School has never been identified by Disciples of Christ or their official spokesmen in any of their official "church publications" as anything other than a "school." Though these publications list the Disciples' benevolences (homes, hospitals, etc.) they do not place the Midway school in this category.

(2) None of the historians who have written from the viewpoint of those opposing missionary societies, so far, as I have ascertained, have indicated the 'institution at Midway was designated as anything except a school.

(3) On the very page of Giovannoli's **Kentucky Female Orphan School** from which the **Advocate** editor cites the "three-fold purpose'; of the School, is found the following:

> "What was in the mind of Pinkerton from the beginning of his 'meditations' on the subject, and that which Parrish and Johnson and their colleagues approved, was not an 'orphanage' or an 'orphan asylum,' but a school for orphan girls equal in dignity and in its prescribed courses of study to 'any seminary of learning or academy within the State'."

(4) In July, 1922, the question of changing the name of the **Kentucky Female Orphan School** was before its Board

of Directors. In his Kentucky Female Orphan School, ,p. 97, Giovannoli makes the following observations:

"The word 'orphan' was the source of the most emphatic objections. Many of the graduates of the School, according to reports, had found that the social stigma which to a measurable degree, attached to some of the old-time 'orphan' homes,' followed them after they left 'K.F.O.S.' Others complained that their diplomas from the Kentucky Female Orphan School, when' submitted with their applications for positions as teachers, had more often than otherwise been an embarrassment, rather than an aid to them, and they were frequently compelled, even in their own or State, to teaching resort to extraordinary means to prove their fitness for teaching.

"Arguments to the contrary were appealing .... The most forceful opposition to the proposed change of name, perhaps, was based upon the theory that the principal appeal for the financial support which had come to the school from the beginning ... had been the fact - fundamental with· the founders .... that the school was established primarily to educate worthy orphan girls and prepare them for useful lives, and that the elimination of the word 'orphan' would in all probability destroy, in an important and material sense, the most valuable asset in the hands of those who were seeking to extend the field of the School's operations."

Notice, please, that the persons charged with financing the school recognized the "money-getting charm" of the term "orphan," for it was considered "in an important and material sense the most valuable asset" the fundraisers possessed! They knew that some things can be done "in the name of an orphan child" that cannot be done "in the name of the Lord"!

(5) Later the name of the Kentucky Female Orphan School was changed and today is a thriving institution of learning

BUILDING ON THE GOOD

called "Midway Junior College and Pinkerton High School."

(6) This institution from its beginning till the present has awarded diplomas to those pupils completing its prescribed course of study. Schools, not "homes," award diplomas and degrees.

(7) The same Campbell-commended L. L. Pinkerton who founded this school supported by churches served as the Chairman of the Convention which gave birth to the American Christian Missionary Society which preaching society was supported from its beginning by many of the churches which contributed to the Kentucky Female Orphan School. Pinkerton opened the Missionary Society convention barely two weeks after opening his church-supported school at Midway.

(8) The same Campbell commended L. L. Pinkerton is credited with introducing instrumental music into church worship. This occurred at the Midway Church in 1859.

(9) The same Campbell-commended Dr. Pinkerton denied the verbal inspiration of the Bible in 1869;

(10) At the time Alexander Campbell referred to Kentucky Female Orphan School as "that home of female orphans" and commended its proprietor in such glowing terms, Campbell himself was serving as president of the American Christian Missionary Society and also Bethany College, both of which were begging and receiving contributions from churches. This was in 1856 — seven years, after the Missionary Society was established and sixteen years after Campbell had founded Bethany. The current **Advocate** editor believes it is scriptural for churches to support schools operated by Christians just as Alexander Campbell did in 1856.

David Lipscomb's Appraisal of A. Campbell's Competency

Interestingly enough, David Lipscomb, worthy predecessor of the current **Advocate** editor, spoke and wrote longer against missionary societies than any other man living at the time the American Christian Missionary Society was formed in 1849. Lipscomb was greatly grieved because the influence which Campbell had once wielded against missionary societies was turned to favor them in Campbell's declining years. In the **Advocate** of April 23, 1884, p. 262, Lipscomb wrote:

"That he afterward worked in Societies we have no disposition to conceal; that in doing it, he violated his own principles, built again the society he destroyed and destroyed that supreme and undivided respect for the word of God, and his appointments which he had vindicated is beyond doubt, true. It represents another case, so pregnant in the history of the church, opposing others, substituting the appointments of the institution of God, yet doing them himself."

Lipscomb did not defend Campbell in his charge, but he sought to explain it. He insisted that Alexander Campbell was never in complete possession of his mental powers as a careful analyst and critical thinker following a trip to Europe in 1847 during which Mr. Campbell's views on slavery had been grossly misrepresented, which event led to his imprisonment and litigation in Scotland only to learn upon setting foot back on American soil that the son of his old age, Wycliffe, described as "the child of his prayers and hopes," had drowned at his father's mill! In his introduction to Campbell's **Familiar Lectures on the Pentateuch**, p. 38, Charles V. Segar, a biographer of Campbell, makes this observation:

"It is said by those who were near him, that Alexander Campbell never was equal to himself after this stroke; but it was long before the admiring world perceived any change."

In the years following 1849 Tolbert Fanning, a former student and ardent admirer of Campbell, became increasingly concerned about the trend of Campbell's thinking on the missionary society question and made a trip to Bethany, Virginia, to discuss the matter with his old teacher. David Lipscomb had studied under Fannine at Franklin College from 1846 to 1849. In the **Advocate** of June 4, 1884, p. 358, Lipscomb wrote of Fanning's report of his trip to sec Campbell as follows:

"I remember well, on his return he stated that he was shocked to find his [Campbell's] mind was so shaken that he could, with difficulty, keep it on one subject; that he could converse in general terms on things he had studied in the past, but that all power of close, connected reasoning was gone; that he had to be continually prompted to keep up an ordinary conversation."

It would appear that the current **Advocate** editor is faced with a dilemma in regard to Alexander Campbell as a witness. (1) If he seeks to make capital of Campbell's commendation of L. L: Pinkerton's project on the basis of its being "that home for female orphans" supported by church contributions and therefore the same in nature as the present-day "homes" he is, at the same time, faced with the fact that both Tolbert Fanning and David Lipscomb, whose editorial chair he now occupies, felt that at the very time Campbell gave his endorsement to the "home" thus operated "all" of Mr. Campbell's "power of close, connected reasoning was gone; that he had to be continually prompted to keep up an ordinary conversation." If he dotes on Campbell as a witness, the editor's predecessors, Tolbert Fanning and David Lipscomb, indict his witness. If Campbell was incompetent, the editor loses his case for the Kentucky Femafo Orphan School being a "home for female orphans" **based on A. Campbell's testimony!** (2) If Mr. Campbell could not reason correctly on the Missionary Society because of his mental condition, why should any person think he could reason correctly that a "school" is a "home"? If Campbell shall be accepted as good authority on church support of orphan homes because he called a "school" a "home," why not accept his testimony in precept and example regarding church support of the Missionary Society? The truth is that Campbell preached and practiced error in calling upon and taking money from churches for schools and missionary societies just as the **Advocate** editor preaches and practices error when he defends churches which support benevolence homes and schools from their treasuries. There is no scriptural authority for either. D. Lipscomb excused A. Campbell on the basis of mental declivity.

Fanning Orphan Schnol: 1884

Another institution prominent in the memory of many yet living was Fanning Orphan School whose existence was due to the generosity of Tolbert Fanning and his wife Charlotte Fanning. It was located on land five miles south of Nashville, Tennessee, purchased by Tolbert Fanning in 1840 and upon which he built and conducted the affairs of Frnnklin College from 1845 forward till its suspension in October, 1865, due to a fire which destroyed its main building. It had been temporarily suspended during the Civil War. In an address delivered by H. R. Moore at a reunion of President Fanning's old students on May 25, 1904, and recorded in James E. Scobey's **Franklin College and Its Influences**, p. 128, the following occurs:

"Their long, useful, and eventful lives were subsequently spent at Elm Crag, the name first applied to their farm and school, next Franklin College and Minerva College, then Hope Institute, now Fanning Orphan School. Pardon me for suggesting that the term 'Orphan' should be dropped. 'Fanning School' is better and more appropriate."

WILDERNESS

In the book referred to above, pp. 381-384, Miss Emma Page makes the following observations on the "History of the Fanning Orphan School":

"... Just before his death, in 1874, Mr. Fanning made a will, giving to his wife all his property and expressing confidence that she would carry out his wishes in regard to it.

"A few years after his death, Mrs. Fanning, acting upon the advice of friends, resolved to set the school in operation before she passed away, that she might witness a portion of the good she believed it was destined to accomplish. She selected, as trustees to carry out her wishes in regard to the school, thirteen brethren of the church of Christ ....

"In her deed of gift to the trustees Mrs. Fanning thus states the purpose of the school she wished to establish:

"'The purpose of this conveyance is to establish a school under the patronage and management of said corporation, wherein white orphan girls may be instructed in books and trained in habits of industry. I am a communicant of the church of Christ, and I wish every person officially connected with the management of this institution to be a member in good standing in said church. The trustees of said school may admit to the school so many destitute orphan girls as the means at their command will allow. They are vested with authority to adopt all needful rules for the government of the school, but I require that the Bible shall be made a regular text-book and shall form a part of the daily study of all the pupils. The pupils must be instructed in household duties, and be required to perform service as cooks, laundresses, dairymaids, housekeepers, etc., so that they may earn in such employment, if necessary, an independent and honest living. The trustees may admit white girls, not orphans, in destitute circumstances, as pupils, on payment of tuition; but no such pupils are to be admitted if such an arrangement shall in the least interfere with the training of the destitute and orphans, who are the peculiar objects of my solicitude.'

"The school was permanently organized February 11, 1884, and opened for pupils the following September."

According to Emma Page (**Franklin College and Its Influences**, p. 383) when Charlotte Fanning deeded to the trustees 160 acres of land "she imposed upon the board of trustees the condition that they should raise a fund equal to the value of the farm and buildings, that the school might be put upon a firm basis. She says that, "this the trustees were able to do by the generosity of many who made contributions — some large, some small -to the work."

In the **Advocate** of January 16, 1884, p. 83, David Lipscomb, a trustee of the Fanning Orphan School, wrote as follows regarding the efforts of the trustees as they moved to put the School into operation:

"While doing what they are able with the means at their command, the trustees proposed to furnish a school at which individuals, churches and associations charitably inclined, may be able to educate destitute orphans in most favorable surroundings at a minimum of cost."

"... This is a work that ought to commend itself to the conscience of every man and woman that desires to help the innocent helpless, and those exposed to ruin from no fault of their own, as well as of all who desire the moral and material wellbeing of the human family."

Lipscomb also said:

"This is a good work. It does not assume the work of the church. It affords means for the church doing its work-the work of educating and training orphan children under the favorable circumstances and at small expense."

Permanent organization of the School was effected February 11, 1884. As the spring of 1884 turned toward summer Lipscomb wrote in the **Advocate** of May 21, p. 327, that the trustees were seeking a qualified superintendent and matron. Among other things he said:

"The trustees will be glad to have benevolent individuals and churches select orphan children around them and make up their minds to help train and educate them for usefulness. The trustees will put the charges at the lowest rate of actual expenses for all who attend, besides giving what aid is in their power to the children ...."

The trustees did not find the superintendent they wanted but with the coming of September the School opened with Miss Emma Page as teacher and Miss Bettie Holiman as matron. Twelve orphan girls were among those enrolled for a five-month term along with about twenty day pupils, according to Miss Page's account. In the **Advocate** of September 3, 1884, David Lipscomb reflected the fact that the institution was a "school," not a modern orphan "home," in these words:

"The trustees ... propose to take destitute orphans, sent by churches, individuals and associations of any kind, at forty dollars per session of five months. Their aim is to take these exactly at cost ....

"... They propose to take children of those able to pay, at fifty dollars per term of five months, charging ten dollars extra for tuition ...."

The account of the School's early years by Miss Page in **Franklin College and Its Influences**, p. 385, confirms the fact that **churches were not making donations to** this institution but were paying for services rendered in exactly the same manner that **parents paid** the same school for services rendered. After all, there is a vast difference in "giving to" any institution and "paying for" its services! Emma Page wrote:

"In the summer of 1885 the trustees elected, as superintendent and matron, Mr. and Mrs. J. S. Hammon. The school increased in numbers greatly during the term. More free pupils were admitted; and parents and guardians, realizing the superiority of such a school over ordinary boarding schools, sent their children or wards there, paying for their board and tuition. In some instances congregations of Christians sent, at their expense, orphan girls to the school, to be trained to usefulness and independence."

Parents sent children "at their expense" and congregations sent orphan girls "at their expense"!

There were those who had known Tolbert Fanning who felt that even the Fanning Orphan School as it existed and functioned did not conform to Fanning's concepts of what a school should be. In a letter to James E. Scobey, appearing in **Franklin College and Its Influences**, pp. 315, 316, P. W. Harsh of Nashville wrote under date of April 3, 1905, as follows:

"I entered the primary department of Franklin College when I was only eight years of age. Shortly after this the main building was burned. The question, 'Why was this building not replaced?' naturally presents itself. The answer to my mind, is clear. Tolbert Fanning had commenced to doubt the owning of church property and the running of denominational schools. I remember having heard him more than once allude to the troubles of Kentucky University by asking: 'Who is to determine what is the Christian Church?' His idea was that the church is a spiritual body, without visible organic union. He hooted at the thought of such a thing. Years ago W. T. Moore, who was preaching in London, said: 'It is time we were taking on organic union.' Mr. Fanning showed that this was foreign and antagonistic to the attempt to restore the primitive church.

"It is my humble opinion that Tolbert Fanning is misrepresented when it is claimed that the Fanning Orphan School and the Nashville Bible School are the outgrowth of his ideas and purposes. He wanted to see industrial schools, and he would have been glad to have set one in motion if he had known how without helping to build another sect. Is it not significant that he individually owned the house in which he worshipped and in which he taught school?"

P. W. Harsh may or may not have properly appraised Fanning's views. It is possible, however, that he did.

Observations

This, then, is a brief account of the Fanning Orphan School as it was purposed by Charlotte Fanning and began functioning. That it was a school, not an orphan "home," is evidenced by the reflections of those who spoke on this point in the early years of that institution. That churches paid for services rendered orphan girls and that other girls, not orphans, might attend school there at a regular tuition is evident from the "deed of gift" whereby Charlotte Fanning conveyed her property to the trustees of Fanning Orphan School, as well as from the words of David Lipscomb, Emma Page and others. Even if it could be shown that several churches contributed to Fanning Orphan School, there is still lacking any evidence to show that this was a general practice of churches, much less a **universal** or **scriptural** practice!

In later years a few churches made outright donations to the School. That any did so while the School was being established and becoming functional, however, I am compelled to deny in view of the evidence available! I have made a rather detailed search through the 1883 and 1884 volumes of the **Gospel Advocate** but find no indication of such contributions by churches. Did churches make donations to widows and their needy children in those days? Yes! There is abundant evidence that churches and individuals supported these objects of charity but none that they supported "homes" or "schools" from their treasuries. The churches had treasuries, but they did not divert their funds to the support of purely private enterprises regardless of their "non-profit" or "good works" implications.

Kentucky Female Orphan School was properly set forth as a "school," not an "orphan home." It graduated girls and awarded diplomas. Fanning Orphan School is properly described as a "school," not an "orphan home." It also awarded diplomas and graduated students. As H. R. Moore pointed out in his "reunion speech," delivered at the 1904 graduation exercises, "the term 'orphan' should be dropped. 'Fanning School' is better and more appropriate."

Summary

To summarize at this point we have discovered the following facts:

1. There is a difference between "orphan schools" and "orphan homes."

2. Orphan schools operated by persons connected with the Restoration Movement date back to 1849.

3. The first "orphan home" officially identified as such by the persons continuing its support became operative in Louisville, Ky., in 1884. It was established by churches identified with the "Disciples of Christ" (Christian Church).

4. The next benevolence organization was the National Benevolence Association founded by the Disciples of Christ and headquartered in St. Louis, Mo., in 1886. It became "national" in actual operation about 1901.

5. The first and oldest orphan "home" currently supported by churches of Christ was Tennessee Orphan Home, chartered in 1909 and formally opened Sept. 5, 1910, approximately fifty years ago.

6. The introduction of missionary societies among the churches brought serious opposition. By the 1880's some churches were dividing and by 1906 there a separate listing in the Federal Census of "Disciples of Christ" and "Churches of Christ."

7. No churches rejecting missionary societies were making donations to orphan homes of any kind at the time of the 1906 Census, so far as I have been able to ascertain. No orphan homes supported only by churches rejecting missionary societies existed in 1906.

CHAPTER IV

General Conditions: 1906 -1935

Lipscomb's Observations 1907

The U. S. Census Bureau conducted a religious census in 1906. Later the Director of the Census wrote David Lipscomb in an effort to clarify certain conflicting reports received in his office regarding listings of preachers and churches. Under date of June 22, 1907, Lipscomb replied and on July 18, 1907, Lipscomb printed his reply on page 457 **of the Gospel Advocate.** He called attention to the "Declaration and Address" of Thomas Campbell in which he had said, "Where the Scriptures speak, we speak; and where the Scriptures are silent, we are silent." Among the extracts quoted by Lipscomb are these: "Nothing ought to be received into the faith or worship of the church, or made a term of communion among Christians, that is not as old as the New Testament" and that men should follow "after the example of the primitive church as exhibited in the New Testament, without any additions whatsoever of human opinions or the inventions of men." Lipscomb continued as follows:

"These show the keynote of the movement ... and the Christians or Disciples increased rapidly and the churches multiplied. As they increased in number and wealth, many desired to become popular also, and sought to adopt the very human inventions that in the beginning of the movement had been oppose? — a general organization of the churches under a missionary society with a moneyed membership, and the adoption of mstrumental music in the worship. This is a subversion of the fundamental principles on which the churches were based.

"Division of sentiment on these and the principle of fidelity to the Scriptures involved in them produce division among the disciples. The policy of the churches being purely congregational, the influences work slowly and the division comes gradually. The parties are distinguished as they call themselves 'conservatives;' and 'progressive,' as they call each other antis and digressives.

"In many places the differences have not as yet resulted in separation. There are some in the conservative churches in sympathy with the progressives, who worship and work with the conservatives because they have no other church facilities. The reverse of this is also true. Many of the conservatives are trying to appropriate the name 'churches of Christ' to distinguish themselves from 'Christian or Disciples' Churches.' But the latter m all their publications and the proceedings of their conventions call themselves 'churches of Christ'—moved, possibly, by the desire to head off the effort of the other party to appropriate the name as distinctive.

"The progressives, through their society organizations, gather and publish statistics that make a show. But they claim not over half of the churches—in all about twelve thousand—as working with them. They claim, and it is probably true, that a number who do not object to their methods fail through indifference to work with them. In a number of churches a few members work with the progressives, a larger number refuse to do so. Yet the church in which only a few members act with the society is counted as one of them. So in Tennessee, where the churches generally oppose all innovations upon the primitive order, they report in their statistics about five hundred and fifty churches and fifty thousand members. I have a list of about eight hundred churches in the State, with thirty-five of the ninety-six counties unreported. These thirty-five counties are sparsely populated mountain counties, with not many churches, still there are near nine hundred churches in the State. The number of members would be a guess. Of these churches, about one hundred work with the progressives.

"While the progressives oppose and refuse to have conservative preachers preach in their houses and to their congregations, and seek to divide and break up the churches they cannot control, and gain possession of their property, yet, for the sake of denominational show, they publish in their yearbooks all the members, preachers, and churches of the conservatives as one with themselves. It is just to say, too, that the conservatives discourage the churches having a progressive preacher to preach for them; as calculated to lead them from fidelity to the Word of God and to introduce discord and division among them: but they never publish their preachers or churches as one with them, as the list of preachers you have shows.

"With this statement, much of which you may think needless, I answer:

"1. There is a distinct people taking the Word of God as their only and sufficient rule of faith, calling their churches 'churches of Christ,' or 'churches of God,' distinct and separate in name, work, and rule of faith from all other bodies or peoples.

"2. They are purely congregational and independent in their policy and work, so have no general meetings or organizations of any kind.

"3. Their aim is to unite all professed Christians 'in the sole purpose of promoting simple, evangelical Christianity as God reveals it in the Scriptures, free from all human opinions and inventions of men.'

"4. Owing to these differences still at work among the churches, there is more or less demoralization in many churches as to how they stand and what their numbers are. I know of no way to obtain the statistics desired other than to get the addresses of the different churches and address a circular asking the number of each church."

Observations

Some of the Lipscomb statement does not pertain to the problem before us, but all of it should prove interesting. Among other things it helps explain why so many American churches using instrumental music and supporting missionary societies are called "Churches of Christ." This nomenclature is especially evident in the North and West. From the foregoing observations, particularly the one by Lipscomb, we draw the following conclusions as descriptive of conditions among the greater portion 'of churches identified as "Churches of Christ" in the 1906 Census:

1. There were approximately six thousand churches rejecting missionary societies and instrumental music in 1907.

2. These 6,000 churches were identified as "antis" by the "digressives."

3. In 1907 Tennessee churches "generally opposed all innovations upon the primitive order."

4. In 1907 out of 900 churches in Tennessee, 800 of them were "opposed to all innovations upon the primitive order."

5. In 1907 in Tennessee these "antis" were "purely congregational and independent in their policy and work" having "no general meetings or organizations of any kind."

6. In 1907, in Tennessee where 800 out of 900 churches were "antis" — "opposed to all innovations upon the primitive

order" —not one of these 800 churches was building or maintaining any kind of benevolence "society" or "home"— orphan or old folks—outside its own congregational organization, because these 800 churches were upurely congregational and dependent" having "no organization of any kind."

7. In 1907, Tennessee did not have within its borders the Tennessee Orphan Home or any other similar organization independent of church control but dependent upon church support, for Tennessee Orphan Home was not chartered till 1909. None will say that Tennessee Orphan Home is "no organization of any kind," and everybody knows that it has never been controlled by any church which is "purely congregational and independent."

8. If any of the 800 Tennessee churches "opposed to all innovations upon the primitive order" or any of the 6,000 churches scattered abroad which the "progressives ... claimed not as working with them" were making donations to any "orphan home" or "benevolence society" in 1907, it would appear that somebody would have recorded this practice by at least one of them! Again, I do not affirm that one or more of these Tennessee "anti-missionary society" churches were not thus using their money. I say that have seen no evidence to this effect, much less anything to indicate such as a "general" practice among the churches "generally opposed to all innovations upon the primitive order."

Tennessee Orphan Home Report: 1911

As pointed out earlier, the Tennessee Orphan Home was chartered in September, 1909, and became operative in October, 1910: In the **Gospel Advocate**, November 9, 1911, pp. 1302-1304, there appears "Tennessee Orphan's Home

Report for Third Quarter" by W. T. Boaz, Superintendent. This report reflects gifts of various kinds and amounts to the institution by individuals and churches. In spite of "help appeals" through the **Advocate** from the Home's beginning, there were only, **twenty-six** Tennessee churches supporting the institution at the time of this report.

Using David Lipscomb's figure of 800 "loyal churches" in Tennessee four years previous (1907), this means that only 3¼ percent of Tennessee churches were involved in this activity in 1911. Twenty-five years later a prominent preacher and **Advocate** writer who urged churches to contribute to both schools and orphanages was to sound a realistic note about the reluctance of churches to support these institutions. In 1935 this man said that churches "everywhere" would not "do the work suggested" until they were "convinced ..., that it is right for churches as such to contribute to these institutions." Please notice how slowly the churches learned what some editors and preachers would have us to believe they have "always" done!

The G. C. Brewer Articles of 1935

In 1933 G. C. Brewer wrote a series of articles on "organizations" in the **Gospel Advocate**. He discussed the right of schools and orphan homes to exist and advocated church support of them. While some interest was observed at that time the movement advocated by Brewer received little enthusiasm or support by churches for either orphan homes or schools.

That relatively few congregations were being motivated to donate the Lord's money to human institutions of any kind and that none felt this more keenly than G. C. Brewer **as late as** 1935 is reflected in one of a series of articles on "The Budget System of Finance" which he wrote in that year. In the **Gospel**

Advocate of August 1, 1935, pp: 722, 730, Brewer made a strong appeal for churches to adopt this system. He called attention to the practice of churches at Memphis, Tennessee, and at Cleburne and Sherman, Texas, while he had labored with them. He said that both the Texas churches had placed Abilene Christian College in the budget for $1,000 per year and had also budgeted two orphan homes at his instigation .... He continued as follows:

> "Just think what the several hundred churches in Middle Tennessee could do for David Lipscomb College if they could get a few of them to systematize their work, to utilize their resources, and to place the school in the budgets for a definite amount. There are enough congregations within a radius of one hundred miles of Nashville to pay David Lipscomb College out of debt, to equip and endow it within ten years if they would only do it. After that it should be self-supporting."

After concluding his 1935 appeal for D. L. C. to be put in the church budgets, he wrote in the closing paragraph the words which reflect that Tennessee churches which "generally opposed all innovations upon the primitive order!" in 1907 were still **"generally opposing all innovations upon the primitive order" in 1935**. They were not "generally" giving from their treasuries to D. L. C., Tennessee Orphan Home, and other human organizations as late as 1935—forty-four years after D. L. C. began, twenty-six years after Tennessee Orphan Home began and nineteen centuries after the church of Christ began—the church which twenty-eight years before "opposed all innovations upon the primitive order." He tells why the Lord's churches were not supporting these human institutions—orphan homes and all—twenty-five years ago!! Observe carefully his reasons. This is what he said:

In the **Gospel Advocate**, August 1, 1935, G. C. Brewer concluded an article as follows:

> "... Before the churches everywhere will do the work suggested in this article they are going to have to be convinced on the following points: (1) that the budget system is scriptural; (2) that it is right to have Christian colleges and orphan homes; (3) that it is right for churches as such to contribute to these institutions .. The members as a whole would very readily take hold of work of this kind with a little instruction from their elders, but there is where the trouble lies. The elders are either not convinced on these things or else they do not know how to set out such a program. The whole trouble lies with the elders. Give the churches proper leadership and they will do a hundred times more than they are doing .... When we have found that [the budget system] to be scriptural, then what is placed in the budget will be left entirely with the local eldership. The congregations may work on the budget system and not support either schools or orphan homes unless they so desire. Personally, I think we should support both schools and homes, and I have so expressed myself in the Gospel Advocate."

Observations

If G. C. Brewer pictured the situation accurately in 1935—twenty-five years ago when there were only about a half dozen independent "Christian" orphan homes in America supported by church donations—upon whom is the reflection for the elders' not being "convinced"? Upon himself? Had he been preaching this doctrine for the thirty-five years of his preaching career prior to 1935'? (Brewer began preaching about 1900.) Was brother Brewer preaching this doctrine of church donations to human institutions when David Lipscomb said in 1907 that the Tennessee churches "generally opposed all innovations upon the primitive order"? Was he preaching it when the first orphan home to be supported by churches of Christ was chartered two years later? Again I ask: upon whom is the unfavorable reflection for churches or their elders not being "convinced" that it "is right for the churches as such to contribute to these institutions"? Who was to blame? Were the **Gospel Advocate** and the Nashville Bible School pushing church support of schools and orphan homes then as they are now? If so, where is the evidence? Had David Lipscomb, E. G. Sewell, M. C. Kurfees, F. B. Srygley, F. W. Smith, H. Leo Boles, and other notable preachers in Tennessee where in 1907 the churches "generally opposed all innovations upon the primitive order" failed the elders and churches of their day in teaching them their duty along these lines? Was this what H. Leo Boles, who first became president of D. L. C. in 1912, was saying in **Sermon Outlines**, edited and published in 1949 by B. C. Goodpasture, when he said that the "mission of the church" is "not to raise money for defraying expenses of human institutions"? If all the opposition to church donations to human institutions is born "of the last ten years," where are the evidences that all these stalwarts of the faith were derelict in their duty of "convincing" elders "that it is right for churches as such to contribute to these institutions" prior to 1935? G. C. Brewer said that neither the churches nor their elders were "convinced" that these things should be done in 1935. If so, is it true, can it possibly be true, that churches of Christ "have **always** supported" orphan homes or any other human institutions?

In his series on "Organizations" in 1933 brother Brewer cited various instances where Alexander Campbell solicited and received church donations for Bethany College in 1853 and following years. Campbell was also serving as president of the American Christian Missionary Society while so doing, it should be recalled. In the same series he mentioned that E. A. Elam had carried repeated requests for help for the Nashville Bible School on the **Advocate** front page during 1907, 1908, and 1909 with the School receiving a few church donations which Elam commended and David Lipscomb sanctioned. This I do not deny but **I also remember two remarkable statements of David Lipscomb** — one about Alexander Campbell's support of the missionary society in the face of earlier opposition and the other about Tennessee churches in 1907. About Campbell he had written in 1884 that in working with the Society "he violated his own principles," and about the Tennessee churches in 1907 he had written that they "generally are opposed to all innovations upon the primitive order" and that they have "no organizations of any kind."

If Lipscomb was such an ardent advocate of church donations to schools and orphan homes while he "opposed all innovations upon the ancient order," why were all the older brethren who were serving as elders in the hundreds of Tennessee churches in 1935 so ignorant and "unconvinced" on church donations to schools and orphan homes **while at the same time** so thoroughly "convinced" that churches should **not** support missionary societies? **Hundreds** of them had known David Lipscomb personally, **multitudes** had heard him preach since they were children and **other hundreds** had studied Bible under him at the Nashville Bible School in addition to having read regularly his writings in the **Gospel Advocate**. Were the **Advocate** of that day and the school which now wears David Lipscomb's name not instructing their readers and pupils that churches **should** donate funds to schools and orphan homes while they should **not** donate to missionary societies? Again I ask: if elders and churches were not "convinced" by 1935 that churches should support these institutions, who had failed in their responsibility of "preaching the word"? Was this a part of the "primitive order" the "restorationists" sought to "restore"? **If so, where may we read about it in the primitive gospel found in the New Testament?**

Perhaps the answer to most of the foregoing questions can be found in the answer to another question which we here present: Is opposition to church support of orphan homes and other human institutions of recent origin?

CHAPTER V

The Opposition Speaks: 1897 -1951

"Behold, How Great a Matter a Little Fire Kindleth!"

Frequently fires kindled with difficulty are ten thousand times more difficult to put out. Once begun they may smoulder and then later burst suddenly into a great conflagration. This has been the story with church support of human institutions of every kind.

Opposition Is Proportionate to Innovation's Intensity

It is also true that any innovation arouses opposition in proportion to the zeal and 'intensity with which its proponents push it upon the minds and hearts of men. Little push means little holdback. For example, little can be found to indicate widespread opposition to sprinkling or pouring for several hundred years after it was first practiced. (251 A. D.) Likewise, centuries passed before instrumental music, first introduced in Christendom in the Seventh Century, was vigorously and widely opposed.

Isolated Cases Do Not Prove General Practice

The fact that relatively little opposition to church donations to orphanages and schools can be found in the' literature of fifty, seventy-five or a hundred years ago does not prove that this practice was either widely or generally accepted by churches. One might as well argue that churches in general went into the missionary society movement from the beginning or that most of them accepted instrumental music as to insist that they generally supported benevolence societies fifty years ago. Here and there voices were heard in opposition to missionary societies and to instrumental music from seventy-five to a hundred years ago, but not until those riding these "hobbies" began 'to push them to the division of churches was there widespread, outspoken opposition. So also goes the story of church support of benevolence homes and schools. As the fire has spread, the fire-fighters have appeared in growing numbers and with strength of opposition.

Scriptural Authority Does Not Need Historical Approval

It is to be expected that those who promote human institutions into church treasuries should appeal to the practice of churches in yesteryears to prove the rightfulness and justice of their cause. If, however, this practice could be sustained by the Scriptures references to later practice would be unnecessary. This even the strongest proponents of this relatively late innovation cannot do, and therefore they resort to human tradition instead of divine truth.

Voices in the Wilderness

The following quotations speak for themselves. Unmistakably they show the attitude of their authors toward the matters mentioned when they spoke the words presented here. The fact that some of them may have changed their views in later years **does not change the fact of their speaking or writing as they did at the dates indicated**. When any person says that all of the opposition to church donations to human institutions was born within the last ten years he necessarily speaks ignorantly or is deliberately misstating the facts.

The following statements cover a period of fifty-five years. Some of them were made as much as thirteen years before the oldest "home" now supported by churches of Christ was established, while most of them came forth as their authors observed the development and influence of these human institutions among and over the churches.

1897 — S. L. **Barker** in sermon on "Mission Work":

" ... This is an infallible guide, and to depart from this is to presume to be wiser than the apostles. The only exceptions to this rule are those things which may be classed under the heads of means, implements and opportunities, which they did not have, in which are included steam, electricity, printing, etc. It is quite sure that they would have used all these had they been available. But whatever they had, or could have had, and did not use were rejected, and, consequently, are prohibited. They had, and used, instrumental music elsewhere, but never in the Christian worship. This was one of the radical changes in the worship. It was used in the Jewish worship, but never in the Christian. Here is the strongest example and precedent for us to leave it out of the Christian worship. They could have founded special benevolent, financial and missionary societies besides the church of the living

God, but they certainly did not, and would not use them now for the same reason that they did not then. They had only the church which the Lord founded, and nothing more; were in it, and 'complete in Christ. If nothing more was needed then, it cannot be needed now'." — J: J. Limerick, **Gospel in Chart and Sermon**, pp. 164, 167

1897 — J. J. Limerick in sermon on "Pure Religion":

"A great many people are very particular about visiting the widows, orphans and afflicted ones. Some churches have societies for such work, and some churches permit their poor and needy to go to the country poorhouse, while they make a big to-do about the poor heathen across the ocean. Such work is not the kind nor the way Christ intended His church should do. Men must obey the gospel of Christ in order to become dead to the world and the societies of the world, and they then will be ways able of to the keep world. themselves unspotted from the world and the ways of the world (Jas. 1:26, 27.)

" ... I say, brethren, it is time for the preachers and bishops to cry aloud and spare not, and, if possible, cleanse the church of Christ of the sin of covetousness. Then will loyal preachers be supported. Then will people obey the gospel of Christ. Then will the church do her duty in caring for the poor, the widows and orphans, and that without the aid of human societies." - J. J. Limerick, **Gospel in Chart and Sermon**, pp. 248, 249

1916 — C. E. Wooldridge:

"Each congregation should make provision for the relief of the needy and suffering of the congregation and the community.

"All this work should be directed by the overseers of the congregation; nor should any part be burdened with special or separate organization." - A. B. Lipscomb, **Christian Treasures**,

Vol. 11, p. 119

1919-C. M. Pullias, article on "Combines in the Church":

" ... That which the church has not the power to do, then, should not be considered. Besides this, we might say this way of a few getting together and saddling on the church of Christ orphan homes and schools or anything else is a very serious thing, and will in the course of time prove to be a curse to the church ....

"A brotherhood paper, or school, or orphanage, or a brotherhood anything else will prove itself to be a dictator and usurper of the church of Christ, and an octopus that grips the interest and life out of the church.

"If you say they make the church more efficient, I answer that man can, then, improve upon what God has made. This I deny. The Lord had a purpose in making the church. He made it to fill a place and do a work and, therefore, it is adequate to such. He also made the church a small, poverty-stricken, insignificant institution in the eyes of the world so designing men would not want it, but so soon as it gets to be respectable with the world the armistice is signed and peace is near, but not the kind of peace God approves. There is, therefore, great danger in human methods and wisdom. 'The wisdom of this world is foolishness with God.' All conventions, associations, societies and even elders' and preachers' meetings may prove to be a curse to the cause they claim to love. There is no combine with the church and human institutions that does not take the life and power from it." - **Tidings of Joy**, July, 1919, p, 1

1930 — A. B. Barrett, founder of Abilene Christian College:

"There ·were no 'brotherhood colleges,' 'church papers,' 'church orphanages,' 'old folk's homes,' and the like, among apostolic congregations ... The churches established by the apostles did not contribute to any organization other than a sister congregation. All 'church' movements should be kept under the local congregation.

"History repeats itself. Following the restoration of the ancient order of things, launched by Stone, Campbell, and others, men of worldly ambition crept in among us .... Individual Christians, any number, may scripturally engage in any worthy work, such as running colleges, papers, and orphanages, and other individual Christians may properly assist them in every proper way; but no local congregation should be called upon, as such, to contribute a thing to any enterprises. Such a call would be out of harmony with the word of the living God. And if any congregation so contributes, it transcends its scriptural prerogatives." - **Gospel Advocate**, March 13, 1930, p. 267

1931-Foy E. Wallace, Jr., editor of Gospel Advocate:

"If it were 'permissible to have a Bible college as an adjunct to the church in the work of education and an orphans' home in the work of benevolence,' we quite agree that it would also be 'permissable' to have 'a missionary society in the work of evangelism.' But the question assumes the point to be proved. Nothing is 'permissible' as an auxillary of the church which is not scriptural. And it is not scriptural for the church to delegate its work, either missionary or benevolent, to boards and organizations other than the church. Bible colleges and instituional orphans' homes cannot be made adjucts of the church, scripturally. The only way the church could scripturally run a school or a home would be for th elocal church to undertake such work through the local organization — elders and deacons — in which case it woul dbe the work of THAT congregation." - Gospel Advocate, July 2, 1931, p. 804

1931 — F. B. Srygley, long-time staff writer and adviser on Gospel

"... In the days of the apostles there were needy people, widows and orphans, just as there are today, and the apostles taught the churches to care for them, and there was no organization or institution by which the churches were tied together in supporting them. Paul directed the church to care for the widows that were widows indeed, and there was nothing said about any institution except the church through which it was to be done. There were famine sufferers in Jerusalem, and their needs were supplied without anything in the way of an institution except the church in Jerusalem." - **Gospel Advocate**, July 9, 1931, p. 828

1934 - F. B. Srygley:

" ... The average denominational preacher seems to think that Christ gave only a few fundamental principles, and allows man to add to it everything in the way of an organization which in his judgment is necessary.

"When men add the things which they think are allowable, they become naturally very much attached to them. They are the creations of man, and man has always loved his own creations .... You will get an argument quicker out of some religionists when you condemn something that man has started than you will by condemning that which is divine. . . .

"It seems that some of the brethren think that there must be some extra organization in order for Christians to teach the Bible on Sunday .... When one contends for such an extra organization, it seems to me he opens the floodgates to everything that anyone thinks we need. The brother who indorses these extra or outside organizations would fare rather poorly in a debate over the missionary society. I know he might argue the fact that these missionary societies take control of the churches; but suppose his opponent should say that it is an abuse of the missionary society, and should promise to help in reforming it at this point. Is it not the tendency of any extra or outside organization to try to control the church?

"But the brethren sometimes argue that the church can organize anything it feels that it needs. I don't grant this, but it is my observation that individuals start these things for the church to support. Who is to say how many and what kind of institutions the churches need? I do not think the church as a divine institution needs any of them, but some of them do need the church, or churches, to support them. As was said by another: 'If the organization of institutions continues, the church will be little but a peg on which to hang. institutions.' We are told again that any number of churches have the right to do collectively what one church has the right to do, and, therefore, churches can be hung together by institutions other than themselves. On its face this seems to be true, but hanging churches together with a separate institution is lacking in divine authority.

"There are, no doubt, divine reasons for not tying them together with any kind of an institution which is not revealed to us ....

"In the early days in the discussion of this matter those in favor of extra organizations argued that there could be no cooperation without organization. But this was not true then, and it is not true now. 'Operate' means to work, and 'co' means together; therefore, when a Christian operates as the Bible directs, he cooperates with every other Christian who operates in the same way. When a church operates as the Head directs, it operates with every other church which operates under the same directions.

" ... Let us spend our time walking in the light of God's truth, and then we will have fellowship with God, with Christ, with apostles, and with all others who walk in the light of the same Word. Let us not get out of step with each other by adding extra organizations to the church, for in so doing we might so far get out of step with God as to be lost." - **Gospel Advocate**, Jan. 11, 1934

When F. B. Srygley died in 1940 the present Advocate editor said of him:

"Like old John Knox, he never feared the face of man. He was loyal to Christ first, last, and all the time. He would not wink at error in the practice of anyone, not even in his most intimate friends." - **Gospel Advocate**, 1940, p. 484

1946 — Guy N. Woods:

"Paul labored at length in the provinces of Macedonia and Achaia .... When these brethren heard of the distress that was occasioned in Judea because of the famiine in those parts, they determined to send relief. There were many poor saints in Jerusalem at this time .... Concerning this contribution, see 1 Corinthians 16:1, 2; 2 Corinthians 8:1, e 9:2. For another such contribution for the poor in Jerusalem see Acts 11:27-30. It should be noted that there was no elaborate organization for the discharge of these charitable functions. The contributions were sent directly to the elders by the churches who raised the offering. This is the New Testament method of functioning. We should be highly suspicious of any scheme that requires the setting up of an organization independent of the church in order to accomplish its work." - **Annual Lesson Commentary**, 1946, p. 338

"The self-sufficiency of the church in organization, work, and worship, and every function required of it by the Lord should be emphasized. This lesson is much needed today. Religious secular organziations are always trying to encroach on the function of the New Testament church, interfere with its obligations, and attempt to discharge some of its functions. The church is the only organization authorized to discharge the responsibilities of the Lord's people. When brethren form organizations independently of the church to do the work of the church, however worthy their aims and right their designs, they are engaged in that which is sinful. - **Idem.**

"In line with the fact that our lesson today deals with the autonomy of the church we point that the contribution here alluded to was raised wholly without the high pressure organization at all; the churches, in their own capacity, raised the funds, and they were gathered by brethren especially appointed for the purpose. This is the Lord's method of raising money, and it will suffice in any case. There is no place for charitable organizations in the word of the New Testament church. It is the only charitable organization that the Lord authorizes or that is needed to do the work the Lord expects His people today to do." -**Ibid.**, p. 340

"No organization is needed to accomplish the work the Lord has qualified the church to do. When men become dissatisified with God's arrangement and set up one of their own, they have already crossed the threshhold to apostasy. Let us be satisfied with the Lord's manner of doing things." - **Ibid.**, p. 341

1951-G. K. Wallace:

"A great deal is being written these days about orphan homes and how they should operate. The appeal has largely been to tradition. Catholic priests say that tradition is equal in authority with the Word of God. The appeal made by many preachers today is to Larimore, Lipscomb, Harding, the the pioneers. The Catholics appeal to the church fathers, and these preachers appeal to the pioneers.

"That the care of orphan children is a responsibility of the church is not denied, except by a few brethren north of the Mason-Dixon line. They affirm that the care of orphan children is an individual matter. Most of my brethren admit, however, that it is a work of the church. If it is a work of the church, we wonder why the church cannot do this work without forming an organization to take over the work of the elders ....

"Elders of a church have the right to hire a superintendent, a matron, a nurse, a cook, a teacher, a dairyman, just as they do to hire a song leader, a preacher, a janitor, or somebody to mow the lawn or fix a window. The New Testament does not contain **officers** such as matrons, nurses, cooks, any more than it contians **officers** called janitors, song leaders, ministers, carpenters, and plumbers; but the elders of the church may hire any and all of these to serve the church.

"The elders of the church may hire someone who is not a member of the church to do a job of work for the church. They may let a contract to some builder to erect a building, and this contractor may use dozens of men, none of whom are members of the church ....

"There is no parallel between colleges and orphan homes. There is a parallel between an orphan home that has a board of trustees other than the elders of the church to do the work of the church, and the United Christian Missionary Society.

"Since it is admitted that children may be cared for by New Testament churches, why is it necessary to have anything other than the church to do it? ...

"Can we still affirm that the Church of Christ is scriptural in name, organization, doctrine, and practice?" - **Gospel Guardian**, May 24, 1951, Vol. III, No. 4, p.p. 1, 3

"I am thankful for the effort that is being made to care for widows and orphans. I do wish that brethren would not set up some **organization** that God did not authorize to do the work of the church. If it is the work of the church, let the church do it. The care of orphans and widows is the work of the church, so let the church do it. The church would do it, too, if preachers would not get out and start an organization unknown to the Bible and beg churches to turn their work over to a human organization. There is no discussion today about the church supporting an orphan home out of the church treasury. The discussion is about the **kind** of a home that is being supported. If it is a work of the church being done by the church and under the direction of God's elders, no one objects to supporting it out of the treasury. If some organizaiton has taken over the work of the church you cannot blame good elders for objecting. **Let the church be the church**." - **Ibid**., August 30, 1951, Vol. III., No. 17, p. 8

"But," asks one, "have not some of these men changed their views within recent years?" This is certainly true if one may judge by some of the recent activities and teachings of two or three of these men. Only four of those quoted yet live. The others did **not** change before they died. The fact remains, however, and shall stand at the judgment of the Great Day that the words of these men reflect what they understood to be the conditions existing and developing **at the time they wrote the words cited above**. Whatever explanations may be made as to changes in views of any of these men (we grant every man this privilege) their words of record in earlier years speak to intelligent and unprejudiced present-day minds what they thought and felt in view of what they claimed they saw **when they spoke**. The innovations they opposed **then**, we oppose **now**. If they were **right then** and have since changed their views they are **wrong now**. If they were wrong then it is conceivable that they could yet be wrong, but of one thing every intelligent person is positive: **they cannot be right then and right now with a change in views between then and now!** Some who once opposed the innovations are in the forefront among the innovators now.

These then are a few of the voices of those who observed the growth of benevolence societies, originally independent of churches in constitution and control but increasingly dependent upon churches for the finances whereby they pursue and promote their. declared interests. These men did not like what they saw. They said so and gave their reasons why.

What has been the effect of all that they were opposing? What has it done to churches of Christ?

CHAPTER VI

The Reality of Division: 1962

Restating the Issue

Before we close this treatise I respectfully solicit my reader's attention to a restatement of the problem which has caused so much heartache and division among brethren. The issue is not that of the duty of Christians or churches to relieve any person—widow, orphan or otherwise—to whom they have an obligation and are therefore responsible. Every person known to me believes that there are such persons and such obligations. Furthermore, the issue is not that of the right of organization—orphan homes, homes for the aged, hospitals or other benevolence societies—to exist independent of church control or support. I know of no person who denies that such institutions have a moral and legal right to exist.

What, then, is the issue? The issue in question form is this: Is there scriptural authority for churches to donate funds to human institutions of any kind?

Those who have witnessed the developments of the last decade know that if such authority were available, it could be produced in one of three ways - by precept, by apostolic example, or by necessary inference. What then has been the effect of churches supporting human institutions?

The answer is found in the gruesome and terribly realistic word **division** with whatever goes with it! Physical families, lifelong friendships, and brotherly love and fellowship have been broken. A once united and prosperous people are divided into warring camps. Sad as the situation is it is unmistakably real, and he who would make himself believe otherwise is only deceiving himself. That hundreds, perhaps thousands, will be lost as a result of the false teaching and the unscriptural division which they have caused or aided is as certain as the Bible foretells the doom of those responsible for offenses contrary to the teaching of God's Word.

Who Is Responsible for the Troubles?

Finally, we ask: who must bear the blame for the sordid condition found in Zion at the present hour?

It should be obvious that persons claiming to "speak where the Scriptures speak" are obligated to produce the Scriptures teaching the right or duty of churches to make donations to human institutions. If they cannot produce the passages called for, they cannot escape the rightful blame for whatever division may result from pushing their unscriptural claims upon churches. If this practice falls within the realm of human judgment, they are morally obligated to show two things: (1) that there is a command of Christ to a local church to relieve the fatherless and widows and (2) that the **making of a donation to a human inistitution** specializing in orphan and/or widow care is a **"method"** whereby the church discharges its duty toward whatever widows and/or orphans Christ has commanded it to relieve. (It is not enough to claim that the human institution is itself a "method of the church," for everybody who things twice knows that the institution itself is not a "method" of any kind any more than a local church is a "method" of any kind.) If it cannot be shown that **a church's making a donation to a human institution** of some kind is merely a "method" whereby the local church obeys God, it necessarily follows that such procedure is not a matter of judgment at all. Rather, such action, i.e., **a church's making donations to human institutions**, is a postive violation of God's law and is therefore properly described as **disobedience to God!**

A few years ago the promoters of the human institutions insisted that church donations to them was merely an expedient, a mere matter of human judgment, one of several "methods" whereby churches of Christ might discharge their duties in caring for the needy within their ranks. Even then they were willing to divide churches rather than be denied their liberty. More recently some of the chief spokesmen for the human institutions calling upon churches for support are saying that the churches cannot "relieve" the fatherless and widows without a "home" apart from the local church. The practical import of this position is that the local church with which you are identified **must** make such contribution under penalty of disobeying God .... In other words, you must either favor church donations to these human societies or you are bound for hell. It matters not how many orphans you may individually feed, clothe and shelter or how many widows you may visit in their affliction. Either you accept the position that churches are acting by God's order when they. make donations to benevolence homes operated by members of the church of Christ or you are a rebel against the God of heaven.

As the institutional question has pressed its way to the front within recent years it has become increasingly apparent that among those carrying institutional banners many are more concerned about having their way in what they claim to be a matter of judgment than, they are about the peace of God's people and the fellowship of the saints. An actual case with identities of the participants not stated illustrates the point.

Church A was at peace. Fatherless children were fed, clothed, sheltered and otherwise cared for by members of Church A who assumed individual responsibility for them. In spite of this action by various Church A members, several other members felt that entire Church A should make donations to Childcare, Inc., an orphan home, located in the same state. What did those insisting on church donations to Childcare, Inc.,. do? Did they send their personal donations to the orphan home and thus permit the church to live in peace and unity? No, they chose to divide the body of Christ instead. They elected to leave Church A and form Church B for the express purpose of being able **as a congregation** to support some orphan "home" — not an orphan, mind you, but an **orphan "home."** They were not supporting Childcare, Inc., even as individuals before leaving Church A and forming Church

B, though they could have done this without disturbing or dividing Church A. While a part of Church A some held out what they would have contributed on Lord's day had Church A been donating to Childcare, Inc. Immediately after forming Church B they cast their money into Church B treasury and sent it to Childcare, Inc.

Who believes that these people were really concerned about suffering children? If they were, why did they not send their money **as individuals** to Childcare, Inc., or to the children themselves while still members of Church A? Who believes that they were really as concerned about the welfare of orphans, the peace of Church A and the fellowship of brethren as they were concerned about espousing the "Cause" of **church support of human institutions**? No fellowship now exists between persons composing Church A and Church B. **Church support of Childcare, Inc., was and remains the dividing wedge.**

We insist that those who have pushed these human institutions upon the churches are responsible for the division resulting from the pushing. Apart from churches the institutions have as much right to exist and operate as does any other private business enterprise whether individual or corporate. **Their right to exist, however, is not the issue. The issue is their right to draw support from churches.** The fact that they are operated by Christians does not change the fact that they are of human origin and therefore unworthy of support by the divine body, the church. The fact that they are constituted of a group of Christians, independent of churches in structure and function and who volunteer their services to supervise the activities of others who are paid employees of the voluntary body politic, does not change the fact that they still constitute a body for which Christ did not die, which. He did not sanctify with His blood, of which He is not head and over which, therefore, He exercises no control whatever. The fact that they may engage in a work of charity and do good in the realm of relieving human misery does not change the gruesome reality of sorrow, heartache and division they have caused by injecting themselves into the divine body. None of their legitimate claims to respectability according to human standards entitles them to church support and therefore to divine approval according to divine standards.

Peace prevailed before these human institutions began sucking the churches. War prevails not over the institutions' right to exist apart from the churches; but war prevails because, while organically apart from the churches, these institutions attach themselves to the churches for succor and support. War will cease and peace will prevailonly when the divine body rids itself of these human parasites. Remove the cause of war and war will cease.

Afterword

I have sometimes been asked if I believe that an orphan "home"constituted as a human board to direct activities under it has aright to exist. Certainly I do! Frequently I have been reported as being "anti-orphan home" and in many instances "anti-orphan." As I read the record of the struggle between those who opposed missionary societies related to churches and the society promoters I can well understand that many persons either willfully or ignorantly misrepresent one's true views. I am not now nor have I ever knowingly spoken one word against the right of any individual or group establishing whatever arrangement of and by themselves might enable that person or group of persons to feed, clothe, shelter and nurse fatherless children for whom they are responsible, I do not understand that this or any other group has a right to impose what they have decided was their responsibility upon other individuals, much less upon the church of my Lord, "for each man shall bear his own burden." (Gal. 6:5.) In 1909 five men in Tennessee constituted themselves by law "a body politic and corporate by the name and style of The Tennessee Orphan Home" for "the education and support of orphan children regardless of sect, creed, or denomination." That they had both moral and legal right to do this I believe. When they thus acted, however, they had no moral or legal right to expect someone else to shoulder the responsibility they had deliberately and aforethoughtedly assumed for themselves any more than I have a right to expect or request somebody else to assume responsibility for my three children. Again, "each man shall bear his own burden." (Gal. 6:5.) If these five men, having assumed the responsibility mentioned, had later fallen upon hard times and had themselves become actual objects of charity to the point that they could not "provide for their own" they would have then been proper objects of charity from their brethren in Christ, not because of their children but because of their own need. "Bear ye one another's burdens, and so fulfill the law of Christ." (Gal. 6:2.) The fact that fifteen men may now be legal successors of the five original incorporators does not change the principle involved. When any group of men assumes the role of a parent they thereby assume the moral responsibility of a parent. Until and unless they personally become objects of charity they have no scriptural right to expect somebody else to do in their stead what they have morally and legally committed themselves to do for the children whose education and support they have assumed ....

It was not until this group of men and their successors, calling themselves a "home," and others of like nature began appealing to churches for donations to do what they originally constituted themselves to do that brethren began to be disturbed and churches began to have serious trouble. When these self-appointed parents cease doing the very thing causing the trouble, the trouble will cease. When they cease calling upon churches for funds to educate and support their own self-selected children and when local churches begin "relieving" whatever objects of charity are theirs through the ministers God has placed in the churches for this very purpose, then and not until then will all strife cease among churches over the benevolence society question.

As enterprises independent of the church benevolence societies ("homes") have a right to exist. When these or similar enterprises begin looking to and calling upon churches of Christ for support and when churches respond, both "homes" and churches have assumed a role for which there is no divine religious authority.

"For we walk by faith, not by sight." (2 Cor. 5:7.)

ADDENDA

A. N. Trice in article, "Law and Expediency," **Gospel Advocate**, March 19, 1931, pp. 314:317:

> "To object to a method of teaching as 'scriptural' when God has not given a method is to set up a rule where God has not established one. We should repect the silence of the Bible; but some of the hairsplitters and objectors seem to delight to pervert the slogan of the Restoration Movement, and, to conform to their views, it should read: 'Where the Bible speaks, I will speak; where the Bible is silent — this is my opportunity to speak my whims, my opinions, and ride any hobby that my fancy may suggest.' ...

"We are taught to feed the hungry, clothe the naked, and visit the fatherless and widows in their affliction but we are not told how this is to be done. Here again we must rely upon expediency, for we have no plan set forth as such in the Scriptures .... Why may we not build an inn, a hospital, an old woman's home, a school, or establish a paper to teach the truth? And why may we not have any of these conducted under a charter from the Senate by a board of trustees or directors? .... .

"Finally, Scripture authority has been demanded for teaching the Bible in schools; for cooperation of churches; for supporting schools from the treasury of the church; for activities other than through the treasury of the local congregation; for maintaining an orphanage or some for the aged; for arranging for a series of gospel meetings, etc. It is freely granted that the affirmant must support his position with evidence, and my answer to this demand is that God requires us to teach His word, to give of our means, to help the poor and needy, to sing and otherwise worship God. Abundant authority is found in the Scriptures for all this. But if one insists on one plan or method to the exclusion of all others, where God does not specify any plan or method, the obligation rests on him to support his position by Scripture evidence and he becomes the affirmant on the point at issue .... Hobby riding and speculation are responsible for much strife and division the alienation of brethren'. the tearing down of churches, schools, etc.; and when these ripen into dogmatism, the result is the tearing down of primitive Christianity and the establishing of sectarianism. Shall we be responsible for the rendmg of the body of Christ? God forbid. 'If any man speak, let him speak as the oracles of God'."

We cite the foregoing to call attention to the fact that A. N. Trice was makmg the same pitch in the **Gospel Advocate** more than thirty years ago and using the same worn out appeal to "expediency" that the orphan home and college-in-the-budget brethren have been makmg more recently and was branding those who opposed his views then as "hobby riders," "hairsplitters," and "objectors" (another word for "antis"). This forever settles the question of whether church support 'of these human institutions was an issue thirty years ago for A. N. Trice wrote a four-page article on the subject at that time.

This, however, is not the end of the story. Two weeks after the Trice article appeared in the Advocate F. B. Srygley, who wrote some fifty years for the Advocate, used the same title, "Law and Expediency," that Trice had used and presented a withering review of the Trice article. Brother Srygley said exactly what some of the rest of us have been trying to get brethren 'to see ever since churches have been dividing over the orphan home question. Here are some of the Srygley observations:

> "While Brother Trice condemns missionary societies through which to preach the gospel, he defends other things with the same arguments the society brethren use with which to defend missionary societies. The question is not that certain things ought to be done, nor is it the how they should be done, but it is the institution or organization through which they are to be done. There is nothing in the New Testament larger than a local church and smaller than the entire body of Christ. I am seeking to make no law, rule, or regulation when I say this. If Brother Trice's article is not used by the society brethren in defense of their societies, it will be because they do not know a good thing when they see it or do not care for Brother Trice's support. The same arguments that Brother Trice makes hav· been made for the societies for the last forty years."

When F. B. Srygley died in 1940, H. Leo. Boles wrote of

him in the **Advocate** of February 15, 1940, p. 148, as follows:

"The last years of his life were given to editorial work of the **Gospel Advocate** .... The writer has been closely associated with him for about thirty years .... No man living today can claim greater loyalty to the church than F. B. Srygley. He has fought more battles for the truth of God, won more victories over error and false teaching than any man now living. He has engaged in more battles for the truth in public debate and preaching the gospel, than any other man of modern times .... Those who read his editorials can bear testimony that he waged a relentless warfare against every encroachment on the truth of God and against the enemies of the church of our Lord.

" ... The writer cannot recall now a single instance where he was on the wrong side of any question that disturbed the peace and happiness of God's people .... He had a clear insight into the intricate problems of the brotherhood. He could analyze with accuracy the problems that disturbed and troubled the churches. He could apply 'scriptural teaching and solve these problems.' ... It fell his lot to deal with problems and situations that called for courage. Brother Srygley never faltered, evaded, or compromised any truth or righteous principle. He knew that the truth in many sections is unpopular, yet he did not shrink from declaring in an effective way the truth. Any enemy that he has was made in fighting for the truth."

Again we call attention to the statement of the present **Advocate** editor's comment regarding. F. B. Srygley when he died. In the **Gospel Advocate**, 1940, p. 484, he wrote:

"Like old John Knox, he never feared the face of man. He was loyal to Christ first, last, and all the time. He would not wink at error in the practice of anyone, not even in his most intimate friends."

BUILDING ON THE GOOD

SOLVING FAMILY PROBLEMS

A SERIES OF STUDIES FOR CONCERNED CHRISTIANS —
OLDER AND YOUNGER, MARRIED AND SINGLE,
PARENTS AND CHILDREN.

By James R. Cope

SOLVING FAMILY PROBLEMS

By
JAMES R. COPE

Copyright, 1971
By
James R. Cope
Revised and Enlarged

Order from Author,
301 Greencastle Ave.,
Temple Terrace, Florida 33617

FOREWORD

Everybody has or will have a domestic problem. Whether husband, wife, father, mother, son, daughter, brother, sister-sooner or later all experience some kind of emotional problem involving moral and spiritual prin ciples.

Thirty-five years as a preacher and the same period as a teacher-admin istrator dealing with every age level from the First Grade through Senior College reveals one indisputable reality - everybody needs help!

Kinsmen in the spirit as well as the flesh should be able to resolve their problems much more easily than those who know not God, and these studies are designed to help all who call on the Lord out of a pure heart as they face the realities of being true to Christ amidst a faithless world wherein the family is under attack and too often losing its identity.

To hundreds of brethren who have encouraged me to make these lessons available in permanent form I am grateful. Beyond this, however, to Georgia Deane, who has been only a faithful wife and Godly mother and to Connie, Cathy and Jim, Jr. ("Butch"), for bringing me all the joys of a happy home I owe a debt I can never pay.

James R. Cope

Temple Terrace, Florida

February 4, 1971

ANOTHER WORD

When the above statement was written, I had delivered this series of lessons six times. When 1971 ends I shall have presented this material in person to 34 different churches across America. Repeated coverage has suggested a few revisions for clarity. Basically, however, this second print ing is the same as the first. I have been greatly encouraged by the plans of some churches to follow my pe.rsonal presentations with classes for parents and others for children while using this arrangement as workbooks for more detailed study of these important matters. In 36 years of preaching I have never seen such a consistently enthusiastic response by my brethren to my efforts. As never before they are seeing the need for this type, mate rial as a vital part of their teaching program. I praise God for the good done.

James R. Cope

October 18, 1971

LESSON NO. 1

CHRIST — THE CHRISTIAN'S AUTHORITY IN ALL RELATIONSHIPS

I. Fleshly Relationships Are Entered by Physical Birth.

A. Domestic (family), civil (governmental) and Adamic (general society) — and without personal choice.

B. Each relationship has distinct identity.

   1. Family - usually an agreement between man (husband) and woman (wife) normally resulting in offspring possessing common fleshly interests with parents.

   2. Civil - consists of rules and non-sanguineous subjects bound by common law and cooperating for mutual protection and projection of common interests.

   3. Adamic - common kinship through Adam, the father of the human race. Its nature prohibits common collective action.

II. Christ Calls For Recognition of His Authority Through the Gospel.

A. Because intelligent man is responsible to his Creator for his actions, he is accountable for his transgression of God's law. Adam and all his descendants who have sinned are guilty before God and need a Savior to restore them to God's favor; hence, the gospel, I Jno. 3:4, Rom. 1:16-3:26; 5:8; 6:1-23.

B. Christ announced His universal authority after He had proved His right to it, Matt. 28:18; Rom. 1:1-4.

C. Apostles and Holy Spirit were to witness to claims of Christ and they did witness, Jno. 14:26; 16:13; 17:17; 15:26, 27; Lk. 24:45-49; Acts 1:8, 26; 2:4, 32, 33; 5:31, 32; 2 Pet. 1:16-18; Eph. 3:1-5; 1 Pet. 1:10-12.

D. Acceptance of Jesus' LORDSHIP was the result of this testimony, Acts 2:36-38.

E. Every baptized believer has committed himself to the control of Christ, 1 Cor. 6:19, 20; 2 Cor. 10:3-5; 1 Jno. 3:18; Jas. 1:21-25;1 Pet. 3:15.

Ill. Respondents to the Gospel Call Are Volunteers.

A. They experience a "new birth," Col. 1:13; Jno. 3:1-7; Matt. 7:21; Lk. 6:46. The figurative language of Jno. 3:5 gives way to the plain language of the law of "Spirit of Life" (Rom. 8:2) as expressed in Mk. 16:15, 16; Acts 2:38; Gal. 3:26, 27.

B. This "in Christ" relationship is a contrast between "old" and "new" things, 2 Cor. 5:17.

  1. The "new man" vs. the "old man," Eph. 4:20-24; Col. 3:9, 10.

  2. "Spiritual death" as "children of wrath" vs. "spiritual blessings" as "sons," Eph. 3:1-5; 2:1-10.

  3. A "new walk" and "new" service, Rom. 6:3-5; 7:4-7.

C. This "in Christ" relationship is **wholly spiritual**, based on spiritual kinship.

  1. A "brotherhood" exists among those who do God's will, Matt.12:48-50 Heb. 2:11, 12, 17; 3:1; 1 Pet. 2:17.

2. Divine love made possible this relationship (Jno. 3:16; 1 Jno. 3:1, 2; 4:9-11, 19) and love is the identifying badge of these spiritual brethren, Jno. 13:34, 35; 1 Jno. 2:7, 8; 4:19.

D. These kinsmen have been "called out" of the world of sin and are identified as "the church" (assembly), Matt. 16:18; Eph. 3:22; 5:23; Col. 1:24. **Together** and **functionally** they are always located geographically, such as, "the churches of Christ," "the churches of Judea in Christ," "the churches of Galatia," and "the church of God which is at Corinth," Rom. 16:16; Gal. 1:22; 1:2; 1 Cor. 1:2.

E. The term **Christian**, meaning "of, or belonging to, Christ," signifies the identity of the "new creature." Usage of the name emphasizes these points:

1. A relationship based on kinship, Acts 11:26.

2. A character (being) identified with the holiness of Christ in contrast to one of sin, Acts 26:28.

3. A life of action identified by doing the will of Christ, 1 Pet. 4:15, 16. **Note:** From these three occurences of **Christian** we may define the word as "a believer baptized into and wearing the name of Christ who partakes of Christ's holiness and performs his work."

IV. The Christian Is Christ's Minister in Every Relationship.

A. By faith Christ indwells the Christian through His word (Eph. 3:17; Rom. 10:17). The Christian sees through the eyes of Jesus, hears through His ears, speaks with His tongue and feels with His hands.

B. The Christian, in turn, indwells every relationship - fleshly and spiritual - as Christ's "light," Phil. 2:12-16.

1. **In the family** the Christian may be a marital companion, parent or child.

   a. **As a husband or wife** the will of Christ controls, Eph. 5:22-33; Col. 3:18, 19.

   b. **As a parent** the will of Christ controls, Eph. 6:4; Col. 3:21; 2 Cor. 12:14.

   c. **As a child** the will of Christ controls, Eph. 6:1-3; Col. 3:20; 1 Tim. 5:4, 8, 16b.

2. **In the civil state** the Christian may be a ruler or subject but always a subject with reference to his ultimate Lord and Master, Rom. 13:1-7; 1 Pet. 2:13-17; Titus 3:1; Acts 5:29; Rom. 12:17, 18.

3. **In the Adamic relationship** the Christian is to love, honor and do good to all men according to Christ's will, Gal. 6:10; Jas. 2:1-12; cf. Lk. 10:25-37; Rom. 13:10; 1 Pet. 2:17.

4. **In the brotherhood relationship** the Christian is to love, honor and do good according to Christ's will, Rom. 12:10; Gal. 5:13; Phil. 2:1-4; 1 Pet. 1:22; 2:17; 1 Thes. 4:9, 10; 5:14, 15: Heb. 13:1; 1 Jno. 4.7

5. **In the congregational relationship** the Christian is to do his part according to the will of Christ, Heb. 10:24, 25; 1 Cor. 11:17-34; Acts 20:7; 1 Cor. 16:1, 2; Eph. 5:18, 19; Col. 3:16, 17; 1 Thes. 5:17, 18; Heb. 13:17; 1 Pet. 5:1-5.

6. **Economics** - the making and use of money - is involved in every other relationship and in this

area also the Christian represents Christ's will, Eph. 4:28; 2 Thes. 3:10-12.

    a. **As servants**, Eph. 6:5-8; Col. 3:22-25.

    b. **As masters**, Eph. 6:9; Col. 4:1.

Questions

1. What relationships are entered by fleshly birth?

2. List some elements of each fleshly relationship.

3. Why does man need a Savior?

4. By what means does man learn of the Savior?

5. What declares Christ's divinity?

6. If Jesus is not divine is there any difference between His authority and

7. In what way did the "witness" of the Holy Spirit differ from that of the apostles regarding the person and work of Jesus?

8. Whose authority did Peter invoke in Acts 2:38?

9. To whose control is every believer baptized into Christ committed?

10. According to John 3:5 and Matthew 7:21 who shall enter the kingdom?

11. Is the plain language of Matthew 7:21 and Mark 16:16 equivalent to the "new birth" of John 3:5?

12. List some "old" and "new" things of a spiritual nature.

13. What kinship is wholly spiritual?

14. Who are brethren "in Christ"?

15. What divine emotion made the "in Christ"

relationship possible?

16. What distinctions may be made between the general brotherhood of believers and a local assembly of saints?

17. What three points are emphasized in the Biblical usage of the word Christian(s)?

18. Memorize the definition of the word Christian.

19. May one properly be called a Christian who lacks any one of the points in this definition?

20. How does Christ indwell the Christian?

21. In what ways do the Christian's eyes, ears, tongue and hands serve Christ?

22. What relationship does the Christian indwell?

23. In reality is there a part-time Christian?

24. Summarize the meaning of the lesson topic, "Christ - the Christian's Authority in All Relationships.

LESSON NO. 2

PARENTAL RESPONSIBILITIES

Introduction

1. Every parental duty is to his own child. This is involved in meaning of word **parent**.

2. Parental duties take many forms yet the Bible gives relatively few rules peculiar to parents.

3. Every blessing has a corresponding duty.

a. Parents deliberately choose their peculiar duties when they choose to be parents.

b. Children do not ask to be born and this makes parental duty all the more serious. Before God parents willingly elect to be re sponsible for the minds, hearts and bodies of their children who did not choose them to exercise such prerogatives. See 1 Tim. 5:8; 2 Cor. 12:14.

c. The duty is a sacred trust. Consider the word **gift**

GOD'S ORDERS FOR PARENTS

PROVOKE NOT TO	WRATH	Rebellion, Eph. 6:4
	DISCOURAGEMENT	Broken spirit, Col. 3:21

BUT NURTURE — Cultivate
"whole training & education of children" (Thayer's definition)

WHAT	MORALS	HOW		WHY
	MINDS		Commands &	OBEDIENCE
	Physical nature		Admonitions	"This is right"
	Mind itself		Reproof	Eph. 6:1
	Social relationships		Punishment	
	Right & Wrong		Encouragement	

Consider also 1 Tim. 5:8; 2 Cor. 12:14

in these pas sages: Gen. 33:5; 48:9; Isa. 8:18.

I. **Two Specific Negatives Addressed to Fathers** - "Provoke not your chil dren to wrath" (Eph. 6:4) and "provoke not your children, that they be not discouraged," (Col. 3:21).

A. **Provoke** means "to irritate beyond measure" in Eph. 6:4 and "stir" in Cor. 3:21 (**Young's Analytical Concordance**).

B. "Wrath" leads to **rebellion** while "discouragement" develops a **broken spirit**.

C. Parents need heavenly wisdom to follow these instructions (see Jas. 1:5, 3:17, 18). Yet wisdom (sound judgment) is dependent upon knowl edge. Plato said, "A man's judgement is no better than his facts."

1. Knowledge of **what** a child does is not enough. A parent must know **why** his child acts and speaks as it does.

2. Understanding a child's nature and factors producing his thinking is necessary if one is not to provoke rebellion or a broken spirit.

D. Some factors affecting a child's state of mind may be:

1. His associates' words and actions.

2. Parents of his friends.

3. Teachers' personality and ideas.

4. T.V., radio, movies, and reading.

5. Social pressures from his peers - Fads in dress, hair styles, hobbies, sports, and other fun activities produce loyalties which may seem silly but with which parents must reckon.

6. Parental failures.

   a. To weigh prayerfully the child's point of view, his good intentions or his social pressures.

   b. To balance **positive** interest and helpfulness against the needed "no-no's."

   c. To make only reasonable demands of the child. Parents must be "just," Micah 6:8; Phil. 4:8.

   d. To correct the child calmly. Anger breeds anger; "Grievous words stir up anger," Prov. 15:1.

   e. To punish in harmony with demands of the offense.

f. To punish when penalty is pledged. Threats should be few but carried out when made. A parent's word of honor is at stake.

g. To recognize that a child's problems are as big and meaningful to him at **his age and stage of development** as a parent's problem is to him/her.

h. To look for and encourage a child's good qualities. He should **never** feel that he can never please his parents and should find his greatest joy in obeying them. See Eph. 6:1. A child should never truthfully say, "My parents are my greatest problem!"

7. A discerning parent will sense what is happening to the ever changing child and identify with the youthful mind, yet with wis dom which can direct without becoming divorced from it. It is tragic when parents forget that they were once young. See I Cor. 13:11; 14:20.

E. Some timely texts:

1. Prov. 17:27 - "He that spareth his words hath knowledge; And he that is of a cool spirit is a man of understanding."

2. Prov. 15:1, 23 - "A soft answer turneth away wrath; But a grievous word stirreth up anger." "A man hath joy in the answer of his mouth; And a word in due season, how good is it!"

3. Prov. 25:11 - "A word fitly spoken is like apples of gold in a network of silver."

4. Prov. 29:20 - "Seest thou a man that is hasty in his words? There is more hope of a fool than of him."

II. **"Nurture in the Chastening and Admonition of the Lord."**

A. **Nurture defined**. Of **prideia**, the Greek word translated "nurture," Thayer says, "the whole training and education of childen (which relates to the cultivation of minds and morals, and employs for this purpose now commands and admonitions, now reproof and punishment)."

B. **Nurture - a parental responsibility - practically expressed.** Consider Prov. 22:6; Deut. 6:5-7.

1. The implementing of this "nurture" rests with the parent - "fathers" are commanded.

2. The limitations of this "nurture" are set for parental guidance - "in the chastening (instruction, training) and admonition (putting into the mind) of the Lord." Parents cannot obey God and ignore these qualifications in their "nurturing."

3. The definition of "nurture" prescribes the **action** to be performed by parents and the areas of involvement; hence, the action and areas of parental responsibility to God and one's own child.

a. **Cultivation of "mind"** - anything for the mind's development which is "of the Lord." (Consider "in the Lord" in Eph. 6:1). This "cultivation" involves:

(1) Physical nature - "the heavens and the earth and the sea and all that in them is" (Gen. 1:1;

Acts 4:24; 17:24). This necessarily includes the child's physical body. (1 Cor. 6:19, 20; 1 Tim. 4:8).

(2) The mind itself - the psyche - with which man thinks, reasons, feels, etc. Whatever is properly "cultural" in litera ture, music, art, etc., is included,. cf. Acts 17:28 - "your own poets." Also 7:22- Moses in "'wisdom of Egyptians."

(3) Social relationships - association with other persons and responsibility of child according to his development. This involves his family, government and general humanity. See Lk. 2:52.

b. **Cultivation of "morals"** - that which regards **right** and **wrong** as defined by God. This involves man's duty to God and to man and deals with "spirit" as well as "mind."

4. The perfect illustration of this "nurture" is seen in the subjection of Jesus to His parents as He "advanced in wisdom (mentally) and stature (physically), and in favor with God (spiritually) and man (socially)" - Luke 2:51, 52.

5. The means of this nurturing are:

a. Commanding and admonishing the child. Eph. 6:4 implies commandments. Consider God's confidence in Abraham (Gen. 18:19). Note Prov. 2:1-5; 3:1-4; 6:20-23.

b. Reproving the child - see Prov. 6:23; 10:17; 12:1; 13:18; 15:5, 10, 31, 32.

    c. Punishing the child - see Prov. 10:13; 13:24; 22:15; 23:13, 14; 29:15.

    d. Encouragement - recognize achievements. See Phil. 4:8.

C. **Parental blindness - effective nurture's greatest obstacle.** (When a child says, "My greatest problem is my parents," it is probably too late to rebridge the chasm of separation.) This blindness takes various forms. Consider these "blind spots":

1. **Parental inconsistencies.**

    a. Between parental practice and parental precepts.

    b. In erratic demands so confusing that the child never knows what to expect.

    c. In discipline because of partiality. Remember Jacob and Joseph (Gen. 37:3, 4-36) and Isaac and Rebecca (Gen. 25:28; 27:1-45).

2. **Parental disagreement** - failure to present a solid front on all matters involving allowable or disallowable behavior by the child. This may well involve day-to-day or periodic permissions, prohibitions and punishment. Noticeable discord between parents on any matter creates uncertainty and possible mistrust by the child. Disagreement on allowables, "no-no's" and penalties will create disloyalty, favoritism, ultimate disciplinary breakdown and may well destroy a marriage. "In union there is strength" applies here also.

3. **Parental injustice** in administering punishment in anger, leaving child to think a parent is revengeful rather than loving. See Eph. 6:4; Col. 3:21.

4. **Parental indulgence** of child's desires. Disregard of punishment of whims which become character traits will cause any child to flaunt parental respect, rebellion and contempt for parents, civil and spiritual authority. Consider Eli's experience. 1 Sam. 2:22-25; 3:3-18. Punishment is never an end in itself but a means to an end. Enforced love through punishment when begun early de velops respect for parents and God's will. See Heb. 12:5-11.

5. **Parental indifference** to the child's real needs for understanding, penalties, rewards, justice and mercy - **all in love.**

6. **Parental stupidity** wherein reason is displaced by emotions, ig norance or dullness of discernment. The following statements point up this problem (These are positive statements. Reflect on their truthfulness.)

  a. True love always works for the child's ultimate welfare, not its temporary pleasure.

  b. An act of a child which mars his character is incomparable to one which disturbs a parent's convenience or personal pleasure. Consider a child's lying, stealing, etc., along with parents' desire to golf, fish, party or even sleep.

  c. A failure to punish a child after warning is (at least could be) a warning to parents that they will ultimately be punished by that same child.

  d. Failure to teach a child self-reliance and initiative is to ex change strength for weakness, sturdiness for instability, inde pendence for insecurity, bravery for cowardice and faith for doubt. It is to confuse rights with responsibilities and make hippies out of potential heroes.

e. Overdoing of a child's accomplishments in his presence and to others is as destructive as failure to take note of his achieve ments at proper time and occasion. One "is as bad as the other if not worse!"

f. Failure to recognize the various stages of a child's physical social development and adjust "nurture" accordingly is to create a freak for the child's would-be buddies to ridicule, a misfit for family friends to pity and to produce a most embar rassing situation to explain!

g. Every "no-no" and every "yes-yes" should be prompted by love and each must find its explanation to the child by a parent who makes the child understand that he/she as a parent is amenable to God for his treatment of his child as is the child amenable to God for its treatment of the parent.

h. A child mature enough to ask an intelligent question is mature enough rightly to expect and receive an intelligent answer.

i. The child who is taught to pray that his parents may "nurture" him in the chastening and admonition of the Lord is learning the meaning of wisdom. "A wise son maketh a glad father."

j. Parental companionship with a child is the surest guarantee of child companionship with parents as the shadows lengthen.

k. The child who does not learn right from wrong from his par ents will probably learn wrong is right through his associates.

I. Learning by earning is good for the head, heart and pocket book. By failure to learn to earn one learns to be a deadbeat or a thief or both.

m. The child not allowed to entertain his friends at home will be entertained by them away from home and to his parents' great sorrow.

n. He who does not learn that he is to requite his parents misses a fundamental law of God. See 1 Tim. 5:4.

o. Parental disagreements in a child's presence creates confusion to use one parent against the other.

p. The child who learns truthfulness and honesty, dependability in responsibility, modesty and courtesy is building that "good name" which "is rather to be chosen than great riches" and the "loving favor" which is more valuable "than silver and gold" (Prov. 22:1).

q. Four steps guarantee absolute failure for parents: the wrong example, a lack of correction, a breakdown in communication, and no teaching of God's word.

NOTE: Parents stupid enough to overlook these perils make "F" on their report card and justly deserve the grade they receive.

Ill. Signposts* of Delinquency: Watch for them in your family!

  A. Extreme faddist appearance and dress.

  B. Constant rudeness and disobedience.

C. Habitual lying.

D. Cruelty to animals.

E. Persistent truancy.

F. Continual unexplained hours of activity.

G. Repeated vandalism.

H. Theft.

I. Possession of illegal weapons.

J. Use of intoxicants or drugs.

*These signposts present the gruesomely clangerous line "that sep arates normal teen frustration from a set course pointing directly to a wasted future." List is taken form **Our Youth and Their Parents** pub lished by the Louisville and Jefferson County Youth Commission, Room #2, City Hall, Louisville, Ky. 40202. Below is another section taken from the same publication.

IV. **Family Understanding Yardstick**

"A. **The National Association of Mental Health** has listed ten basic needs· of youth - criteria necessary to support the healthy growth of a young person through his transition years between childhood and manhood.

1. ACCEPTANCE- Every young person needs to believe his parents like him for himself; that they like him all the time and not only when he acts according to their ideals of the way a child should act; that they always accept him, though they may not always approve of the things he does.

2. CONTROL - Youth needs to know that there are limits to what he is permitted to do and that his

parents will hold him to those limits; he must be taught self-control to avoid hurting himself and others when he feels jealous or angry.

3. FAITH - Youth needs a set of moral standards to live by, a belief in human values, kindness, courage, honesty, generosity, and justice.

4. GUIDANCE - Youth needs to have friendly help in learning how to behave toward persons and things; grown-ups around him should show by example how to get along with others.

5. INDEPENDENCE - Youth needs to know his parents have con fidence in him and will help him develop his ability to do good things for himself and others.

6. LOVE - Youth needs to know his parents love him, want him and enjoy him; that he matters to someone and that there are people around him who care what happens to him.

7. PRAISE - Every young person needs approval. Youth, like adults, needs "pat on the back" for something good they have accomplished. It is not small; it is important to youth.

8. PROTECTION - Youth needs to know his parents want him safe from harm; that they will help him when he feels a strange or frightening situation.

9. RECOGNITION - Every young person needs to be recognized for what he is inside and outside the home. Consider him in plan ning a new home, buying furniture, a new car, or going on a vacation.

10. SECURITY - Youth needs to know his home is a place of safety; that his parents will be around in time of need, that he does be long to, and is an important member of the family.

B. **HOW DO YOU MEASURE UP?**

1. Does he know that he has a special place as an important mem ber of your family which no one else could ever fill; can he rely on your always liking him for himself even when you don't like some of the things he does?

2. Does he understand the necessity of discipline and that you will hold him to certain determined limits; has he been helped to develop self-control in all of his personal relationships?

3. Have you shown him by example the importance of honesty, kindness, courage, generosity_ and justice; does he understand the value of moral standards and their significance in his everyday life?

4. Has he been given guidance for making sound choices of responsible action outside the home under conflicting pressures; does he respect the rights of others in normal daily relationships?

5. Have you helped him understand that increased independence carries with it increased responsibility; does he believe that you trust him to do right within the limits of his experience?

6. Does your child know that you love and want him; does he believe in his heart that he truly matters to you and that you care what happens to him?

7. Do you praise his efforts so that he enjoys the challenge of new projects that prove his worthiness to his family and community; do you help him accept his failures as well as his successes and encourage him to investigate new experiences within the boundaries of good judgment?

8. Does he know that your concern for his safety comes from your love for him; that you will help him always as he takes new steps?

9. Do you always consider him in planning activities and making important decisions that will affect the family; does he feel free to express his ideas and contribute to discussions?

10. Is he sure that you are concerned for his safety and understand the many influences that can affect him outside your home? Does he know you will always protect him in time of crisis?

Most parents cannot answer an unqualified "yes" to all of these yardstick questions, but all parents should be aware of the great responsi bility inherent in these questions.

Questions

1. What is primarily implied in the word **parent**?
2. What corresponds to blessings?
3. What duties are automatic when two people become parents?
4. What is there about the birth of a child which makes parenthood serious?
5. What do children as a "gift" of the Lord imply?
6. What does "provoke" mean?

7. What are some factors which demand parental kindness and under standing of a child's thinking?

8. What often produces actions and reactions which adults consider silly?

9. In those situations (#8) what problem do parents face?

10. What are the two basic results of provoking (irritating, stirring) a child?

11. What thought is common to Proverbs 15:1, 23; 17:27; 25:11; 29:20?

12. What is the result of a wrathful parental chastizing of a child?

13. What should a parent never have said **truthfully** of him by a child?

14. What points of understanding will help prevent parental provoking of their children?

15. List three ways in which parents may provoke children.

16. Quote Proverbs 22:6.

17. Who is told to "nurture" children?

18. Whose children are directly involved in this command?

19. What two basic qualities of the child are to be "cultivated" by parents?

20. What are some things in which the mind is to be cultivated? (Be able to cite supporting scriptures.)

21. What is meant by **morals**?

22. Who alone ultimately determines moral "right" and "wrong"?

23. What four elements are involved in perfect nurture?

24. What are four means of accomplishing the nurturing God requires of parents?

25. When is it probably too late for parents to nurture a child effectively?

26. What is probably parents' greatest obstacle in effecting proper nurture of their children?

27. List six "blind spots" in parental nurturing.

28. What do you consider the most common inconsistency in nurturinga child?

29. What results when a child observes marked discord between its parents

30. What may cause a child to think a parent is revengeful rather than loving?

31. What will cause a child to flaunt all authority?

32. What results from parental indifference to a child's real needs?

33. In your judgment what are the five most glaring marks of parental stupidity?

34. Can you discuss intelligently the reasons behind the ten "signposts of delinquency" and the "ten basic needs of youth" listed under "Family Understanding Yardstick"? Study them carefully.

LESSON NO. 3

DISCIPLINE IN THE FAMILY

Introduction

Had God intended for children to control parents, He would have arranged for them to bear and care for them accordingly.

The Scriptures show God's wisdom and order. Read these: Eph. 6:4; Exod. 20:12; Prov. 30:17; Rom. 1:30; 2 Tim. 3:2. The latter two texts emphasize the result of children's disregard for parental authority.

Satan wins a major victory over parents and robs the child when he can destroy the following:

1. Parental love and pity, Tit. 2:4; Psa. 103:13.

2. Material provisions, 2 Cor. 12:14; 1 Tim. 5:8; Eph. 4:28.

3. Parental nurture of children, Eph. 6:4; Col. 3:21. cf. Heb. 12:5-8. Some of his temptations are found in irritating family situations, questions about the divinity of Jesus, the origin of life, origin of the universe, the need for prayer, Bible study, church attendance, dancing, petting, drinking intoxicants, dope, obscene pictures and dress, and vulgar speech.

Thoughtful parents will be alert to Satan's wiles.

I. **What Is Meant by Discipline?**

A. Discipline is "the treatment suited to a disciple."

B. The word **disciple** basically means "a learner," i.e., "a taught or trained one" (Young's **Analytical Concordance**). In Biblical usage it comes to mean "a follower." There were "the disciples of John" and "disciples of the Pharisees" (Mk. 2:18). Most of its 270 New Testament occurrences refer to followers of Jesus. Isa. 8:16 is its only occurrence in the Old Testament.

C. Our subject restricts us to persons in the family relationship. Here we are considering discipline as treatment that is for the best inter est and ultimate good of one who is learning or being taught. Punish ment is only one phase of discipline.

D. The design of discipline is to produce obedience in purpose and fact. Parental authority should be with firmness to make obedience advisable, with wisdom to make obedience natural and with love to make obedience pleasant.

E. Discipline must begin early. See 2 Tim. 1:5; 3:14, 15.

II. Some Elements of Discipline. These should be recognized by both parents and children.

A. A sense of responsibility must be learned - Lamentations 3:27.

B. Example must be prominent.

1. Children are great imitators, Ezek. 16:44.

2. Solomon was admonished to follow David's example, 1 Kgs. 3:14.

3. Paul admonished to this end, 1 Cor. 11:1.

4. "I'd rather see a sermon than hear one ... "

C. Precept in commands, instruction and admonition must be in evi dence, Gen. 18:19; Deut. 4:9, 10; 6:7; 11:19; Ps. 18:1-4.

D. Correction is a divinely recognized principle, Heb. 12:5-11.

   1. It is needed, Prov. 19:18; 22:15; 23:13, 14; 29:15-17.

   2. It should always harmonize with God's will, Eph. 6-4.

   3. It should always be consistent with love, Prov. 3:11, 12.

III. **God's Plan for the Child in the Child-Parent Relationship Is Two-fold.**

A. Obedience to parents: "Children, obey your parents in the Lord, for this is right," Eph. 6:1.

   1. Obedience " in the Lord" is obedience to the Lord. Consider Col. 3:20-24, noticing especially "fearing the Lord," "Ye serve the Lord Christ," "as unto the Lord."

      a. No child may disregard God's will in favor of human will for "We must obey God rather than men," Acts 5:29. cf. Lk. 2:51, 52.

      b. Parents must cause the child to recognize the sovereignty 0f God in all things all the time and that the parent himself is disobeying God when he fails to discipline his child.

   2. Causing the child to obey and to "obey from the heart" is the design and object of discipline. A sense of right and wrong must be imparted to the child by the parent. This is done by word and example (See Deut. 6:6-9). Consider these: lying vs. truth-telling; stealing vs. honesty; murder vs. life's sanctity; vulgarity and forni cation vs. purity

of mind and body; covetousness vs. cheerful stewardship.

3. Obedience to God in all relationships must be instilled into the child. Consider these: child-parent; citizen-government; employee (servant)-employer (master); pupil-teacher; brother-sister; wife husband.

B. Honor of parents: "Honor thy father and mother," Eph. 6:2.

1. Consider direct order in 1 Tim. 5:4, 8, 16a.

2. Jesus applied this command to mean children are to "provide for" their parents. See Mark 7:1-13, especially verses 9-13.

3. There is "honor" to bestow in addition to material things which money cannot buy. Consider tenderness, conversation of news or memory, a loving kiss, arm around the shoulder of a father or mother, a fond embrace, an automobile drive. "It's the little things that count." Children shall and should "rise up and call her" - the worthy mother - "blessed." See Prov. 31:10-31.

Questions

1. List several areas wherein Satan's temptations are found.

2. What will thoughtful parents teach children about Satan's will?

3. What do Rom. 1:30 and 2 Tim. 3:2 reflect about children's attitude toward parents?

4. When does Satan win a major victory over parents?

5. Define **discipline**.

6. What is the design of discipline?

7. Is discipline always punitive?

8. List four elements of discipline.

9. What are the two primary commands God addresses to children regard ing parents?

10. What is equivalent to obedience "in the Lord"?

11. Should a parent teach a child that he (parent) is obeying God when he disciplines the child? Discuss.

12. How diligently were Israelite parents to discipline their children?

13. List several moral matters about which parents should teach children.

14. What are some relationships in which the child should be taught obedi ence to God?

15. Mark 7:1-13 what interpretation did Jesus give to the command, "Honor thy father and mother"?

16. Does "honoring" parents involve more than providing material comforts for them?

17. What does "requite" mean?

18. Will one ever be able to fully requite one's parents?

19. What are some things money cannot buy?

NATURAL STAGES OF DEVELOPMENT TO RECOGNIZE IN CHILDREN*

1. INFANCY (1-6 years)

Dependent. Irresponsible, wiggler, rapid growth, short-span activities. Guided play most important in training.

434

Major Interests. Self, subjective.

Imitative. He learns by playing a part. Loves rhythm activities such as flying birds, swaying trees, marching children.

Motivations. Largely by pleasure and advantage, often by coercion. Control must be largely external.

Major Life Pattern. Habits, feelings, attitudes are being taught, and caught - so much so that some religionists say that if given a child till it is seven years old they have no fear of its departing from the training they give. It is a time when home influence is strongest and most exclusive.

Limitations. The child has a limited vocabulary. It learns by "seeing," "touching" and pointing out things. The child is limited 'in coordina tion. He has poor use of his small muscles for drawing, coloring, cut ting, etc. Must have adult aid. He fears the new. The 2 and 3 year old must be wooed rather than forced into group activity.

2. CHILDHOOD (6-12 years)

Dependent. Still somewhat dependent, but more or less imitative. Active, imaginative, keen memory.

Intellectual Interests. This is a time when intellectual interests are easily developed -   the time·to   instill important facts and principles to be appreciated in later years.

Major Interests. It is a time when parents are heroes, paragons, oracles. Or it could be some other hero. Bible characters are important at this time in their lives. ·They are curious and collectors. The child at this age is enthusiastic about the mysterious; codes, object lessons are ata high peak; projects and collections of one sort or another are a part of life. He belongs to something, and is about ready to come into the church.

General. Control is largely authoritative. And possessive. Idealistic. Gang spirit and rivalry. Girls dislike boys, and boys detest sissy girls.

3. ADOLESCENCE (12-18 years).

    This is a crucial age — some have termed it an "age of crisis." It is a transition from childhood to adulthood — and is approached rather slowlv.

    Critical Period. This age is characterized by instability, inconsistency, unpredictableness, independence, criticalness, dissatisfaction, resentment of restraint, egotism, vanity - a time that tries both parents and the growing person. It is a time when children need the sympathetic understanding of both parents.

    Ideals. This is a time when ideals develop, with hero worship and idealistic imitation at their peak -   b o y s appealed to by advanture - by action, power, courage; and girls by romance -   by the strange and wonderful, with emphasis on the passive virtues of love and devotion under trying circumstances.

    Transitions. Adolescence is a time when childhood dependences and ways of life are abandoned more or less for good. This cannot be achieved without conflict and confused feelings - moodiness, !onli ness, self-doubt. It takes years for this transition to adulthood to ap proach a degree of stability. Between the ages of 9 and 12 - the period of pre-adolescence - the child loses some of the charm and tractability of childhood; he begins to gripe about accustomed routines at home, to resist rules and challenge regulations. His language and habits become sloppy. His attentions and concentration suffer; his homework becomes an ordeal. In every way the pre-adolescents and parents get on each other's nerves. The child at this age is at war with time. Girls mature some one to three years earlier than boys. The adolescent swings rapidly from independence to dependence and back; he is fearful one day, over-confident the next; he is moody, over sensitive, never quite sure of himself.

Identity. At this stage the child is no longer "parent-centered" but is "other-centered." It is a time of struggle emotionally. The counsel of parents is less sought, often resisted. Often a teacher or other adult serves as the adolescent's model. It is at this state of sexual maturity that the young person's love needs are directed away from his family to members of the opposite sex outside. The fact that he begins to withdraw his affections from those nearest him makes him rather lonely and intensely self-centered. It is at this period that conscience is awakened, a period of emotional interest in religion, and when conversations are most numerous. It is a time of choosing certain areas of identity such as mates, religious identity, schools, groups of one sort or another. During this time of sexual maturation, it is normal for young people to find themselves engaging in sexual experimentation such as petting, necking, kissing, dancing and other forms common in this area.

Guidance. Parents must realize that great changes have been wrought since they were boys and girls and try to place themselves in their children's position. However careful and tactful parents may be, there will come inevitable clashes. However the adolescent behaves, he still very much needs his parents. More than anything else, the adoles cent needs his parents' trust in his essential goodness. And the parent still bears the responsibility for his adolescent.

* The above is from P. D. Wilmeth, <u>The Christian Home</u>, pp 63, 64, with permission of the author.

LESSON NO. 4

CHRIST IN THE HOME

Introduction

We know the mind of Christ (Phil. Les:5) only as we hear His words and observe His deeds as given by the Four Gospels and conveyed by other inspired writers. Let us observe some revealing situations and statements.

I.   Christ in His Own Home

    A. Our Lord's disposition toward obedience in His youthful years, Lk. 2:51. cf. Eph. 6:1-3.

    B. Jesus' interpretation of the Fifth Commandment, Mk. 7:1-13. cf. 1 Tim. 5:4, 8, 16.

II. Christ in the Home of Others, -Lk. 10:38-42.

    A. Jesus taught as He had occasion.

    B. This story shows where emphasis should be placed. cf. Matt. 6:33.

III. The Sanctity of Marriage, Matt. 19:9.

IV. The Rule That Always Works, 1 Cor. 13:4-8. cf. Eph. 5-22-33.

Questions

1. How may one person know the mind of another?

2. How only may one know the mind of Christ?

3. What one expression shows Jesus' attitude toward parental authority?

4. What lesson should children learn from this example of Jesus?

5. What does Ephesians 6:1-3 require of children?

6. According to Mark 7:1-13, what did certain Jews teach and practice which set aside God's command, "Honor thy father and mother"?

7. Whose house is mentioned in Luke 10:38-42?

8. Did Martha sin by "serving" in her house?

9. What mistake was Martha making?

10. What "good part" was Mary choosing?

11. What did Jesus command in Matt. 6:33?

12. What is the common point of emphasis in Matt. 6:33 and Luke 10:42?

13. What did Jesus forbid in Matt. 19:9?

14. Who has a right to alter Jesus' teaching on putting away one's companion?

15. According to Ephesians 5:22-33, what attitude should husband and wife have toward each other?

16. What rule mentioned in 1 Cor. 13:4-8 never fails?

17. List those qualities which are always found in true love.

18. Is there any reason to think love will fail when honestly practiced by all members of a family?

LESSON NO. 5

RECREATION- HOW SHALL A CHRISTIAN CHOOSE?

Introduction

The Industrial Age with its 40-hour work week and the urbanization of American living habits have left most persons with approximately 68 hours each week not spent sleeping (56 hrs.) or "in church" (4 hrs.). The Christian must use this time for good or evil. Which shall it be?

I. **Some Primary Considerations**.

A. The distinction between dissipation - that which tears down or de stroys - and recreation, literally, re-creation - that which builds up or renews physical energies after labor has tired the body and mental energies after toil has wearied the mind.

B. Jesus set the example for rest when He said to His disciples, "Come ye yourselves apart into a desert place, and re.st awhile," Mk. 6:31.

C. The Christian needs to keep two thoughts before himself always

1. "Prove all things; hold fast that which is good," 1 Thes. 5:21. cf. 2 Cor. 13:5.

2. "Avoid every form of evil," 1 Thes. 5:22.

II. **Tests for Helping a Christian Choose His Recreation.**

NOTE: No one person can know all the specific activities in which all Christians may participate without embracing evil. That which may be right for one could possibly be wrong for another de pending on circumstances. Rom. 14:23 deals with the individual conscience.

A. Does it hurt my body? 1 Cor. 6:19.

B. Is it within my financial means?

    1. I am a steward (1 Cor. 4:2. cf. 1 Pet. 4:10).

    2. Care of mind and body should be a budgetary consideration. It involves the "whole man."

C. Does it appeal to the indecent within me?

    1. There is a difference between the "old man" and the "new man" in his practice, Eph. 4:17; Col. 3:1-14; Gal. 5:17, 19-21.

    2. Proper thinking will help here. See Phil. 4:8; 2 Cor. 10:5; Rom. 12:1, 2.

D. Does it identify me with evil companions?

    1. Which way is the good influence flowing? 1 Cor. 15:33.

    2. Constant association with worldly-minded persons makes spiritual concern difficult. It dulls the percreption.

E. Does it hurt my influence?

    1. I am responsible for my good name. Prov. 22:1.

    2. I must be concerned about my weaker brother. 1 Cor. 8:13; 10:32; Rom. 14:21; 1 Tim. 4:12.

F. Does it harm me spiritually?

    1. What does it do to my friendship with God? He must always be first. Matt. 6:33; 22:37, 38. cf. Lk. 8:14.

    2. The acid test: would I ask Jesus to go with me and

participate? See Acts 5:29.

3. The Christian, young or old, must and can, by God's grace, stand against social pressure. See Mk. 14:66-72; 1 Cor. 10:12, 13; Eph. 6:10-18.

Questions

1. What is "leisure time"?

2. Must a Christian engage in evil to "prove all things"? If not, how shall he "prove" anything and everything?

3. What is the difference between recreation and dissipation?

4. What example did Jesus establish regarding recreation?

5. What does Rom. 14:23 teach regarding one's conscience?

6. Who dwells in a Christian's body?

7. What is a Christian to do with his body?

8. List some things which may dishonor one's body.

9. What is required of stewards?

10. How do you know it is right to spend money on recreation?

11. What is meant by indecency?

12. May a Christian ever give way to indecency or sensuality without sin? If so, when, where and how?

13. Can a Christian control his thoughts?

14. What may evil companionships do?

15. Does association with evil men mean sin to the Christian who associates?

16. How may Jesus' action in Luke 15:1, 2 be harmonized with 2 Cor. 6:14ff.?

17. How may Christians be "salt" (Matt. 5:14) unless they contact the world?

18. When is a Christian's saving power lost?

19. Is there any material wealth or social prestige as important as a good name?

20. What attitude must a Christian have toward a "weak brother"?

21. Who must be considered first always and everywhere?

22. What is an appropriate question to apply to every situation a Christian faces?

23. How may a Christian overcome temptation?

LESSON NO. 6

PROBLEMS OF YOUNG CHRISTIANS

Introduction

There is no difference between the young people of today and any other time in the world's history as regards their basic physical, mental and emotional drives.

Morally and spiritually men have always been amenable to God in whose image they are made. This is the area of human experience which concerns the young Christian and the older Christian more than any other because of the area of specific accountability to God who made him and be fore whom he must stand in the day of judgment

(2 Cor. 5:10, Heb. 9:27, Acts 17:30, 31). The manner therefore in which the Christian uses his mind and body will determine what eventually happens to both.

I. The Young Christian's Faith.

    A. It comes from hearing God's word, Rom. 10:17.

    B. By it he/she walks as long as he/she walks with God, 2 Cor. 5:7; 1 Jno. 5:4.

    C. God makes no distinction regarding the belief of an older or younger Christian about anything. All Christians, regardless of age, are bound by the same spiritual laws in every relationship common to all. The word of Christ binds all Christians to do His will everywhere and all the time.

II. Some Divine Observations and Admonitions to Youth.

    A. Eccl. 12:1 - "Remember also thy Creator in the days of thy youth, before the evil days come, and the years draw night, when thou shalt say, I have no pleasure in them."

    B. 2 Tim. 3:15 - "And that from a babe thou hast known the sacred writings which are able to make thee wise unto salvation through faith which is in Christ Jesus.

    2 Tim. 3:16- "Every scripture inspired of God is also profitable for reproof, for correction, for instuction which is in righteousness:

    2 Tim. 3:17 - "that the man of God may be complete, furnished completely unto every good work."

    C. 1 Tim. 5:1, 2 - "Rebuke not an elder, but exhort him as a father; the younger men as brethren; the elder women as mothers; the younger as sisters, in all purity."

D. 1 Tim. 4:12 - "Let no man despise thy youth; but be thou an en sample to them that believe in word, in manner of life, in love, in faith, in purity."

E. 2 Tim 2:22 - "But flee youthful lusts, and follow after righteousness, faith, love, peace with them that call on the Lord out of a pure heart."

F. Tit. 2:4 - "that they may train the young women to love their hus bands, to love their children, not blasphemed:

Tit. 2:6 - "the younger men likewise exhort to be sober-minded: Tit. 2:7 - "in all things showing thyself an ensample of good works; in thy doctrine showing uncorruptness, gravity,

Tit. 2:8 - "sound speech, that cannot be condemned; that he that is of the contrary part may be ashamed."

G. 1 Tim. 5:17 - "I desire therefore that the younger widows marry, bear children, rule the household, give no occasion to the adversary for reviling."

III. Some Problems of Young People.

A. The problem of conscience.

1. Every true Christian recognizes that he belongs to Christ - "Ye are not your own, for ye are bought with a price" (1 Cor. 6:19, 20), that he is answerable to Christ (2 Cor. 5:10) and that to delib erately do what he believes to be sinful is to "defile" the con science (Tit. 1:15, 16; 1 Cor. 8:7) and to "sear" it (1 Tim. 4:2). Nothing is more destructive to a tender conscience than repeated disregard of its cry to the Christian, "You have done wrong! You have sinned! You are not in the

favor of God because you have not done what you knew was right!" Regarding such indifferent matters as eating meats we are told the effect of engaging in **doubtful** practices. God's word says, "He that doubteth is damned if he eat, because he eateth not of faith: for whatsoever is not of faith is sin" (Rom. 14:23).

2. With the young Christian, as with the older Christian, there must be one fundamental question in every situation in every relation ship of life. The question is not: "What do I want to do?" or "What gives me immediate pleasure or fun? or "What will give me the approval of and set me in good standing with my associates?" It is from these alternatives that the Christian turns when on his own, alone with God, he says, "I will do right!"

B. Problems affecting the family from within the family.

1. **Self**. Can it be that I am my own greatest obstacle in having a peaceful, happy family life? Have. I ever really taken a look at myself in the mirror of reality? Have I x-rayed my own mind and heart? Do I have a monopoly on honesty while only older persons possess a monoply on hypocrisy? Is my parent any more ·obligated than I to tell the truth and keep his good name above reproach? Is not God's law of righteousness equally binding on younger and older Christians?

2. **Problem of communication**. Is there truly a "generation gap" between young Christians and their parents? If so, why and whose fault is it?

Is it because young Christians don't understand their parents or that the parents don't understand their children or both? Have school teachers, newspapers, magazines and TV pro grams built up an imaginary barrier between childrern and par- ents? Even if a communication "gap" exists between parents and youth who are non-Chrirstians, does it necessarily follow that the same condition exists between young Christians and their par ents? If one really feels a "gap" exists between himself and his parents, whose duty is it to take the first step to solve the prob lem - the one who is ignorant of it or the one who recognizes the problem? Have I cut off communication with them?

3. **Parents**. Do they understand me? Have I given occasion for their distrusting me? Have I always levelled with them? Are they un reasonable? Do they take time for my things which are important to me? Do I love them -   really? What evidence can I present to prove my love for them? What shows their love to me? Am I impudent? Harsh? Rebellious? Critical? Do I consider my attitude and actions toward my parents in harmony with Ephesians 6:1-3? If not, why not? Am I willing to discuss unselfishly my problem with my parents and "keep my cool" while doing so? Am I being as honest with them as I expect them to be with me?

4. **Brother(s) and/or sister(s)**. Why do we quarrel? Am I contributing to the fussing? Do I treat them with fairness I expect of them? Do I **really try** to understand them in light of their age?

5. **Grandparents**. Do I owe them anything? What will please me when I'm their age? Do I hurt their feelings? Do I tell them about my friends, fun and general school and social life? Do I ever hug and kiss them? Do I ever ask them to tell about their own lives when young as I am now? Do I ever ask their moral or spiritual advice?

6. **Finances**. Am I aware of the obligations my parents must meet on their financial income? Have I ever asked them to tell me about the financial situation of our family - how much is spent for food, clothing, shelter, medical bills, automobile, insurance, taxes, interest on debts, repayment of debts, church contributions and plans for financing my own and the other children's college education? Do I look for jobs to help relieve my family's financial burden? Do I complain because my friends have finer clothes or houses? (How must such make my parents feel?) What can I do to help the financial situation in my family? Do I insist on using a family car when I could as well walk?

7. **Friends**. Do I insist on bringing friends to our house against the known disapproval of my parents? Do my parents always know the person I am dating? Do I insist on visiting another friend's home when my parents disapprove? Does the dress style or hair style of my friends embarrass my parents?

C. **Problems of the Spirit**. Read Rom. 8:5-14; 12:1, 2, 9-21; 1 Cor. 13:1-7; Gal. 5:16, 17, 22-25; Eph. 4:17-24, 28; 5:2, 8-21; 1 Thes. 5:12-24; 1 Pet. 2:5, 9; Eph.

6:10-18; 2 Tim. 3:16, 17; 1 Cor. 2:12, 13; 2 Cor. 11:2, 3; 1 Pet. 5:8.

1. **The Christian's life is Spirit controlled by the word of God.**

2. **The Christian is under relentless attack.** The young Christian lives in a culture whose greatest emphasis is upon material things - the **things** money will buy. The youth who chooses to live for Christ also chooses to fight a never-ending battle against the "pull" of the **people and things** of this present evil age which can (without dependence upon God) and will (without dependence upon God) completely engulf his mind and spirit and ultimately extract every vestige of spiritual interest and life from him. Some of these forces challenge his intellect, seeking to create doubt regarding the existence, revelation and workings of God while others challenge his spiritual zeal, growth and development in the image of Christ.

3. **Problems of intellectual honesty.**

    a. **The divinity of Jesus Christ** (Matt. 16:13-18; Jno. 7:12; Jno. 1:1-4, 14, 18). Did Jesus of Nazareth really live? Did He die for my sins? How can there be any connection between His death 19 centuries ago with my sense of guilt now? On what reason able basis shall I accept Him and His claim to control my heart and life in this scientific age? Did He really rise from a sealed militarily guarded tomb? Was He really God in fleshly form? Was he and is He eternal?

b. **The inspiration of the Bible** (2 Tim. 3:16, 17, cf. 2 Pet. 3:16). Is this book really from God or is it like any other book - wholly a human production? What evidences proclaim it to be from God and not a compendium of fables and "old wives tales"? Does it really harmonize with scientific knowledge or does true science contradict it? How shall one know that those who wrote the Bible always told the truth? Is the Bible filled with contradictions?

c. **The existence of physical life on earth** (Gen. 1-3, esp. 1:26, 27; 2:7). What of man's origin? Was man created physically up right as he now is with power of reason, judgment and with a conscience - a sense of right and wrong? Or has man evolved from a single cell over many billions of years? Did all plant and animal life originate with one single sexless cell in the sea and is man, therefore, a distant relative to the cocklebur, cockleshell, and cockroach?

d. **The origin of the physical universe** (Gen. 1, 2; Psm. 19:1-6; Heb. 11:3; 2 Pet. 3:1-14). Whence came all the innumerable planetary systems? Did they just happen? Is the perfect in ternal and external order of the various systems the result of a master designer hand at work or is the existence of these bodies and their operation in time and space all by sheer chance?

4. **Problems of spiritual growth.** Read 1 Pet. 2:1, 2; 2 Pet. 3:18.

a. **Private prayer**. Does God really answer prayer? Does God do things when a devout Christian prays that He would not other wise do? How does prayer help God's child? Is prayer like a power switch or sedative to be used when emergencies arise? Are there conditions one must meet for his prayer to be answered? If so, what are they?

b. **Bible reading and study**. Does God have messages which will give information and understanding in dealing with daily living in a world of conflicting voices? Is God's word really food for my soul as bread is for my body? Does the Bible tell me how to avoid evil and be good and do good? Will knowledge and practice of Biblical precepts strengthen me in dealing with right and wrong, understanding the other person's views and in leading others to Christ?

c. **Public worship**. Does observing the Lord's supper with fellow Christians and singing and praying with them really make me a better person? If not, why should we "go to church"? Does my presence encourage others "to love and good works"? Does one really gain any spiritual blessing by joining others in praising God? Is worship an end in itself or a means to an end? If the latter, what does it enable one eventually to achieve?

d. **Money**. Shall a young Christian think of his money (an allow ance or earned) as a gift from God? Does one have any re sponsibility to use it for anything except food, clothing and dates? Does he really achieve any conscious blessing from giving into the treasury to help others preach the gospel, to relieve needy saints or to help keep the local church program alive? Why should one share with anybody else? What good comes from giving away one's money?

e. **Sickness**. Shall one ever consider physical or emotional sickness as a blessing? If so, how? Shall a robust youth become embittered when a freak accident injures him either tempo rarily or for life? Shall he blame his injury on God? How can a Christian turn infirmity into a blessing for self and others?

f. **Death**. Does death in the family or among friends mean God is cruel and unjust? Shall God be blamed for death's entrance among friends and relatives of the young Christian? What shall be a young Christian's attitude toward death? Shall death sober or embitter? What does death say to the young person?

g. **Responsibility to the lost**. As one pledged to Christ, does a young Christian have any obligation to reach non-Christians? Is his responsibility different toward sinners than that of an older Christian? Does youth have opportunities to reach their friends as do older persons? Will God hold one accountable for his time and efforts?

h. **Dealing with the religions of others.** How shall one approach friends with the gospel? Shall he approach them with an arrogant "I-have-the-truth-and-you're-going-to-hell" attitude? Shall a young Christian ask another to study with him? Shall a Christian disregard the religion of one he or she may marry? Is there an obligation here? If so, what is it? Is a Christian able to refute error and teach the truth without knowledge of both? Can a young Christian learn from the experience of older Christians regarding the handling of a situation?

i. **Class teaching.** Does a young Christian frequently have oppor tunity to teach Bible classes to small children or younger teen agers? Should they take advantage of the opportunity? Shall one beg off when requested even though he or she finds time to participate in various social and school activities and per haps hold a money-making job? May one improve his spiritual maturity by meeting this challenge?

j. **Public service.** Shall a young Christian man refuse any oppor tunity to better equip himself for greater usefulness publicly? When asked to lead prayer, read the Scriptures, make a talk, teach a class, serve or preside at the Lord's table, lead singing or perform any other service, should he not do it? Does God require less interest and effort of the younger than the older? Shall one think only of self, only of others, or both as he con templates the Lord's greatest meaningfulness to others and himself?

D. **Problems of the flesh**.

1. The Christian is under a sacred pledge to Christ his Lord to control the desires of his flesh **through his mind**. Yet these desires are played upon by Satan as **Satan tempts him**. Study these Scriptures: Jas. 1:13-15; 1 Cor. 10:13; Rom. 7:18-25; 2 Cor. 10:3-5; 11:2, 3; Rom. 8:1-10; 12:1, 2; Phil. 2:5; 4:8.

2. Satan is helpless to induce the mind to yield to his temptations through the flesh **as long as** Christ through His word controls the Christian's mind. Study carefully 2 Cor. 11:2, 3, especially verse 3, and 2 Cor. 10:3-5, especially verse 5. There can be no moral responsibility apart from the mind. When the mind of a Christian yields itself to the control of Satan he becomes "carnally (fleshly) minded" (Rom. 8-6; 1 Cor. 3:1-4). This is the mind which, under Satan's direction, produces "works of the flesh" as described in Gal. 5:19-21.

3. Some works of the flesh as listed in Galatians 5:19-21:

   a. **Immorality**- fornication, uncleanness, lasciviousness.

   b. **Irreligion** - idolatry, sorcery.

   c. **Disposition** - enmities, strife, jealousies, wraths, factions, di visions, parties, envyings.

   d. **Excess** - drunkenness, revellings.

4. **Questions**: Under which of the foregoing shall a young Christian place the following?

   a. Drinking intoxicants? Why list it thus?

   b. "Pot" (dope)? Why list it thus?

   c. Dancing involving close body contact? Why list it thus?

   d. Dancing involving sensually suggestive girations? Why list it thus?

   e. Petting, fondling? Why list it thus?

   f. Pornography (obscene, sensually suggestive pictures)? Why list it thus?

   g. Words (written, spoken) producing vulgar, salacious thoughts? Why list it thus?

   h. Nakedness? Why list it thus?

   i. Scanty (mini) attire? Why list it thus?

   j. Tight-fitting, exposing-rather-than-concealing clothing? Why list it thus?

   k. Placing otherwise innocent pleasure above worship? Why list it thus?

   I. Using a fortune-teller? Why list it thus?

   m. One who desires evil to come to another? Why list it thus?

   n. Following a man rather than God? Why list it thus?

   o. Willingness to split a church over non-essentials? Why list it thus?

   p. Effort to build up self by another's downfall Why list it thus?

q. Uncontrolled speech? Why list it thus?

May a Christian (one who rightly wears Christ's name, exemplifies His holiness and performs His works) engage in any of these things without throwing off Christ as the King of his heart and Lord of his life? If so, how may it be justified? "Am I my brother's keeper?" See 1 Cor. 8:13. Am I to be concerned about my exam ple and good name? See 1 Cor. 10:31-33; Prov. 22:1; 1 Tim. 4:12.

E. **Problems of Physical health**.

1. **Developing bodies**. Should one ask one of his/her parents about obvious changes in his/her body - what these changes signify, how they should be handled? Are desires for sex abnormal? How should they be handled? If father or mother can't be approached on such matters, who can?

2. **Sickness**. Should one report every ailment to his parents? How should persistent pain or soreness be handled? Are tired eyes and/or continuing headaches following long reading a danger signals? Are fainting spells symptoms of a serious disease or malady? To whom should one go for counsel?

3. **Physical abnormalities**. Is there an unnatural growth on the phys ical body or obvious to touch within the body? Shall sprains, torn muscles and ligaments be reported and handled by parents and/or physician? Are severe pains in the chest or abdomen promptly handled? If a limp, blindness, deafness, or impediment in speech exist from birth or develop with age, how shall they be handled and from whom shall advice be obtained?

4. **Work and recreation**. Is physical labor too heavy, hours too many or job unsuitable to size and/ or age of the worker? Are there hazards to proper body functioning on or off the job? To whom shall one go for discussion? Is the worker re-creating his physical and mental energies after toil has worn the body and concern has wearied the mind by rest, in sleep, or change of scenery, or change in type of activity from work situations? Where my help be found for such discussions?

F. **Problems of mental growth.**

1. **Formal schooling**. Should a junior or senior high student be con cerned about what he wants to follow as a life's occupation? If so, what courses should be taken to help reach this goal? Who shall advise? Shall parents be consulted? What shall a good student do when other students interfere with study situations? Shall he report it? To whom? What if a teacher "gets it in" for a student? How handle?

2. **Self-stimulation - travel, reading, painting, etc**. How shall one find materials needed to enlarge mental stimulation during vaca tion or out-of-school periods? If travel in U.S.A. or abroad is afforded special groups, how shall financially able student learn about it? What if family finances are not able to meet the desire? Can something else be done?

G. **Problems of preparation**.

1. **Higher education**. What should be the primary concern of a young Christian regarding choice of

college he will attend? Should moral and spiritual atmosphere and teaching available be the first consideration? What thought should be given to "big" colleges, "name" colleges, athletics, sororities and fraternities? Should one think in terms of type of life-companion (Christian or non-Christian) he will probably meet in the college he attends? Is this really important? Why?

2. **Preparation for marriage**. Outside of deciding for Christ to be Lord of his life, is there a more important decision affecting one's future than the choice of a life-companion? Should much thought and prayer be given to these marriage matters: its purposes? its indissolubility? its religious liabilities and assets? its responsi bilites and rights? possible differences between husband and wife intellectually,'· educationally, economically, age, size, racially? possible differences in attitudes toward having and caring for children, aged or ill in-laws and toward working wives and mothers, the planning and handling of finances, and what shall be allowed in the home in the form of social activities, entertainment, etc.? What role will the Bible, prayer, and Christ's people play in the family? How shall husband-wife differences be resolved? Shall known differences be settled before or after marriage?

3. **Preparation for occupation**. Should one go blindly ahead in plans for a certain type job without taking aptitude. tests for possible job fitness? Shall one plan in terms of the job that pays the most money? Shall one pray as he plans that God will lead him into whatever realm of economic security that will

be most compatible with spiritual ideals? May a Christian ever properly overlook Matt. 6:33? What does this text mean? Is there ever a second place for Jesus Christ in a Christian's heart and life plans?

Questions

1. Wherein is modern youth the same as others of other ages?

2. Why is a Christian primarily concerned about spiritual and moral matters?

3. With what area does conscience deal?

4. Why is the use of a Christian's mmd and body so important?

5. Whence cometh faith?

6. How relative is faith in the life of a Christian with reference to God and the world?

7. Does God require an older Christian to believe anything that He does not equally require of a younger Christian?

8. Specify several matters of equal importance to the faith of young and old.

9. How often, where and how long is a Christian amenable to God?

10. When should one remember his Creator?

11. How long had Timothy been taught the sacred writings?

12. For what four things are the Scriptures profitable?

13. How should a young Christian treat older men and women and younger men and women?

14. What is the import of the word "despise" in 1 Tim. 4:12?

15. What was Timothy to flee?

16. What role does the conscience play when one sins?

17. May a Christian ever violate his conscience without sin?

18. What should be the basic question of every Christian facing any problem?

19. List seven problems affecting the family from within the family.

20. Which of the seven problems affecting the family do you consider most important? Why?

21. Who controls the Christian's life and through what medium?

22. What is the great emphasis of our modern culture?

23. What two areas within the young Christian's experience do the forces of this present evil age challenge?

24. List four problems involving intellectual honesty.

25. List ten problems of spiritual growth.

26. What is Satan's only avenue of attack upon the Christian?

27. Through what quality of man is the flesh controlled.

28. When does Satan gain control of a person?

29. What is the word describing the mind which Satan directs?

30. List four major divisions of the works of the flesh mentioned in Gal. 5:19-21 and sub-divide each one.

31. According to 1 Pet. 3:1-6, what should be the ornamentation of a Christian woman?

32. Will the adornment of a woman's heart have anything to do with her manner of dress? If so, what will be the effect?

33. Does a Christian have any responsibility toward his brother as regards his own conduct?

34. List four problems of physical health.

35. List two problems of mental growth.

36. List three problems of preparation.

37. List any problems not covered in the outline or these questions with which a young Christian must deal.

LESSON NO. 7

A YOUNG CHRISTIAN'S FAITH IN A FAITHLESS WORLD

Introduction.

Every age has its problems. See Plato (4th Century B.C.).

No evidence that the real disease is different from any other age, i.e., lack of respect for authority - parental, civil, spiritual.

Older persons understand youth problems because they were once young but many parents exert little influence because they are too busy working and playing and partying to care. This does not excuse youth for disobeying God. Bible tells of many young people - Daniel, David, Samuel, Joseph, Paul, Jesus, Timothy, Mary, Rhoda.

I. Some Permanent Realities.

A. No difference in youth's intelligence today and ever.

B. No difference in great decisions youth makes now and previously- occupation, marriage, spiritual values.

C. No difference in basic youth desires and drives now and previously.

    1. Jealousy, anger and murder since Cain's day.

    2. Drunkenness, rebellion and "long hair" since Absalom's day.

    3. Lust and rape since Amnon forced his sister Tamar and sons of Eli prostituted priestly office.

    4. Restlessness, self-will and resentment since prodigal son and elder brother's day, Lk. 15:11ff.

    5. "Youthful lusts" were and are destructive of Christ's image ina young Christian, 2 Tim. 2:22.

D. No difference between faith of younger and older Christian. Age has nothing to do with faith regarding God, Christ, gospel, Holy Spirit, baptism, church, worship, marriage morality and civic duty.

E. No difference in God's expectation of youth's behavior today and previously 1 Tim. 5:1, 2; 4:16; Tim. 2:22; Titus 2:6; 1 Pet. 5:5; Eph. 6:1-3.

F. No difference in the working of time's effect upon today's youth - it will bear the responsibilities of tomorrow's world, all of them, in government; in business, industry, education, professions, etc.; in moral conduct; in church activity - teaching, guidance, etc.

Note: What one **believes** will determine **what** he **does**!

II. **Problems Challenging Modern Youth Peculiar to Their Generation.**

A. More information about more things to challenge them than that of all other generations combined.

B. More and speedier communication media to relay information about and relate them to all others of earth; hence, each with his own problem for all others to consider - this means more opportunities for service.

C. More and speedier transportation facilities enabling on-scene contact within hours. Over 14,000 passports issued daily for U. S. citi zens to travel abroad. Think of on-spot impressions.

D. Racial tensions - an issue in every community and many homes.

E. A tragedy of moral decadence of which they are both recipients and perpetuators.

1. Family deterioration.

a. Easy divorce (1 in 4 marriages ends in divorce and annulment) - 500,000 annually.

b. Abrogation of educational responsibilities to T.V. and public schools.

c. Parents (including many mothers who work) place more value on material things than on moral and spiritual training includ ing higher education at hands of Christians.

d. Parental permissiveness toward (1) social activities in public schools where moral issues are involved, (2) unlimited auto usage, (3) immodest dress and (4) familiarity between sexes.

e. Behavior pattern of parents before children. See Melvin Munn, Halt Crime, p. 43.

2. School liberties.

a. Teaching of organic evolution. See Munn, Halt Crime, p. 55.

b. Progress has come to mean lack of discipline or guidance; hence, eliminated concept of propriety and impropriety. See Louria, The Drug Scene, pp. 19-21.

3. Inability of government leaders to deal decisively and as states men rather than as politicians with problems of our times. This manifests itself in:

a. Non-commitment - e.g., hippyism.

b. Contempt for law. See Louria, ibid, pp. 21-23.

Ill. Youth's Ultimate Problem Is Same as Ever- Belief vs. Unbelief!

A. This separates all regardless of age.

B. This was problem of ancient Israel (Heb. 3:13 ff.); Thomas, the Eleven, Saul of Tarsus.

C. This is battle of the ages - divine revelation vs. human wisdom.

D. CERTAIN ISSUES which must be settled:

NOTE: Theoretically these have been settled prior to baptism, yet many young Christians find their earlier acceptance of such matters put to the test. The divine order is "prove all things; hold fast that which is good. Abstain from every form of evil" 1 Thess. 5:21, 22.

1. CREATION VS. EVOLUTION - See Heb. 11:2; Gen. 1:1. Cf. virgin

birth vs. theory of evolution.

2. SPIRITUALITY VS. MATERIALISM -

Rom. 8:5-17; Col. 3:1-4,

12-25; Jas. 3:17; 4:4.

Gal. 5:16-24	(comfort)
Eph. 4:17; 5:21	(pleasure) physical things are
1 Cor. 6:9-11	(wealth) highest goals.
Rom. 1:18; 2:2	Cf. 1 Jno. 2:15

3. MORALITY VS. SITUATIONALISM -

only one thing is intrinsically good love! See Fletcher, **Situation Ethics**; Barnett's, **The New Theology and Morality**.

IV. **Abiding Values**. (See 1 Jno. 5:4)

A. God, Mal. 3:6

    B. Son of God, Heb. 13:8

    C. Word of God, Matt. 24:35; 1 Pet. 1:23

    D. Kingdom of God, Dan. 2:44; Heb. 12:28

Questions

1. Are youth problems peculiar to this age? Why do you think so?

2. What is the real disease producing the basic problems of youth and general society?

3. Why should older persons be in position to understand youth problems?

4. Does a young Christian have a right to disobey God's will simply be- cause his parents do not practice what they preach?

5. List some young people whose lives the Bible presents.

6. Briefly state six realities common to youth in all ages.

7. What Biblical incidents reflect a perversion of youth's desires and drives?

8. List five areas challenging modern youth which are primarily peculiar to the present generation.

9. What is the present total number of divorces and annulments in the United States each year?

10. To what two media of information have many parents abrogated their educational responsibilities?

11. What does emphasis on material things rather than on moral and spiritual training have to do with the moral decadence of the present age?

12. What four areas of paternal permissiveness have affected the moral decadence of this age?

13. Does parental behavior in the presence of children affect their conduct?

14. What effect does the teaching of organic evolution have on one's ' attitude toward morals?

15. What has progress come to mean with many parents and schools?

16. In what manner has inability of government leaders to deal decisively with problems of our times manifested itself?

17. What is the battle of the ages as regards the young Christian's ulti mate problem of salvation?

18. What are three major issues facirig the young Christian?

19. What are the four abiding values which have meaning to every Christian?

20. What overcomes the world and is the means to eternal life?

MATERIALS OF OTHERS FREQUENTLY USED

The materials below are frequently requested by those who hear them in connection with these studies. In most instances their authors are un known but identified if identity has been available.

BABY

Where did you come from, Baby dear?
Out of everywhere into here.
Where did you get your eyes so blue?
Out of the sky as I came through.
What makes the light in them sparkle and spin?
Some of the starry spikes left in.
Where did you get that little tear?
I found it waiting when I got here.
What makes your forehead so smooth and high?
A soft hand stroked it as I went by.
What makes your cheek like a warm, white rose?
I saw something better than anyone knows.
Whence that three-cornered smile of bliss?
Three angels gave me at once a kiss.
Where did you get this pearly ear?
God spoke, and it came out to hear.
Where did you get those arms and hands?
Love made itself into hooks and bands.
Feet, whence did you come, you darling things?
From the same box as the cherubs' wings.
How did they all come to be you?
God thought about me, and so I grew.
But how did you come to us, you dear?
God thought about you, and so I am here.

George MacDonald

THE LITTLE CHAP THAT FOLLOWS ME

A careful man, I ought to be;
 A little fellow follows me;
I do not dare to go astray
 For fear he'll go the self-same way.
I cannot once escape his eyes;
 Whatever he sees me do, he tries;
Like me, he says, he's going to be;
 That little chap that follows me.
He thinks that I am good and fine,
 Believes in every word of mine;
The bad in me, he must not see;
 My life to him must an example be.
I must remember, as I go
 Through summer's sun and winter's snow,
I'm building for the years to be,
 For that little chap that follows me.

YOUR NAME

You got it from your father;
 It was all he had to give.
So it's yours to use and cherish
 For as long as you may live.
If you lose the watch he gave you
 It can always be replaced;
But a black mark on your name, Son,
 Can never be erased.
It was clean the day you took it,
 And a worthy name to bear.
When he got it from his father,
 There was no dishonor there.
So make sure you guard it wisely,
 After all is said and done.
You'll be glad the name is spotless
 When you give it to your Son.

BEAUTIFUL HANDS

Such beautiful, beautiful hands,
 They're neither white nor small;
And you, I know, would scarcely think
 That they were fair at all.
I've looked on hands whose form and hue
 A sculptor's dream might be,
Yet are these aged, wrinkled hands
 Most beautiful to me.

Such beautiful, beautiful hands!
 Though heart were weary and sad
These patient hands kept toiling on
 That the children might be glad.
I almost weep when looking back
 To childhood's distant day!
I think how these hands rested not
 When children were at their play.

Such beautiful, beautiful hands!
 They're growing feeble now,
And time and pain have left their mark
 On head, and heart and brow.
Alas! Alas! The nearing time -
 And the sad, sad day to me,
When 'neath the daisies, out of sight,
 These hands must folded be.

But, oh! beyond the shadowy lands,
 Where all is bright and fair,
I know full well those dear old hands
 Will palms of victory bear;
Where crystal streams, through sadless years
 Flow over golden sands,
And where the old are young again,
 I'll clasp my mother's hands.

Ellen M. H. Gatos

NEGLECT

A story is told of a young man who stood at the bar of justice to be sentenced for forgery. The judge had known the young man from child hood, for his father had been a famous legal light and his work on the Law of Trusts was the most exhaustive work on the subject. "Do you remember your father," asked the judge, sternly, "that father whom you have disgrac ed?" The prisoner answered, "I remember him perfectly. When I went to him for advice or companionship, he would look up from his book on the Law of Trusts and say, 'Run away, boy, I am busy.' My father finished his book, and here I am." The great lawyer had neglected his own trust with awful results.

- Public Speakers Library

MUTUAL HELP

The family is a school of mutual help. Each member depends on every other. Today the robust father holds the "wee laddie" on his knee, or leads him up the stairway of that schoolroom in which he is to be taught his alphabet. But there is a tomorrow coming by and by when the lisper of the ABC will be tbe master of a home of his own - with an infirm, gray haired parent dozing away his sunset years in an armchair. Each helps the other when and where the help is most needed. And every word and deed of unselfish love, comes back in blessings on its author. God puts helpless babes, and infirm parents into our families for this purpose (among others) that the strong may bear the burden of the weak, and in bearing them may grow stronger themselves in Bible graces.

-Cuyler.

CHILDREN WON'T WAIT!

by Helen M. Young

There is a time to anticipate the baby's coming,
  a time to consult a doctor;
A time to plan a diet and exercise,
  a time to gather a layette.
There is a time to wonder at the ways of God,
  knowing this is the destiny for which I was created;
A time to dream of what this child may become,
A time to pray that God will teach me how to train this child which
I bear
A time to prepare myself that I might nurture his soul.
But soon there comes the time for birth,
For children won't wait.
There is a time for night feeding,
  and colic and formulas.
There is a time for rocking and a time for walking the floor,
A time for patience and self-sacrifice,
A time to show him that his new world is a world of love and goodness
and dependability.
There is a time to ponder what he is -
  not a toy, but a person, an individual -
  a soul made in God's image.
There is a time to consider my steward ship. I cannot possess him.
He is not mine. I have been chosen to care for him, to love him, to
enjoy him, to nurture him, and to answer to God.
I resolve to do my best for him,
For children won't wait.
There is a time to hold him close
  and tell him the sweetest story ever told:
A time to show him God in earth and sky and flower,
  to teach him to wonder and reverence.
There is a time to leave the dishes, to swing him in the park,
To run a race, to draw a picture, to catch a butterfly, to give him
  happy comradeship.
There is a time to point the way, to teach his infant lips to pray,
To teach his heart to love God's word, to love God's day
For children won't wait.

Solving Family Problems by James Cope

There is a time to sing instead of grumble,
  to smile instead of frown,
To kiss away the tears and laugh at broken dishes.
A time to share with him my best in attitudes -
  a love of life, a love of God, a love of family.
There is a time to answer his questions, all his questions.
Because there may come a time when he will not want my answers.
There is a time to teach him so patiently to obey,
  to put his toys away.
There is a time to teach him the beauty of duty,
  the habit of Bible study,
The joy of worship at home, the peace of prayer.
  For children won't wait.
There is a time to watch him bravely go to school,
  to miss him underfoot,
And to know that other minds have his attention,
  but that I will be there to answer his call when he comes home,
And to listen eagerly to the story of his day.
There is a time to teach him independence,
  responsibility, self-reliance.
To be firm but friendly, to discipline with love.
For soon, so soon, there will be a time to let him go,
  the apron strings untied,
For children won't wait.
There is a time to treasure every fleeting minute of his childhood.
Just eighteen precious years to inspire and train him.
I will not exchange this birthright for a mess of pottage called social
  position, or business or professional reputation, or a pay check.
An hour of concern today may save years of heartache tomorrow,
The house will wait, the dishes will wait, the new room can wait,
But children won't wait.
There will be a time when there will be no slamming of doors, no toys
on the stairs, no childhood quarrels, no fingerprints on the wallpaper.
Then I may look back with joy and not regret.
There will be a time to concentrate on service outside my home;
On visiting the sick, the bereaved, the discouraged, the untaught;
To give myself to the "least of these." There will be a time to look back
and know that these years of motherhood were not wasted.
I pray there will be a time to see him an upright and an honest man,
loving God and serving all.

God, give me wisdom to see that today is my day with my children.
There is no unimportant moment in their lives.
May I know that no other career is so precious,
No other work so rewarding,
No other task too urgent.
May I not defer it nor neglect it,
But by Thy Spirit accept it gladly,
joyously, and by Thy grace realize
That the time is short and my time is now.
For children won't wait.

MYSELF

I have to live with myself and so
 I want to be fit for myself to know.
I want to be able as days go by
 Always to look myself straight in the eye.
I don't want to stand with the setting sun
 And hate myself for the things I've done;
But I want to go on with my head erect,
 I want to deserve all men's respect
And here in the struggle for fame and pelf,
 I want to be able to like myself.
I don't want to look at myself and know
 That I am blunder and bluster and empty show.
I never can hide myself from me.;
 I see what others may never see.
I know what others may never know.
 I never can fool myself and so
Whatever happens I want to be
 Self-respecting and conscience-free.

A BOY TO TRAIN

The man who has a boy to train,
 Has work to keep him night and day.
There's much to him he must explain,
 And many a doubt to clear away;
His task is one which calls for tact
 And friendship of the finest kind,

Because, with every word and act,
 He molds the little fellow's mind.
He must be careful of his speech,
 For careless words are quickly learned;
He must be wise enough to teach
 What corners may be safely turned.

-Edgar A. Guest

TWO BUILDERS

"A builder builded.a temple
He wrought it with care and skill
Pillars and groins and arches,
Were fashioned to meet his will.
And men said when they saw its beauty:
'It shall never know decay,
Great is thy skill, 0, builder,
Thy fame shall endure for aye.'

A teacher builded a temple.
She wrought it with skill and care,
Forming each pillar with patience, Laying each stone with care.
None saw the unceasing effort
None knew the marvelous plan,
For the temple the teacher builded
Was unseen by the eyes of man.

Gone is the builder's temple
Crumbled into dust,
Pillars and groins and arches,
Food for consuming rust.
But the temple the teacher builded
Shall endure while the ages roll,
For the beautiful unseen temple
Was the child's immortal soul."

THE BAD EXAMPLE

He whipped his boy for lying,
And his cheeks were flaming red,
And of course there's no denying
There was truth in what he said
That a liar's always hated.
But the little fellow knew
That his father often stated
Many things that were untrue.
He caught the youngster cheating
And he sent him up to bed,
And it's useless now repeating
All the bitter things he said;
He talked of honor loudly,
As a lesson to be learned,
And forgot he'd boasted proudly
Of the cunning tricks he'd turned.
He heard the youngster swearing
And he punished him again -
He'd have no boy as daring
As to utter words profane.
Yet the youngster could have told him,
Poor misguided little elf,
That it seemed unfair to scold him
When he often cursed himself.
All in vain is splendid preaching,
And the noble things we say,
All our talk is wasted teaching
If we do not lead the way.
We can never, by reviewing
All the sermons on the shelves
Keep the younger hands from doing
What we often do ourselves.

Cope "Solving Family Problems" Series

August 8-15, 1970	Danville Road – Decatur, AL Lynn Hedrick (2 times)
November 21-22, 1970	Valley Station – Louisville, KY
January 1-3, 1971	Expressway – Louisville, KY John Clark (32 times)
January 9-10, 1971	Southeast – Akron, OH Morris Norman
January 16-17, 1971	Palmetto, FL Paul Branch
January 23-24, 1971	Fort Myers, FL Danny Towe
February 5-7, 1971	Hillview, Nashville, TN Billy Adcock
February 21-23, 1971	Valley, Phoenix, AZ Ken Morris
February, 27-28, 1971	Spring & Delta, Long Beach, CA Ford Carpenter
March 1-5, 1971	Venice, CA John Collins
March 6-7, 1971	Brea, CA Ted Beaver
March 12-14, 1971	Beaver Dam, KY B. G. Hope

March 19-21, 1971	Seminole, Tampa, FL
	Barney Keith
March 22-28, 1971	Jonesboro, AR
	Jimmy Yopp
April 4-May31 1971	Lake Wire, Lakeland, FL
April 2, 16-18, 1971	Lakeshore, Jacksonville, FL
	C. L. Overturff
May 7-9, 1971	Tomlinson Run, PA
	Bill Calame
June, 1971	Bartow, FL
	Jim Cope
June 11-13, 1971	Tuckerman, AR
	Earl Kimbrough
July 9-11, 1971	Westside, Marion, IN
	Cecil Willis
July 19-25, 1971	Greencastle, IN
	Jim Sanders
August 6-8, 1971	Gainesville, FL
	Roy Foutz
August 20-22, 1971	Par Avenue, Orlando, FL
	Royce Chandler
Sept. 17-19, 1971	Toronto, Ohio
Sept.. 27-Oct. 1	Mahoney Ave, Plant City, FL
	Jerry Eubanks
Oct. 8-10, 1971	Zion, IL
	Dale Smelser
Oct. 15-17, 1971	Haynes St.; Dayton, OH
	Abe Martin

Oct. 22-24, 1971	East Memphis, TN Don Basset
Oct. 25-28, 1971	Arlington, TX Hubert Moss Jr.
Oct. 29-31, 1971	Floral Heights; Wichita Falls, TX Hayse Reneau
Nov. 5-7, 1971	Palatka, FL C. L. Overturff Jr.
Nov. 12-15, 1971	Trussville, AL R. A. Ginn
Nov. 19-21, 1971	Embry Hills; Atlanta, GA David Tant
Dec. 10-12, 1971	Racine, WI Elmo Wilson
Jan. 7-9, 1972	Newbern, TN Mason Harris (51 times)
Jan. 14-16, 1972	Spring & Blaine; St. Louis, MO Gordon Wilson
Jan. 21-23, 1972	Brandon, FL Harry Rice
Jan. 28-30, 1972	Lafayette, LA
Feb. 4-6, 1972	Franklin Road; Nashville, TN Harold Howard
Feb. 11-13, 1972	Snapfinger Rd.; Decatur, AL H. S. (Sparky) Owen
Feb. 18-20, 1972	North Seattle, WA Bill Radke
Feb. 20-25, 1972	Sumner, WA Paul Hawthorne

Feb. 26-27, 1972	Ontario, CA Bob Bolton
Feb. 28-Mar 3, 1972	Tustin, CA Charles Limburg
Mar. 4-5, 1972	Northside; Tucson, AZ Bill Moseley
Mar. 10-12, 1972	Waycross, GA Dwight Edwards
Mar. 17-19, 1972	Gashland; Kansas City, MO Calvin Essry
Mar. 24-26, 1972	77th Street; Birmingham, AL Harold Comer
Mar. 31-Apr. 2, 1972	Holden Heights; Orlando, FL Oaks Gowen
April 8-9, 1972	Burbank Manor; Chicago, IL Dorval McClister
April 14-16, 1972	Manslick Road; Louisville, KY Connie Adams
April 21-23, 1972	Bell Sci; Houston, TX W. R. Jones
April 29-30, 1972	Harding Street; Hollywood, FL Guy Roberson
May 6-7, 1972	Osprey, FL Don Hastings
May 8-14, 1972	Univ. Heights; Murfreesboro, TN Bob Bunting
May 26-28, 1972	Paden City, WV Weldon Warnock

June 3-4, 1972	Edna, TX Herbert Thornton
June 10-11, 1972	Taylor; Greenville, SC Larry Dickens
June 18-22, 1972	San Bernardino, CA R. J. Stevens
June 23-26, 1972	Bellflower, CA Ken Marrs
July 3-6, 1972	F.C. Summer Lectures
July 8-9, 1972	Haleyville, AL Gary Patton
July 14-16, 1972	Owensboro, KY A. C. Grider
July 21-23, 1972	Flagstaff, AZ
July 24-26, 1972	Cottonwood, AZ Wayne McDaniel
July 28-30, 1972	Boston St.; Aurora, CO Hoyt Houchen
Aug. 6-10, 1972	Liberty St.; Lexington, KY Walter Stevens
Aug. 11-13, 1972	Warner Robbins, GA Wiley Adams
Aug. 18-20, 1972	Griffith, IN
Aug. 27-31, 1972	Palm River; Tampa, FL Colly Caldwell
Sep. 2-3, 1972	Wauchula, FL Wayne Cobia

Sep. 9-10, 1972	Virginia Beach, VA Jack Gibbert
Sep. 17-21, 1972	Temple Terrace, FL Irven Himmel
Sep. 23-24, 1972	Annandale, VA
Sep. 29-Oct.1	Fair Lawn, N.J. James L. Finney
Oct. 20-22, 1972	E. Columbus, MS Weldon Warnock
Oct. 27-29, 1972	Jordan Park; Huntsville, AL Herschel Patton
Nov. 1-5, 1972	North Boulevard; Tampa, FL Paul Andrews
Nov. 10-12, 1972	Southside; Tulsa, OK
Nov. 15-19, 1972	Lakeland Hills; Lakeland, FL Ferrell Jenkins
Nov. 24-26, 1972	N. Washington St.;Russellville AL John Swatzell
Dec. 1-3, 1972	Perry, FL J. Ed Nowlin
Dec. 9-10, 1972	Southwest; Miami, FL Ed Walker
Dec. 15-17, 1972	Gay Meadows; Montgomery, AL Carroll Puckett
Dec. 29-31, 1972	Chiefland, FL Elmo Hazelwood
Jan. 9-11, 1973	Disston Ave.; St. Petersburg, FL Claude Wilsford (45 times)

Jan. 12-14, 1973   West End; Richmond, VA
Bobby Graham

Jan. 28-Feb. 1, 1973   Lutz, FL
Bobby Andrews

Feb. 2-4, 1973   West End; Franklin, TN
Rufus Clifford

Feb. 9-11, 1973   Old Wire Rd.; Fayettville, AR

Feb. 16-18, 1973   Jackson Heights; Columbia, TN
Sam Binkley

Feb. 19-23, 1973   Caldwell, ID
Ken Sterling

Feb. 24-25, 1973   South Salem, OR
Peter J. Wilson

Feb. 26-March 3, 1973   Alameda, CA
Olen Holderby

March 4-7, 1973   Fresno, CA
Denton Thompson

March 8-11, 1973   West Anaheim, CA
Gilbert Copeland

March 17-18, 1973   Albertville, AL
Caroll Sutton

March 23-25, 1973   6th Street; Pine Bluff, AR
Leonard Tyler

March 30-April 1, 1973 East Florence, AL
Bob Harkrider

April 6-8, 1973   Arch Street; Little Rock, AR
Eugene Britnell

April 15-18, 1973   University; Tampa, FL
Guy Roberson

April 20-22, 1973	Haynesville, LA Rayford Petty
April 27-29, 1973	Westside; Tallahassie, FL Conway Skinner
May 4-6, 1973	Caprock; Lubbock, TX Grover Stevens
May 11-13, 1973	Caesarea; Georgetown, KY Joe Hill
May 26-27, 1973	Hendersonville, TN Bill Hawkins
June 8-10, 1973	Fairview; Birmingham, AL James Shear
June 17-20, 1973	West Ave.; San Antonio, TX Jim Ward
June 22-24, 1973	Trazevant St.; Memphis, TN Leslie E. Sloan
June 29-July 1, 1973	Bald Knob, AR James Smelser
July 6-8, 1973	12th St.; Bowling Green, KY James P. Miller
July 9-15, 1973	Green's Chapel, KY Wayne Gary
July 20-22, 1973	Eastside; Las Vegas, NV Terrel Cook
July 27-29, 1973	Parkview; Kermit, TX Royce Bell
August 5-8, 1973	Danville, KY Royce Chandler

August 10-12, 1973	St. Charles, MO Luther Martin
August 17-19, 1973	Trenton, FL Doug Black & Jack Linsay
Sept. 14-16, 1973	Lewisville, TX Robert Farish
Sept. 21-23, 1973	Romulus, MI L. A. Mott
Oct. 7, 1973	Easton Rd; Dallas, TX Bryan Vinson, Jr.
Oct. 8-11, 1973	Sacramento, CA Bill Fling
Oct. 12-13, 1973	Sparks, NV Bill Young
Oct. 14-18, 1973	Tucson, AZ Bill Mosley
Oct. 19-21, 1973	Valley; Phoenix, AZ John Coffman
Nov. 2-4, 1973	Saraland, AL Owen Calvert
Nov. 9-11, 1973	Lawrenceville, GA Steve Bobbit
Nov. 16-18, 1973	Inglenook Dr.; Birmingham, AL Hugh Davis
Dec. 2-4, 1973	South 45th St; Fort Smith, AR George Jones
Dec. 7-9, 1973	Central; Ocala, FL Colin Williamson

Dec. 14-16, 1973	Greenwood, IN
	Tom Wheeler
Jan. 4-6, 1974	Jerry Whitson Rd.; Cookeville, TN
	Harold Griffin (25 times)
Jan. 11-13, 1974	Crane, TX
	Jim Sanders
Jan. 18-20, 1974	Honeysuckle Rd.; Dothan, AL
	Joe Corley
Jan. 24-27, 1974	Hercules Ave.; Clearwater, FL
	Ricky Smith
Feb. 1-3, 1974	North Ridgedale, OH
Feb. 8-10, 1974	Eastside; Athens, AL
	Sewell Hall
Feb. 15-17, 1974	Oak Grove; McDavid, FL
	Cheryl Schmid
March 1-3, 1974	Vivian Road; Kansas City, MO
	Norman Sewell
March 4-7, 1974	Renfore, WA
	Harold Trimble
March 9-10, 1974	160 St.; Portland, OR
	Arnold Schnabel
March 15-17, 1974	Penole, CA
	B. T. Raulieu
March 29-31, 197 4	Pinson, AL
	Bob Tuten
April 19-21, 1974	Thayer St.; Akron, OH
	Morris Norman

April 26-28, 1974	Eastside; Denton, TX Jesse Jenkins
May 3-5, 1974	Chipley, FL Roy Whitworth
May 10-12, 1974	East Hill; Pensacola, FL Pete McKee
July 14-17, 1974	Lyons Chapel; Tompkinsville, KY Earl Robertson
August 16-18, 1974	Eau Galllie; Melbourne, FL Jack Frost, Jr.
Sep. 12-15, 1974	Elgin, IL Billy Boyd
Oct. 3-6, 1974	Huntington, TX Oliver Murray
Nov. 3-6, 1974	Wonsley Ave.; Austin, TX Kent Ellis
Nov. 7-10, 1974	South Loop; Crocket, TX Bruce James
Nov. 15-17, 1974	Libertyville, ILL Ken Murphy
Dec. 6-8, 1974	West Booneville, MS Bill Ward
Dec. 13-15, 1974	Jordan Ontario Canada
Jan. 12-15, 1975	Timberland Dr.; Lufkin, TX Dean Bullock (17 times)
Feb. 21-23, 1975	Cobra Dr.; Springs, CO
Feb. 24-27, 1975	Carmichel, CA Ed Broulette

Feb. 28-March 2, 1975	Winnetca Ave; Canoga, Park, CA Ford Carpenter
March 7-9, 1975	Hardlng Heights; Houston, TX Ed Whidden
April 4-6, 1975	Westside; Athens, AL Doyle Banta
April 18-20, 1975	Imhoff Ave.; Port Arthur, TX Bill Cavender
June 20-22, 1975	Warrenton, MO John Berlise
June 23-25, 1975	Rochester, MN Gary Hargis
June 27-29, 1975	Newton, NC Giles Painter
Aug. 3-5, 1975	Jonestown, TX Barry Pennington
Aug. 8-10, 1975	Portage, IN Ron Griffin
Sep. 19-21, 1975	South Cullman, AL O. C. Birdwell
Sep. 25-28, 1975	Eastside; Indianapolis, IN L. A. Stauffer
Oct. 19-22, 1975	East Central; Tulsa, OK
Oct. 23-26, 1975	Northeast; Austin, TX
Oct. 27-29, 1975	North Irving, TX Warren Cheatham
Feb. 27-29, 1976	Studebaker, Rd; Long Beach, CA J. T. Smith (11 times)

March 11-14, 1976	Corrigan, TX Jimmy Stevens
April 9-11, 1976	New Smyrna Beach, FL Raford Petty
April 15-21, 1976	Plainfield, IN Olin Kern
May 16-18, 1976	Camden, AR
May 21-23, 1976	Duke St.; Nashville, TN Bill Oneal
May 24-28, 1976	Covington, GA Harvey Buttrey
June 13-16, 1976	Greenville, TX Bill Miller
Oct. 8-10, 1976	Eastside; Marshall, TX Ken Williams
Dec. 3-5, 1976	Park Forest; Baton Rouge, LA Bill Crews
Dec. 10-12, 1976	Merritt Island, FL James P. Miller
Jan. 14-16, 1977	Southside; Pasadena, TX Dee Bowman (13 times)
Feb. 4-6, 1977	Jackson, MS Gary White
April 15-17, 1977	Oak Avenue; Dickson, TN Billy Ashworth
May 9-12, 1977	Emerado, ND Gary Hargis
May 27-29, 1977	Panama City Beach, FL Fred Liggin

June 3-5, 1977	Greggton; Longview, TX Earnest Finley
June 7-10, 1977 (radio)	Antioch; Woodbury, TN David Arnold
June 13-16, 1977	Galena, IN Willis Kay
July 29-31, 1977	Chapel Hill, TN Alvin Walker
Sept. 26-30, 1977	Claremore, OK Scott Young
Nov. 4-6, 1977	Meridian, MS Horace Huggins
Dec. 2-4, 1977	Ft. Myers, FL Danny Tams
Dec. 9-11, 1977	Boca Raton, FL Dempsey Collins
Jan. 1, 1978 (Sundays)	Antioch; Tampa, FL James R. Cope (11 times)
Feb. 17-19, 1978	Hickory Heights; Lewisburg, TN Gilbert Holt
March 3-5, 1978	Freemont, CA Pat Broaddus
March 17-19, 1978	Tillman's Corner; Mobile, AL J. W. Evans
April 29-30, 1978	Roswell; Atlanta, GA David Tant
May 21-25, 1978	Thomasville, GA
June 5-9, 1978	Greenville, TX Terrell Cook

June 18-21, 1978	Rose Hill; Columbus, GA Frank Jamerson
July 30-Aug. 2, 1978	Benton, IL Bill Cunningham
Sep. 6-8, 1978	Milton, VT Keith Clayton
Sep. 27-29, 1978	Wellsburg, WV Owen Thomas
Jan. 12-14, 1979	Auburn, AL Dave Bradford (11 times)
Feb. 2-4, 1979	Hillsboro, OH Bill Pierce
Feb. 15-18, 1979	Oxnard, CA Ken Adams
Feb. 23-25, 1979	Carmichel, CA Jim Puterbaugh
March 2-4, 1979	Beaver Dan, KY Tom Wheeler
April 10-15, 1979	Worthington, OH Grant Caldwell
May 18-20, 1979	Arlington, TX Dan Petty
May 25-27, 1979	Winslow, AZ Sonny Marrs
Sep. 21-23, 1979	Tupelo, MS William Ward
Nov. 9-11, 1979	Vestavia; Birmingham, AL David Claypool

Nov. 23-25, 1979	Grenada, MS Bill James
Jan. 7-11, 1980	West Bradenton, FL
Feb. 17-20, 1980	Sierra Vista; Fresno, CA Olen Holderby
Feb. 22-24, 1980	Ontario, CA Landon Hope
Feb. 25-28, 1980	Northland; Flagstaff, AZ Roy Tinnik
Feb. 29, 1980	Winslow, AZ (cancelled; chest pain)
Sept. 14, 1980	Skyview; Pinellas County, FL Buddy Payne
Nov. 16-18, 1980	Percell, OK E. Paul Price
Nov. 20-23, 1980	Southside; Greenville, TX Galen Evans & Jack Howard
Feb. 2-6, 1981	Zepherhills, FL Edgar Srygley
Aug. 28-30, 1981	Palmetto, FL Ken Weliever
Oct. 30-Nov. 1, 1981	Virginia Beach, VA Doug Lyell
Nov. 2-6, 1981	Moody; Birmingham, AL Tim Sutton
Feb. 19-21, 1982	Brandon, MS Jim Allen
May 21-23, 1982	College Park; Deer Park, TX Bill Collett & David Crawford

Sept. 5-9, 1982	Forest Hills; Tampa, FL
Oct. 24-29, 1982	Texarkana, AR Terrell Cook
Feb. 11-13, 1983	Ocala, FL Steve Hudgins
March 27-April 1, 1983	Athens, GA Bill Weston
Oct. 31-Nov. 6, 1983	Benton, IL Vernon Ford
June 15-17, 1984	Greencastle, IN Morris Hafley
Nov. 5-10, 1984	Connor, GA James Shear
Dec. 9-14, 1984	Glendale, AZ Jerry Cook
March 29-31, 1985	Duncanville, TX Jack Hogart
May 6-10, 1985	Ft. White, FL
May 17-19, 1985	Trillacoochee, FL Don Hastings
June 2-6, 1985	Pine Mountain Valley, GA John Madrigal
June 10-14, 1985	Collegeview; Florence, AL Harold Comer
Aug. 25-28, 1985	Broadview Hgts; Okla. City OK James Lusby
June 27-29, 1986	Smyrna Beach, FL Richard Parham

BUILDING ON THE GOOD

October 19-22, 1986	Colorado Springs, CO
	James L. Finney
November 20-21, 1987	Washington, NJ

Index

www.ingramcontent.com/pod-product-compliance
Lightning Source LLC
Chambersburg PA
CBHW051128120626
46547CB00012B/718

9781965356173